Quennell, Peter
Byron, a self portrait

DATE DUE

BYRON
A Self-Portrait

LORD BYRON.

BYRON
A Self-Portrait

LETTERS AND DIARIES
1798 TO 1824

WITH HITHERTO UNPUBLISHED LETTERS
IN TWO VOLUMES EDITED BY

PETER QUENNELL

★

VOLUME I

★

NEW YORK
HUMANITIES PRESS
1967

First Published in 1950

Reprinted 1967 by
HUMANITIES PRESS, INC.
by arrangement with
John Murray (Publishers) Ltd.

Printed in U.S.A. by
NOBLE OFFSET PRINTERS, INC.
NEW YORK 3, N. Y.

CONTENTS

VOLUME I

★

VOLUME II

★ ★

NOTE : *Unpublished letters are marked by a star ; letters to which passages
have been restored, by a dagger.*

FOREWORD

Ay me! what perils do environ
The man that meddles with Lord Byron!

murmured a volatile acquaintance caught in the web of the strange Byronic destiny. It is a complaint that every biographer of Byron must now and then have echoed; for, although Byron is the most alluring of themes, and although there is no other great man who appears at first sight to reveal himself more readily, his character, if we study him closely enough and follow him hard enough, often seems, as our knowledge increases, to be among the most elusive. We possess a vast quantity of information about his habits, tastes and antecedents; and yet, it may presently strike us, some essential clues are lacking. We know much, possibly too much, about his various troubled love-affairs; but we can only guess at the nature of that decisive early experience which caused him to feel that he had anticipated adult life, and that he had begun to squander his capital before he had reached an age when he could gather in the interest. Other problems are equally insoluble. Byron, who had an odd, at times a slightly distorted, sense of humour, was never averse from mystifying his intimates; and that he might mystify readers yet unborn was an idea that, in freakish and provocative moods, evidently appealed to him. Their correspondence, he wrote to his friend Lady Melbourne, on November 6th, 1812, might be expected to " puzzle posterity " when, after a hundred years' interval, it eventually burst forth!

That particular section of his private papers (edited and published by John Murray under the title of *Lord Byron's Correspondence*) as he had prophesied finally burst upon the world in 1922. It added not a little to our understanding of his temperament, and heightened the impression made by his *Letters and Journals*, edited in six volumes by R. E. Prothero (later Lord Ernle) at the end of the last century. But a mass of documents, some of them unusually illuminating, still remained unpublished. A large number are preserved at

vii

50 Albemarle Street, in a house that Byron often visited, among the Murray archives: others repose in the British Museum, or have been acquired by collections, both private and public, in England and America. Because the pleasures of becoming acquainted with Byron far outweigh the perils, we have been tempted to make a new selection of the poet's scattered prose-writings, the letters he dashed off to his friends and the wonderful diaries and journals in which, for his own amusement, he composed a partial and fragmentary, but extremely vivid, self-portrait. Together with material already published, we have included fifty-six letters hitherto unprinted; while to the published text of some thirty-six we have restored passages, ranging in length from a few lines to several solid paragraphs, suppressed or omitted by Byron's previous editors. It has been a stimulating, at times a perplexing, task. So strong was Byron's personality that everything he produced, down to the smallest and least studied notes, seems impregnated with his character; and his was a character that, however attentively we observe it, at length defies analysis. Thus he was the most self-conscious of men; yet the chief characteristic of his private outpourings is their reckless spontaneity. He did not labour to create an effect; yet he can seldom have been unaware of the effect he was creating. He was usually prepared to live for the moment, but always inclined to see the moment against a background of eternity: for his religious sense, though undeveloped, was strong and ineradicable. Opportunist and amorous adventurer, he had in him the makings (as Walter Scott once remarked) of an ascetic and a devotee.

All these aspects of his temperament appear in rapid succession, sometimes brightly, sometimes flickeringly, throughout the pages of his correspondence. We watch the evolution of a human being—from the little boy who informs his aunt, Mrs. Parker, that the " potatoes are now ready ", and the angry schoolboy bursting with a complication of adolescent grievances, to the disillusioned and exhausted man, struggling to perform an impossible task amid the gloom of Missolonghi, while rain thrashes down into the muddy street and the Suliot mercenaries in the courtyard chant their dismal war-songs. He grows up; he changes perpetually; yet neither triumph nor disgrace, neither satisfaction nor disillusionment, can alter or obliterate the underlying outline. He was a fatalist. " Like Sylla ", he wrote in *Detached Thoughts*, the journal of miscellaneous reflections he compiled in 1821, " I have always believed that all things depended upon Fortune, and nothing upon ourselves. I am not aware of any one thought or action worthy of being called good to myself or others, which is not to be attributed to the Good Goddess, Fortune ! " But his pagan fatalism had a Christian colouring. Brought up by a Calvinist nurse, he never quite shook off the dogma of predestination in which he had been educated ; and to these ideas a strain of private superstition gave added picturesqueness. All the Byrons, he was convinced, were doomed—the " Wicked Lord ", " Foulweather Jack " (the admiral whose mere presence seemed to have attracted hurricanes) and himself, offspring of a handsome, dissolute father and a foolish, ill-educated, violent-tempered mother. They shared a mysterious ancestral curse. To those whom he loved, Byron sometimes asserted, his love was always fatal.

With these hereditary factors Byron, at least as a young man, combined a strain of vehement personal ambition and romantic self-assertiveness. Take, for example, this passage from a letter (hitherto unpublished) written to his mother from Harrow, presumably during the year 1804: " I . . . am equal ", he rages, " if not superior to most of my school-fellows, and if my fortune is narrow it is my misfortune, not my fault. But, however, the way *to riches, to greatness* lies before me. I can, I will cut myself a path through the world or perish in the attempt. . . . I will carve myself a passage to Grandeur, but never with Dishonour. These, Madam, are my intentions."

Yet Byron the arch-Romantic is but a single aspect of the complex and fascinating being whom his private letters show us. Equally conspicuous is Byron the man of the world— rake and diner-out and jocular companion, than whom (as he was wont to observe, somewhat plaintively, when the dark Byronic legend became too oppressive or too embarrassing) nobody could laugh more ! Byron's correspondence, on the other hand, does not deserve attention merely because it builds up into the portrait of an extraordinarily gifted and unusually complex personality ; it is also memorable because this intimate record of his moods and thoughts and doings is conveyed in a prose-style at once sensitive and vigorous, a style which is frequently slipshod but at times rises to the height of imaginative literature. The letters of Pope, Gray and Walpole are deliberate works of art, copied out and carefully revised and often begged back from the recipient for further literary polishing. Byron, however, agreed with Dorothy Osborne that the real charm of a letter was its freedom from any deliberate literary artifice ; " all letters [she had remarked] . . . should be free and easy as one's discourse, not studied as an oration, nor made up of hard words like a charm ". Byron's epistles have always this quality : at their best, they are admirable *talk*—delivered by a talker of genius, who had explored life energetically and mused upon it passionately, even though (as his detractors may suggest) he had not seen it steadily. English prose is much the richer for the constant need Byron felt, whether at home or abroad, to communicate his feelings ; and it is an odd fact that the most eloquent appreciation of his merits as a letter-writer should have been composed neither by a contemporary nor -by a twentieth-century admirer, but by a great Victorian prophet. Ruskin's criticism is both just and generous. In the eighth chapter of *Praeterita*, after describing the benefit that during his youth he had received from Byron's poetry, he proceeds to expatiate at considerable length on the virtues of his prose-work :

" Read . . .", Ruskin advises, " the sentence on Sheridan, in his letter to Thomas Moore, from Venice, June 1st (or dawn of June 2nd !), 1818. ' The Whigs abuse him ; however, he never left them, and such blunderers deserve neither credit nor compassion. As for his creditors,—remember, Sheridan *never had* a shilling, and was thrown, with great powers and passions, into the thick of the world, and placed upon the pinnacle of success, with no other external means to support him in his elevation. Did Fox * * * *pay his* debts ? or did Sheridan take a subscription ? Was the * *'s drunkenness more excusable than his ? Were his intrigues more notorious than those of all his contemporaries ? and is his memory to be blasted and theirs respected ? Don't let yourself be led away by clamour, but compare him with the coalitioner Fox, and the pensioner

Burke, as a man of principle; and with ten hundred thousand in personal views; and with none in talent, for he beat them all *out* and *out*. Without means, without connexion, without character (which might be false at first, and make him mad afterwards from desperation), he beat them all, in all he ever attempted. But, alas poor human nature! Good-night or rather, morning. It is four, and the dawn gleams over the Grand Canal, and unshadows the Rialto '.

" Now, observe, that passage is noble primarily because it contains the utmost number that will come together into the space, of absolutely just, wise, and kind thoughts. But it is more than noble, it is *perfect*, because the quantity it holds is not artificially or intricately concentrated, but with the serene swiftness of a smith's hammer-strokes on hot iron ; and with choice of terms which, each in its place, will convey far more than they mean in the dictionary. Thus, ' however ' is used instead of ' yet ', because it stands for ' howsoever ', or, in full, for ' yet whatever they did '. ' Thick ' of society, because it means, not merely the crowd, but the *fog* of it; ' ten hundred thousand ' instead of ' a million ', or ' a thousand thousand ', to take the sublimity out of the number, and make us feel that it is a number of nobodies. . . . Finally, the dawn ' un-shadows '—lessens the shadow on—the Rialto, but does not *gleam* on that, as on the broad water. . . .

". . . Here at last ", Ruskin concludes, now discussing Byron's prose and verse as facets of the same genius, " I had found a man who spoke only of what he had seen, and known ; and spoke without exaggeration, without mystery, without enmity. ' That *is* so ;—make what you will of it ! ' "

Ruskin's tastes were commendably catholic. All his inherited puritanism did not debar him from conceding Byron's splendid qualities, though they were the qualities of a mind to which his own intelligence bore very little likeness. But each writer had a superb descriptive gift; and for sheer evocative and descriptive skill Byron's letters composed in Italy— especially the letters written from Venice—would be difficult to improve on. In a few sentences he produced an impression which the average novelist might fail to achieve in many laboured paragraphs :

" That she had a sufficient regard for me in her wild way, I had many reasons to believe. I will mention one. In the autumn, one day, going to the Lido with my Gondoliers, we were overtaken by a heavy Squall, and the Gondola put in peril—hats blown away, boat filling, oar lost, tumbling sea, thunder, rain in torrents, night coming, and wind encreasing. On our return, after a tight struggle, I found her on the open steps of the Mocenigo palace, on the Grand Canal, with her great black eyes flashing through her tears, and the long dark hair, which was streaming drenched with rain over her brows and breast. She was perfectly exposed to the storm; and the wind blowing her hair and dress about her tall thin figure, and the lightning flashing round her, with the waves rolling at her feet, made her look like Medea alighted from her chariot, or the Sibyl of the tempest that was rolling around her, the only living thing within hail at that moment except ourselves. . . . Her joy at seeing me again was moderately mixed with ferocity, and gave me the idea of a tigress over her recovered Cubs."

But no less beguiling than his broadly dramatic strokes is the verbal wit that Byron compresses into two or three words, or into a single telling epithet. Certain phrases constantly recur to the memory, so felicitous is their summing-up of some familiar human situation. The charm of these jokes is very often their apparent slightness; and we are reminded that George Bryan Brummell, whose wit struck always a glancing blow, had been one of Byron's early masters. Thus, on September 21st, 1813, describing for Lady Melbourne's benefit the not excessively comfortable household of his friends the Websters, he remarks that " the place is very well, and quiet, and *the children only scream in a low voice*. . . ." And, elsewhere, portraying a Venetian mistress: ". . . She is pretty as an Antelope, is but two-and-twenty years old, has the large, black, Oriental eyes, with the Italian countenance, and dark glossy hair, of the curl and colour of Lady Jersey's. . . . But her great merit is finding out mine—*there is nothing so amiable as discernment*."

Elsewhere a robust satirical humour, expressed in some comic or ludicrous image, suddenly reveals itself. Byron was accounted excellent company by friends who met him in a laughing mood, and with whom he felt sufficiently at his ease to discard the haughty and supercilious attitude he sometimes adopted in mixed or hostile gatherings. Then there was no hint of the Byronic melancholy, no indication that this muscular, talkative and curly-headed young man had any relationship with the misanthropic wanderer depicted in *Childe Harold*. But, if it is true that he was seldom serious for long, and that his habitual flippancy shocked solemn admirers of the stamp of Lady Blessington, who found that he loved to gossip and rarely troubled to philosophise, it is also true that the strain of melancholy which ran through his nature was deep-rooted and pervasive. It was at least as genuine as his flippant and ribald humour. Byron himself accepted both sides of his temperament, but did not try to reconcile them. Both coloured his epistolary prose-style, and contribute to the feeling of fascination with which we turn his pages. But where is the *real* Byron? we are occasionally tempted to ask. Are we to look for this elusive personage among the rich diversity of letters he sent to Hobhouse, Moore and Kinnaird, in which he emerges as a generous and warm-hearted friend, though, when crossed or disappointed, markedly petulant and short-tempered : among the rancorous letters received by his wife : the tender letters to Augusta Leigh : or in his protestations to the other women with whom his fortune linked him? Nowhere is Byron revealed in so many contradictory aspects as in his attitude towards the opposite sex. Women had dominated his life : he laughed at and pitied and adored and often affected to despise them. " There is something to me ", he recorded, " very softening in the presence of a woman— some strange influence, even if one is not in love with them —which I cannot at all account for. . . ." Yet if we except the letters to Augusta Leigh and Lady Melbourne, we find little evidence of strong affection and numerous traces, as disillusionment grew upon him, of boredom and satiety. To Teresa Guiccioli he was undoubtedly devoted; but there is a disconcerting contrast between the carefully penned declara- tions—copy-book productions in the author's best Italian—with which at frequent intervals her romantic lover favoured her, and his irreverent account to Hoppner and Kinnaird of the progress of their intimacy. No lover could be less loyal, no writer less consistent. Yet his inconsistency and emotional instability were as much a part of Byron's character as his melancholy, his fatalism or his wild romantic yearnings ; and in his collected correspondence all are fully set forth—and set forth with a freedom and freshness, even with a kind of shamelessness, rarely equalled and never surpassed in European literature. He may not reveal the whole of himself, but he gives us more than any English letter-writer had previously attempted. Indeed, he had more to give. His nature, with its disorderly abundance, its bewildering assemblage of mean and noble attributes, was, as his contemporaries guessed, in the most genuine sense inimitable ; and, when he died, young and old understood that a light had been extinguished. " Byron is dead. . . . Byron is dead ", scratched the boyish Tennyson, half stupefied by the news, upon the sandstone slabs of a deserted quarry. " Gentlemen, Lord Byron is dead ! " announced the Duke of Rutland to a gathering of local fox-hunters : and the country gentlemen abandoned their banquet and silently, unquestioningly trooped home.

BIBLIOGRAPHICAL NOTE

This selection of Byron's letters and journals includes forty-nine letters hitherto unpublished, and thirty-eight not hitherto published in full. Unpublished letters are marked by a star ; letters to which passages have been restored, by a dagger. A list of sources will be found at the end of the second volume. Many of the manuscripts used by Moore have subsequently disappeared, and his omissions therefore remain. In the interests of propriety, certain brief passages, not in themselves important, have been deleted from letters, of which the manuscript still exists, at the request of their present owners ; otherwise every letter appears in its entirety. Nothing, however, has been omitted which throws real light on Byron's career or character. These omissions, like Moore's, are denoted by asterisks. Byron's spelling has been preserved, except where it seemed likely to confuse the general reader.

The printed sources which have been drawn upon are *Correspondence of Lord Byron*, by R. C. Dallas; *Letters and Journals of Lord Byron*, by Thomas Moore; *Byron's Letters and Journals*, edited by R. E. Prothero; *Astarte*, by the Earl of Lovelace; *Lord Byron's Correspondence*, edited by John Murray; *Recollections of a Long Life*, by Lord Broughton; *The Life and Letters of Anne Isabella, Lady Noel Byron*, by Ethel Colburn Mayne; *The Last Attachment*, by the Marchesa Iris Origo. For permission to print unpublished material, we are indebted to the legal personal representative of Lord Byron's Estate, who controls Byron copyrights, apart from some controlled by Sir John Murray, and to owners of Byroniana who have allowed us to make use of their manuscripts; the Trustees of the British Museum; Mr. Russell Ellice; the Count Carlo Gamba; Henry E. Huntingdon Library; Rare Books Collections, the University of Texas and Professor Cline; the Lord Kinnaird; the Marquess of Lansdowne; Sir John Murray; the Historical Society of Pennsylvania; the Pierpont Morgan Library; Yale University Library. The editor wishes to express his gratitude for the generous assistance that he has throughout received; to Mr. Harold Nicolson, and especially to Miss Lilian Mattingly, the author of the index. Finally, he would like to put on record his deep indebtedness to his friend, Mr. John Grey Murray, with whom, in surroundings that the poet knew well, he has passed so many agreeable evening hours. Thanks to Mr. Murray's help, encouragement and sympathetic insight into editorial frailties, sessions at 50 Albemarle Street, beneath the eye of Byron's portrait, have frequently assumed an almost festive colouring.

NOTE TO SECOND PRINTING

Since the appearance of the first edition, Dr. Ehrsam of New York University has been kind enough to draw our attention to evidence proving conclusively that a letter purporting to have been addressed to Sir Godfrey Webster from Pisa on April 12th, 1822, is one of the forgeries of G. G. Byron. Another letter has been inserted in its place. To Professor L. A. Marchand of Rutgers University, New Jersey, we are particularly indebted for several important corrections and suggestions.

1
Childhood and Youth
January 1798 to July 1811

George Gordon Lord Byron was born on January 22nd, 1788, at 16 Holles Street, London, the son of Captain John Byron and of his second wife, the former Miss Catherine Gordon of Gight, once a substantial Scottish heiress. By his previous marriage—to the divorced Lady Carmarthen—Captain Byron had a single surviving child, Augusta, subsequently married to her cousin, Colonel George Leigh. His first marriage was brief; his second was ill-fated. A gambler and spend-thrift, by 1786 he had run through his wife's fortune and was obliged to go abroad, where he eventually died in squalor and poverty at Valenciennes. Mrs. Byron had meanwhile returned to London, and thence fell back upon Aberdeen. In that place, amid gloomy and poverty-stricken surroundings, exposed to the tempestuous whims of his ungovernable mother, the little lame boy received his early education. Then, in 1798, his grand-uncle, the " Wicked Lord ", died at Newstead Abbey, and mother and son travelled south to Nottinghamshire to claim the new lord's half-ruined and much-encumbered heritage, the Newstead estates and the disputed Rochdale property. They could not hope to inhabit Newstead itself: the house was dilapidated; their resources were meagre; and for many years they were obliged to make do with a small and unpretentious house in the adjacent town of Southwell. During 1801 Byron was sent to Harrow. At school he made a number of close friends, Clare, Dorset, Delawarr, Wingfield and Long, for whom the feelings he experienced were passionately possessive, ran into several storms, played cricket and swam, but scamped his academic tasks. At home he became desperately enamoured of Mary Chaworth, the " Morning Star of Annesley ", who made light of his protestations and married a dissolute local squire. He would also seem to have had some revealing and disconcerting adventures among the mercenary young ladies whom he met in Southwell drawing-rooms.

Having left Harrow, he went up to Cambridge in the autumn of 1805. At the University, besides his protégé *John Edleston, his friends were Charles Skinner Matthews, Scrope Davies and John Cam Hobhouse. All were high-spirited young men; and it was with their encouragement that, during this period of his life, Byron took his first enthusiastic steps in London dissipation. He was already deep in debt when he came down from Cambridge in July 1808.* English Bards and Scotch Reviewers (*to which he had been provoked by the unkind reception of his juvenile poems,* Hours of Idleness) *appeared in May 1809; and that same spring he gathered his Cambridge friends at Newstead, there to hold profane revels in a romantic mediaeval setting. The Newstead party was to be his farewell to England. In July he sailed from Falmouth, accompanied by John Cam Hobhouse, and visited Portugal, Spain, Sardinia, Malta, Constantinople, Athens and the countries of the Near East. Hobhouse presently returned to England; but Byron remained abroad, eagerly absorbing new impressions and tasting new enjoyments, for exactly two years.*

TO MRS. PARKER[1]   *Newstead Abbey, Nov. 8th, 1798*

DEAR MADAM,—My Mamma being unable to write herself desires I will let you know that the potatoes are now ready and you are welcome to them whenever you please.

She begs you will ask Mrs. Parkyns if she would wish the poney to go round by Nottingham or to go home the nearest way as it is now quite well but too small to carry me.

---

[1] The recipient of this letter, written by Byron at the age of ten years and ten months, was his aunt, Mrs. Parker, born Charlotte Augusta Byron, the mother of Margaret, one of his earliest loves.

3

I have sent a young Rabbit which I beg Miss Frances will accept off and which I promised to send before. My Mamma desires her best compliments to you all in which I join.

I am, Dear Aunt, yours sincerely, BYRON

I hope you will excuse all blunders as it is the first letter I ever wrote.

TO HIS MOTHER   *Harrow-on-the-Hill, Sunday, May 1st, 1803*

MY DEAR MOTHER,—I received your Letter the other day. And am happy to hear you are well. I hope you will find Newstead in as favorable a state as you can wish. I wish you would write to Sheldrake to tell him to make haste with my shoes. I am sorry to say that Mr. Henry Drury has behaved himself to me in a manner I neither *can* nor *will bear.* He has seized now an opportunity of showing his resentment towards me. To day in church I was talking to a Boy who was sitting next me ; *that* perhaps was not right, but hear what followed. After Church he spoke not a word to me, but he took this Boy to his pupil room, where he abused me in a most violent manner, called me *blackguard,* said he *would* and *could* have me expelled from the School, and bade me thank his *Charity* that *prevented* him ; this was the Message he sent me, to which I shall return no answer, but submit my case to *you* and those you may think *fit* to *consult.* Is this fit usage for any body ! had I *stole* or behaved in the most *abominable* way to him, his language could not have been more outrageous. What must the boys think of me to hear such a Message ordered to be delivered to me by a *Master ?* Better let him take away my life than ruin my *Character.* My Conscience acquits me of ever *meriting* expulsion at this School ; I have been *idle* and I certainly ought not to talk in church, but I have never done a mean action at this School to him or *any one.* If I had done anything so *heinous,* why should he allow me to stay at the School ? Why should he himself be so *criminal* as to overlook faults which merit the *appellation* of a *blackguard ?* If he had

4

had it in his power to have me expelled, he would long ago have *done* it ; as it is, he has done *worse*. If I am treated in this Manner, I will not stay at this *School*. I write you that I will not as yet appeal to Dr. Drury ; [1] his son's influence is more than mine and *justice* would be *refused* me. Remember I told you, when I *left* you at *Bath*, that he would seize every means and opportunity of revenge, not for leaving him so much as the mortification he suffered, because I begged you to let me leave him. If I had been the Blackguard he talks of, why did he not of his own accord refuse to keep me as his *pupil* ? You know Dr. Drury's first letter, in it were these Words : " My son and Lord Byron have had some disagreements ; but I hope that his future behaviour will render a change of Tutors unnecessary ". Last time I was here but a short time, and though he endeavoured, he could find nothing to abuse me in. Among other things I forgot to tell you he said he had a great mind to expel the boy for speaking to me, and that if he ever again spoke to me he would expel him. Let him explain his meaning ; he abused me, but he neither did nor can mention anything bad of me, further than what every boy else in the School has done. I fear him not ; but let him explain his meaning ; 'tis all I ask. I beg you will write to Dr. Drury to let him know what I have said. He has behaved to me, as also Mr. Evans, very kindly. If you do not take notice of this, I will leave the School myself ; but I am sure *you* will not see me *ill treated* ; better that I should suffer anything than this. I believe you will be tired by this time of reading my letter, but, if you love me, you will now show it. Pray write me immediately. I shall ever remain,

Your affectionate Son, Byron

P.S.—Hargreaves Hanson [2] desires his love to you and hopes you are very well. I am not in want of any money so will not ask you for any. God bless, bless you.

---

[1] The Reverend Joseph Drury, D.D., was Head-master of Harrow from 1784 to 1805. He was assisted by his son Henry, who afterwards became the poet's close friend.

[2] Son of John Hanson, London solicitor and the Byrons' man of business. He had three sons, Charles, Hargreaves (Byron's contemporary at Harrow) and Newton, and a daughter, Mary Anne, whom the poet gave away when, in 1814, she married the weak-witted Earl of Portsmouth.

TO THE HON. AUGUSTA BYRON   *Burgage Manor*
                                         March 22d, 1804

Although, My ever Dear Augusta, I have hitherto appeared
remiss in replying to your kind and affectionate letters; yet I hope
you will not attribute my neglect to a want of affection, but rather
to a shyness naturally inherent in my Disposition.   I will now endeavour as amply as lies in my power to repay your kindness, and
for the Future I hope you will consider me not only as *a Brother*
but as your warmest and most affectionate *Friend,* and if ever
Circumstances should require it your *protector.*   Recollect, My
Dearest Sister, that you are *the nearest relation* I have in *the world
both by the ties of Blood* and *affection.*   If there is anything in which I
can serve you, you have only to mention it ; Trust to your Brother,
and be assured he will never betray your confidence.   When You
see my Cousin and future Brother George Leigh,[1] tell him that
I already consider him as my Friend, for whoever is beloved by
you, my amiable Sister, will always be equally Dear to me.

I arrived here today at 2 o'clock after a fatiguing Journey,
I found my Mother perfectly well.   She desires to be kindly
remembered to you ; as she is just now Gone out to an assembly,
I have taken the first opportunity to write to you, I hope she
will not return immediately ; for if she was to take it into her
head to peruse my epistle, there is one part of it which would
produce from her a panegyric on *a friend of yours,* not at all
agreeable to me, and I fancy, *not particularly delightful to you.*
If you see Lord Sidney Osborne I beg you will remember me
to him ; I fancy he has almost forgot me by this time, for it
is rather more than a year Since I had the pleasure of Seeing
him.—Also remember me to poor old Murray ;[2] tell him we
will see that something is to be done for him, for *while I live
he shall never be abandoned In his old Age.*   Write to me Soon,
my Dear Augusta, And do not forget to love me, In the meantime, I remain, more than words can express, your ever
sincere, affectionate   Brother and Friend, BYRON

P.S.—Do not forget to knit the purse you promised me,
Adieu my beloved Sister.

---

[1] Byron's half-sister married her first cousin, Colonel George Leigh of the
Tenth Dragoons, in 1807.

[2] Joe Murray, an old servant of the Byron family, to whom Byron afterwards
made a small allowance.

TO THE HON. AUGUSTA BYRON

Southwell, March 26th, 1804

I received your affectionate letter, my ever Dear Sister, yesterday and I now hasten to comply with your injunction by answering it as soon as possible. Not, my Dear Girl, that it can be in the least irksome to me to write to you, on the Contrary it will always prove my Greatest pleasure, but I am sorry that I am afraid my correspondence will not prove the most entertaining, for I have nothing that I can relate to you, except my affection for you, which I can never sufficiently express, therefore I should tire you, before I had half satisfied myself. Ah, How unhappy I have hitherto been in being so long separated from so amiable a Sister ? but fortune has now sufficiently atoned by discovering to me a relation whom I love, a Friend in whom I can confide. In both these lights, my Dear Augusta, I shall ever look upon you, and I hope you will never find your Brother unworthy of your affection and Friendship.

I am as you may imagine a little dull here ; not being on terms of intimacy with Lord Grey [1] I avoid Newstead, and my resources of amusement are Books, and writing to my Augusta, which, wherever I am, will always constitute my Greatest pleasure. I am not reconciled to Lord Grey, *and I never will*. He was once my *Greatest Friend*, my reasons for ceasing that Friendship are such as I cannot explain, not even to you, my Dear Sister, (although were they to be made known to any body, you would be the first,) but they will ever remain hidden in my own breast.

They are Good ones, however, for although I am *violent* I am not *capricious* in my *attachments*. My mother disapproves of my quarrelling with him, but if she knew the cause (which she never will know,) She would reproach me no more. He Has forfeited all *title to my esteem*, but I hold him in too much *contempt* ever *to hate him*. My mother desires to be kindly

[1] Newstead Abbey was let to Lord Grey de Ruthyn from 1803 to 1808. Some light on this quarrel is shed by Hobhouse's pencil note scribbled in the margin of Moore's *Life*. While Mrs. Byron was established at Southwell, Byron often visited Newstead and was on friendly terms with his tenant. " . . . A circumstance occurred during this intimacy [Hobhouse records] which certainly had much effect on his future morals."

remembered to you. I shall soon be in town to resume my studies at Harrow ; I will certainly call upon you in my way up. Present my respects to Mrs. Harcourt ; I am Glad to hear that I am in her Good Graces for I shall always esteem her on account of her behaviour to you, my Dear Girl. Pray tell me If you see Lord S. Osborne, and how he is ; what little I know of him I like very much and If we were better acquainted I doubt not I should like him still better. Do not forget to tell me how Murray is. As to your Future prospects, my Dear Girl, *may they be happy!* I am sure you deserve Happiness and if *you* do not meet with it I shall begin to think it is " a bad world we live in ". Write to me soon. I am impatient to hear from you. God bless you, My amiable Augusta, I remain,

Your ever affectionate Brother and Friend, BYRON

TO THE HON. AUGUSTA BYRON *Burgage Manor,*
August 18th, 1804

MY DEAREST AUGUSTA,—I seize this interval of my *amiable* mother's absence this afternoon, again to inform you, or rather to desire to be informed by you, of what is going on. For my own part I can send nothing to amuse you, excepting a repetition of my complaints against my tormentor, whose *diabolical* disposition (pardon me for staining my paper with so harsh a word) seems to increase with age, and to acquire new force with Time. The more I see of her the more my dislike augments ; nor can I so entirely conquer the appearance of it, as to prevent her from perceiving my opinion ; this, so far from calming the Gale, blows it into a *hurricane*, which threatens to destroy everything, till exhausted by its own violence, it is lulled into a sullen torpor, which, after a short period, is again roused into fresh and renewed phrenzy, to me most terrible, and to every other Spectator astonishing. She then declares that she plainly sees I hate her, that I am leagued with her bitter enemies, viz. Yourself, L^d C[arlisle] [1] and Mr. H[anson],

---

[1] Lord Carlisle, former gambler, dandy and friend of George Selwyn, had become Byron's guardian in 1799. He was connected with the Byron family on his mother's side.

8

and, as I never Dissemble or contradict her, we are all *honoured* with a multiplicity of epithets, too *numerous*, and some of them too *gross*, to be repeated.   In this society, and in this amusing and instructive manner, have I dragged out a weary fortnight, and am condemned to pass another or three weeks as happily as the former.   No captive Negro, or Prisoner of war, ever looked forward to their emancipation, and return to Liberty with more Joy, and with more lingering expectation, than I do to my escape from this maternal bondage, and this accursed place, which is the region of dullness itself, and more stupid than the banks of Lethe, though it possesses contrary qualities to the river of oblivion, as the detested scenes I now witness, make me regret the happier ones already passed, and wish their restoration.

Such Augusta is the happy life I now lead, such my *amusements*.   I wander about hating everything I behold, and if I remained here a few months longer, I should become, what with *envy, spleen and all uncharitableness*, a complete *misanthrope*, but notwithstanding this,

Believe me, Dearest Augusta, ever yours, etc., etc., BYRON

TO HIS MOTHER *   [*Harrow-on-the-Hill, 1804 ?*]

MY DEAR MOTHER,—I received your letter and was very glad to hear that you are well.   I am very comfortable here as far as relates to my Comrades, but I have got into two or three scrapes with Drury and the other Masters, which are not very convenient.   The other day as he was reprimanding me (perhaps very properly) for my misdeeds he uttered the following words, " it is not probable that from your age and situation in the School your Friends will permit you to remain longer than Summer.   But because you are about to leave Harrow, it is no reason you are to make the house a scene of riot and confusion."   This and much more said the Doctor ; and I am informed from creditable authority that Dr. Drury, Mr. Evans and Martin Drury said I was a *Blackguard*.   That Martin Drury said so I *know*, but I am inclined to doubt the authenticity of the report as to the rest.   Perhaps it is true, perhaps not. But thank God they may call me a Blackguard, but they can never make me one. If Dr. Drury can bring one boy or any one else to say that I have committed a dishonourable action, and to prove it, I am content. But otherwise I am stigmatized without a cause, and I disdain and despise the malicious efforts of him and his Brother. His Brother Martin not Henry Drury (whom I will do the justice to say has never since last year interfered with me) is continually reproaching me with the narrowness of my fortune, to what end I know not ; his intentions may be good, but his manner is disagreeable. I see no reason why I am to be reproached with it. I have as much money, as many clothes, and in every respect of appearance am equal if not superior to most of my schoolfellows, and if my fortune is narrow it is my misfortune, not my fault. But, however, the way *to riches*, *to greatness* lies before me. I can, I will cut myself a path through the world or perish in the attempt. Others have begun life with nothing and ended greatly. And shall I, who have a competent if not a large fortune, remain idle ? No, I will carve myself the passage to Grandeur, but never with Dishonour. These, Madam, are my intentions. But why this upstart Son of a Button maker is to reproach me about an estate which, however, is far superior to his own, I know not. But that he should call me a Blackguard is far worse. On account of the former, I can blame only Mr. Hanson (and that officious friend Lord Grey de Ruthyn, whom I shall ever consider as my most inveterate enemy). It is a mere trifle, but the latter I cannot bear. I have not deserved it, and I will not be insulted with impunity. Mr. Martin Drury rides out with his son, sees me at a distance on a poney which I hired to go to the bathing place which is too far for me to walk. He calls out, tells his son I am a Blackguard. This son, who is no friend of mine, comes home, relates the story to his companions, possibly with a few exaggerations. But however the greatest part was true, and I am to be considered as such a person by my comrades. It shall not be. I will say no more. I only hope you will take this into your consideration and remove me at Summer from a place where I am goaded with insults by those from whom I have little deserved it.

I remain your affectionate Son, BYRON

TO THE HON. AUGUSTA BYRON   *Harrow-on-the-Hill,*
                                        October 25th, 1804

MY DEAR AUGUSTA,—In compliance with your wishes, as well as gratitude for your affectionate letter, I proceed as soon as possible to answer it ; I am glad to hear that *any body* gives a good account of me ; but from the quarter you mention, I should imagine it was exaggerated. That you are unhappy, my dear Sister, makes me so also ; were it in my power to relieve your sorrows you would soon recover your spirits ; as it is, I sympathize better than you yourself expect. But really, after all (pardon me my dear Sister), I feel a little inclined to laugh at you, for love, in my humble opinion, is utter nonsense, a mere jargon of compliments, romance, and deceit ; now, for my part, had I fifty mistresses, I should in the course of a fortnight, forget them all, and, if by any chance I ever recollected one, should laugh at it as a dream, and bless my stars, for delivering me from the hands of the little mischievous Blind God. Can't you drive this Cousin of ours out of your pretty little head (for as to *hearts* I think they are out of the question), or if you are so far gone, why don't you give old L'Harpagon (I mean the General) the slip, and take a trip to Scotland, you are now pretty near the Borders. Be sure to Remember me to my formal Guardy Lord Carlisle, whose magisterial presence I have not been into for some years, nor have I any ambition to attain so great an honour. As to your favourite Lady Gertrude, I don't remember her ; pray, is she handsome ? I dare say she is, for although they are a *disagreeable*, *formal*, *stiff* Generation, yet they have by no means plain *persons*, I remember Lady Cawdor was a sweet, pretty woman ; pray, does your sentimental Gertrude resemble her ? I have heard that the duchess of Rutland was handsome also, but we will say nothing about her temper, as I hate Scandal.

Adieu, my pretty Sister, forgive my levity, write soon, and God bless you.

I remain, your very affectionate Brother, BYRON

P.S.—I left my mother at Southwell, some time since, in a monstrous pet with you for not writing. I am sorry to say the old lady and myself don't agree like lambs in a meadow, but I believe it is all my own fault, I am rather too fidgety, which my precise mama objects to, we differ, then argue, and to my shame be it spoken fall out a *little*, however after a storm comes a calm ; what's become of our aunt the amiable antiquated Sophia ? is she yet in the land of the living, or does she sing psalms with the *Blessed* in the other world. Adieu. I am happy enough and Comfortable here. My friends are not numerous, but select ; among them I rank as the principal Lord Delawarr,[1] who is very amiable and my particular friend ; do you know the family at all ? Lady Delawarr is frequently in town, perhaps you may have seen her ; if she resembles her son she is the most amiable woman in Europe. I have plenty of acquaintances, but I reckon them as mere Blanks. Adieu, my dear Augusta.

TO THE HON. AUGUSTA BYRON   *Harrow-on-the-Hill,*
                                Novr., Saturday, 17th, 1804

I am glad to hear, My dear Sister, that you like Castle Howard so well, I have no doubt what you say is true and that Lord C[arlisle] is much more amiable than he has been represented to me. Never having been much with him and always hearing him reviled, it was hardly possible I should have conceived a very *great friendship* for his L^dship. My mother, you inform me, commends my *amiable disposition* and *good understanding* ; if she does this to you, it is a great deal more than I ever hear myself, for the one or the other is always found fault with, and I am told to copy the *excellent pattern* which I see before me in *herself*. You have got an invitation too, you may accept it if you please, but if you value your own comfort, and like a pleasant situation, I advise you to avoid Southwell.—I thank you, My dear Augusta, for your readiness to assist me, and will in some manner avail myself of it ; I do not however wish to be separated from *her* entirely,

[1] Lord Delawarr, like Lord Clare, was one of the bevy of good-looking younger companions whom Byron collected around himself at Harrow.

but not to be so much with her as I hitherto have been, for I do believe she likes me ; she manifests that in many instances, particularly with regard to money, which I never want, and have as much as I desire. But her conduct is so strange, her caprices so impossible to be complied with, her passions so outrageous, that the evil quite overbalances her *agreeable qualities*. Amongst other things I forgot to mention a most *ungovernable appetite* for Scandal, which she never can govern, and employs most of her time abroad, in displaying the faults, and censuring the foibles, of her acquaintance ; therefore I do not wonder, that my precious Aunt, comes in for her share of encomiums ; This however is nothing to what happens when my conduct admits of animadversion ; " then comes the tug of war ". My whole family from the conquest are upbraided ! myself abused, and I am told that what little accomplishments I possess either in mind or body are derived from her and *her alone*.

When I leave Harrow I know not ; that depends on her nod ; I like it very well. The master Dr. Drury, is the most amiable *clergyman* I ever knew ; he unites the Gentleman with the Scholar, without affectation or pedantry, what little I have learnt I owe to him alone, nor is it his fault that it was not more. I shall always remember his instructions with Gratitude, and cherish a hope that it may one day be in my power to repay the numerous obligations, I am under ; to him or some of his family.

Our holidays come on in about a fortnight. I however have not mentioned that to my mother, nor do I intend it ; but if I can, I shall contrive to evade going to Southwell. Depend upon it I will not approach her for some time to come if it is in my power to avoid it, but she must not know, that it is my wish to be absent. I hope you will excuse my sending so short a letter, but the Bell has just rung to summon us together. Write Soon, and believe me,

Ever your affectionate Brother, BYRON

I am afraid you will have some difficulty in decyphering my epistles, but *that* I know you will excuse. Adieu. Remember me to Ld Carlisle.

TO THE HON. AUGUSTA BYRON   *Burgage Manor,*
                                          April 23d, 1805

MY DEAREST AUGUSTA,—I presume by this time, that
you are safely arrived at the Earl's, at least I *hope* so ; nor
shall I feel myself perfectly easy, till I have the pleasure of
hearing from yourself of your safety.   I myself shall set out
for town this day (Tuesday) week, and intend waiting upon
you on Thursday at farthest ; in the mean time I must console
myself as well as I can ; and I am sure, no unhappy mortal
ever required much more consolation than I do at present.
You as well as myself know the *sweet* and *amiable* temper of a
certain personage to whom I am nearly related ; of *course*,
the pleasure I have enjoyed during my vacation, (although
it has been greater than I expected) yet has not been so *super-
abundant* as to make me wish to stay a day longer than I can
avoid.   However, notwithstanding the dullness of the place,
and certain *unpleasant things* that occur In a family not a hundred
miles distant from Southwell, I contrived to pass my time in
peace, till to day, when unhappily, In a most inadvertent
manner, I said that Southwell was not *peculiarly* to my taste ;
but however, I merely expressed this in common conversation,
without speaking disrespectfully of the *sweet* town ; (which,
between you and I, I wish was swallowed up by an earthquake,
provided my *Eloquent mother* was not in it).   No sooner had the
unlucky sentence, which I believe was prompted by my evil
Genius, escaped my lips, than I was treated with an Oration
in the *ancient style*, which I have often so *pathetically* described
to you, unequalled by any thing of *modern* or *antique* date ;
nay the *Philippics* against Lᵈ Melville [1] were nothing to it ;
one would really Imagine, to have heard the *Good Lady*, that
I was a most *treasonable culprit*, but thank St. Peter, after undergoing this *Purgatory* for the last hour, it is at length blown over,
and I have sat down under these *pleasing impressions* to address
you, so that I am afraid my epistle will not be the most entertaining.   I assure you upon my *honour*, jesting apart, I have
never been so *scurrilously*, and *violently* abused by any person,

---

[1] Henry Dundas, created Viscount Melville in 1802, was accused in 1805 of
misdemeanours connected with the accounts of the naval department.   He stood
trial in Westminster Hall during the following year and was acquitted on all
charges.

as by that woman, whom I think I am to call mother, by that being who gave me birth, to whom I ought to look up with veneration and respect, but whom I am sorry I cannot love or admire. Within one little hour, I have not only heard myself, but have heard my *whole family*, by the father's side, *stigmatized* in terms that the *blackest malevolence* would perhaps shrink from, and that too in words you would be shocked to hear. Such, Augusta, such is my mother ; *my mother !* I disclaim her from this time, and although I cannot help treating her with respect, I cannot reverence, as I ought to do, that parent who by her outrageous conduct forfeits all title to filial affection. To you, Augusta, I must look up, as my nearest relation, to you I must confide what I cannot mention to others, and I am sure you will pity me ; but I entreat you to keep this a secret, nor expose that unhappy failing of this woman, which I must bear with patience. I would be very sorry to have it discovered, as I have only one week more, for the present. In the mean time you may write to me with the greatest safety, as she would not open any of my letters, even from you. I entreat then that you will favour me with an answer to this. I hope however to have the pleasure of seeing you on the day appointed, but If you could contrive any way that I may avoid being asked to dinner by L⁴ C. I would be obliged to you, as I hate strangers. Adieu, my Beloved Sister,

　　　　　　　　　　　　　　I remain ever yours, BYRON

TO THE HON. AUGUSTA BYRON　　　　　[Address cut out],
　　　　　　　　　　　　　　　　　Tuesday, July 2d, 1805

MY DEAREST AUGUSTA,—I am just returned from Cambridge, where I have been to enter myself at Trinity College. —Thursday is our Speechday at Harrow, and as I forgot to remind you of its approach, previous to our first declamation, I have given you *timely* notice this time. If you intend doing me the *honour* of attending, I would recommend you not to come without a Gentleman, as I shall be too much engaged all the morning to take care of you, and I should not imagine you would admire *stalking* about by yourself. You had better be there by 12 o'clock as we begin at 1, and I should like to procure you a good place ; Harrow is 11 miles from town, it will just make a *comfortable* mornings drive for you. I don't know how you are to come, but for *Godsake* bring as few women with you as possible. I would wish you to Write me an answer immediately, that I may know on Thursday morning, whether you will drive over or not, and I will arrange my other engagements accordingly. I *beg, Madam,* you may make your appearance in one of his Lordships most *dashing* carriages, as our Harrow *etiquette,* admits of nothing but the most *superb* vehicles, on our Grand *Festivals.* In the mean time, believe me, dearest Augusta,

Your affectionate Brother, BYRON

TO JOHN HANSON *Harrow, 8 July, 1805*

MY DEAR SIR,—I have just received a Letter from my Mother, in which she talks of coming to Town about the *commencement* of our Holidays. If she does, it will be impossible for me to call on *my Sister,* previous to my leaving it, and at the same time I cannot conceive˙ what the Deuce she can want at this season in London. I have written to tell her that my Holidays commence on the 6th of August, but however, July the 31ˢᵗ is the proper day.—I beg that if you cannot find some means to keep her in the Country that you at least will connive at this deception which I can palliate, and then I shall be down in the country before she knows where I am. My reasons for this are, that I do *not wish* to be detained in Town so uncomfortably as I know I shall be if I remain with her ; that *I do wish* to see my Sister ; and in the next place she can just as well come to Town after my return to Notts, as I don't desire to be dragged about according to her caprice, and there are some other causes I think unnecessary to be now mentioned. If you will only contrive by settling this business (if it is in your power), or if that is impossible, not mention anything about the day our Holidays commence, of which you can be easily supposed not to be informed : if, I repeat, you can by any means prevent this Mother from executing her purposes, believe me, you will greatly oblige

Yours truly, BYRON

TO CHARLES O. GORDON [1]　　*Burgage Manor, Southwell, Notts,*
August 4, 1805

Although I am greatly afraid, my Dearest Gordon, that you will not receive this epistle till you return from Abergeldie, (as your letter stated that you would be at Ledbury on Thursday next) yet, that is not my fault, for I have not deferred answering yours a moment, and, as I have just now concluded my Journey, my first, and, I trust you will believe me when I say, most pleasing occupation will be to write to you.

We have played the Eton and were most confoundedly beat; however it was some comfort to me that I got 11 notches the 1st Innings and 7 the 2d, which was more than any of our side except Brockman and Ipswich could contrive to hit. After the match we dined together, and were extremely friendly, not a single discordant word was uttered by either party. To be sure, we were most of us rather drunk and went together to the Haymarket Theatre, where we kicked up a row, As you may suppose, when so many Harrovians and Etonians met at one place; I was one of seven in a single hackney, 4 Eton and 3 Harrow, and then we all got into the same box, and the consequence was that such a devil of a noise arose that none of our neighbours could hear a word of the drama, at which, not being *highly delighted*, they began to quarrel with us, and we nearly came to a *battle royal*. How I got home after the play God knows. I hardly recollect, as my brain was so much confused by the heat, the row, and the wine I drank, that I could not remember in the morning how I found my way to bed.

The rain was so incessant in the evening that we could hardly get our Jarveys, which was the cause of so many being stowed into one. I saw young Twilt, your brother, with

---

[1] Charles Gordon was one of Byron's " juniors and favourites " at Harrow, whom he " spoilt by indulgence ".

Malet, and saw also an old schoolfellow of mine whom I had not beheld for six years, but he was not the one whom you were so good as to enquire after for me, and for which I return you my sincere thanks. I set off last night at eight o'clock to my mother's, and am just arrived this afternoon, and have not delayed a second in thanking you for so soon fulfilling my request that you would correspond with me. My address at Cambridge will be Trinity College, but I shall not go there till the 20th of October. You may continue to direct your letters here, when I go to Hampshire which will not be till you have returned to Harrow. I will send my address previous to my departure from my mother's. I agree with you in the hope that we shall continue our correspondence for a long time. I trust, my dearest friend, that it will only be interrupted by our being some time or other in the same place or under the same roof, as, when I have finished my *Classical Labour*, and my minority is expired, I shall expect you to be a frequent visitor to Newstead Abbey, my seat in this country which is about 12 miles from my mother's house where I now am. There I can show you plenty of hunting, shooting and fishing, and be assured no one ever will be more welcome guest than yourself—nor is there any one whose correspondence can give me more pleasure, or whose friendship yield me greater delight than yours, sweet, dearest Charles, believe me, will always be the sentiments of

Yours most affectionately, BYRON

TO CHARLES O. GORDON   *Burgage Manor, August 14, 1805*

Believe me, my dearest Charles, no letter from you can ever be unentertaining or dull, at least to me; on the contrary they will always be productive of the highest pleasure as often as you think proper to gratify me by your correspondence. My answer to your first was addressed to Ledbury; and I fear you will not receive it till you return from your tour, which I hope may answer your expectation in every respect; I recollect some years ago passing near Abergeldie in an excursion through the Highlands, it was at that time a most beautiful place.

I suppose you will soon have a view of the eternal snows that summit the top of Lachin y Gair, which towers so majestically above the rest of our *Northern Alps*. I still remember with pleasure the admiration which filled my mind, when I first beheld it, and further on the dark frowning mountains which rise near Invercauld, together with the romantic rocks that overshadow Mar Lodge, a seat of Lord Fife's, and the cataract of the Dee, which dashes down the declivity with impetuous violence in the grounds adjoining to the House. All these I presume you will soon see, so that it is unnecessary for me to expatiate further on the subject. I sincerely wish that every happiness may attend you in your progress. I have given you an account of our match in my epistle to Herefordshire. We unfortunately lost it. I got 11 notches the first innings and 7 the 2d, making 18 in all, which was more runs than any of our side (except Ipswich) could make. Brockman also scored 18. After the match we dined together and were very convivial. In the evening we proceeded to the play.

TO THE HON. AUGUSTA BYRON   *Trin. Coll.*
                             [*Wednesday*], *Novr. 6th, 1805*

MY DEAR AUGUSTA,—As might be supposed I like a College Life extremely, especially as I have escaped the Trammels or rather *Fetters* of my domestic Tyrant Mrs. Byron, who continued to plague me during my visit in July and September. I am now most pleasantly situated in *Super*excellent Rooms, flanked on one side by my Tutor, on the other by an old Fellow, both of whom are rather checks upon my *vivacity*. I am allowed 500 a year, a Servant and Horse, so Feel as independent as a German Prince who coins his own Cash, or a Cherokee Chief who coins no Cash at all, but enjoys what is more precious, Liberty. I talk in raptures of that *Goddess* because my amiable Mama was so despotic. I am afraid the Specimens I have lately given her of my Spirit, and determination to submit to no more unreasonable demands, (or the insults which follow a refusal to obey her implicitly whether right or wrong,) have given high offence, as I had a most *fiery* Letter from the *Court* at *Southwell* on Tuesday, because I would not turn off my Servant, (whom I had not the least reason to distrust, and who had an excellent Character from his last Master) at her suggestion, from some caprice she had taken into her head. I sent back to the Epistle, which was couched in *elegant* terms, a severe answer, which so nettled her Ladyship, that after reading it, she returned it in a Cover without deigning a Syllable in return.

The Letter and my answer you shall behold when you next see me, that you may judge of the Comparative merits of Each. I shall let her go on in the *Heroics*, till she cools, without taking the least notice. Her Behaviour to me for the last two Years neither merits my respect, nor deserves my affection. I am comfortable here, and having one of the best allowances in College, go on Gaily, but not extravagantly. I need scarcely inform you that I am not the least obliged to Mrs. B. for it, as it comes off my property, and She refused to fit out a single thing for me from her own pocket ; my Furniture is paid for, and she has moreover a handsome addition made to her own income, which I do not in the least regret, as I would wish her to be happy, but by *no means* to live with me in *person*. The sweets of her society I have already drunk to the last dregs, I hope we shall meet on more affectionate Terms, or meet no more.

But why do I say *meet*? her temper precludes every idea of happiness, and therefore in future I shall avoid her *hospitable* mansion, though she has the folly to suppose She is to be mistress of my house when I come of [age].¹ I must apologize to you for the [dullness?] ¹ of this letter, but to tell you the [truth] ¹ [the effects] ¹ of last nights Claret have no[t gone] ¹ out of my head, as I supped with a large party. I suppose that Fool Hanson in his *vulgar* Idiom, by the word Jolly did not mean Fat, but High Spirits, for so far from increasing I have lost one pound in a fortnight as I find by being regularly weighed.

Adieu, Dearest Augusta. [Signature cut out.]

TO JOHN HANSON   *Trinity College, Cambridge, Novr. 30, 1805*

SIR,—After the contents of your epistle, you will probably be less surprized at my answer, than I have been at many points

¹ Words torn out with the seal.

of yours; never was I more astonished than at the perusal, for I confess I expected very different treatment. Your *indirect* charge of Dissipation does not affect me, nor do I fear the strictest inquiry into my conduct; neither here nor at *Harrow* have I disgraced myself, the " Metropolis " and the " Cloisters " are alike unconscious of my debauchery, and on the plains of *merry Sherwood* I have experienced *Misery* alone; in July I visited them for the last time. Mrs. Byron and myself are now totally separated, injured by her, I sought refuge with Strangers, too late I see my error, for how was kindness to be expected from *others*, when denied by a *parent*? In you, Sir, I imagined I had found an Instructor; for your advice I thank you; the Hospitality of yourself and Mrs. H. on many occasions I shall always gratefully remember, for I am not of opinion that even present injustice can cancel past obligations. Before I proceed, it will be necessary to say a few words concerning Mrs. Byron; you hinted a probability of her appearance at Trinity; the instant I hear of her arrival I quit Cambridge, though *Rustication* or *Expulsion* be the consequence. Many a weary week of *torment* have I passed with her, nor have I forgot the insulting *Epithets* with which myself, my *Sister*, my *father* and my *Family* have been repeatedly reviled.

To return to you, Sir, though I feel obliged by your hospitality, etc., etc., in the present instance I have been completely deceived. When I came down to College, and even previous to that period I stipulated that not only my Furniture, but even my Gowns and Books, should be paid for that I might set out free from *Debt*. Now with all the *Sang Froid* of your profession you tell me, that not only I shall not be permitted to repair my rooms (which was at first agreed to) but that I shall not even be indemnified for my present expence. In one word, hear my determination. I will *never* pay for them out of my allowance, and the Disgrace will not attach to me but to *those* by whom I have been deceived. Still, Sir, not even the Shadow of dishonour shall reflect on *my* Name, for I will see that the Bills are discharged; whether by you or not is to me indifferent, so that the men I employ are not the victims of my Imprudence or your Duplicity. I have ordered nothing extravagant; every man in College is allowed to fit up his rooms; mine are secured to me during my residence which will probably be some time, and in rendering them decent I am more praiseworthy than culpable. The money I requested was but a secondary consideration; as a *Lawyer* you were not obliged to advance it till due; as a *Friend* the request might have been complied with. When it is required at Xmas I shall expect the demand will be answered. In the course of my letter I perhaps have expressed more asperity than I intended, it is my nature to feel warmly, nor shall any consideration of interest or Fear ever deter me from giving vent to my Sentiments, when injured, whether by a Sovereign or a Subject.

I remain, etc., etc., BYRON

TO THE HON. AUGUSTA BYRON   *16, Piccadilly,*
                                  Decr. 27th, 1805

MY DEAR AUGUSTA,—You will doubtless be surprised to see a second epistle so close upon the arrival of the first, (especially as it is not my custom) but the Business I mentioned rather mysteriously in my last compels me again to proceed. But before I disclose it, I must require the most inviolable Secrecy, for if ever I find that it has transpired, all confidence, all Friendship between us has concluded. I do not mean this exordium as a threat to induce you to comply with my request but merely (whether you accede or not) to keep it a Secret. And although your compliance would essentially oblige me, yet, believe me, my esteem will not be diminished by your Refusal; nor shall I suffer a complaint to escape. The Affair is briefly thus; like all other young men just let loose, and especially one as I am, freed from the worse than bondage of my maternal home, I have been extravagant, and consequently am in want of Money. You will probably now imagine that I am going to apply to you for some. No, if you would offer me thousands, I declare solemnly that I would without hesitation refuse, nor would I accept them were I in danger of Starvation. All I expect or wish is, that you will be joint Security with me for a few Hundreds a person (one of the money lending tribe) has offered to advance in case I can bring forward any collateral guarantee that he will not be a loser, the reason of this requisition is my being a Minor, and might refuse to discharge a debt contracted in my nonage. If I live till the period of my minority expires, you cannot doubt my paying, as I have property to the amount of 100 times the sum I am about to raise; if, as I think rather probable, a pistol or a Fever cuts short the thread of my existence, you will receive half the *Dross* saved since I was ten years old, and can be no great loser by discharging a debt of 7 or £800 from as many thousands. It is far from my Breast to exact any promise from you that would be detrimental, or tend to lower me in your opinion. If you suppose this leads to either of those consequences, forgive my impertinence and bury it in oblivion. I have many Friends, most of them in the same predicament with myself; to those who are not, I am too proud to apply, for I hate obligation; my Relations you know I *detest*; who then is there that I can address on the subject but yourself? to you therefore I appeal, and if I am disappointed, at least let me not be tormented by the advice of Guardians, and let silence rule your Resolution. I know you will think me foolish, if not criminal; but tell me so yourself, and do not rehearse my failings to others, no, not even to that proud Grandee the Earl, who, whatever his qualities may be, is certainly not amiable, and that Chattering puppy Hanson would make still less allowance for the foibles of a Boy. I am now trying the experiment, whether a woman can retain a secret; let me not be deceived. If you have the least doubt of my integrity, or that you run too great a Risk, do not hesitate in your refusal. Adieu. I expect an answer with impatience, believe me, whether you accede or not,

[Signature cut out.]

P.S.—I apologize for the numerous errors probably enveloped in this cover; the temper of my mind at present, and the hurry I have written in, must plead for pardon. Adieu.

TO JOHN M. B. PIGOT[1]   *16 Piccadilly, August 9, 1806*

MY DEAR PIGOT,—Many thanks for your amusing narrative
of the last proceedings of my amiable Alecto, who now begins
to feel the effects of her folly. I have just received a penitential
epistle, to which, apprehensive of pursuit, I have despatched
a moderate answer, with a *kind* of promise to return in a fortnight;—this, however (*entre nous*), I never mean to fulfil.
Her soft warblings must have delighted her auditors, her higher
notes being particularly musical, and on a calm moonlight
evening would be heard to great advantage. Had I been
present as a spectator, nothing would have pleased me more;
but to have come forward as one of the *dramatis personæ*—St.
Dominic defend me from such a scene! Seriously, your
mother has laid me under great obligations, and you, with the
rest of your family, merit my warmest thanks for your kind
connivance at my escape from " Mrs. Byron *furiosa* ".

Oh! for the pen of Ariosto to rehearse, in epic, the scolding
of that momentous eve,—or rather, let me invoke the shade of
Dante to inspire me, for none but the author of the Inferno
could properly preside over such an attempt. But, perhaps,
where the pen might fail, the pencil would succeed. What a
group!—Mrs. B. the principal figure; you cramming your
ears with cotton, as the only antidote to total deafness; Mrs.
—— in vain endeavouring to mitigate the wrath of the lioness
robbed of her whelp; and last, though not least, Elizabeth and
Wousky,—wonderful to relate!—both deprived of their parts
of speech, and bringing up the rear in mute astonishment.
How did S. B. receive the intelligence? How many *puns* did
he utter on so *facetious* an event? In your next inform me on
this point, and what excuse you made to A. You are probably,
by this time, tired of deciphering this hieroglyphical letter;—
like Tony Lumpkin, you will pronounce mine to be " a damned
up and down hand." All Southwell, without doubt, is involved
in amazement. *Apropos*, how does my blue-eyed nun, the
fair * *? Is she " *robed in sable garb of woe* "?

Here I remain at least a week or ten days; previous to

---

[1] His friendship with the Pigot family, which included John Pigot and his
sister, Elizabeth Bridget, was one of the few agreeable features of Byron's life at
Southwell. Miss Pigot, who survived till 1866, remembered him as a " fat,
bashful boy, with his hair combed straight over his forehead. . . ."

my departure you shall receive my address, but what it will be I have not determined. My lodgings must be kept secret from Mrs. B. You may present my compliments to her, and say any attempt to pursue me will fail, as I have taken measures to retreat immediately to Portsmouth, on the first intimation of her removal from Southwell. You may add, I have proceeded to a friend's house in the country, there to remain a fortnight.

I have now *blotted* (I must not say written) a complete double letter, and in return shall expect a *monstrous budget*. Without doubt, the dames of Southwell reprobate the pernicious example I have shown, and tremble lest their *babes* should disobey their mandates, and quit, in dudgeon, their mammas on any grievance. Adieu. When you begin your next, drop the " lordship ", and put " Byron " in its place.

Believe me yours, etc., BYRON

TO THE EARL OF CLARE[1]   *Southwell, Notts, February 6, 1807*

MY DEAREST CLARE,—Were I to make all the apologies necessary to atone for my late negligence, you would justly say you had received a petition instead of a letter, as it would be filled with prayers for forgiveness; but instead of this, I will acknowledge my *sins* at once, and I trust to your friendship and generosity rather than to my own excuses. Though my health is not perfectly re-established, I am out of all danger, and have recovered every thing but my spirits, which are subject to depression. You will be astonished to hear I have lately written to Delawarr, for the purpose of explaining (as far as possible without involving some *old friends* of mine in the business) the cause of my behaviour to him during my last residence at Harrow (nearly two years ago), which you will recollect was rather " *en cavalier* ". Since that period, I have discovered he was treated with injustice both by those who misrepresented his conduct, and by me in consequence of their suggestions. I have therefore made all the reparation

---

[1] Of all his Harrow friendships, that with Lord Clare lasted longest, and was remembered by Byron with most tenderness and gratitude.

in my power, by apologizing for my mistake, though with very faint hopes of success; indeed I never expected any answer, but desired one for form's sake; *that* has not yet arrived, and most probably never will. However, I have *eased* my own *conscience* by the atonement, which is humiliating enough to one of my disposition; yet I could not have slept satisfied with the reflection of having, *even unintentionally*, injured any individual. I have done all that could be done to repair the injury, and there the affair must end. Whether we renew our intimacy or not is of very trivial consequence.

My time has lately been much occupied with very different pursuits. I have been *transporting* a servant, who cheated me,— rather a disagreeable event;—performing in private theatricals; —publishing a volume of poems (at the request of my friends, for their perusal);—making love,—and taking physic. The two last amusements have not had the best effect in the world; for my attentions have been divided amongst so many fair damsels, and the drugs I swallow are of such variety in their composition, that between Venus and Æsculapius I am harassed to death. However, I have still leisure to devote some hours to the recollections of past, regretted friendships, and in the interval to take the advantage of the moment, to assure you how much I am, and ever will be, my dearest Clare,

Your truly attached and sincere BYRON

TO JOHN HANSON *Southwell, April 2nd, 1807*

DEAR SIR,—Before I proceed in Reply to the other parts of your Epistle, allow me to congratulate you on the *Accession* of *Dignity* and *profit*, which will doubtless accrue, from your official appointment.

You was fortunate in obtaining possession at so critical a period; your patrons " exeunt omnes ". I trust they will soon supersede the Cyphers, their successors. The Reestablishment of your health is another happy event, and, though *secondary* in my *Statement*, is by no means so in my *Wishes*. As to our Feuds, they are purely *official*, the natural consequence of our relative Situations, but as little connected with *personal animosity*, as the *Florid Declamations* of *parliamentary Demagogues*. I return you my thanks for your favorable opinion of my muse; I have lately been honoured with many very flattering literary critiques, from men of high Reputation in the Sciences, particularly Lord Woodhous[lee] and Henry Mackenzie, both *Scots* and of great Eminence as *Authors* themselves. I have received also some most favorable Testimonies from *Cambridge*. This you will *marvel* at, as indeed I did myself. Encouraged by these and several other Encomiums, I am about to publish a volume at large; this will be very different from the present; the amatory effusions (not to be wondered at from the *dissipated* Life I have led) will be cut out, and others substituted. I coincide with you in opinion that the *Poet* yields to the *orator*; but as nothing can be done in the latter capacity till the expiration of my *Minority*, the former occupies my present attention, and both *ancients* and *moderns* have declared that the two pursuits are so nearly similar as to require in a great measure the same Talents, and he who excels in the one, would on application succeed in the other. Lyttelton, Glover, and Young (who was a celebrated Preacher and a Bard) are instances of the kind. *Sheridan* and *Fox* also; *these* are *great Names*. I may imitate, I can never equal them.

You speak of the *Charms* of Southwell; the *place* I *abhor*. The Fact is I remain here because I can appear no where else, being *completely done* up. *Wine* and *Women* have *dished* your *humble Servant*, not a *Sou* to be *had*; all *over*; condemned to exist (I cannot say live) at this *Crater* of Dullness till my *Lease* of *Infancy* expires. To appear at Cambridge is impossible; no money even to pay my College expences. You will be surprized to hear I am grown *very thin*; however it is the *Fact*, so much so, that the people here think I am *going*. I have lost 18 LB in my weight, that is one Stone and 4 pounds since January, this was ascertained last Wednesday, on account of a *Bet* with an acquaintance. However don't be alarmed; I have taken every means to accomplish the end, by violent exercise and Fasting, as I found myself too plump. I shall continue my Exertions, having no other amusement; I wear *seven* Waistcoats and a great Coat, run, and play at cricket in this Dress, till quite exhausted by excessive perspiration, use the hot Bath daily; eat only a quarter of a pound of Butcher's Meat in

27

24 hours, no Suppers or Breakfast, only one Meal a Day ; drink no malt liquor, but a little Wine, and take Physic occasionally. By these means my *Ribs* display Skin of no great Thickness, and my Clothes have been taken in nearly *half a yard*. Do you believe me now?

Adieu. Remembrance to Spouse and the Acorns.

Yours ever, BYRON

TO ELIZABETH BRIDGET PIGOT   *Cambridge, June 30, 1807*

" Better late than never, Pal " is a saying of which you know the origin, and as it is applicable on the present occasion, you will excuse its conspicuous place in the front of my epistle. I am almost superannuated here. My old friends (with the exception of a very few) all departed, and I am preparing to follow them, but remain till Monday to be present at three *Oratorios*, two *Concerts*, a *Fair*, and a Ball. I find I am not only *thinner* but *taller* by an inch since my last visit. I was obliged to tell every body my *name*, nobody having the least recollection of my *visage*, or person. Even the hero of *my Cornelian* [1] (who is now sitting *vis-à-vis* reading a volume of my *Poetics*) passed me in Trinity walks without recognising me in the least, and was thunderstruck at the alteration which had taken place in my countenance, etc., etc. Some say I look *better*, others *worse*, but all agree I am *thinner*,—more I do not require. I have lost two pounds in my weight since I left your *cursed, detestable*, and *abhorred* abode of *scandal*, where, excepting yourself and John Becher,[2] I care not if the whole race were consigned to the *Pit* of *Acheron*, which I would visit in person rather than contaminate my *sandals* with the polluted dust of Southwell. *Seriously*, unless obliged by the *emptiness* of my purse to revisit Mrs. B., you will see me no more.

On Monday I depart for London. I quit Cambridge with little regret, because our *set* are *vanished*, and my *musical protégé* before mentioned has left the choir, and is stationed in a mer-

[1] John Edleston, a Cambridge chorister, whom Byron adopted as his protégé, and to whom he presented a Cornelian heart.

[2] The Reverend John Becher, another Southwell friend and an intimate of the Pigot family.

cantile house of considerable eminence in the metropolis. You may have heard me observe he is exactly to an hour two years younger than myself. I found him grown considerably, and as you will suppose, very glad to see his former *Patron*. He is nearly my height, very *thin*, very fair complexion, dark eyes, and light locks. My opinion of his mind you already know ;—I hope I shall never have occasion to change it. Every body here conceives me to be an *invalid*. The University at present is very gay from the fêtes of divers kinds. I supped out last night, but eat (or ate) nothing, sipped a bottle of claret, went to bed at two, and rose at eight. I have commenced early rising, and find it agrees with me. The Masters and the Fellows all very *polite*, but look a little *askance*—don't much admire *lampoons*—truth always disagreeable.

Write, and tell me how the inhabitants of your *Menagerie* go *on*, and if my publication goes *off* well : do the quadrupeds *growl?* Apropos, my bull-dog is deceased—" Flesh both of cur and man is grass ". Address your answer to Cambridge. If I am gone, it will be forwarded. Sad news just arrived— Russians beat—a bad set, eat nothing but *oil*, consequently must melt before a *hard fire*. I get awkward in my academic habiliments for want of practice. Got up in a window to hear the oratorio at St. Mary's, popped down in the middle of the *Messiah*, tore a *woeful* rent in the back of my best black silk gown, and damaged an egregious pair of breeches. Mem.— never tumble from a church window during service. Adieu, dear * * * * ! do not remember me to any body :—to *forget* and be forgotten by the people of Southwell is all I aspire to.

TO ELIZABETH BRIDGET PIGOT   *Trin. Coll. Camb.*
                                  July 5, 1807

Since my last letter I have determined to reside *another year* at Granta, as my rooms, etc., etc., are finished in great style, several old friends come up again, and many new ac- quaintances made ; consequently my inclination leads me forward, and I shall return to college in October if still *alive*. My life here has been one continued routine of dissipation—

out at different places every day, engaged to more dinners, etc., etc., than my *stay* would permit me to fulfil. At this moment I write with a bottle of claret in my *head* and *tears* in my *eyes*; for I have just parted with my " *Cornelian* ", who spent the evening with me. As it was our last interview, I postponed my engagement to devote the hours of the *Sabbath* to friendship :—Edleston and I have separated for the present, and my mind is a chaos of hope and sorrow. To-morrow I set out for London : you will address your answer to " Gordon's Hotel, Albemarle Street ", where I *sojourn* during my visit to the metropolis.

I rejoice to hear you are interested in my *protégé*; he has been my *almost constant* associate since October, 1805, when I entered Trinity College. His *voice* first attracted my attention, his *countenance* fixed it, and his *manners* attached me to him for ever. He departs for a *mercantile house* in *town* in October, and we shall probably not meet till the expiration of my minority, when I shall leave to his decision either entering as a *partner* through my interest, or residing with me altogether. Of course he would in his present frame of mind prefer the *latter*, but he may alter his opinion previous to that period ;—however, he shall have his choice. I certainly love him more than any human being, and neither time nor distance have had the least effect on my (in general) changeable disposition. In short, we shall put *Lady E. Butler* and *Miss Ponsonby* [1] to the blush, *Pylades* and *Orestes* out of countenance, and want nothing but a catastrophe like *Nisus* and *Euryalus*, to give *Jonathan* and *David* the " go by ". He certainly is perhaps more attached to *me* than even I am in return. During the whole of my residence at Cambridge we met every day, summer and winter, without passing *one* tiresome moment, and separated each time with increasing reluctance. I hope you will one day see us together. He is the only being I esteem, though I *like* many.

The Marquis of Tavistock was down the other day; I supped with him at his tutor's—entirely a Whig party. The opposition muster strong here now, and Lord Hartington, the Duke of Leinster, etc., etc., are to join us in October, so every thing will be *splendid*. The *music* is all over at present. Met

[1] Those " two dear inseparable inimitables ", the celebrated " Ladies of Llangollen ".

with another "*accidency*"—upset a butter-boat in the lap of
a lady—look'd very *blue*—*spectators* grinned—"curse 'em!"
Apropos, sorry to say, been *drunk* every day, and not quite
sober yet—however, touch no meat, nothing but fish, soup, and
vegetables, consequently it does me no harm—sad dogs all
the *Cantabs*. Mem.—*we mean* to reform next January. This
place is a *monotony of endless variety*—like it—hate Southwell.
Has Ridge sold well? or do the ancients demur? What ladies
have bought?

Saw a girl at St. Mary's the image of Anne * * *, thought
it was her—all in the wrong—the lady stared, so did I—I
blushed, so did *not* the lady,—sad thing—wish women had *more
modesty*. Talking of women, puts me in mind of my terrier
Fanny—how is she? Got a headache, must go to bed, up early
in the morning to travel. My *protégé* breakfasts with me;
parting spoils my appetite—excepting from Southwell. Mem.
I hate Southwell.

Yours, etc.

TO ELIZABETH BRIDGET PIGOT　　　　*Gordon's Hotel,
July 13, 1807*

You write most excellent epistles—a fig for other correspondents, with their nonsensical apologies for "*knowing nought about
it*",—you send me a delightful budget. I am here in a perpetual vortex of dissipation (very pleasant for all that), and,
strange to tell, I get thinner, being now below eleven stone
considerably. Stay in town a *month*, perhaps six weeks, trip
into Essex, and then, as a favour, *irradiate* Southwell for three
days with the light of my countenance; but nothing shall ever
make me *reside* there again. I positively return to Cambridge
in October; we are to be uncommonly gay, or in truth I
should *cut* the University. An extraordinary circumstance
occurred to me at Cambridge; a girl so very like * * made her
appearance, that nothing but the most *minute inspection* could
have undeceived me. I wish I had asked if *she* had ever been
at H * * *

What the devil would Ridge [1] have? is not fifty in a fort-night, before the advertisements, a sufficient sale? I hear many of the London booksellers have them, and Crosby has sent copies to the principal watering places. Are they liked or not in Southwell? * * * * * I wish Boatswain [2] had *swallowed* Damon! How is Bran? by the immortal gods, Bran ought to be a *Count* of the *Holy Roman Empire*.

The intelligence of London cannot be interesting to you, who have rusticated all your life—the annals of routs, riots, balls and boxing-matches, cards and crim. cons., parliamentary discussion, political details, masquerades, mechanics, Argyle Street Institution and aquatic races, love and lotteries, Brookes's and Buonaparte, opera-singers and oratorios, wine, women, wax-work, and weathercocks, can't accord with your *insulated* ideas of decorum and other *silly expressions* not inserted in *our vocabulary*.

Oh! Southwell, Southwell, how I rejoice to have left thee, and how I curse the heavy hours I dragged along, for so many months, among the Mohawks who inhabit your kraals!—However, one thing I do not regret, which is having *pared off* a sufficient quantity of flesh to enable me to slip into " an eel-skin ", and vie with the *slim* beaux of modern times; though I am sorry to say, it seems to be the mode amongst *gentlemen* to grow *fat*, and I am told I am at least fourteen pound below the fashion. However, I *decrease* instead of en-larging, which is extraordinary, as *violent* exercise in London is impracticable; but I attribute the *phenomenon* to our *evening squeezes* at public and private parties. I heard from Ridge this morning (the 14th, my letter was begun yesterday): he says the poems go on as well as can be wished; the seventy-five sent to town are circulated, and a demand for fifty more com-plied with, the day he dated his epistle, though the advertise-ments are not yet half published. Adieu.

[1] Byron's first collection of juvenile verses, published in 1806 and entitled *Fugitive Pieces*, had been suppressed on the advice of the Reverend John Becher. During the next year it was followed by a second, *Poems on Various Occasions*, issued anonymously, and during the summer months by a third, *Hours of Idleness*, which received considerable notice. All three were published by S. & J. Ridge of Newark.

[2] Boatswain, Byron's big black-and-white Newfoundland dog, died during the following year and was buried in the garden vault at Newstead, where the poet afterwards directed that he was himself to lie.

P.S.—Lord Carlisle, on receiving my poems, sent, before he opened the book, a tolerably handsome letter :—I have not heard from him since. His opinions I neither know nor care about : if he is the least insolent, I shall enrol him with *Butler* and the other worthies. He is in Yorkshire, poor man ! and very ill ! He said he had not had time to read the contents, but thought it necessary to acknowledge the receipt of the volume immediately. Perhaps the Earl " *bears no brother near the throne* ",—*if so*, I will make his *sceptre* totter *in his hands*.— Adieu !

TO ELIZABETH BRIDGET PIGOT   *August 2, 1807*

London begins to disgorge its contents—town is empty— consequently I can scribble at leisure, as occupations are less numerous. In a fortnight I shall depart to fulfil a country engagement ; but expect two epistles from you previous to that period. Ridge does not proceed rapidly in Notts—very possible. In town things wear a more promising aspect, and a man whose works are praised by *reviewers*, admired by *duchesses*, and sold by every bookseller of the metropolis, does not dedicate much consideration to *rustic readers*. I have now a review before me, entitled *Literary Recreations* where my *bardship* is applauded far beyond my deserts. I know nothing of the critic, but think *him* a very discerning gentleman, and *myself* a devilish *clever* fellow. His critique pleases me particularly, because it is of great length, and a proper quantum of censure is administered, just to give an agreeable *relish* to the praise. You know I hate insipid, unqualified, common-place compliment. If you would wish to see it, order the 13th Number of *Literary Recreations* for the last month. I assure you I have not the most distant idea of the writer of the article—it is printed in a periodical publication—and though I have written a paper (a review of Wordsworth), which appears in the same work, I am ignorant of every other person concerned in it—even the editor, whose name I have not heard. My cousin, Lord Alexander Gordon, who resided in the same hotel, told me his mother, her Grace of Gordon, requested he would introduce my *Poetical* Lordship to her *Highness*, as she had bought my volume, admired it exceedingly, in common with the rest of the fashionable world, and wished to claim her relationship with the author. I was unluckily engaged on an excursion for some days afterwards; and, as the Duchess was on the eve of departing for Scotland, I have postponed my introduction till the winter, when I shall favour the lady, *whose taste I shall not dispute*, with my most sublime and edifying conversation. She is now in the Highlands, and Alexander took his departure, a few days ago, for the same *blessed* seat of " *dark rolling winds* ".

Crosby, my London publisher, has disposed of his second importation, and has sent to Ridge for a *third*—at least so he says. In every bookseller's window I see my *own name*, and *say nothing*, but enjoy my fame in secret. My last reviewer kindly requests me to alter my determination of writing no more : and " A Friend to the Cause of Literature " begs I will *gratify* the *public* with some new work " at no very distant period ". Who would not be a bard?—that is to say, if all critics would be so polite. However, the others will pay me off, I doubt not, for this *gentle* encouragement. If so, have at 'em? By the by, I have written at my intervals of leisure, after two in the morning, 380 lines in blank verse, of Bosworth Field. I have luckily got Hutton's account. I shall extend the poem to eight or ten books, and shall have finished it in a year. Whether it will be published or not must depend on circumstances. So much for *egotism* ! My *laurels* have turned my brain, but the *cooling acids* of forthcoming criticism will probably restore me to *modesty*.

Southwell is a damned place—I have done with it—at least in all probability; excepting yourself, I esteem no one within its precincts. You were my only *rational* companion; and in plain truth, I had more respect for you than the whole *bevy*, with whose foibles I amused myself in compliance with their prevailing propensities. You gave yourself more trouble with me and my manuscripts than a thousand *dolls* would have done. Believe me, I have not forgotten your good nature in *this circle* of *sin*, and one day I trust I shall be able to evince my gratitude. Adieu.

Yours, etc.

P.S.—Remember me to Dr. P.

On Sunday next I set off for the Highlands. A friend of mine accompanies me in my carriage to Edinburgh. There we shall leave it, and proceed in a *tandem* (a species of open carriage) through the western passes to Inverary, where we shall purchase *shelties*, to enable us to view places inaccessible to *vehicular conveyances*. On the coast we shall hire a vessel, and visit the most remarkable of the Hebrides ; and, if we have time and favourable weather, mean to sail as far as Iceland, only 300 miles from the northern extremity of Caledonia, to peep at *Hecla*. This last intention you will keep a secret, as my nice *mamma* would imagine I was on a Voyage of *Discovery*, and raise the accustomed *maternal warwhoop*.

Last week I swam in the Thames from Lambeth through the two bridges, Westminster and Blackfriars, a distance, including the different turns and tracks made on the way, of three miles ! You see I am in excellent training in case of a *squall* at sea. I mean to collect all the Erse traditions, poems, etc., etc., and translate, or expand the subject to fill a volume, which may appear next spring under the denomination of " *The Highland Harp* ", or some title equally *picturesque*. Of Bosworth Field, one book is finished, another just began. It will be a work of three or four years, and most probably never *conclude*. What would you say to some stanzas on Mount Hecla? they would be written at least with *fire*. How is the immortal Bran? and the Phœnix of canine quadrupeds, Boatswain? I have lately purchased a thorough-bred bull-dog, worthy to be the coadjutor of the aforesaid celestials—his name is *Smut* !—" Bear it, ye breezes, on your *balmy* wings ".

Write to me before I set off, I conjure you, by the fifth rib of your grandfather. Ridge goes on well with the books— I thought that worthy had not done much in the country. In town they have been very successful ; Carpenter (Moore's publisher) told me a few days ago they sold all their's im-mediately, and had several enquiries made since, which, from the books being gone, they could not supply. The Duke of York, the Marchioness of Headfort, the Duchess of Gordon, etc., etc., were among the purchasers ; and Crosby says the circulation will be still more extensive in the winter, the summer season being very bad for a sale, as most people are absent from London. However, they have gone off extremely well altogether. I shall pass very near you on my journey through Newark, but cannot approach. Don't tell this to Mrs. B, who supposes I travel a different road. If you have a letter, order it to be left at Ridge's shop, where I shall call, or the post-office, Newark, about six or eight in the evening. If your brother would ride over, I should be devilish glad to see him—he can return the same night, or sup with us and go home the next morning—the Kingston Arms is my inn. Adieu.

Yours ever, BYRON

TO LORD CLARE *   *Cambridge, August 20th, 1807*

MY DEAR CLARE,—What apology will be adequate to atone for my offence I know not. I can only say your letters would not have remained so long unnoticed, had I received them previous to my arrival at this place after an absence of 10 months when your kind epistles were diligently perused. Here they had waited for 6 months, and from them I received the first intimation of your departure from Harrow. Since *we* met, they tell me I am grown taller and so much thinner from illness and violent exercise that many who had lived with me in habits of intimacy, even old *school fellows*, found great difficulty in acknowledging me to be the *same person*. Indeed I ought to be *thin* for I weigh less by *three stone* and 9 *pounds* than I did 6 months ago. My weight was then 14 stone and 6 lbs. It is now 10 *stone* 11 lbs !!!

I believe I saw you and your brother a few weeks since passing through Bond Street in a lady's carriage. I was *only* a pedestrian and escaped your notice. The Poems you were pleased to mention have been published about 6 weeks. My bookseller tells me he has sold a great number. When we meet I shall be happy to present a copy for your inspection. The present volume differs very materially from the one printed privately last winter; several poems published in the former are withheld from the latter, which however contains many more pieces, original and translated, and is of considerably larger size. When you answer this (if I can expect so much after my apparent, yet unintentional, neglect) address the reply to Trinity College, where I remain another year. Illness prevented my residence for the last twelve months. I have heard 3 times from Delawarr, that is to say, *twice* more often than I expected, or indeed desired, for, though I formerly liked him, long absence and our serious quarrel entirely destroyed the seeds of affection once *deeply* sown. I addressed him merely to explain the mistaken grounds on which he had acted, without (as I plainly told him) any view to a reconciliation. This produced a reply, etc., etc. In short the affair was compromised and we are what the World commonly call *friends*. Long may we be so, but never so intimate as before. Indeed, I shall take care we are not much together, and I doubt not D's inclinations are not more violently bent on a renewal of our acquaintance than my own. All things considered, how should it be otherwise?

I have never seen Harrow since the last day I spent there with your Lordship; next summer, *we old Harrow men* will favour the *little* Boys, our successors, with a visit. I hope this letter will find you *safe*. I saw in the morning paper a long account of robbery etc. etc. committed on the persons of *sundry Majors, Colonels* and Esquires, passing from *Lady Clare's* to *Limerick*. From such banditti the *Lord* deliver your *carcase* and *habitation*, you may exclaim with Pope in his Imitation of Spenser " Bad Neighbourhood I ween ". I am now setting off for the Highlands of Scotland [1] and expect your answer on my return to Cambridge. Have we any chance of meeting next winter? I shall pass some time in Town, where you will probably spend your vacation. Present my remembrances to Brother Richard and believe me, dearest Clare, yours ever affectly

BYRON

---

[1] Byron's often postponed journey to Scotland became, we are told, a joke among his friends.

TO ELIZABETH BRIDGET PIGOT   *Trinity College, Cambridge,*
                                        October 26, 1807

MY DEAR ELIZABETH,—Fatigued with sitting up till four in
the morning for the last two days at hazard, I take up my
pen to inquire how your highness and the rest of my female
acquaintance at the seat of archiepiscopal grandeur go on.   I
know I deserve a scolding for my negligence in not writing
more frequently; but racing up and down the country for
these last three months, how was it possible to fulfil the duties
of a correspondent?   Fixed at last for six months, I write, as
thin as ever (not having gained an ounce since my reduction),
and rather in better humour;—but, after all, Southwell was
a detestable residence.   Thank St. Dominica, I have done
with it: I have been twice within eight miles of it, but could
not prevail on myself to *suffocate* in its heavy atmosphere.   This
place is wretched enough—a villainous chaos of din and
drunkenness, nothing but hazard and burgundy, hunting,
mathematics, and Newmarket, riot and racing.   Yet it is a
paradise compared with the eternal dulness of Southwell.
Oh! the misery of doing nothing but make *love*, *enemies*, and
verses.

Next January (but this is *entre nous only*, and pray let it be
so, or my maternal persecutor will be throwing her tomahawk
at any of my curious projects), I am going to *sea* for four or
five months, with my cousin Captain Bettesworth, who commands the *Tartar*, the finest frigate in the navy.   I have seen
most scenes, and wish to look at a naval life.   We are going
probably to the Mediterranean, or to the West Indies, or—to
the devil; and if there is a possibility of taking me to the latter,
Bettesworth will do it; for he has received four and twenty
wounds in different places, and at this moment possesses a
letter from the late Lord Nelson, stating Bettesworth as the
only officer in the navy who had more wounds than himself.

I have got a new friend, the finest in the world, a *tame bear*.
When I brought him here, they asked me what I meant to do
with him, and my reply was, "he should *sit* for a *fellowship*".
Sherard will explain the meaning of the sentence, if it is
ambiguous.   This answer delighted them not.   We have
several parties here, and this evening a large assortment of

jockeys, gamblers, boxers, authors, parsons, and poets, sup with me,—a precious mixture, but they go on well together; and for me, I am a *spice* of every thing except a jockey; by the bye, I was dismounted again the other day.

Thank your brother in my name for his treatise. I have written 214 pages of a novel—one poem of 380 lines,[1] to be published (without my name) in a few weeks, with notes,—560 lines of Bosworth Field, and 250 lines of another poem in rhyme, besides half a dozen smaller pieces. The poem to be published is a Satire. *Apropos*, I have been praised to the skies in the *Critical Review*, and abused greatly in another publication. So much the better, they tell me, for the sale of the book: it keeps up controversy, and prevents it being forgotten. Besides, the first men of all ages have had their share, nor do the humblest escape;—so I bear it like a philosopher. It is odd two opposite critiques came out on the same day, and out of five pages of abuse, my censor only quotes *two lines* from different poems, in support of his opinion. Now, the proper way to *cut up*, it to quote long passages, and make them appear absurd, because simple allegation is no proof. On the other hand, there are seven pages of praise, and more than *my modesty* will allow said on the subject. Adieu.

P.S.—Write, write, write!!!

TO JOHN CAM HOBHOUSE †   *Dorant's, February 27th, 1808*

DEAR HOBHOUSE,—I write to you to explain a foolish circumstance, which has arisen from some words uttered by me before Pearce and Brown, when I was devoured with Chagrin, and almost insane with the fumes of, not " last night's Punch " but that evening's wine. In consequence of a misconception of something on my part, I mentioned an intention of withdrawing my name from the Whig Club. This I hear has been broached, and perhaps in a moment of Intoxication and passion such might be my idea, but *soberly* I have no such design, particularly as I could not abandon my principles,

---

[1] *English Bards*, printed but not published, which subsequently formed the basis of *English Bards and Scotch Reviewers*.

even if I renounced the society with whom I have the honour to be united in sentiments which I never will disavow. This I beg you will explain to the members as publicly as possible, but should not this be sufficient, and they think proper to erase my name, be it so. I only request that in this case they will recollect I shall become a *Tory* of *their own making*. I shall expect your answer on this point with some impatience. Now a few words on the subject of my own conduct.

* * * * * * *

As an author, I am cut to atoms by the E—— Review. It is just out, and has completely demolished my little fabric of fame. This is rather scurvy treatment from a Whig Review, but politics and poetry are different things, and I am no adept in either. I therefore submit in Silence.

Scrope Davies is meandering about London, feeding upon Leg of Beef Soup, and frequenting the British Forum. He has given up hazard, as also a considerable sum at the same time. Altamont is a good deal with me. Last night at the Opera Masquerade, we supped with seven whores, a *Bawd* and a *Ballet master*, in Madame Catalani's apartment behind the Scenes, (of course Catalani was *not* there). I have some thoughts of purchasing d'Egville's pupils : they would fill a glorious Haram.

I do not write often, but I like to receive letters. When therefore you are disposed to philosophize, no one standeth more in need of precepts of all sorts than

Yours very truly BYRON

TO JOHN CAM HOBHOUSE *   *Dorant's, March 26th 1808*

DEAR HOBHOUSE,—I have sent Fletcher to Cambridge for various purposes, and he has this *dispatch* for you. I am still living with my Dalilah, who has only two faults, unpardonable in a woman—she can read and write. Greet in my name the Bilious Birdmore. If you journey this way, I shall be glad to furnish you with Bread and Salt.

The university still chew the Cud of my degree. Please

God they shall swallow it, though Inflammation be the consequence.

I am leading a quiet though debauched life.

Yours very truly, BYRON

TO THE REV. JOHN BECHER   *Dorant's, March 28, 1808*

I have lately received a copy of the new edition from Ridge, and it is high time for me to return my best thanks to you for the trouble you have taken in the superintendence. This I do most sincerely, and only regret that Ridge has not seconded you as I could wish,—at least, in the bindings, paper, etc., of the copy he sent to me. Perhaps those for the public may be more respectable in such articles.

You have seen the *Edinburgh Review*, of course. I regret that Mrs. Byron is so much annoyed. For my own part, these " paper bullets of the brain " have only taught me to stand fire ; and, as I have been lucky enough upon the whole, my repose and appetite are not discomposed. Pratt, the gleaner, author, poet, etc., etc., addressed a long rhyming epistle to me on the subject, by way of consolation ; but it was not well done, so I do not send it, though the name of the man might make it go down. The E. R⁸ have not performed their task well ; at least the literati tell me this ; and I think *I* could write a more sarcastic critique on *myself* than any yet published. For instance, instead of the remark,—ill-natured enough, but not keen,—about Macpherson, I (quoad reviewers) could have said, " Alas, this imitation only proves the assertion of Dr. Johnson, that many men, women, and *children*, could write such poetry as Ossian's ".

I am *thin* and in exercise. During the spring or summer I trust we shall meet. I hear Lord Ruthyn leaves Newstead in April. As soon as he quits it for ever, I wish much you would take a ride over, survey the mansion, and give me your candid opinion on the most advisable mode of proceeding with regard to the *house*. *Entre nous*, I am cursedly dipped ; my debts, *every* thing inclusive, will be nine or ten thousand before I am twenty-one. But I have reason to think my property will turn

out better than general expectation may conceive. Of Newstead I have little hope or care; but Hanson, my agent,
intimated my Lancashire property was worth three Newsteads.
I believe we have it hollow; though the defendants are pro-
tracting the surrender, if possible, till after my majority, for
the purpose of forming some arrangement with me, thinking
I shall probably prefer a sum in hand to a reversion. Newstead
I may *sell*;—perhaps I will not,—though of that more anon.
I will come down in May or June.

Yours most truly, etc.

TO JOHN CAM HOBHOUSE *   *Dorant's, April 15th 1808*

MY DEAR HOBHOUSE,—I proceed as usual turning the
twenty four hours to the best account, particularly the nocturnal
moiety. My Belles would probably differ, were they together.
But one is *with* me, and the other *for* me—or any body else,
I dare say, in my absence. * * * * * * I have been well about
a fortnight, and I trust shall continue so, but I am sadly meagre,
and vigilant. Alas! for the Shepherd and his Lambkin!
How cursedly absurd such proceedings appear compared with
your chastity and my Carnality.

I shall be in Cambridge next month to graduate. The first
night I went out after my illness I got into a Row and gave a
fellow at the theatre my address and a black eye, after pugilising
with him and his friend, on their refusing to name their place
of Residence; they were kicked out into the Piazzas. I was
very weak and languid, but managed to keep these youths
at Bay, till a person whom I don't know engaged one, and I
then contended singly with the other, till the above consequence
ensued. Scrope Davies is at Portsmouth. I form one of a very
sad set, consisting of Capt. Wallace, Sir Godfrey, Sir B.
Graham, and other sensual Sinners. We have kept it up with
the most laudable systematic profligacy. Sir G. is with his
regiment at present, to the sorrow of his Confederates. I have
given up *play* altogether. I saw Mahon last night. He made
one of a party of ten * * * * *.

When do you come to town? I long to see you. Adieu.

Yours very truly, BYRON

TO FRANCIS HODGSON   *Newstead Abbey, Notts, Nov. 3, 1808*

My dear Hodgson,—I expected to have heard ere this the event of your interview with the mysterious Mr. Haynes, my volunteer correspondent; however, as I had no business to trouble you with the adjustment of my concerns with that illustrious stranger, I have no right to complain of your silence.

You have of course seen Drury, in all the pleasing palpitations of anticipated wedlock. Well! he has still something to look forward to, and his present extacies are certainly enviable. "Peace be with him and with his spirit", and his flesh also, at least just now. . . .

Hobhouse and your humble are still here. Hobhouse hunts, etc., and I do nothing; we dined the other day with a neighbouring Esquire (not Collet of Staines), and regretted your absence, as the Bouquet of Staines was scarcely to be compared to our last "feast of reason". You know, laughing is the sign of a rational animal; so says Dr. Smollett. I think so, too, but unluckily my spirits don't always keep pace with my opinions. I had not so much scope for risibility the other day as I could have wished, for I was seated near a woman, to whom, when a boy, I was as much attached as boys generally are, and more than a man should be. I knew this before I went, and was determined to be valiant, and converse with *sang froid*; but instead I forgot my valour and my nonchalance, and never opened my lips even to laugh, far less to speak, and the lady was almost as absurd as myself, which made both the object of more observation than if we had conducted ourselves with easy indifference. You will think all this great nonsense; if you had seen it, you would have thought it still more ridiculous. What fools we are! We cry for a plaything, which, like children, we are never satisfied with till we break open, though like them we cannot get rid of it by putting it in the fire.

I have tried for Gifford's *Epistle to Pindar*, and the bookseller says the copies were cut up for *waste paper*; if you can procure me a copy I shall be much obliged. Adieu!

Believe me, my dear Sir, yours ever sincerely, Byron

TO FRANCIS HODGSON   *Newstead Abbey, Notts.,*
                                           Nov. 18th, 1808

MY DEAR HODGSON,—Boatswain is dead! He expired in
a state of madness on the 10th after suffering much, yet re-
taining all the gentleness of his nature to the last, never
attempting to do the least injury to any one near him. I have
now lost every thing except old Murray. . . .

I sent some game to Drury lately, which I hope escaped
the scrutiny of the mutineers. I trust the letter to Claridge [1]
was equally fortunate (after being put in the post by you at
London) as it contained some cash, which my correspondent,
notwithstanding the patriotic fervour of the moment, might
not chuse to submit to the inspection of the William Tells and
Gracchi of the day.

If my songs have produced the *glorious* effects you mention,
I shall be a complete Tyrtaeus, though I am sorry to say I
resemble that interesting Harper more in his person than
Poesy. I only lament that Drury's conjecture should be more
facetious than well founded. Nothing could give me greater
glee than to suppose it was perfectly correct. It is singular
enough that Wingfield and Keynis [?] were both my fags at
Harrow, and they have now obtained that honour to which
their master aspired in vain. I have written to Government
for letters etc. Won't you come and broach a farewell batch
at Xmas? Can't you " tice Drury into the woods and afterwards devour him "? This day twelvemonth, Deo favente,
I shall be crossing Mount Caucasus. Is your information of
Jeffrey's proposal to Southey well authenticated? If so, pray
favour both with a few couplets in your satire. I should be too
happy to think Gifford had troubled . . . [sentence missing]
. . . could discover if he really wrote the " exposé " in your
possession. My Rhymes on the Bards are forthcoming. Tell
Drury he must purchase a copy. I can't afford to give away.
Hobhouse and myself nearly suffocated a person in the Bath
yesterday, by way of ascertaining the soundings. I was obliged
to jump in and extricate the Drownee. Drury will find a
letter from me at Harrow, which I hope he will answer. If
still at Cambridge, greet him with an embrace. Hobhouse

[1] John Claridge, a former Harrow favourite.

presents all sorts of remembrances to both. But, the words of
Gaffer Thumb, " I can no more ".

Believe me, dear H. yours [Signature missing.]

TO JOHN HANSON   *Newstead Abbey, Notts.,*
                                            November 18th, 1808

DEAR SIR,—I am truly glad to hear your health is re-
instated. As for my affairs I am sure you will do your best, and,
though I should be glad to get rid of my Lancashire property
for an equivalent in money, I shall not take any steps of that
nature without good advice and mature consideration.

I am (as I have already told you) going abroad in the
spring; for this I have many reasons. In the first place, I
wish to study India and Asiatic policy and manners. I am
young, tolerably vigorous, abstemious in my way of living;
I have no pleasure in fashionable dissipation, and I am determined to take a wider field than is customary with travellers.
If I return, my judgment will be more mature, and I shall still
be young enough for politics. With regard to expence,
travelling through the East is rather inconvenient than expensive : it is not like the tour of Europe, you undergo hardship,
but incur little hazard of spending money. If I live here I
must have my house in town, a separate house for Mrs. Byron;
I must keep horses, etc., etc. When I go abroad I place Mrs.
Byron at Newstead (there is one great expence saved), I have
no horses to keep. A voyage to India will take me six months,
and if I had a dozen attendants cannot cost me five hundred
pounds ; and you will agree with me that a like term of months
in England would lead me into four times that expenditure. I
have written to Government for letters and permission of the
Company, so you see I am *serious*.

You honour my debts ; they amount to perhaps twelve
thousand pounds, and I shall require perhaps three or four
thousand at setting out, with credit on a Bengal agent. This
you must manage for me. If my resources are not adequate
to the supply I must *sell*, but *not Newstead*. I will at least
transmit that to the next Lord. My debts must be paid, if

possible, in February. I shall leave my affairs to the care of *trustees*, of whom, with your acquiescence, I shall *name you* one, Mr. Parker another, and two more, on whom I am not yet determined.

Pray let me hear from you soon. Remember me to Mrs. Hanson, whom I hope to see on her return. Present my best respects to the young lady, and believe me, etc.,

BYRON

TO FRANCIS HODGSON　　　　　*Newstead Abbey, Notts.,*
Nov. 27, 1808

MY DEAR SIR,—Boatswain is to be buried in a vault waiting for myself. I have also written an epitaph, which I would send, were it not for two reasons: one is, that it is too long for a letter; and the other, that I hope you will some day read it on the spot where it will be engraved.

You discomfort me with the intelligence of the real orthodoxy of the Arch-fiend's name, but alas! it must stand with me at present; if ever I have an opportunity of correcting, I shall liken him to Geoffrey of Monmouth, a noted liar in his way, and perhaps a more correct prototype than the Carnifex of James II.

I do not think the composition of your poem " a sufficing reason " for not keeping your promise of a Christmas visit. Why not come? I will never disturb you in your moments of inspiration; and if you wish to collect any materials for the *scenery*, Hardwicke (where Mary was confined for several years) is not eight miles distant, and, independent of the interest you must take in it as her vindicator, is a most beautiful and venerable object of curiosity. I shall take it very ill if you do not come; my mansion is improving in comfort, and, when you require solitude, I shall have an apartment devoted to the purpose of receiving your poetical reveries.

I have heard from our Drury; he says little of the Row, which I regret: indeed I would have sacrificed much to have contributed in any way (as a schoolboy) to its consummation; but Butler survives, and thirteen boys have been expelled in

46

vain. Davies is not here, but Hobhouse hunts as usual, and your humble servant " drags at each remove a lengthened chain ". I have heard from his Grace of Portland on the subject of my expedition : he talks of difficulties ; by the gods ! if he throws any in my way I will next session ring such a peal in his ears,

> That he shall wish the fiery Dane
> Had rather been his guest again.

You do not tell me if Gifford is really my commentator : it is too good to be true, for I know nothing would gratify my vanity so much as the reality ; even the idea is too precious to part with.

I shall expect you here ; let me have no more excuses. Hobhouse desires his best remembrance. We are now lingering over our evening potations. I have extended my letter further than I ought, and beg you will excuse it ; on the opposite page I send you some stanzas I wrote off on being questioned by a former flame as to my motives for quitting this country. You are the first reader. Hobhouse hates everything of the kind, therefore I do not show them to him. Adieu !

Believe me, yours very sincerely, BYRON

TO THE HON. AUGUSTA LEIGH   *Newstead Abbey, Notts.,*
Novr. 30th 1808

My DEAREST AUGUSTA,—I return you my best thanks for making me an uncle, and forgive the sex this time ; but the next *must* be a nephew. You will be happy to hear my Lancashire property is likely to prove extremely valuable : indeed my pecuniary affairs are altogether far superior to my expectations or any other person's. If I would *sell*, my income would probably be six thousand per annum ; but I will not part at least with Newstead, or indeed with the other, which is of a nature to increase in value yearly. I am living here *alone*, which suits my inclinations better than society of any kind. Mrs. Byron I have shaken off for two years, and I shall not resume her yoke in future, I am afraid my disposition will suffer in your estimation; but I never can forgive that woman, or breathe in comfort under the same roof.

I am a very unlucky fellow, for I think I had naturally not a bad heart; but it has been so bent, twisted, and trampled on, that it has now become as hard as a Highlander's heelpiece.

I do not know that much alteration has taken place in my person, except that I am grown much thinner, and somewhat taller! I saw Col. Leigh at Brighton in July, where I should have been glad to have seen you; I only know your husband by sight, though I am acquainted with many of the Tenth. Indeed my relations are those whom I know the least, and in most instances, I am not very anxious to improve the acquaintance. I hope you are quite recovered, I shall be in town in January to take my seat, and will call, if convenient; let me hear from you before.

[Signature cut off]

TO WILLIAM HARNESS [1]   *8 St. James's Street,*
                                               March 18, 1809

There was no necessity for your excuses; if you have time and inclination to write, " for what we receive, the " Lord make us thankful ",—if I do not hear from you, I console myself with the idea that you are much more agreeably employed.

I send down to you by this post a certain Satire lately published, and in return for the three and sixpence expenditure upon it, only beg that if you should guess the author, you will keep his name secret; at least for the present. London is full of the Duke's business.[2] The Commons have been at it these last three nights, and are not yet come to a decision. I do not know if the affair will be brought before our House, unless in the shape of an impeachment. If it makes its appearance in a debatable form, I believe I shall be tempted to say

[1] " A *Harrow* man ", one of several friends whom Byron described at different periods as ' earliest ' and ' dearest '.

[2] The inquiry into charges of corruption brought against the Duke of York, as Commander-in-Chief, and his mistress, Mary Ann Clarke. See also note on letter to Lady Melbourne, Sept. 13th, 1812.

something on the subject.—I am glad to hear you like Cambridge : firstly, because, to know that you are happy is pleasant to one who wishes you all possible sublunary enjoyment ; and, secondly, I admire the morality of the sentiment. *Alma mater* was to me *injusta noverca* ; and the old beldam only gave me my M.A. degree because she could not avoid it.—You know what a farce a noble Cantab. must perform.

I am going abroad, if possible, in the spring, and before I depart I am collecting the pictures of my most intimate schoolfellows ; I have already a few, and shall want yours, or my cabinet will be incomplete. I have employed one of the first miniature painters of the day to take them, of course, at my own expense, as I never allow my acquaintance to incur the least expenditure to gratify a whim of mine. To mention this may seem indelicate ; but when I tell you a friend of ours first refused to sit, under the idea that he was to disburse on the occasion, you will see that it is necessary to state these preliminaries to prevent the recurrence of any similar mistake. I shall see you in time, and will carry you to the *limner*. It will be a tax on your patience for a week ; but pray excuse it, as it is possible the resemblance may be the sole trace I shall be able to preserve of our past friendship and acquaintance. Just now it seems foolish enough ; but in a few years, when some of us are dead, and others are separated by inevitable circumstances, it will be a kind of satisfaction to retain in these images of the living the idea of our former selves, and, to contemplate, in the resemblances of the dead, all that remains of judgment, feeling and a host of passions. But all this will be dull enough for you, and so good night ; and, to end my chapter, or rather my homily,

Believe me, my dear H., yours most affectionately.

TO HIS MOTHER   *Falmouth, June 22, 1809*

DEAR MOTHER,—I am about to sail in a few days ; probably before this reaches you. Fletcher begged so hard, that I have continued him in my service. If he does not behave well abroad, I will send him back in a *transport*. I have a

German servant (who has been with Mr. Wilbraham in Persia before, and was strongly recommended to me by Dr. Butler, of Harrow), Robert [1] and William ; they constitute my whole suite. I have letters in plenty :—you shall hear from me at the different ports I touch upon ; but you must not be alarmed if my letters miscarry. The Continent is in a fine state—an insurrection has broken out at Paris, and the Austrians are beating Buonaparte—the Tyrolese have risen.

There is a picture of me in oil, to be sent down to Newstead soon.—I wish the Miss Pigots had something better to do than carry my miniatures to Nottingham to copy. Now they have done it, you may ask them to copy the others, which are greater favourites than my own. As to money matters, I am ruined— at least till Rochdale is sold ; and if that does not turn out well, I shall enter into the Austrian or Russian service—perhaps the Turkish, if I like their manners. The world is all before me, and I leave England without regret, and without a wish to revisit any thing it contains, except *yourself*, and your present residence.

Believe me, yours ever sincerely

P.S.—Pray tell Mr. Rushton his son is well, and doing well ; so is Murray, indeed better than I ever saw him ; he will be back in about a month. I ought to add the leaving Murray to my few regrets, as his age perhaps will prevent my seeing him again. Robert I take with me ; I like him, because, like myself, he seems a friendless animal.

TO EDWARD ELLICE *   *Falmouth, June 25th, 1809*

DEAR ELLICE,[2]—You will think me a very sad dog for not having written a long acknowledgment of what I really feel viz. a sincere sense of the many favours I have received at your hands concerning my coming Tour. But if you knew the hurry I have been in and the natural laziness of my disposition, you would excuse an omission which cannot be attributed to neglect or ingratitude.

---

[1] Robert Rushton, Byron's servant and sparring-partner.
[2] Edward (" Bear ") Ellice afterwards sat as Member for Coventry.

I beg you will now accept my very hearty thanks for the divers troubles you have had on my account, which I am sure no person but yourself would have taken for so worthless an animal. I am afraid I shall never have any opportunity of repaying them, except by a promise that they shall not be repeated.

We are waiting here for a wind and other necessaries. Nothing of moment has occurred in the town save the castigation of one of the fair sex at a Cart's tail yesterday morn, whose hands had been guilty of " picking and stealing " and whose tongue of " evil speaking " for she stole a Cock and *damned* the corporation. She was much whipped, but exceeding impenitent. I shall say nothing of Falmouth because I know it, and you don't, a very good reason for being silent as I can say nothing in its favour, or you hear anything that would be agreeable. The Inhabitants both female and male, at least the young ones, are remarkably handsome, and how the devil they come to be so is the marvel! for the place is apparently not favourable to Beauty. The Claret is good, and Quakers [?] plentiful, so are Herrings salt and fresh. There is a port called St. Mawes off the harbour, which we were nearly taken up on a suspicion of having carried by storm. It is well defended by one able-bodied man of eighty years old, six ancient demi-culverins that would exceedingly annoy anybody except an enemy, and parapet walls which would withstand at least half a dozen kicks of any given grenadier in the kingdom of France.

Adieu, believe me your obliged and sincere BYRON

TO FRANCIS HODGSON   *Lisbon, July 16, 1809*

Thus far have we pursued our route, and seen all sorts of marvellous sights, palaces, convents, etc.;—which, being to be heard in my friend Hobhouse's forthcoming Book of Travels, I shall not anticipate by smuggling any account whatsoever to you in a private and clandestine manner. I must just observe, that the village of Cintra in Estremadura is the most beautiful, perhaps, in the world.

I am very happy here, because I loves oranges, and talks bad Latin to the monks, who understand it, as it is like their own,—and I goes into society (with my pocket-pistols), and I swims in the Tagus all across at once, and I rides on an ass or a mule, and swears Portuguese, and have got a diarrhœa and bites from the mosquitoes. But what of that? Comfort must not be expected by folks that go a pleasuring.

When the Portuguese are pertinacious, I say *Carracho!*— the great oath of the grandees, that very well supplies the place of " Damme ",—and, when dissatisfied with my neighbour, I pronounce him *Ambra di merdo*. With these two phrases, and a third, *Avra bouro*, which signifieth " Get an ass ", I am universally understood to be a person of degree and a master of languages. How merrily we lives that travellers be !—if we had food and raiment. But, in sober sadness, any thing is better than England, and I am infinitely amused with my pilgrimage as far as it has gone.

To-morrow we start to ride post near 400 miles as far as Gibraltar, where we embark for Melita and Byzantium. A letter to Malta will find me, or to be forwarded, if I am absent. Pray embrace the Drury and Dwyer, and all the Ephesians you encounter. I am writing with Butler's donative pencil, which makes my bad hand worse. Excuse illegibility.

Hodgson ! send me the news, and the deaths and defeats and capital crimes and the misfortunes of one's friends ; and let us hear of literary matters, and the controversies and the criticisms. All this will be pleasant—*Suave mari magno*, etc. Talking of that, I have been sea-sick, and sick of the sea. Adieu.

Yours faithfully, etc.

TO HIS MOTHER   *Gibraltar, August 11th, 1809*

DEAR MOTHER,—I have been so much occupied since my departure from England, that till I could address you at length I have forborne writing altogether. As I have now passed through Portugal, and a considerable part of Spain, and have leisure at this place, I shall endeavour to give you a short detail of my movements.

We sailed from Falmouth on the 2nd of July, reached Lisbon after a very favourable passage of four days and a half, and took up our abode in that city. It has been often described without being worthy of description; for, except the view from the Tagus, which is beautiful, and some fine churches and convents, it contains little but filthy streets, and more filthy inhabitants. To make amends for this, the village of Cintra, about fifteen miles from the capital, is, perhaps in every respect, the most delightful in Europe; it contains beauties of every description, natural and artificial. Palaces and gardens rising in the midst of rocks, cataracts, and precipices; convents on stupendous heights—a distant view of the sea and the Tagus; and, besides (though that is a secondary consideration), is remarkable as the scene of Sir Hew Dalrymple's Convention.[1] It unites in itself all the wildness of the western highlands, with the verdure of the south of France. Near this place, about ten miles to the right, is the palace of Mafra, the boast of Portugal, as it might be of any other country, in point of magnificence without elegance. There is a convent annexed; the monks, who possess large revenues, are courteous enough, and understand Latin, so that we had a long conversation: they have a large library, and asked me if the *English* had *any books* in their country?

I sent my baggage, and part of the servants, by sea to Gibraltar, and travelled on horseback from Aldea Galbega (the first stage from Lisbon, which is only accessible by water) to Seville (one of the most famous cities in Spain) where the Government called the Junta is now held. The distance to Seville is nearly four hundred miles, and to Cadiz almost ninety farther towards the coast. I had orders from the governments, and every possible accommodation on the road, as an English nobleman, in an English uniform, is a very respectable personage in Spain at present. The horses are remarkably good, and the roads (I assure you upon my honour, for you will hardly believe it) very far superior to the best English roads, without the smallest toll or turnpike. You will suppose this when I rode post to Seville, in four days, through this parching country in the midst of summer, without fatigue or annoyance.

[1] The Convention of Cintra, by which Junot evacuated Portugal, had been signed on August 31st, 1808.

Seville is a beautiful town; though the streets are narrow, they are clean. We lodged in the house of two Spanish un-married ladies, who possess *six* houses in Seville, and gave me a curious specimen of Spanish manners. They are women of character, and the eldest a fine woman, the youngest pretty, but not so good a figure as Donna Josepha. The freedom of manner, which is general here, astonished me not a little; and in the course of further observation, I find that reserve is not the characteristic of the Spanish belles, who are, in general, very handsome, with large black eyes, and very fine forms. The eldest honoured your *unworthy* son with very particular attention, embracing him with great tenderness at parting (I was there but three days), after cutting off a lock of his hair, and presenting him with one of her own, about three feet in length,[1] which I send, and beg you will retain till my return. Her last words were, *Adios, tu hermoso! me gusto mucho*—" Adieu, you pretty fellow! you please me much ". She offered me a share of her apartment, which my *virtue* induced me to decline; she laughed, and said I had some English *amante* (lover), and added that she was going to be married to an officer in the Spanish Army.

I left Seville, and rode on to Cadiz, through a beautiful country. At *Xeres*, where the sherry we drink is made, I met a great merchant—a Mr. Gordon of Scotland—who was ex-tremely polite, and favoured me with the inspection of his vaults and cellars, so that I quaffed at the fountain head.

Cadiz, sweet Cadiz, is the most delightful town I ever beheld, very different from our English cities in every respect except cleanliness (and it is as clean as London), but still beautiful, and full of the finest women in Spain, the Cadiz belles being the Lancashire witches of their land. Just as I was introduced and began to like the grandees, I was forced to leave it for this cursed place; but before I return to England I will visit it again. The night before I left it, I sat in the box at the opera with Admiral Cordova's family; he is the commander whom Lord St. Vincent defeated in 1797, and has an aged wife and a fine daughter, Sennorita Cordova. The girl is very pretty, in the Spanish style; in my opinion, by no means

[1] This relic is still preserved among Byronic archives by the poet's publisher at 50 Albemarle Street.

inferior to the English in charms, and certainly superior in fascination. Long black hair, dark languishing eyes, *clear* olive complexions, and forms more graceful in motion than can be conceived by an Englishman used to the drowsy, listless air of his countrywomen, added to the most becoming dress, and, at the same time, the most decent in the world, render a Spanish beauty irresistible.

I beg leave to observe that intrigue here is the business of life ; when a woman marries she throws off all restraint, but I believe their conduct is chaste enough before. If you make a proposal, which in England will bring a box on the ear from the meekest of virgins, to a Spanish girl, she thanks you for the honour you intend her, and replies, " Wait till I am married, and I shall be too happy ". This is literally and strictly true.

Miss Cordova and her little brother understood a little French, and, after regretting my ignorance of the Spanish, she proposed to become my preceptress in that language. I could only reply by a low bow, and express my regret that I quitted Cadiz too soon to permit me to make the progress which would doubtless attend my studies under so charming a directress. I was standing at the back of the box, which resembles our Opera boxes, (the theatre is large and finely decorated, the music admirable,) in the manner which Englishmen generally adopt, for fear of incommoding the ladies in front, when this fair Spaniard dispossessed an old woman (an aunt or a duenna) of her chair, and commanded me to be seated next herself, at a tolerable distance from her mamma. At the close of the performance I withdrew, and was lounging with a party of men in the passage, when, *en passant*, the lady turned round and called me, and I had the honour of attending her to the admiral's mansion. I have an invitation on my return to Cadiz, which I shall accept if I repass through the country on my return from Asia.

I have met Sir John Carr, Knight Errant, at Seville and Cadiz. He is a pleasant man. I like the Spaniards much. You have heard of the battle near Madrid, and in England they would call it a victory—a pretty victory ! Two hundred officers and five thousand men killed, all English, and the French in as great force as ever. I should have joined the army, but we have no time to lose before we get up the Mediterranean and Archipelago. I am going over to Africa tomorrow; it is only six miles from this fortress. My next stage is Cagliari in Sardinia, where I shall be presented to His Majesty. I have a most superb uniform as a court dress, indispensable in travelling.

August 13.—I have not yet been to Africa—the wind is contrary—but I dined yesterday at Algesiras, with Lady Westmorland, where I met General Castanos, the celebrated Spanish leader in the late and present war. To-day I dine with him. He has offered me letters to Tetuan in Barbary, for the principal Moors, and I am to have the house for a few days of one of the great men, which was intended for Lady W., whose health will not permit her to cross the Straits.

August 15.—I could not dine with Castanos yesterday, but this afternoon I had that honour. He is pleasant and, for aught I know to the contrary, clever. I cannot go to Barbary. The Malta packet sails to-morrow, and myself in it. Admiral Purvis, with whom I dined at Cadiz, gave me a passage in a frigate to Gibraltar, but we have no ship of war destined for Malta at present. The packets sail fast, and have good accommodation. You shall hear from me on our route.

Joe Murray delivers this; I have sent him and the boy back. Pray show the lad kindness, as he is my great favourite; I would have taken him on, * * * Say this to his father, who may otherwise think he has behaved ill.

I hope this will find you well. Believe me,

Yours ever sincerely, BYRON

P.S.—So Lord G[rey de Ruthyn] is married to a rustic. Well done! If I wed, I will bring home a Sultana, with half a dozen cities for a dowry, and reconcile you to an Ottoman daughter-in-law, with a bushel of pearls not larger than ostrich eggs, or smaller than walnuts.

TO HIS MOTHER *Malta, September 15, 1809*

DEAR MOTHER,—Though I have a very short time to spare, being to sail immediately for Greece, I cannot avoid taking an opportunity of telling you that I am well. I have been in Malta a short time, and have found the inhabitants hospitable and pleasant.

This letter is committed to the charge of a very extraordinary woman, whom you have doubtless heard of, Mrs. Spencer Smith,[1] of whose escape the Marquis de Salvo published a narrative a few years ago. She has since been shipwrecked, and her life has been from its commencement so fertile in remarkable incidents, that in a romance they would appear improbable. She was born at Constantinople, where her father, Baron Herbert, was Austrian Ambassador; married unhappily, yet has never been impeached in point of character; excited the vengeance of Buonaparte by a part in some conspiracy; several times risked her life; and is not yet twenty-five. She is here on her way to England, to join her husband, being obliged to leave Trieste, where she was paying a visit to her mother, by the approach of the French, and embarks soon in a ship of war. Since my arrival here, I have had scarcely any other companion. I have found her very pretty, very accomplished, and extremely eccentric. Buonaparte is even now so incensed against her, that her life would be in some danger if she were taken prisoner a second time.

You have seen Murray and Robert by this time, and received my letter. Little has happened since that date. I have touched at Cagliari in Sardinia, and at Girgenti in Sicily, and embark to-morrow for Patras, from whence I proceed to Yanina, where Ali Pacha holds his court. So I shall soon be among the Mussulmans. Adieu.

Believe me, with sincerity, yours ever, BYRON

TO CAPTAIN CARY, A.D.C.   *3, Strada di Torni* [*Malta*], *September 18th 1809*

SIR,—The marked insolence of your behaviour to me the first time I had the honour of meeting you at table, I should

---

[1] The adventurous Mrs. Spencer Smith, wife of the British Minister at Stuttgart and the " Florence " of *Childe Harold*, caused Byron some emotional perturbation during his stay in Malta. According to Galt, " he affected a passion for her, but it was only Platonic. She, however, beguiled him of his valuable yellow diamond ring."

have passed over from respect to the General, had I not been informed that you have since mentioned my name in a public company with comments not to be tolerated, more particularly after the circumstance to which I allude. I have only just heard this, or I should not have postponed this letter to so late a period. As the vessel in which I am to embark must sail the first change of wind, the sooner our business is arranged the better. To-morrow morning at 6 will be the best hour, at any place you think proper, as I do not know where the officers and *gentlemen* settle these affairs in your island.

The favour of an immediate answer will oblige

Your obedient servant, BYRON

TO HIS MOTHER *Prevesa, November 12, 1809*

MY DEAR MOTHER,—I have now been some time in Turkey: this place is on the coast, but I have traversed the interior of the province of Albania on a visit to the Pacha. I left Malta in the *Spider*, a brig of war, on the 21st of September, and arrived in eight days at Prevesa. I thence have been about 150 miles, as far as Tepaleen, his Highness's country palace, where I stayed three days. The name of the Pacha is *Ali*, and he is considered a man of the first abilities: he governs the whole of Albania (the ancient Illyricum), Epirus, and part of Macedonia. His son, Vely Pacha, to whom he has given me letters, governs the Morea, and has great influence in Egypt; in short, he is one of the most powerful men in the Ottoman empire. When I reached Yanina, the capital, after a journey of three days over the mountains, through a country of the most picturesque beauty, I found that Ali Pacha was with his army in Illyricum, besieging Ibrahim Pacha in the castle of Berat. He had heard that an Englishman of rank was in his dominions, and had left orders in Yanina with the commandant to provide a house, and supply me with every kind of necessary *gratis*; and, though I have been allowed to make presents to the slaves, etc., I have not been permitted to pay for a single article of household consumption.

I rode out on the vizier's horses, and saw the palaces of

himself and grandsons: they are splendid, but too much ornamented with silk and gold. I then went over the mountains through Zitza, a village with a Greek monastery (where I slept on my return), in the most beautiful situation (always excepting Cintra, in Portugal) I ever beheld. In nine days I reached Tepaleen. Our journey was much prolonged by the torrents that had fallen from the mountains, and intersected the roads. I shall never forget the singular scene on entering Tepaleen at five in the afternoon, as the sun was going down. It brought to my mind (with some change of *dress*, however) Scott's description of Branksome Castle in his *Lay*, and the feudal system. The Albanians, in their dresses, (the most magnificent in the world, consisting of a long *white kilt*, gold-worked cloak, crimson velvet gold-laced jacket and waistcoat, silver-mounted pistols and daggers,) the Tartars with their high caps, the Turks in their vast pelisses and turbans, the soldiers and black slaves with the horses, the former in groups in an immense large open gallery in front of the palace, the latter placed in a kind of cloister below it, two hundred steeds ready caparisoned to move in a moment, couriers entering or passing out with the despatches, the kettle-drums beating, boys calling the hour from the minaret of the mosque, altogether, with the singular appearance of the building itself, formed a new and delightful spectacle to a stranger. I was conducted to a very handsome apartment, and my health inquired after by the vizier's secretary, *à-la-mode Turque*!

The next day I was introduced to Ali Pacha. I was dressed in a full suit of staff uniform, with a very magnificent sabre, etc. The vizier received me in a large room paved with marble; a fountain was playing in the centre; the apartment was surrounded by scarlet ottomans. He received me standing, a wonderful compliment from a Mussulman, and made me sit down on his right hand. I have a Greek interpreter for general use, but a physician of Ali's named Femlario, who understands Latin, acted for me on this occasion. His first question was, why, at so early an age, I left my country?— (the Turks have no idea of travelling for amusement). He then said, the English minister, Captain Leake, had told him I was of a great family, and desired his respects to my mother; which I now, in the name of Ali Pacha, present to you. He said he was certain I was a man of birth, because I had small ears, curling hair, and little white hands, and expressed himself pleased with my appearance and garb. He told me to consider him as a father whilst I was in Turkey, and said he looked on me as his son. Indeed, he treated me like a child, sending me almonds and sugared sherbet, fruit and sweetmeats, twenty times a day. He begged me to visit him often, and at night, when he was at leisure. I then, after coffee and pipes, retired for the first time. I saw him thrice afterwards. It is singular that the Turks, who have no hereditary dignities, and few great families, except the Sultans, pay so much respect to birth; for I found my pedigree more regarded than my title.

To-day I saw the remains of the town of Actium, near which Antony lost the world, in a small bay, where two frigates could hardly manœuvre: a broken wall is the sole remnant. On another part of the gulf stand the ruins of Nicopolis, built by Augustus in honour of his victory. Last night I was at a Greek marriage; but this and a thousand things more I have neither time nor *space* to describe.

His highness is sixty years old, very fat, and not tall, but with a fine face, light blue eyes, and a white beard; his manner is very kind, and at the same time he possesses that dignity which I find universal amongst the Turks. He has the appearance of anything but his real character, for he is a remorseless tyrant, guilty of the most horrible cruelties, very brave, and so good a general that they call him the Mahometan Buonaparte. Napoleon has twice offered to make him King of Epirus, but he prefers the English interest, and abhors the French, as he himself told me. He is of so much consequence, that he is much courted by both, the Albanians being the most warlike subjects of the Sultan, though Ali is only nominally dependent on the Porte; he has been a mighty warrior, but is as barbarous as he is successful, roasting rebels, etc., etc. Buonaparte sent him a snuff-box with his picture. He said the snuff-box was very well, but the picture he could excuse, as he neither liked it nor the original. His ideas of judging of a man's birth from ears, hands, etc., were curious enough. To me he was, indeed, a father, giving me letters, guards, and every possible accommodation. Our next conversations were of war and travelling, politics and England. He called my

Albanian soldier, who attends me, and told him to protect me
at all hazard; his name is Viscillie, and, like all the Albanians,
he is brave, rigidly honest, and faithful; but they are cruel,
though not treacherous, and have several vices but no mean-
nesses. They are, perhaps, the most beautiful race, in point of
countenance, in the world; their women are sometimes handsome also, but they are treated like slaves, *beaten*, and, in short,
complete beasts of burden; they plough, dig, and sow. I
found them carrying wood, and actually repairing the highways.
The men are all soldiers, and war and the chase their sole
occupations. The women are the labourers, which after all
is no great hardship in so delightful a climate. Yesterday, the
11th of November, I bathed in the sea; to-day is so hot that
I am writing in a shady room of the English consul's, with
three doors wide open, no fire, or even *fireplace*, in the house,
except for culinary purposes.

I am going to-morrow, with a guard of fifty men, to Patras
in the Morea, and thence to Athens, where I shall winter.
Two days ago I was nearly lost in a Turkish ship of war, owing
to the ignorance of the captain and crew, though the storm was
not violent. Fletcher yelled after his wife, the Greeks called
on all the saints, the Mussulmans on Alla; the captain burst
into tears and ran below deck, telling us to call on God; the
sails were split, the main-yard shivered, the wind blowing
fresh, the night setting in, and all our chance was to make
Corfu, which is in possession of the French, or (as Fletcher
pathetically termed it) " a watery grave ". I did what I
could to console Fletcher, but finding him incorrigible,
wrapped myself up in my Albanian capote (an immense
cloak), and lay down on deck to wait the worst. I have learnt
to philosophise in my travels; and if I had not, complaint was
useless. Luckily the wind abated, and only drove us on the
coast of Suli, on the main land, where we landed, and proceeded, by the help of the natives, to Prevesa again; but I
shall not trust Turkish sailors in future, though the Pacha had
ordered one of his own galliots to take me to Patras. I am
therefore going as far as Missolonghi by land, and there have
only to cross a small gulf to get to Patras.

Fletcher's next epistle will be full of marvels. We were one
night lost for nine hours in the mountains in a thunder-storm,

and since nearly wrecked. In both cases Fletcher was sorely
bewildered, from apprehensions of famine and banditti in the
first, and drowning in the second instance. His eyes were a
little hurt by the lightning, or crying (I don't know which),
but are now recovered. When you write, address to me at
Mr. Strané's, English consul, Patras, Morea.

I could tell you I know not how many incidents that I
think would amuse you, but they crowd on my mind as much
as they would swell my paper, and I can neither arrange them
in the one, nor put them down on the other, except in the greatest confusion. I like the Albanians much ; they are not all
Turks ; some tribes are Christians. But their religion makes
little difference in their manner or conduct. They are esteemed
the best troops in the Turkish service. I lived on my route,
two days at once, and three days again, in a barrack at Salora,
and never found soldiers so tolerable, though I have been in the
garrisons of Gibraltar and Malta, and seen Spanish, French,
Sicilian, and British troops in abundance. I have had nothing
stolen, and was always welcome to their provision and milk.
Not a week ago an Albanian chief, (every village has its chief,
who is called Primate,) after helping us out of the Turkish
galley in her distress, feeding us, and lodging my suite, consisting of Fletcher, a Greek, two Athenians, a Greek priest,
and my companion, Mr. Hobhouse, refused any compensation
but a written paper stating that I was well received ; and when
I pressed him to accept a few sequins, " No," he replied ;
" I wish you to love me, not to pay me ". These are his
words.

It is astonishing how far money goes in this country. While
I was in the capital I had nothing to pay by the vizier's order ;
but since, though I have generally had sixteen horses, and
generally six or seven men, the expense has not been *half* as
much as staying only three weeks in Malta, though Sir A.
Ball, the governor, gave me a house for nothing, and I had only
one servant. By the by, I expect Hanson to remit regularly ;
for I am not about to stay in this province for ever. Let him
write to me at Mr. Strané's, English consul, Patras. The fact
is, the fertility of the plains is wonderful, and specie is scarce,
which makes this remarkable cheapness. I am going to
Athens, to study modern Greek, which differs much from the

ancient, though radically similar. I have no desire to return to England, nor shall I, unless compelled by absolute want, and Hanson's neglect; but I shall not enter into Asia for a year or two, as I have much to see in Greece, and I may perhaps cross into Africa, at least the Egyptian part. Fletcher, like all Englishmen, is very much dissatisfied, though a little reconciled to the Turks by a present of eighty piastres from the vizier, which, if you consider every thing, and the value of specie here, is nearly worth ten guineas English. He has suffered nothing but from cold, heat, and vermin, which those who lie in cottages and cross mountains in a cold country must undergo, and of which I have equally partaken with himself; but he is not valiant, and is afraid of robbers and tempests. I have no one to be remembered to in England, and wish to hear nothing from it, but that you are well, and a letter or two on business from Hanson, whom you may tell to write. I will write when I can, and beg you to believe me,

Your affectionate son, BYRON

P.S.—I have some very " magnifiques " Albanian dresses, the only expensive articles in this country. They cost fifty guineas each, and have so much gold, they would cost in England two hundred.

I have been introduced to Hussein Bey, and Mahmout Pacha, both little boys, grandchildren of Ali, at Yanina; they are totally unlike our lads, have painted complexions like rouged dowagers, large black eyes, and features perfectly regular. They are the prettiest little animals I ever saw, and are broken into the court ceremonies already. The Turkish salute is a slight inclination of the head, with the hand on the heart; intimates always kiss. Mahmout is ten years old, and hopes to see me again; we are friends without understanding each other, like many other folks, though from a different cause. He has given me a letter to his father in the Morea, to whom I have also letters from Ali Pacha.

TO HENRY DRURY   Salsette *frigate, May 3, 1810*

My DEAR DRURY,—When I left England, nearly a year ago, you requested me to write to you—I will do so. I have crossed Portugal, traversed the south of Spain, visited Sardinia, Sicily, Malta, and thence passed into Turkey, where I am still wandering. I first landed in Albania, the ancient Epirus, where we penetrated as far as Mount Tomarit—excellently treated by the chief Ali Pacha,—and, after journeying through Illyria, Chaonia, etc., crossed the Gulf of Actium, with a guard of fifty Albanians, and passed the Achelous in our route through Acarnania and Ætolia. We stopped a short time in the Morea, crossed the Gulf of Lepanto, and landed at the foot of Parnassus;—saw all that Delphi retains, and so on to Thébes and Athens, at which last we remained ten weeks.

His Majesty's ship, *Pylades*, brought us to Smyrna; but not before we had topographised Attica, including, of course, Marathon and the Sunian promontory. From Smyrna to the Troad (which we visited when at anchor, for a fortnight, off the tomb of Antilochus) was our next stage; and now we are in the Dardanelles, waiting for a wind to proceed to Constantinople.

This morning I *swam* from *Sestos* to *Abydos*. The immediate distance is not above a mile, but the current renders it hazardous;—so much so that I doubt whether Leander's conjugal affection must not have been a little chilled in his passage to Paradise. I attempted it a week ago, and failed,—owing to the north wind, and the wonderful rapidity of the tide,— though I have been from my childhood a strong swimmer. But, this morning being calmer, I succeeded, and crossed the " broad Hellespont " in an hour and ten minutes.

Well, my dear sir, I have left my home, and seen part of Africa and Asia, and a tolerable portion of Europe. I have been with generals and admirals, princes and pashas, governors and ungovernables,—but I have not time or paper to expatiate. I wish to let you know that I live with a friendly remembrance of you, and a hope to meet you again; and if I do this as shortly as possible, attribute it to any thing but forgetfulness.

Greece, ancient and modern, you know too well to require description. Albania, indeed, I have seen more of than any Englishman (except a Mr. Leake), for it is a country rarely visited, from the savage character of the natives, though abounding in more natural beauties than the classical regions of Greece,—which, however, are still eminently beautiful,

64

particularly Delphi and Cape Colonna in Attica. Yet these
are nothing to parts of Illyria and Epirus, where places without
a name, and rivers not laid down in maps, may, one day, when
more known, be justly esteemed superior subjects, for the
pencil and the pen, to the dry ditch of the Ilissus and the bogs
of Bœotia.

The Troad is a fine field for conjecture and snipe-shooting,
and a good sportsman and an ingenious scholar may exercise
their feet and faculties to great advantage upon the spot;—
or, if they prefer riding, lose their way (as I did) in a cursed
quagmire of the Scamander, who wriggles about as if the
Dardan virgins still offered their wonted tribute. The only
vestige of Troy, or her destroyers, are the barrows supposed
to contain the carcasses of Achilles, Antilochus, Ajax, etc.;—
but Mount Ida is still in high feather, though the shepherds
are now-a-days not much like Ganymede. But why should I
say more of these things? are they not written in the *Boke* of
Gell? [1] and has not Hobhouse got a journal? I keep none, as
I have renounced scribbling.

I see not much difference between ourselves and the Turks,
save that we have * * and they have none—that they have
long dresses, and we short, and that we talk much, and they
little. They are sensible people. Ali Pacha told me he was
sure I was a man of rank, because I had *small ears* and *hands*,
and *curling hair*. By the by, I speak the Romaic, or modern
Greek, tolerably. It does not differ from the ancient dialects
so much as you would conceive; but the pronunciation is
diametrically opposite. Of verse, except in rhyme, they have
no idea.

I like the Greeks, who are plausible rascals,—with all the
Turkish vices, without their courage. However, some are
brave, and all are beautiful, very much resembling the busts
of Alcibiades;—the women not quite so handsome. I can
swear in Turkish; but, except one horrible oath, and " pimp ",
and " bread ", and " water ", I have got no great vocabulary
in that language. They are extremely polite to strangers of
any rank, properly protected; and as I have two servants and
two soldiers, we get on with great *éclat*. We have been occasion-

---

[1] Sir William Gell was the author of *Topography of Troy, Geography and Antiquities of Ithaca,* etc.

ally in danger of thieves, and once of shipwreck,—but always escaped.

Of Spain I sent some account to our Hodgson, but have subsequently written to no one, save notes to relations and lawyers, to keep them out of my premises. I mean to give up all connection, on my return, with many of my best friends— as I supposed them—and to snarl all my life. But I hope to have one good-humoured laugh with you, and to embrace Dwyer, and pledge Hodgson, before I commence cynicism.

Tell Dr. Butler I am now writing with the gold pen he gave me before I left England, which is the reason my scrawl is more unintelligible than usual. I have been at Athens, and seen plenty of these reeds for scribbling, some of which he refused to bestow upon me, because topographic Gell had brought them from Attica. But I will not describe,—no—you must be satisfied with simple detail till my return, and then we will unfold the flood-gates of colloquy. I am in a thirty-six gun frigate, going up to fetch Bob Adair from Constantinople, who will have the honour to carry this letter.

And so Hobhouse's *boke*[1] is out, with some sentimental sing-song of my own to fill up,—and how does it take, eh? and where the devil is the second edition of my Satire,[2] with additions? and my name on the title page? and more lines tagged to the end, with a new exordium and what not, hot from my anvil before I cleared the Channel? The Mediterranean and the Atlantic roll between me and criticism ; and the thunders of the Hyperborean Review are deafened by the roar of the Hellespont.

Remember me to Claridge, if not translated to college, and present to Hodgson assurances of my high consideration. Now, you will ask, what shall I do next? and I answer, I do not know. I may return in a few months, but I have intents and projects after visiting Constantinople.—Hobhouse, however, will probably be back in September.

On the 2d of July we have left Albion one year—*oblitus meorum obliviscendus et illis*. I was sick of my own country, and not much prepossessed in favour of any other ; but I

---

[1] *Imitations and Translations from the Ancient and Modern Classics* contained sixty-five pieces, nine by Byron's hand.

[2] *English Bards and Scotch Reviewers*, published by James Cawthorn.

" drag on my chain " without " lengthening it at each remove."
I am like the Jolly Miller, caring for nobody, and not cared for.
All countries are much the same in my eyes. I smoke, and
stare at mountains, and twirl my mustachios very independently.
I miss no comforts, and the musquitoes that rack the morbid
frame of H. have, luckily for me, little effect on mine, because
I live more temperately.

I omitted Ephesus in my catalogue, which I visited during
my sojourn at Smyrna ; but the Temple has almost perished,
and St. Paul need not trouble himself to epistolise the present
brood of Ephesians, who have converted a large church built
entirely of marble into a mosque, and I don't know that the
edifice looks the worse for it.

My paper is full, and my ink ebbing—good afternoon !
If you address to me at Malta, the letter will be forwarded
wherever I may be. H. greets you ; he pines for his poetry,—
at least, some tidings of it. I almost forgot to tell you that I
am dying for love of three Greek girls at Athens, sisters. I
lived in the same house. Teresa,[1] Mariana, and Katinka,
are the names of these divinities,—all of them under fifteen.

Your ταπεινοτατος δουλος, BYRON

TO FRANCIS HODGSON *Salsette frigate, in the Dardanelles,*
off Abydos, May 5, 1810

I am on my way to Constantinople, after a tour through
Greece, Epirus, etc., and part of Asia Minor, some particulars
of which I have just communicated to our friend and host,
H. Drury. With these, then, I shall not trouble you ; but as
you will perhaps be pleased to hear that I am well, etc., I take
the opportunity of our ambassador's return to forward the
few lines I have time to despatch. We have undergone some
inconveniences, and incurred partial perils, but no events
worthy of communication, unless you will deem it one that two
days ago I swam from Sestos to Abydos. This, with a few
alarms from robbers, and some danger of shipwreck in a Turkish
galliot six months ago, a visit to a Pacha, a passion for a married

---

[1] Teresa Macri was, of course, the " Maid of Athens ".

woman at Malta, a challenge to an officer, an attachment to three Greek girls at Athens, with a great deal of buffoonery and fine prospects, form all that has distinguished my progress since my departure from Spain.

Hobhouse rhymes and journalises; I stare and do nothing —unless smoking can be deemed an active amusement. The Turks take too much care of their women to permit them to be scrutinised; but I have lived a good deal with the Greeks, whose modern dialect I can converse in enough for my purposes. With the Turks I have also some male acquaintances—female society is out of the question. I have been very well treated by the Pachas and Governors, and have no complaint to make of any kind. Hobhouse will one day inform you of all our adventures—were I to attempt the recital, neither *my* paper nor *your* patience would hold out during the operation.

Nobody, save yourself, has written to me since I left England; but indeed I did not request it. I except my relations, who write quite as often as I wish. Of Hobhouse's volume I know nothing, except that it is out; and of my second edition I do not even know *that*, and certainly do not, at this distance, interest myself in the matter. I hope you and Bland roll down the stream of sale with rapidity.

Of my return I cannot positively speak, but think it probable Hobhouse will precede me in that respect. We have been very nearly one year abroad. I should wish to gaze away another, at least, in these evergreen climates; but I fear business, law business, the worst of employments, will recall me previous to that period, if not very quickly. If so, you shall have due notice.

I hope you will find me an altered personage,—I do not mean in body, but in manner, for I begin to find out that nothing but virtue will do in this damned world. I am tolerably sick of vice, which I have tried in its agreeable varieties, and mean, on my return, to cut all my dissolute acquaintance, leave off wine and carnal company, and betake myself to politics and decorum. I am very serious and cynical, and a good deal disposed to moralise; but fortunately for you the coming homily is cut off by default of pen and defection of paper.

Good morrow! If you write, address to me at Malta,

whence your letters will be forwarded. You need not remember me to any body, but believe me,

Yours with all faith, BYRON

Constantinople, May 15, 1810

P.S.—MY DEAR H.,—The date of my postscript " will prate to you of my whereabouts ". We anchored between the Seven Towers and the Seraglio on the 13th, and yesterday settled ashore. The ambassador is laid up ; but the secretary does the honours of the palace, and we have a general invitation to his palace. In a short time he has his leave of audience, and we accompany him in our uniforms to the Sultan, etc., and in a few days I am to visit the Captain Pacha with the commander of our frigate. I have seen enough of their Pashas already ; but I wish to have a view of the Sultan, the last of the Ottoman race.

Of Constantinople you have Gibbon's description, very correct as far as I have seen. The mosques I shall have a firman to visit. I shall most probably (*Deo volente*), after a full inspection of Stamboul, bend my course homewards ; but this is uncertain. I have seen the most interesting parts, particularly Albania, where few Franks have ever been, and all the most celebrated ruins of Greece and Ionia.

Of England I know nothing, hear nothing, and can find no person better informed on the subject than myself. I this moment drink your health in a bumper of hock ; Hobhouse fills and empties to the same ; do you and Drury pledge us in a pint of any liquid you please—vinegar will bear the nearest resemblance to that which I have just swallowed to your name ; but when we meet again the draught shall be mended and the wine also.

Yours ever, B.

TO HIS MOTHER †   *Constantinople, June 28, 1810*

MY DEAR MOTHER,—I regret to perceive by your last letter that several of mine have not arrived, particularly a very long one written in November last from Albania, where

I was on a visit to the Pacha of that province. Fletcher has also written to his spouse perpetually.

Mr. Hobhouse, who will forward or deliver this, and is on his return to England, can inform you of our different movements, but I am very uncertain as to my own return. He will probably be down in Notts. some time or other; but Fletcher, whom I send back as an incumbrance (English servants are sad travellers), will supply his place in the interim, and describe our travels, which have been tolerably extensive.

I have written twice briefly from this capital, from Smyrna, from Athens and other parts of Greece; from Albania, the Pacha of which province desired his respects to my mother, and said he was sure I was a man of high birth because I had small ears, curling hair, and white hands!!! He was very kind to me, begged me to consider him as a father, and gave me a guard of forty soldiers through the forests of Acarnania. But of this and other circumstances I have written to you at large, and yet hope you will receive my letters.

I remember Mahmout Pacha, the grandson of Ali Pacha, at Yanina, (a little fellow of ten years of age, with large black eyes, which our ladies would purchase at any price, and those regular features which distinguish the Turks,) asked me how I came to travel so young, without anybody to take care of me. This question was put by the little man with all the gravity of threescore. I cannot now write copiously; I have only time to tell you that I have passed many a fatiguing, but never a tedious moment; and all that I am afraid of is that I shall contract a gypsylike wandering disposition, which will make home tiresome to me: this, I am told, is very common with men in the habit of peregrination, and, indeed, I feel it so. On the 3d of May I swam from *Sestos* to *Abydos*. You know the story of Leander, but I had no *Hero* to receive me at landing.

I also passed a fortnight on the Troad. The tombs of Achilles and Æsyetes still exist in large barrows, similar to those you have doubtless seen in the North. The other day I was at Belgrade (a village in these environs), to see the house built on the same site as Lady Mary Wortley's. By-the-by, her ladyship, as far as I can judge, has lied, but not half so much as any other woman would have done in the same situation.

I have been in all the principal mosques by the virtue of a firman : this is a favour rarely permitted to Infidels, but the ambassador's departure obtained it for us. I have been up the Bosphorus into the Black Sea, round the walls of the city, and, indeed, I know more of it by sight than I do of London. I hope to amuse you some winter's evening with the details, but at present you must excuse me ;—I am not able to write long letters in June. I return to spend my summer in Greece. I shall not proceed further into Asia, as I have visited Smyrna, Ephesus and the Troad. I write often, but you must not be alarmed when you do not receive my letters ; consider we have no regular post farther than Malta, where I beg you will in future send your letters, and not to this city.

Fletcher is a poor creature, and requires comforts that I can dispense with. He is very sick of his travels, but you must not believe his account of the country. He sighs for ale, and idleness, and a wife, and the devil knows what besides. I have not been disappointed or disgusted. I have lived with the highest and the lowest. I have been for days in a Pacha's palace, and have passed many a night in a cowhouse, and I find the people inoffensive and kind. I have also passed some time with the principal Greeks in the Morea and Livadia, and, though inferior to the Turks, they are better than the Spaniards, who, in their turn, excel the Portuguese. Of Constantinople you will find many descriptions in different travels ; but Lady Mary Wortley errs strangely when she says, " St. Paul's would cut a strange figure by St. Sophia's ". I have been in both, surveyed them inside and out attentively. St. Sophia's is undoubtedly the most interesting from its immense antiquity, and the circumstance of all the Greek emperors, from Justinian, having been crowned there, and several murdered at the altar, besides the Turkish Sultans who attend it regularly. But it is inferior in beauty and size to some of the mosques, particularly " Soleyman ", etc., and not to be mentioned in the same page with St. Paul's (I speak like a *Cockney*). However, I prefer the Gothic cathedral of Seville to St. Paul's, St. Sophia's, and any religious building I have ever seen.

The walls of the Seraglio are like the walls of Newstead gardens, only higher, and much in the same *order* ; but the ride by the walls of the city, on the land side, is beautiful.

Imagine four miles of immense triple battlements, covered with ivy, surmounted with 218 towers, and, on the other side of the road, Turkish burying-grounds (the loveliest spots on earth), full of enormous cypresses. I have seen the ruins of Athens, of Ephesus, and Delphi. I have traversed great part of Turkey, and many other parts of Europe, and some of Asia; but I never beheld a work of nature or art which yielded an impression like the prospect on each side from the Seven Towers to the end of the Golden Horn.

Now for England. You have not received my friend Hobhouse's volume of poesy: it has been published several months; you ought to read it. I am glad to hear of the progress of *English Bards,* etc. Of course, you observed I have made great additions to the new edition. Have you received my picture from Sanders, Vigo Lane, London? It was finished and paid for long before I left England: pray, send for it. You seem to be a mighty reader of magazines: where do you pick up all this intelligence, quotations, etc., etc.? Though I was happy to obtain my seat without the assistance of Lord Carlisle, I had no measures to keep with a man who declined interfering as my relation on that occasion, and I have done with him, though I regret distressing Mrs. Leigh, poor thing!—I hope she is happy.

It is my opinion that Mr. B * * ought to marry Miss R * *. Our first duty is not to do evil; but, alas! that is impossible: our next is to repair it, if in our power. The girl is his equal: if she were his inferior, a sum of money and provision for the child would be some, though a poor, compensation: as it is, he should marry her. I will have no gay deceivers on my estate, and I shall not allow my tenants a privilege I do not permit myself—*that* of debauching each other's daughters. God knows, I have been guilty of many excesses; but, as I have laid down a resolution to reform, and lately kept it, I expect this Lothario to follow the example, and begin by restoring this girl to society, or, by the beard of my father! he shall hear of it. Pray take some notice of Robert, who will miss his master; poor boy, he was very unwilling to return. I trust you are well and happy. It will be a pleasure to hear from you.

Believe me, yours very sincerely, BYRON

P.S.—How is Joe Murray?

P.S.—I open my letter again to tell you that Fletcher having petitioned to accompany me into the Morea, I have taken him with me, contrary to the intention expressed in my letter.

TO EDWARD ELLICE*   *Constantinople, July, 4th, 1810*

MY DEAR ELLICE,—I seize the occasion of Mr. Adair's return to convey my congratulations on your marriage, (for I hear you have taken unto yourself a wife) these, though somewhat of the latest, will arrive at a time when you must be more sensible of their value, as having full experience of matrimony and its concomitant blessings. Hobhouse is returning, but I am going back to Greece. To that loquacious traveller I refer you for all our adventures, but I must beg leave to mention to you as a feat that I have swum from Sestos to Abydos.

I hear your friend Brougham is in the lower house mouthing at the ministry. Notwithstanding my enmity against him and the dogs without faith with whom he is critically connected, I wish him success. You remember, he would not believe that *I* had written my pestilent Satire. Now that was very cruel and unlike me, for the moment I read his speech I believed it to be *his* entire from Exordium to Peroration. My fellow traveller Hobby, who is posting to your country full of marvels, has, as you no doubt know, put forth a volume of Poesy, which I do exhort you and all your acquaintance who may be possessed of a dormant half-guinea to purchase, and he himself (when he is worth so much money) will in return buy rhyme at the same rate from any of the said persons who shall please to be poetical. *My* work, it seems, has frisked through another edition with my name prefixed to it, despite of the advice of all my friends, who were fearful I should be cut off in the flower of my youth by an Insurrection in Grub street. Now I mean to live a long time in defiance of pens or penknives.

I suppose by this time you have become a bitter politician. I hope in no very long time to be amongst you, but I have one or two little things to adjust in the Morea before I sail. We have been in Portugal, Spain, Sardinia, Sicily, Malta, Albania, Greece, Asia Minor, and seen the Troad, Athens, Ephesus and sundry cities with names that would choak you, but I spare you. I shall not proceed into Persia, as I prophesied in rather too great a hurry, but having satiated my curiosity in this metropolis quietly repair home—and then—I hope you will be glad to see me, and I will have a speech ready for your spouse, and marry myself, seeing I have such excellent encouragement. Present my humble service to your brethren, and my cousin Trunnion. I am sorry to hear that my sister Mrs. Leigh is annoyed at my attack on the Earl of C[arlisle], though I had motives enough to justify any measures against that silly old man. Had I been aware that she would have laid it to heart, I would have cast my pen and poem both into the flames, and, in good truth (if she knew the feelings of us scribblers) no small sacrifice. But the mischief is done, Lord forgive me ! This it is to have tender-hearted she-relations. If I had been lucky enough to be a bastard, I might have abused everybody to my dying-day, and *nobody never* the *worser*. I have sent no descriptions to you of these parts, because you know the Mackenzies and other vagrant people who have told you all . . . about them. I address this to Brookes's, supposing marriage to have driven you from Park Street. I have nothing left to wish you but an heir, of whose Papa I remain

the obliged and very sincere friend, BYRON

TO JOHN CAM HOBHOUSE † *Patras, July 29th, 1810*

DEAR HOBHOUSE,—The same day which saw me ashore at Zea, set me forth once more upon the high seas, where I had the pleasure of seeing the frigate in the *Doldrums* by the light of sun and moon. Before daybreak I got into the Attics at Thaskalio, hence I dispatched men to Keratia for horses, and in ten hours from landing I was at Athens. There I was greeted by my Lord Sligo, and next day Messrs. North, Knight, and Fazakerly paid me formal visits. Sligo has a brig with

50 men who won't work, 12 guns that refuse to go off, and
sails that have cut every wind except a contrary one, and then
they are as willing as may be.   He is sick of the concern, but
an engagement of six months prevents him from parting with
this precious ark.   He *would* travel with me to Corinth, though
as you may suppose I was already heartily disgusted with
travelling in company.   He has "en suite" a painter, a
captain, a gentleman misinterpreter (who boxes with the
painter), besides sundry idle English varlets.   We were obliged
to have twenty-nine horses in all.   The captain and the
Drogueman were left at Athens to kill bullocks for the crew, and
the Marquis and the limner, with a ragged Turk by way of
Tartar, and the ship's carpenter in the capacity of linguist,
with two servants (one of whom had the gripes) clothed both
in leather breeches (the thermometer 125°!!), followed over
the hills and far away.   On our route, the poor limner in these
gentle latitudes was ever and anon condemned to bask for
half-an-hour, that he might produce what he himself termed a
"bellissimo sketche" (pardon the orthography of the last
word) of the surrounding country.   You may also suppose that
a man of the Marchese's kidney was not very easy in his seat.
As for the *servants*, they and their *leather breeches* were equally
immovable at the end of the first stage.   Fletcher, too, with
his usual acuteness, contrived at Megara to ram his damned
clumsy foot into a boiling tea-kettle.   At Corinth we separated,
the M[arquis] for Tripolitza, I for Patras.   Thus far the
ridiculous part of my narrative belongs to others, now comes
my turn.   At Vostitza I found my dearly-beloved Eustathius,
ready to follow me not only to England, but to Terra Incognita, if so be my compass pointed that way.   This was *four*
days ago: at present affairs are a little changed.   The next
morning I found the dear soul upon horseback clothed very
sprucely in Greek Garments, with those ambrosial curls
hanging down his amiable back, and to my utter astonishment,
and the great abomination of Fletcher, a *parasol* in his hand
to save his complexion from the heat.   However, in spite of
the *Parasol* on we travelled very much enamoured, as it should
seem, till we got to Patras, where Strané received us into his
new house where I now scribble.   Next day he went to visit
some accursed cousin and the day after we had a grand quarrel.

Strané said I spoilt him. I said nothing; the child was as froward as an unbroken colt, and Strané's Janizary said I must not be surprised, for he was too *true* a *Greek* not to be disagreeable. I think I never in my life took so much pains to please any one, or succeeded so ill. I particularly avoided every thing which *could possibly give* the *least offence* in *any manner*. Somebody says, that those who try to please will please. This I know not; but I am sure that no one likes to fail in the attempt. At present he goes back to his father, though he is now become more tractable. Our *parting* was vastly pathetic, as many kisses as would have sufficed for a boarding school, and embraces enough to have ruined the character of a county in England, besides tears (not on *my* part) and expressions of " Tenerezza " to a vast amount. All this and the warmth of the weather has quite overcome me. Tomorrow I will continue. At present, " to bed ", " to bed ", " to bed ". The youth insists on seeing me tomorrow, the issue of which interview you shall hear. I wish you a pleasant sleep.

July 30th, 1810

I hope you have slept well. I have only dozed. For this last six days I have slept little and eaten less. The heat has burnt me brown, and as for Fletcher he is a walking Cinder. My new Greek acquaintance has called thrice, and we improve vastly. In good truth, so it ought to be, for I have quite exhausted my poor powers of pleasing, which God knows are little enough, Lord help me ! We are to go on to Tripolitza and Athens together. I do not know what has put him into such good humour unless it is some Sal Volatile I administered for his headache, and a green shade instead of that effeminate parasol. But so it is. We have *redintegrated* (a new *word* for you) our affections at a great rate. Now is not all this very ridiculous? Pray tell Matthews. It would do his heart good to see me travelling with my Tartar, Albanians, Buffo, Fletcher and this amiable παιδη prancing by my side. Strané hath got a steed which I have bought, full of spirit, I assure you, and very handsome accoutrements. My *account* with him was as I stated on board the Salsette. Here hath just arrived the Chirugeon of the Spider from Zante, who will take this letter

to Malta. I hope it will find you warm. You cannot conceive
what a delightful companion you are now you are gone.
Sligo has told me some things that ought to set you and me
by the ears, but they shan't; and as a proof of it, I won't tell
you what they are till we meet, but in the meantime I exhort
you to behave well in polite society. His Lordship has been
very kind, and as I crossed the Isthmus of Corinth, offered if
I chose to take me to that of Darien, but I liked it not, for you
have cured me of " villainous company ".

I am about—after a Giro of the Morea—to move to
Athens again, and thence I know not where; perhaps to
Englonde, Malta, Sicily, Ægypt, or the Low Countries. I
suppose you are at Malta or Palermo. I amuse myself alone
very much to my satisfaction, riding, bathing, sweating,
hearing Mr. Paul's musical clock, looking at his red breeches;
we visit him every evening. There he is, playing at stopper
with the old Cogia Bachi. When these amusements fail,
there is my Greek to quarrel with, and a sopha to tumble upon.
Nourse and Dacres had been at Athens scribbling all sorts
of ribaldry over my old apartment, where Sligo, before my
arrival, had added to your B.A. an A.S.S., and scrawled the
compliments of Jackson, Deville, Miss Cameron, and " *I am
very unappy Sam Jennings* ". Wallace is incarcerated, and wanted
Sligo to bail him, at the " Bell and Savage ", Fleet Rules.
The news are not surprising. What think you? Write to
me from Malta, the Mediterranean, or Ingleterra, to care of
ὁ μονόλοο Στράνε.

Have you cleansed my pistols? and dined with the
" *Gineral* "? My compliments to the church of St. John's,
and peace to the ashes of Ball. How is the Skipper? I have
drank his cherry-brandy, and his rum has floated over half the
Morea. Plaudite et valete.

Yours ever, BYRON

TO JOHN CAM HOBHOUSE†   *Tripolitza, August 16th, 1810*

DEAR HOBHOUSE,—I am on the rack of setting off for
Argos amidst the usual creaking, swearing, loading, and

neighing of sixteen horses and as many men, serrugees included. You have probably received one letter dated Patras, and I send this at a venture. Vely Pasha received me even better than his father did, though he is to join the Sultan, and the city is full of troops and confusion, which, as he said, prevented him from paying proper attention. He has given me a very pretty horse, and a most particular invitation to meet him at Larissa, which last is singular enough, as he recommended a different route to Lord Sligo, who asked leave to accompany him to the Danube. I asked no such thing, but on his enquiry where I meant to go, and receiving for answer that I was about to return to Albania, for the purpose of penetrating higher up the country, he replied, " No, you must not take that route, but go round by Larissa, where I shall remain some time, on my way. I will send to Athens, and you shall join me ; we will eat and drink and go a hunting." He said he wished all the old men (specifying under that epithet North, Forresti, and Strané,) to go to his father, but the young ones to come to him, to use his own expression, " Vecchio con Vecchio, Giovane con Giovane ". He honoured me with the appellations of his *friend* and *brother*, and hoped that we should be on good terms, not for a few days but for life. All this is very well, but he has an awkward manner of throwing his arm round one's waist, and squeezing one's hand in *public* which is a high compliment, but very much embarrasses " *ingenuous youth* ".

The first time I saw him he received me *standing*, accompanied me at my departure to the door of the audience chamber, and told me I was a παλικαρι and an εὔμορφω παίδι. He asked if I did not think it very proper that as *young* men (he has a *beard* down to his middle) we should live together, with a variety of other sayings, which made Strané stare, and puzzled me in my replies. He was very facetious with Andreas and Viscillie, and recommended that my Albanians' heads should be cut off if they behaved ill. I shall write to you from Larissa, and inform you of our proceedings in that city. In the meantime I sojourn at Athens. I have sent Eustathius back to his home ; he plagued my soul out with his whims, and is besides subject to *epileptic* fits (tell *M.* this) which made him a perplexing companion ; in *other* matters he was very tolerable,

I mean as to his learning, being well versed in the Ellenics.
You remember Nicolo at Athens, Lusieri's wife's brother.
Give my *compliments* to *Matthews*, from whom I expect a con-
gratulatory letter.   I have a thousand anecdotes for him and
you, but at present, τί να κάμω ?   I have neither time nor space,
but in the words of Dawes, " I have things in store ".   I have
scribbled thus much.   Where shall I send it?   Why, to Malta
or Paternoster Row.   Hobby, you wretch, how is the Miscellany?   that damned and damnable work.   What has the
learned world said to your Paradoxes?   I hope you did not
forget the importance of Monogamy.   Strané has just arrived
with bags of piastres, so that I must conclude by the usual
phrase of

Yours, etc. etc., BYRON

P.S.—You knew young Bossari at Yanina ; he is a piece of
Ali Pacha's ! !   Well did Horace write " Nil Admirari ".

TO JOHN CAM HOBHOUSE †   *The Convent, Athens,*
                                    August 23rd, 1810

MY DEAR HOBHOUSE,—Lord Sligo's unmanageable brig
being remanded to Malta, with a large quantity of vases,
amounting in value (according to the depreciation of Fauriel)
to one hundred and fifty piastres, I cannot resist the temptation
of assailing you in this third letter, which I trust will find you
better than your deserts, and no worse than my wishes can
make you.   I have girated the Morea, and was presented with
a very fine horse (a stallion), and honoured with a number
of squeezes and speeches by Velly Pasha, besides a most
pressing invitation to meet him at Larissa in his way to the
wars.   But of these things I have written already.   I returned
to Athens by Argos, where I found Lord Sligo with a painter,
who has got a fever with sketching at midday, and a dragoman
who has actually lied himself into a lockjaw.   I grieve to say
the Marchese has done a number of young things, because
I believe him to be a clever, and I am sure he is a good man.
I am most auspiciously settled in the Convent, which is more
commodious than any tenement I have yet occupied, with

room for my *suite*; and it is by no means solitary, seeing there is not only " il Padre Abbate ", but his " schuola ", consisting of six " Ragazzi ", all my most particular allies. These gentlemen being almost (saving Fauvel and Lusieri) my only associates, it is but proper their character, religion, and morals, should be described. Of this goodly company three are Catholics, and three are Greeks, which schismatics I have already set a boxing to the great amusement of the Father, who rejoices to see the Catholics conquer. Their names are Barthelemi, Giuseppè, *Nicolo*, Yani, and two anonymous, at least in my memory. Of these, Barthelemi is a " simplice Fanciullo ", according to the account of the Father, whose favourite is Giuseppè, who sleeps in the lantern of Demosthenes. We have nothing but riot from noon to night.

The first time I mingled with these sylphs, after about two minutes' reconnoitring, the amiable Signor Barthelemi, without any previous notice, seated himself by me, and after observing by way of compliment that my " Signoria " was the " piu bello " of his English acquaintance, saluted me on the left cheek, for which freedom being reproved by Giuseppè, who very properly informed him that I was " $\mu\epsilon\gamma\acute{a}\lambda os$ "; he told him I was his " $\phi\acute{\iota}\lambda os$ ", and " by his beard " he would do so again, adding, in reply to the question " $\delta\iota\grave{a}$ $\tau\grave{\iota}$ $\dot{a}\sigma\pi\acute{a}\sigma\epsilon\tau\epsilon$?" " you see he laughs ", as in good truth I did heartily. But my friend, as you may easily imagine, is Nicolo, who, by-the-by, is my Italian master, and we are already very philosophical. I am his " Padrone " and his " amico ", and the Lord knows what besides. It is about two hours since, that, after informing me he was most desirous to follow *him* (that is me) over the world, he concluded by telling me it was proper for us not only to live, but " morire insieme ". The latter I hope to avoid—as much of the former as he pleases. I am awakened in the morning by those imps shouting " Venite abasso ", and the friar gravely observes it is " bisogno bastonare " everybody before the studies can possibly commence. Besides these lads, my suite,—to which I have added a Tartar and a youth to look after my two new saddle horses,—my suite, I say, are very obstreperous, and drink skinfuls of Zean wine at eight paras the olne daily. Then we have several Albanian women washing in the " giardino ", whose hours of relaxation are spent in running pins into Fletcher's backside. "*Damnata di mi, if I have seen such a spectaculo in my way from Viterbo.*" In short, what with the *women*, and the *boys*, and the *suite*, we are very disorderly. But I am vastly happy and childish, and shall have a world of anecdotes for you and the "citoyen".

Intrigue flourishes: the old woman, Theresa's mother, was mad enough to imagine I was going to marry the girl; but I have better amusement. Andreas is fooling with Dudu, as usual, and Mariana has made a conquest of Dervise Tahiri; Vircillie, Fletcher and Sullee, my new Tartar, have each a mistress—"Vive l'Amour".

I am learning Italian, and this day translated an ode of Horace, "Exegi monumentum", into that language. I chatter with everybody, good or bad, and tradute prayers out of the mass ritual; but my lessons, though very long, are sadly interrupted by scamperings, and eating fruit, and peltings and playings; and I am in fact at school again, and make as little improvement now as I did then, my time being wasted in the same way.

However, it is too good to last; I am going to make a second tour of Attica with Lusieri, who is a new ally of mine, and Nicolo goes with me at his own most pressing solicitation, "per mare per terras". "Forse" you may see us in Inghilterra, but "non so, come, etc." For the present, good-even, Buona sera a vos signoria. Bacio le mani:—August 24th, 1810.

I am about to take my daily ride to the Piræus, where I swim for an hour despite of the heat; here hath been an Englishman ycleped Watson, who died and is buried in the Tempio of Theseus. I knew him not, but I am told that the surgeon of Lord Sligo's brig slew him with an improper potion, and a cold bath.

Lord Sligo's crew are sadly addicted to liquor. He is in some apprehension of a scrape with the Navy concerning certain mariners of the King's ships.

He himself is now at Argos with his hospital, but intends to winter in Athens. I think he will be sick of it, poor soul, he has all the indecision of your humble servant, without the relish for the ridiculous which makes my life supportable.

I wish you were here to partake of a number of waggeries, which you can hardly find in the gun-room or in Grub Street, but then you are so very crabbed and disagreeable, that when the laugh is over I rejoice in your absence. After all, I do love thee, Hobby, thou hast so many good qualities, and so many bad ones, it is impossible to live with or without thee.

Nine in the Evening.

I have, as usual, swum across the Piræus, the Signor Nicolo also laved, but he makes as bad a hand in the water as L'Abbé Hyacinth at Falmouth; it is a curious thing that the Turks when they bathe wear their lower garments, as your humble servant always doth, but the Greeks not; however, questo Giovane e vergognó [sic].

Lord Sligo's surgeon has assisted very materially the malignant fever now fashionable here; another man *dead* to-day, two men a week, like fighting Bob Acres in the country. Fauriel says he is like the surgeon whom the Venetians fitted out against the Turks, with whom they were then at war.

I have been employed the greater part of today in conjugating the verb " ασπαζω " (which word being Ellenic as well as Romaic may find a place in the *Citoyen's* Lexicon). I assure you my progress is rapid, but like Caesar " nil actum reputans dum quid superesset agendum ", I must arrive at the [indecipherable], and then I will write to ——. I hope to escape the fever, at least till I finish this affair, and then it is welcome to try. I don't think without its friend the drunken Pothecary it has any chance. Take a quotation:—" Et Lycam *nigris* oculis, nigroque *crine* decorum ".

yours and the *Sieur's* ever, B.

TO JOHN CAM HOBHOUSE †   *Patras, September 25th, 1810*

MY DEAR HOBHOUSE,—I am at present in a very ridiculous situation, under the hands of Dr. Romanelli, and a fever which hath confined me to my bed for these three days past, but by the blessing of God and two glysters, I am now able to sit up, but much debilitated. I will describe my situation in a parody on Pope's lines on the Duke of Buckingham, the which I composed during an interval for your edification.

On a cold room's cold floor, within a bed
Of iron, with three coverlids like lead,

A coat and breeches dangling o'er a nook,
Where sits a doctor and prescribes a puke,
Poor B—r—n sweats,—alas ! how changed from him,
So plump in feature, and so round in limb,
Grinning and gay in Newstead's monkish fane,
The scene of profanation, and champagne,
Or just as gay with scribblers in a ring
Of twenty hungry authors banqueting.
No whore to fondle left of half a score,
Yet one thing left him, which he values more,
Here victor of a fever, and its friends,
Physicians and their art, his lordship *mends*.

I have been vomited and purged according to rule, and as my
fever has almost subsided, I hope to weather this bout, which
has been pretty tight, I assure you.   Yet if I do fall by the
Glyster pipe of Romanelli, recollect my injunction.

Odious ! in boards, 'twould any Bard provoke
(Were the last words that dying Byron spoke) ;
No, let some charming cuts and frontispiece
Adorn my volume, and the sale increase.
One would not be unpublished when one's dead,
And, Hobhouse, let my works be bound in *Red*.

TO JOHN CAM HOBHOUSE†   *Patras, October 2nd, 1810*

DEAR YANI,—By this second date you will perceive that
I have been again ill.   Indeed I have had this fever very
violently, and five days bed-riding with Emetics, glysters,
Bark, and all the host of Physic shewed how vain were my
former hopes of complete recovery.   But being well toasted
and watered etc., I shall endeavour to conclude this letter of
two beginnings, which I must do quickly and attend poor
Nicolo who has waited on me day and night till he is worse than
I was and is now undergoing the same process for his recovery.
I believe you recollect him.   He is the brother of Lusieri's
spouse, and has been with me nearly two months, at his
particular request.   He is now my sole dragoman (I have
commenced Italian), for the moment I received yours Andreas

was dismissed at the instance of Dominus Magelli. I have made a tolerable tour of the Morea, and visited Vely Pasha, who gave me a very pretty horse.

The other day I went to Olympia. Argos, Napoli, and Mantinea I saw in my route to and from Tripolitza.

I have seen a good deal of Lord Sligo; by the bye, there is a silly report all over the Morea, that he and I quarrelled, fought, and were wounded at Argos, there is not a word of truth in it from beginning to end.

If I kept any journal your request would be immediately complied with, but I have none.

Vely is gone to the Danube. I have been here on business with Strané, but the moment Nicolo and myself are enough recovered to set out, I shall proceed again to Athens. I lodge in the convent.

Perhaps I am in possession of anecdotes that would amuse you and the Citoyen, but I must defer the detail till we meet, I have written to you three times since I left you in Zea, and direct my letters to Ridgways, where I presume you will be found on Sundays. You are now in England. What you tell me of the Miscellany grieves me (in spite of Rochefoucault); I commend your design of not letting the public off so easily; come out as a tourist, prose must go down.

But don't ask half a guinea for your next book. Consider, half a guinea carries a man to the Opera, and if he goes to Hookham's, 'tis odds but he buys more tickets than books, aye, and cheaper too; try seven shillings, Mr. Hobhouse, seven shillings, sir, stick to that, and let me tell you, when you have received seven hundred seven shilling pieces, they will cut a figure on your little deal writing-table. I have a regard for you, sir, and out of it, I beg you to strike off the odd three and sixpence.

I have nothing to request in England; everybody with whom I am at all connected seems asleep; as far as regards me, I shan't awake them. Hanson you may just fillup on the nose, and ask him from me if he is insane, not to have answered my letters. As to the others, their conduct is optional, and I have nothing to say. I shall certainly be in England in a few months, perhaps before, but I do not wish this to go forth, as it will only make Hanson more dilatory. If you hear anything you will write, and I will apprise you of my intentions as they rise and subside, for it would be very absurd in me to pretend to any regular plan. You have no doubt, a deal to do and say and hear and reply; wishing you well through it,

I am yours very sincerely etc., BYRON

TO JOHN CAM HOBHOUSE †   *Patras, Morea, October 4th, 1810*

MY DEAR HOBHOUSE,—I wrote to you two days ago, but the weather and my friend Strané's conversation being much the same, and my ally Nicolo in bed with a fever, I think I may as well talk to you, the rather, as you can't answer me; and excite my wrath with impertinent observations, at least for three months to come. I will try not to say the same things I have set down in my other letter of the 2nd, but I can't promise, as my poor head is still giddy with my late fever. I saw the Lady Hesther Stanhope [1] at Athens, and do not admire " that dangerous thing a female wit ". She told me (take her own words) that she had given you a good set-down at Malta, in some disputation about the Navy; from this, of course, I readily inferred the contrary, or in the words of an *acquaintance* of ours, that " you had the best of it ". She evinced a similar disposition to *argufy* with me, which I avoided by either laughing or yielding. I despise the sex too much to squabble with them, and I rather wonder you should allow a woman to draw you into a contest, in which, however, I am sure you had the advantage, she abuses you so bitterly. I have seen too little of the Lady to form any decisive opinion, but I have discovered nothing different from other she-things, except a great disregard of received notions in her conversation as well as conduct. I don't know whether this will recommend her to our sex, but I am sure it won't to her own. She is going on to Constantinople. Ali Pacha is in a scrape. Ibrahim Pacha and the Pacha of Scutari have come down upon him with 20,000 Gegdes and Albanians, retaken Berat, and threaten Tepaleni. Adam Bey

---

[1] The celebrated Lady Hester Stanhope was at this time travelling through European Turkey. The impression that Byron made upon her was not entirely favourable. " One time [she remarked] he was mopish, and nobody was to speak to him; another, he was for being jocular with everybody. . . . He had a great deal of vice in his looks. . . ."

is dead, Vely Pacha was on his way to the Danube, but has gone off suddenly to Yanina, and all Albania is in an uproar. The mountains we crossed last year are the scene of warfare, and there is nothing but carnage and cutting of throats. In my other letter I mentioned that Vely had given me a fine horse. On my late visit he received me with great pomp, standing, conducted me to the door with his arm round my waist, and a variety of civilities, invited me to meet him at Larissa and see his army, which I should have accepted, had not this rupture with Ibrahim taken place. Sultan Mahmout is in a phrenzy because Vely has not joined the army. We have a report here, that the Russians have beaten the Turks and taken Muchtar Pacha prisoner, but it is a Greek Bazaar rumour and not to be believed. I have now treated you with a dish of Turkish politics. You have by this time gotten into England, and your ears and mouth are full of " Reform Burdett, Gale Jones, minority, last night's division, dissolution of Parliament, battle in Portugal ", and all the cream of forty newspapers.

In my t'other letter, to which I am perpetually obliged to refer, I have offered some moving topics on the head of your *Miscellany*, the neglect of which I attribute to the half guinea annexed as the indispensable equivalent for the said volume. Now I do hope, notwithstanding that exorbitant demand, that on your return you will find it selling, or, what is better, sold, in consequence of which you will be able to face the public with your new volume, if that intention still subsists. My journal, did I keep one, should be yours. As it is I can only offer my sincere wishes for your success, if you will believe it possible for a brother scribbler to be sincere on such an occasion. Will you execute a commission for me? Lord Sligo tells me it was the intention of Miller in Albemarle Street to send by him a letter to me, which he stated to be of consequence. Now I have no concern with Mr. M. except a bill which I hope is paid before this time; will you visit the said M. and if it be a pecuniary matter, refer him to Hanson, and if not, tell me what he means, or forward his letter. I have just received an epistle from Galt, with a Candist poem, which it seems I am to forward to you. This I would willingly do, but it is too large for a letter, and too small for a parcel, and besides appears to be damned nonsense, from all which considerations

I will deliver it in person. It is entitled the " Fair Shepherd-
ess ", or rather " Herdswoman " ; if you don't like the translation take the original title ' ἡ βοσκοπουλα ". Galt also writes
something not very intelligible about a " Spartan State paper "
which by his account is everything but Laconic. Now the
said Sparta having some years ceased to be a state, what the
devil does he mean by a paper? he also adds mysteriously that
the *affair* not being concluded, he cannot at present apply for it.
Now, Hobhouse, are you mad? or is he? Are these documents
for Longman and Co.? Spartan state papers! and Cretan
rhymes! indeed these circumstances superadded to his house
at Mycene (whither I am invited) and his Levant wines,
make me suspect his sanity.

Athens is at present infested with English people, but they
are moving, *Dio bendetto!* I am returning to pass a month or
two ; I think the spring will see me in England, but do not let
this transpire, nor cease to urge the most dilatory of mortals,
Hanson. I have some idea of purchasing the Island of Ithaca ;
I suppose you will add me to the Levant lunatics. I shall be
glad to hear from your Signoria of your welfare, politics, and
literature. Tell M. that I have obtained above two hundred
[word indecipherable] and am almost tired of them ; for the
history of these he must wait my return, as after many attempts
I have given up the idea of conveying information on paper.
You know the monastery of Mendele ; it was there I made
myself master of the first. Your last letter closes pathetically
with a postscript about a nosegay ; I advise you to introduce
that into your next sentimental novel. I am sure I did not suspect
you of any fine feelings, and I believe you were laughing, but
you are welcome. *Vale* ; " I can no more ", like Lord Grizzle.

Yours, Μπαίρων

TO JOHN CAM HOBHOUSE   *Capuchin Convent, Athens,*
                                            January 10th, 1811

DEAR HOBHOUSE,—I have written at intervals several
letters, some of which it is probable you have received. Two
have arrived of yours, dated Malta and Cagliari, and I conceive there be others *on* the sea, or *in* it, for you must have been

months in England. Since your departure from the Cyclades I have been principally in Attica, which I have traversed more than once, besides two tours in the Morea, of the particulars of which Mr. Fletcher, now on his voyage with despatches, will apprise you. Here be many English, and there have been more, with all of whom I have been and *am* on dining terms, and we have had balls and a variety of fooleries with the females of Athens. I am very undecided in my intentions, though stationary enough, as you perceive by my date. I sometimes think of moving homewards in spring, and sometimes of not moving at all till I have worn out my shoes, which are all as good as new. Hanson has at last written, and wants me to sell Newstead. I *will not*; and though I have in more than one letter to you requested you to corroborate and assist this *negative*, I beg in this and all subsequent communications, to entreat you to tell him and all whom it may concern, that I will not sell my patrimony. I suppose, however, the adjustment of that, and other damned affairs will drag me to England. Well, sir, and I suppose you are holding forth to your acquaintance, on the subject of your travels, and they are all very glad to see you, and you have been tipsy and loquacious as usual on such occasions, and are just beginning to subside into the old track of living, after shaking about sixty pairs of hands, and seeing the play and such like, all of which must be very new to a voyager from the Levant. You will present my respects to Matthews and Davies, who is I hear about to throw himself away on a rich wife, and none of the seemliest, according to my reporter. Pray what profits make ye of the Miscellany? Eh, eh! I warrant you now, you are preparing a tome of travel for the press. I have no journal, or you should have it to abet your design. I am now tolerable in Italian, and am studying the Romaic under a master, being obliged to cashier my Latin with my last dragoman, and betake myself to the moderns. I have sent a bark to Smyrna in the faint hope of letters, and shall not fill up this sheet till its return.

January 14th, 1811

My boat is returned with some newspapers, and duplicates of letters already arrived. None from you, but all in good time. I shall certainly not (without something very novel occurs), move towards your Island till spring, nor even then if I receive any further remittances, a business which I hope you did not fail to urge to my agent. You have, I humbly presume, forwarded all my epistles to their respective destinations. I certainly wish to hear how you go on, and what plan you have chalked out. Five and twenty is almost too late in life for anything but the Senate, or the Church. I wish you was a parson, or a counsellor-at-law; by the bye Lord Erskine did not commence till nearly thirty. I do not think your sire so blameable; the fault lies of course with the stepdame; the old story; Baillie has got rid of his " injusta noverca ", see what it is to have luck! As you are fond of scribbling, and are said to have a talent that way, why don't you, and *Matthews*, and some other wits, undertake some periodical, hebdomadal or diurnal concern, I leave you to find out what, but I think you might bring such a scheme to bear. Fyott is this day arrived from Mount Athos (" ἅγιον ὄρος "), he has discovered nothing to signify in the manuscript way; Graham and Haygarth are to depart shortly, one for Stamboul, Haygarth for Sicily. I shall send this by the latter. Galt is in Pera, full of his Sour Wine Company speculation. I shall look at him in Mycenæ, in the " Prima Vera ". He sent me a Candiot poem for you, but being the worst Romaic, and the vilest nonsense ever seen, it was not worth the carriage. As you know Athens and all its peculiarities, I shall not afflict you with description. I have three horses (one a gift of Vely Pasha), and live rather better and cheaper than last winter. I see a good deal of the English, and Lusieri, chiefly of late, and have had no disputes with anyone. I am tranquil, and as contented as I suppose one can be in any situation. I have also a Bavarian Baron and celebrated painter, taking views for me.

Yours very affectionately and truly, B——

[Written inside the wrapper]   *January 17th, 1811*

P.S.—This goes by Haygarth, who moves in a few days to Malta, by way of the Morea and Zante. Graham is off too.

I stay till spring, at all events till I receive letters, which as usual take their time on the way. Good-night, you port-drinking fellow. I am just returned from dining with Haygarth.

TO HIS MOTHER   *Athens, January 14, 1811*

MY DEAR MADAM,—I seize an occasion to write as usual, shortly, but frequently, as the arrival of letters, where there exists no regular communication, is, of course, very precarious. I have received, at different intervals, several of yours, but generally six months after date ; some sooner, some later, and, though lately tolerably stationary, the delays appear just the same. I have lately made several small tours of some hundred or two miles about the Morea, Attica, etc., as I have finished my grand giro by the Troad, Constantinople, etc., and am returned down again to Athens. I believe I have mentioned to you more than once that I swam (in imitation of Leander, though without his lady) across the Hellespont, from Sestos to Abydos. Of this, and all other particulars, Fletcher, whom I have sent home with papers, etc., will apprise you. I cannot find that he is any loss ; being tolerably master of the Italian and modern Greek languages, which last I am also studying with a master, I can order and discourse more than enough for a reasonable man. Besides, the perpetual lamentations after beef and beer, the stupid, bigoted contempt for every thing foreign, and insurmountable incapacity of acquiring even a few words of any language, rendered him, like all other English servants, an incumbrance. I do assure you, the plague of speaking for him, the comforts he required (more than myself by far), the pilaws (a Turkish dish of rice and meat) which he could not eat, the wines which he could not drink, the beds where he could not sleep, and the long list of calamities, such as stumbling horses, want of *tea!!!* etc., which assailed him, would have made a lasting source of laughter to a spectator, and inconvenience to a master. After all, the man is honest enough, and, in Christendom, capable enough ; but in Turkey, Lord forgive me ! my Albanian soldiers, my Tartars and Jannissary, worked for him and us too, as my friend Hobhouse can testify.

It is probable I may steer homewards in spring; but to enable me to do that, I must have remittances. My own funds would have lasted me very well; but I was obliged to assist a friend, who, I know, will pay me; but, in the mean time, I am out of pocket. At present, I do not care to venture a winter's voyage, even if I were otherwise tired of travelling; but I am so convinced of the advantages of looking at mankind instead of reading about them, and the bitter effects of staying at home with all the narrow prejudices of an islander, that I think there should be a law amongst us, to set our young men abroad, for a term, among the few allies our wars have left us.

Here I see and have conversed with French, Italians, Germans, Danes, Greeks, Turks, Americans, etc., etc., etc.; and without losing sight of my own, I can judge of the countries and manners of others. Where I see the superiority of England (which, by the by, we are a good deal mistaken about in many things), I am pleased, and where I find her inferior, I am at least enlightened. Now, I might have stayed, smoked in your towns, or fogged in your country, a century, without being sure of this, and without acquiring any thing more useful or amusing at home. I keep no journal, nor have I any intention of scribbling my travels. I have done with authorship, and if, in my last production, I have convinced the critics or the world I was something more than they took me for, I am satisfied; nor will I hazard *that reputation* by a future effort. It is true I have some others in manuscript, but I leave them for those who come after me; and, if deemed worth publishing, they may serve to prolong my memory when I myself shall cease to remember. I have a famous Bavarian artist taking some views of Athens, etc., etc., for me. This will be better than scribbling, a disease I hope myself cured of. I hope, on my return, to lead a quiet, recluse life, but God knows and does best for us all; at least, so they say, and I have nothing to object, as, on the whole, I have no reason to complain of my lot. I am convinced, however, that men do more harm to themselves than ever the devil could do to them. I trust this will find you well, and as happy as we can be; you will, at least, be pleased to hear I am so, and

Yours ever

TO JOHN CAM HOBHOUSE *   *Athens, March 5th, 1811*

DEAR HOBHOUSE,—Two English gentlemen after 7 years captivity in France having made their escape through Bosnia, and having arrived here in their way home, I shall follow up my last letter with the present which will be conveyed by these runaways whose names are Cazenove [?].

I am this moment come out of the Turkish Bath, which is an immense luxury to me, though I am afraid it would not suit you at all, there being a great deal of rubbing, sweating, and *washing* (your aversion) to go through, which I indulge in every other day. . . . I cannot sufficiently admire the punctuality and success with which you have written to me in reward for my numerous communications, the last of which must have arrived with the nincompoop Fletcher. Since my last letter, 27 ult, I have begun an Imitation of the " De Arte Poetica " of Horace (in rhyme of course) and have translated or rather varied about 200 lines and shall probably finish it for lack of other argument. The Horace I found in the convent where I have sojourned some months.

Ever since my fever in the Morea in Septr. of which I wrote you an account, my health has been changing in the most tramontane way. I have been fat, and thin (as I am at present) and had a cough and a catarrh and the piles and be damned to them, and I have had pains in my side and left off animal food, which last has done me some service. But I expect great things from the coming summer and if well and wealthy shall go to Jerusalem, for which I have a firman.

Dun Hanson, and tell him, he won't persuade me to sell Newstead, unless something particular occurs. If I sell it, I live abroad; if not, I come home; and I have no intention of selling it, but the contrary. The English here and myself are on very good terms. We have balls and dinners frequently. As I told you before, no letters have arrived from anybody. Consequently I know nothing of you, or Matthews, or the Miscellany. I have seen English papers of October, which say little or nothing; but I have lately sent a Battello [?] to Smyrna in hopes of hearing from my vagabond connections. I don't think you will see me before July, and if things go on to my wish, not for another year. I take it for granted all this time that you are arrived in England, as the Salsette has returned these six months to Smyrna, but your silence makes me rather doubt it. You see, you were mistaken in your conjectures on the subject of my return, and I have remanded Fletcher, whom I by no means miss, unless it be by having less confusion than usual in my wardrobe and household. I got your Malta and Cagliari letters, but I expected you would have written from England, though I can excuse a little delay and drunkenness on your first arrival. I feel also interested in your plans. I want to know what you are doing, saying, and writing, whether your domestic affairs go on to your satisfaction, and having heard all this, I should be glad to be informed of Matthieu, who I suppose was pleased to see you again. As for my own affairs, I don't want to hear of them unless they shine a little brighter than in June last, when I received a jocose account of their inextricability from Mr. H., who might as well have kept his good things for a better opportunity. If he remits a round sum, I will take that and his wit in good part; but I can't allow any naggery from Temple Bar without an adequate remuneration, particularly as three thousand miles (according to Fletcher's invariable calculation from the moment he *cleared* the *channel*) are too long for a repartee. I am at present out of spirits, having just lost a particular friend; poor dear Dr. Bronstedt of Copenhagen (who lost half his rix dollars by our cursed bombardment) is lately gone to Constantinople. We used to tipple punch and talk politics; Sandford Graham is also gone. But then there are more coming.

Pray have you sent Mrs. Pigot a copy of the Miscellany? Have you sent my letters to their proper places? Have you fulfilled my commissions? And how d'ye do?

Yours ever very truly, BYRON

TO JOHN CAM HOBHOUSE†   Volage, *frigate, at Sea,*
                                        June 19th, 1811

MY DEAR HOBHOUSE,—In the gentle dullness of a summer voyage I shall converse with you for half-an-hour.

We left Malta on the 2nd, with three other frigates, inclusive of the Lissa prizes, and we are on our way, they to glory, and I to what God pleases. I am recovered from my Tertian, but neither my health nor my hitherto hoydenish spirits are as rampant as usual. I received at Malta your letters, which I have answered; and I have succeeded in the discovery and embarkation of your memorable marbles; they shall be brought to town or left in proper care at Portsmouth, till you can arrange their removal.

I am accompanied by two Greek servants, both middle-aged men, and one is Demetrius your old mis-interpreter. I have letters for you from Cockerell, whom I left well with other Franks. My own antiquities consist of four *tortoises*, and four *Skulls*, all taken out of ancient sarcophagi. Our health is very lackadaisycal. I have a *, and Sr. Demetrius a * *, the fatal consequence of some forty " Sculamente ". I shall put off all account of my Winter in Athens, which was most social and fantastical, as also all my marchings and countermarchings, till our meeting, and indulge in speculation on my prospects in your Country. I shall first endeavour to repair my irreparable affairs, and it seems I must set out for Lancashire, for I shall neither have coals nor comfort till I visit Rochdale in person. I wish you would meet me or tell me where to meet you, as I wish to consult you on various subjects, besides the pleasure I shall experience in your society.

With regard to all *Dross* business between us, don't think of it till it is most perfectly convenient. I would rather you did not think of it at all, but as I know your sentiments on the subject, I shall not annoy you by such a proposition.

You tell me fine things—very fine things—on the *literary* " *lay* ", I suppose from your natural knowledge of our weak side, and with a view to set me *marble-hunting*, by dint of compliment. I have, as I told you before, completed an Imitation of Horace, " Ad Pisones ", addressed to you, and to be published forthwith, as you will readily conjecture.

I hope the Miscellany mends in sale. Its failure must be attributed to that accursed " Walsh-ean " preface, which the Citoyen M. would recommend, and you see what it has come to. M[atthe]ws has written to me; thank him, and say further I shall have great pleasure in gratifying his curiosity, which, however, he must not raise too high.

You talk of the militia—Santissimi Coglioni!—the militia at five-and-twenty; boys over your head, and brutes under you, mess, country-quarters, courts-martial, and quelling of riots. If you will be mad or martial ('tis the same thing) go to Portugal again, and I will go with you (for I have some serious thoughts of it, if matters are intricate at home), but don't waste your time in mere *holiday* soldiering, as Major Sturgeon would call it. I am writing all this time without knowing your address. However I shall send as usual to Ridgways, who will forward my present as he has done the other letters. Fletcher must have arrived some time. I sent him off in November. He was useless and in the way, and in every respect I did better without him. How goes on "La Bagatelle"? Have you met with any clubbable persons with a sufficient tincture of Literature for your purpose. You have not been in London, it should seem. I shall proceed there from Portsmouth to Reddish's or Dorant's for a few days, and afterwards to Newstead, and most probably abroad again as soon as my arrangements will admit. Ld. Sligo is on his way home; I left him at Malta in quarantine. Bruce is gone or going to Persia; he is a singular being; on the night he left Athens he made me a profession of friendship, on the extremity of the Piræus, the only one I ever received in my life, and certainly very unexpected, for I had done nothing to deserve it. Whitbread (in Peter Pindar's visit from George Guelph) says he is too old for a *knight*, and I am too old for a friend, at least a new one. Tell M[atthews] I have bade adieu to every species of affection, and may say with Horace, " Me jam nec fœmina ", etc., he will finish the lines. Seriously, I can't think, for the soul of me, what possessed Michael, for, like the Rovers, " a sudden thought struck him ". We had dined together, so I know he was not drunk; but the truth is, he is a little chivalrous and romantic, and is smitten with unimaginable fantasies ever since his connection with Lady H. Stanhope. However, both her ladyship and he were very polite, and asked me to go on with them a second time to Constantinople; but having been there once, and preferring *philosophy* at Athens, I staid in my convent. Matthews tells me that Jeffrey[1] means to review your book; if he does, it

---

[1] Lord Jeffrey, editor of the *Edinburgh Review*.

will do you good, one way or the other, but I think it probable
he will praise you. Have you nothing new for the press?
Don't be discouraged by the Miscellany, but throw the blame
on your friends, and the preface, and Matthews, and me, and
the damned trash of your auxiliaries. There is something
very impudent in my offering this pert consolation, but I hope
you will stand in no need of it, and begin to receive half-
guineas at a rare rate; by-the-bye, would not seven-and-
sixpence have sold and sounded better? Matthews has been
advising you to philosophize at Cambridge—do, and I'll
join you for a time, and we will tipple and talk Matthews to
death with our travels, and jest and squabble, and be as insipid
as the best of them.

Bold Webster [1] (by way of keeping up that epithet, I suppose)
has married, and, *bolder* still, a sister of Ld. V^t Valentia, and,
boldest of all, has published letters to the Commr. in Chief!
Corpo di Caio Mario! what will the world come to? I take
this to be one of the newest events " under the sun ".

Had he no friend, no relation, no pitying monitor to snatch
the manuscript from one devil to save it from the other? Pray
are the letters in prose or verse? I have gossiped away till
we are off Cape St. Vincent, and I am puzzled what to say
next, or rather to ask, for my letter is a string of questions,
quite forgetting you can't answer my Catechism. I am dull,
" dull as the last new comedy " (*vide* Goldsmith's " Good
Natured Man "), though Capt. Hornby is a gentlemanly and
pleasant man, and a Salamander in his profession, fight
anything; but as I have got all the particulars of his late action
out of him, I don't know what to ask *him* next any more than
you. But we are infested in the cabin by another passenger,
a teller of tough stories, all about himself. I could laugh at
him were there anybody to laugh with; as it is, I yawn and
swear to myself, and take refuge in the quarter gallery; thank
God he is now asleep, or I should be worried with impertinence.
His name is Thomas, and he is Staff- or Stuff- Apothecary to
General Oakes, who has rammed him down our throats for
the voyage, and a bitter Bolus he is, that's the truth on't. But
I long for land, and then for a post-chaise, and I believe my

---

[1] James Wedderburn Webster, an irrepressibly foolish personage, whose wife,
Lady Frances, was destined to play a part in Byron's later career.

enjoyments will end there, for I have no other pleasure to expect that I know of.

We have had a tedious passage, all except the Straits, where we had an easterly gale, and glided through the gut like an oil Glyster. Dear Hobby, you must excuse all this facetiousness, which I should not have let loose if I knew what the devil to do, but I am so out of spirits, and hopes, and humour, and pocket, and health, that you must bear with my merriment, my only resource against a Calentura. Write to me; I am now going to patrole the melancholy deck. God be wi' ye!

Yours always, B.

[On the envelope]

P.S.—Take a mouthful of Saltwater poetry, by a Tar on the late Lissa Victory.

> If I had an e*di*cation
> I'd sing your praise more large,
> But I'm only a common foremast Jack
> On board of *the le Volage!!!!!*

TO HIS MOTHER   *Volage frigate, at sea, June 25, 1811*

DEAR MOTHER,—This letter, which will be forwarded on our arrival at Portsmouth, probably about the 4th of July, is begun about twenty-three days after our departure from Malta. I have just been two years (to a day, on the 2d of July) absent from England, and I return to it with much the same feelings which prevailed on my departure, viz. indifference; but within that apathy I certainly do not comprise yourself, as I will prove by every means in my power. You will be good enough to get my apartments ready at Newstead; but don't disturb yourself, on any account, particularly mine, nor consider me in any other light than as a visiter. I must only inform you that for a long time I have been restricted to an entire vegetable diet, neither fish nor flesh coming within my regimen; so I expect a powerful stock of potatoes, greens, and biscuit; I drink no wine. I have two servants, middle-aged men, and both Greeks. It is my intention to proceed first to town, to see Mr. Hanson, and thence to Newstead, on my way to Rochdale. I have only to beg you will not forget my diet, which it is very necessary for me to observe. I am well in health, as I have generally been, with the exception of two agues, both of which I quickly got over.

My plans will so much depend on circumstances, that I shall not venture to lay down an opinion on the subject. My prospects are not very promising, but I suppose we shall wrestle through life like our neighbours; indeed, by Hanson's last advices, I have some apprehension of finding Newstead dismantled by Messrs. Brothers, etc., and he seems determined to force me into selling it, but he will be baffled. I don't suppose I shall be much pestered with visiters; but if I am, you must receive them, for I am determined to have nobody breaking in upon my retirement: you know that I never was fond of society, and I am less so than before. I have brought you a shawl, and a quantity of attar of roses, but these I must smuggle, if possible. I trust to find my library in tolerable order.

Fletcher is no doubt arrived. I shall separate the mill from Mr. B * *'s farm, for his son is too gay a deceiver to inherit both, and place Fletcher in it, who has served me faithfully, and whose wife is a good woman; besides, it is necessary to sober young Mr. B * *, or he will people the parish with bastards. In a word, if he had seduced a dairy-maid, he might have found something like an apology; but the girl is his equal, and in high life or low life reparation is made in such circumstances. But I shall not interfere further than (like Buonaparte) by dismembering Mr. B.'s *kingdom*, and erecting part of it into a principality for field-marshal Fletcher! I hope you govern my little *empire* and its sad load of national debt with a wary hand. To drop my metaphor, I beg leave to subscribe myself

Yours ever, BYRON

P.S. July 14.—This letter was written to be sent from Portsmouth, but, on arriving there, the squadron was ordered to the Nore, from whence I shall forward it. This I have not done before, supposing you might be alarmed by the interval mentioned in the letter being longer than expected between our arrival in port and my appearance at Newstead.

TO R. C. DALLAS   Volage *Frigate, at sea, June 28, 1811*

After two years' absence (to a day, on the 2d of July, before which we shall not arrive at Portsmouth), I am retracing my way to England. I have, as you know, spent the greater part of that period in Turkey, except two months in Spain and Portugal, which were then accessible. I have seen every thing most remarkable in Turkey, particularly the Troad, Greece, Constantinople, and Albania, into which last region very few have penetrated so high as Hobhouse and myself. I don't know that I have done anything to distinguish me from other voyagers, unless you will reckon my swimming from Sestos to Abydos, on May 3d, 1810, a tolerable feat for a *modern*.

I am coming back with little prospect of pleasure at home, and with a body a little shaken by one or two smart fevers, but a spirit I hope yet unbroken. My affairs, it seems, are considerably involved, and much business must be done with lawyers, colliers, farmers, and creditors. Now this, to a man who hates bustle as he hates a bishop, is a serious concern. But enough of my home department.

I find I have been scolding Cawthorn without a cause, as I found two parcels with two letters from you on my return to Malta. By these it appears you have not received a letter from Constantinople, addressed to Longman's, but it was of no consequence.

My Satire, it seems, is in a fourth edition, a success rather above the middling run, but not much for a production which, from its topics, must be temporary, and of course be successful at first, or not at all. At this period, when I can think and act more coolly, I regret that I have written it, though I shall probably find it forgotten by all except those whom it has offended. My friend Hobhouse's *Miscellany* has not succeeded; but he himself writes so good-humouredly on the subject, I don't know whether to laugh or cry with him. He met with your son at Cadiz, of whom he speaks highly.

Yours and Pratt's *protégé*, Blacket, the cobbler, is dead, in spite of his rhymes, and is probably one of the instances where death has saved a man from damnation. You were the ruin of that poor fellow amongst you : had it not been for his patrons, he might now have been in very good plight, shoe- (not verse-) making ; but you have made him immortal with a vengeance. I write this, supposing poetry, patronage, and strong waters, to have been the death of him. If you are in town in or about the beginning of July, you will find me at Dorant's, in Albemarle Street, glad to see you. I have an imitation of Horace's *Art of Poetry* ready for Cawthorn, but don't let that deter you, for I sha'n't inflict it upon you. You know I never read my rhymes to visiters. I shall quit town in a few days for Notts., and thence to Rochdale. I shall send this the moment we arrive in harbour, that is a week hence.

Yours ever sincerely, BYRON

TO HENRY DRURY   *Volage frigate, off Ushant, July 17, 1811*

MY DEAR DRURY,—After two years' absence (on the 2d) and some odd days, I am approaching your country. The day of our arrival you will see by the outside date of my letter. At present, we are becalmed comfortably, close to Brest Harbour ;—I have never been so near it since I left Duck Puddle. We left Malta thirty-four days ago, and have had a tedious passage of it. You will either see or hear from or of me, soon after the receipt of this, as I pass through town to repair my irreparable affairs ; and thence I want to go to Notts. and raise rents, and to Lancs. and sell collieries, and back to London and pay debts,—for it seems I shall neither have coals nor comfort till I go down to Rochdale in person.

I have brought home some marbles for Hobhouse ;—for myself, four ancient Athenian skulls, dug out of sarcophagi— a phial of Attic hemlock—four live tortoises—a greyhound (died on the passage)—two live Greek servants, one an Athen- ian, t'other a *Yaniote*, who can speak nothing but Romaic and Italian—and *myself*, as Moses in the *Vicar of Wakefield* says, *slily*, and I may say it too, for I have as little cause to boast of my expedition as he had of his to the fair.

I wrote to you from the Cyanean Rocks to tell you I had swam from Sestos to Abydos—have you received my letter? Hobhouse went to England to fish up his *Miscellany*, which foundered (so he tells me) in the Gulph of Lethe. I daresay it capsized with the vile goods of his contributory friends, for his own share was very portable. However, I hope he will either weigh up or set sail with a fresh cargo, and a luckier vessel. Hodgson, I suppose, is four deep by this time. What would he have given to have seen, like me, the *real Parnassus*, where I robbed the Bishop of Chrisso of a book of geography! —but this I only call plagiarism, as it was done within an hour's ride of Delphi.

2
The Years of Fame
August 1811 to January 1815

Byron returned to England in a mood of deep despondency. He regretted the past and dreaded the future: the friends he had loved were scattered, and the prospect he had to face was decidedly unpromising. Very soon his fears were justified. News reached him that his mother was seriously ill: before he could gain Newstead, he learned that on August 1st, 1811, her violent, unhappy, foolish life had ended. Though he had never loved her, he was exceedingly shocked by her death. Then, before her funeral procession had left the Abbey, he received a letter telling him that his great friend, Charles Skinner Matthews, had been drowned while bathing near Cambridge. In desperation, he appealed to another Cambridge friend, Scrope Davies: " Some curse ", he declared, " hangs over me and mine. My mother lies a corpse in this house; one of my best friends is drowned in a ditch. . . . Come to me, Scrope, I am almost desolate—left almost alone in the world. . . ."

He was not long to remain uncomforted; for the poem which he had brought back with him from Greece, and had handed to a serviceable admirer and remote family connection, Robert Charles Dallas, was going through the printing-press. Byron attached no special importance to these Spenserian stanzas; but Dallas had praised them warmly and, once entrusted with the manuscript, after trying in vain a less enterprising publisher, had submitted them to John Murray who presently accepted them. Childe Harold's Pilgrimage was published at the end of February or the beginning of March 1812—a few days after the poet had delivered his vigorous maiden speech in the House of Lords—and proved immediately successful. The author became the lion of the season, the hero of every drawing-room and the talk of every dinner-table. From loneliness, poverty and obscurity, he was raised overnight to the height of fame and fashion.

Byron's letters give a vivid and detailed account of the adventures of this period : his entanglement with Lady Caroline Lamb, for which he was in some measure consoled by his friendship with her mother-in-law, Lady Melbourne ; his escape from Lady Caroline's furious infatuation into the maternal arms of Lady Oxford; his inconclusive passage with Lady Frances Webster, which was reported at length for Lady Melbourne's benefit; finally, that " strange summer adventure ", as to the nature of which the student of Byron's biography must form his own conclusions. Whatever it was, this " new scrape " caused his well-wishers, particularly Lady Melbourne and his half-sister, Augusta Leigh, many anxious moments. An unusually grave scandal seemed to be impending ; Byron's state of mind was volcanic ; and they agreed that the sooner he was married off—to a suitable, sensible and well-endowed young woman—the better for their peace of mind. Byron himself-was prepared to admit that they were right. The candidate eventually selected was Anne Isabella (or Annabella) Milbanke, the daughter of Lady Melbourne's brother, Sir Ralph Milbanke of Seaham, a highly educated girl of very decided views and rigid moral principles. Byron's first proposal was refused; a second proposal was accepted. He was married at Seaham on January 2nd, 1815.

TO JOHN M. B. PIGOT   *Newport Pagnell, August 2, 1811*

MY DEAR DOCTOR,—My poor mother died yesterday ! and I am on my way from town to attend her to the family vault. I heard *one* day of her illness, the *next* of her death. Thank God her last moments were most tranquil. I am told she was in little pain, and not aware of her situation. I now feel the truth of Mr. Gray's observation, " That we can only have *one* mother ". Peace be with her ! I have to thank you for your expressions of regard ; and as in six weeks I shall be in Lancashire on business, I may extend to Liverpool and Chester, —at least I shall endeavour.

If it will be any satisfaction, I have to inform you that in November next the Editor of the *Scourge* [1] will be tried for two different libels on the late Mrs. B. and myself (the decease of Mrs. B. makes no difference in the proceedings) ; and as he is guilty, by his very foolish and unfounded assertion of a breach of privilege, he will be prosecuted with the utmost rigour.

I inform you of this, as you seem interested in the affair, which is now in the hands of the Attorney-general.

I shall remain at Newstead the greater part of this month, where I shall be happy to hear from you, after my two years' absence in the East.

I am, dear Pigot, yours very truly, BYRON

TO SCROPE BERDMORE DAVIES *Newstead Abbey,*
August 7, 1811

MY DEAREST DAVIES,—Some curse hangs over me and mine. My mother lies a corpse in this house ; one of my best friends is drowned in a ditch. What can I say, or think, or do? I received a letter from him the day before yesterday. My dear Scrope, if you can spare a moment, do come down to me— I want a friend. Matthews's last letter was written on *Friday* —on Saturday he was not. In ability, who was like Matthews? How did we all shrink before him? You do me but justice in saying, I would have risked my paltry existence to have preserved his. This very evening did I mean to write, inviting him, as I invite you, my very dear friend, to visit me. God forgive —— for his apathy ! What will our poor Hobhouse feel? His letters breathe but of Matthews. Come to me, Scrope, I am almost desolate—left almost alone in the world— I had but you, and H., and M., and let me enjoy the survivors

[1] The attack on Byron in the *Scourge* was the work of a journalist named Hewson Clarke, who had been mentioned abusively in *English Bards.* Clarke retaliated by describing Byron as the " illegitimate descendant of a murderer " and asserting that Mrs. Byron passed her " days and nights . . . in the delirium of drunkenness ".

whilst I can.   Poor M., in his letter of Friday, speaks of his intended contest for Cambridge, and a speedy journey to London.   Write or come, but come if you can, or one or both.

Yours ever.

TO JOHN CAM HOBHOUSE   *Newstead Abbey, August 10th, 1811*

My DEAR HOBHOUSE,—From Davies I had already received the death of Matthews, and from M. *a letter* dated the *day* before his *death*.   In that letter he mentions you, and as it was perhaps the last he ever wrote, you will derive a poor consolation from hearing that he spoke of you with that affectionate familiarity, so much more pleasing from those we love, than the highest encomiums of the world.

My dwelling you already know is the house of mourning, and I am really so much bewildered with the different shocks I have sustained, that I can hardly reduce myself to reason by the most frivolous occupations.   My poor friend, J. Wingfield, my mother, and your best friend (and surely not the worst of mine), C. S. M., have disappeared in one little month, since *my return*, and without my seeing *either*, though I have *heard* from *all*.   There is to me something so incomprehensible in death, that I can neither speak nor think on the subject. Indeed, when I looked on the mass of corruption which was the being from whence I sprung, I doubted within myself whether I *was*, or she *was not*.   I have lost her who gave me being, and some of those who made that being a blessing.   I have neither hopes nor fears beyond the grave, yet if there is within us " a spark of that Celestial fire ", M[atthews] has already " mingled with the gods ".

In the room where I now write (flanked by the *skulls* you have seen so often) did you and Matthews and myself pass some joyous unprofitable evenings, and here we will drink to his memory, which though it cannot reach the dead, will soothe the survivors, and to them only death can be an evil. I can neither receive nor administer consolation ; time will do it for us ; in the interim let me see or hear from you, if possible both.   I am very lonely, and should think myself miserable were it not for a kind of hysterical merriment, which I can neither account for nor conquer; but strange as it is, I do laugh, and heartily, wondering at myself while I sustain it. I have tried reading, and boxing, and swimming, and writing, and rising early, and sitting late, and water, and wine, with a number of ineffectual remedies, and here I am, wretched, but not " melancholy or gentleman-like ".

My dear " *Cam of the Cornish* " (Matthews's last expression ! !) may man or God give you the happiness which I wish rather than expect you may attain; believe me, none living are more sincerely yours than

BYRON

TO R. C. DALLAS   *Newstead Abbey, Notts., August 12, 1811*

Peace be with the dead ! Regret cannot wake them. With a sigh to the departed, let us resume the dull business of life, in the certainty that we also shall have our repose. Besides her who gave me being, I have lost more than one who made that being tolerable.—The best friend of my friend Hobhouse, Matthews, a man of the first talents, and also not the worst of my narrow circle, has perished miserably in the muddy waves of the Cam, always fatal to genius :—my poor school-fellow, Wingfield, at Coimbra—within a month; and whilst I had heard from *all three*, but not seen *one*. Matthews wrote to me the very day before his death; and though I feel for his fate, I am still more anxious for Hobhouse, who, I very much fear, will hardly retain his senses : his letters to me since the event have been most incoherent. But let this pass; we shall all one day pass along with the rest—the world is too full of such things, and our very sorrow is selfish.

I received a letter from you, which my late occupations prevented me from duly noticing.—I hope your friends and family will long hold together. I shall be glad to hear from you, on business, on commonplace, or any thing, or nothing— but death—I am already too familiar with the dead. It is strange that I look on the skulls which stand beside me (I have always had *four* in my study) without emotion, but I

cannot strip the features of those I have known of their fleshy
covering, even in idea, without a hideous sensation; but the
worms are less ceremonious.—Surely, the Romans did well
when they burned the dead.—I shall be happy to hear from
you, and am,

Yours, etc.

TO JOHN CAM HOBHOUSE   *Newstead Abbey, August 30th, 1811*

MY DEAR HOBHOUSE,—Scrope Davies has been here and
seemed as much affected by late events as could be expected,
from one who has lived so much in the world.   His society was
(as it always wont to be) very reviving, but now he is gone,
and I am solitary and sullen.

Not a scrap of paper has been found at Cambridge, which
is singular.   I can hardly agree with you in a wish to forget,
I love to remember the dead, for we see only the virtues, and
when our best friends are thus removed, we become reconciled
to our own prospects, and " long to be with them, and at rest ".

I think when your mind is more calm you ought to write
his epitaph, and we will erect to his memory a monument
in some appropriate place.   I do not know any other who
would do him justice; indeed, it is *your right*, and perhaps your
duty.

Then " give his fame to the winds, and let the harp sigh
over his narrow house "; you are now in the land of Ossian.

In the poem which I wrote abroad, and is now in the
hands of Murray the bookseller for publication, at the close
of the first canto, which treats of Spain, I have two stanzas
in commemoration of W[ingfield], who died at Coimbra;
and in a note to those, having occasion to mention the loss
of three persons very dear to me, in so very short a time, I
have added a very short sentence or two on the subject of our
friend; which, though they can neither add to his credit or
satisfaction, will at least show my own pride in the acquaintance of such a man.

Your book goes on well, and I trust will answer your
purpose and my expectations.   Demetrius has made out a

most formidable vocabulary, on which I wait for further orders.

I do not know who is your deputy in town; perhaps Baillie, or Shepherd. I have had a letter from Bankes, of the patronising kind, where I am invited to " *one* of *my places in Wales!!* "

I am going to Lancs., and am in daily expectation of Hanson to back me; and I mean to marry, prudently if possible; that is, wealthily; I can't afford anything to Love.

I wish you were here; but you *will* be *here*, and we shall laugh again as usual, and be very miserable dogs for all that.

My sister writes me melancholy letters; things are not going on well there, but mismanagement is the hereditary epidemic of our brood.

Hodgson is battening on " Laver Moor, Herefordshire ", Davies at Harrowgate.

I am to visit him in October at King's Coll.

Dallas is running to and from Mortlake, with his pocket full of proofs of *all* his *friends*, who are all scribblers and make him a packhorse.

I am here boxing in a Turkish pelisse to prevent obesity, and as usual very much yours,

BYRON

TO THE HON. AUGUSTA LEIGH   *Newstead Abbey,*
                                   August 30th, 1811

My dear Augusta,—The embarrassments you mention in your last letter I never heard of before, but that disease is epidemic in our family. Neither have I been apprised of any of the changes at which you hint, indeed how should I? On the borders of the Black Sea, we heard only of the Russians. So you have much to tell, and all will be novelty.

I don't know what Scrope Davies meant by telling you I liked Children. I abominate the sight of them so much that I have always had the greatest respect for the character of Herod. But, as my house here is large enough for us all, we should go on very well, and I need not tell you that I long to see *you*. I really do not perceive any thing so formidable in a Journey hither of two days, but all this comes of Matrimony, you have a Nurse and all the etcæteras of a family. Well, I must marry to repair the ravages of myself and prodigal ancestry, but if I am ever so unfortunate as to be presented with an Heir, instead of a *Rattle* he shall be provided with a *Gag*.

I shall perhaps be able to accept D's invitation to Cambridge, but I fear my stay in Lancashire will be prolonged, I proceed there in the 2ᵈ week in Sepᵗʳ to arrange my coal concerns, and then if I can't persuade some wealthy dowdy to ennoble the dirty puddle of her mercantile Blood,—why—I shall leave England and all its clouds for the East again ; I am very sick of it already. Joe has been getting well of a disease that would have killed a troop of horse ; he promises to bear away the palm of longevity from old Parr. As you won't come, you will write ; I long to hear all those unutterable things, being utterly unable to guess at any of them, unless they concern *your* relative the Thane of Carlisle,—though I had great hopes we had done with him.

I have little to add that you do not already know, and being quite alone, have no great variety of incident to gossip with ; I am but rarely pestered with visiters, and the few I have I get rid of as soon as possible. I will now take leave of you in the Jargon of 1794. " Health and *Fraternity!* "

Yours alway, B.

TO THE HON. AUGUSTA LEIGH   *Newstead Abbey,*
                                        Sept. 2ᵈ, 1811

MY DEAR AUGUSTA,—I wrote you a vastly dutiful letter since my answer to your second epistle, and I now write you a third, for which you have to thank Silence and Solitude. Mr. Hanson comes hither on the 14ᵗʰ, and I am going to Rochdale on business, but that need not prevent you from coming here, you will find Joe, and the house and the cellar and all therein very much at your Service.

As to Lady B., when I discover one rich enough to suit

me and foolish enough to have me, I will give her leave to make me miserable if she can. Money is the magnet ; as to Women, one is as well as another, the older the better, we have then a chance of getting her to Heaven. So, your Spouse does not like brats better than myself; now those who beget them have no right to find fault, but *I* may rail with great propriety.

My " Satire ! "—I am glad it made you laugh for Somebody told me in Greece that you was angry, and I was sorry, as you were perhaps the only person whom I did *not* want to *make angry.*

But how you will make *me laugh* I don't know, for it is a vastly *serious* subject to me I assure you ; therefore take care, or I shall hitch *you* into the next Edition to make up our family party. Nothing so fretful, so despicable as a Scribbler, see what *I* am, and what a parcel of Scoundrels I have brought about my ears, and what language I have been obliged to treat them with to deal with them in their own way ;—all this comes of Authorship, but now I am in for it, and shall be at war with Grubstreet, till I find some better amusement.

You will write to me your Intentions and may almost depend on my being at Cambridge in October. You say you mean to be etc. in the *Autumn* ; I should be glad to know what you call this present Season, it would be Winter in every other Country which I have seen. If we meet in October we will travel in my *Vis.* and can have a cage for the children and a cart for the Nurse. Or perhaps we can forward them by the Canal. Do let us know all about it, your " *bright thought* " is a little clouded, like the Moon in this preposterous climate. Good even, Child.

Yours ever, B.

TO FRANCIS HODGSON   *Newstead Abbey, Sept. 3, 1811*

My dear Hodgson,—I will have nothing to do with your immortality; we are miserable enough in this life, without the absurdity of speculating upon another. If men are to live, why die at all? and if they die, why disturb the sweet and sound sleep that " knows no waking "?   " Post Mortem nihil est, ipsaque Mors nihil . . . quæris quo jaceas post obitum loco? Quo *non* Nata jacent."

As to revealed religion, Christ came to save men; but a good Pagan will go to heaven, and a bad Nazarene to hell; " Argal " (I argue like the gravedigger) why are not all men Christians? or why are any? If mankind may be saved who never heard or dreamt, at Timbuctoo, Otaheite, Terra Incognita, etc., of Galilee and its Prophet, Christianity is of no avail: if they cannot be saved without, why are not all orthodox? It is a little hard to send a man preaching to Judæa, and leave the rest of the world—Negers and what not—*dark* as their complexions, without a ray of light for so many years to lead them on high; and who will believe that God will damn men for not knowing what they were never taught? I hope I am sincere; I was so at least on a bed of sickness in a far-distant country, when I had neither friend, nor comforter, nor hope, to sustain me. I looked to death as a relief from pain, without a wish for an after-life, but a confidence that the God who punishes in this existence had left that last asylum for the weary.

Ὃν ὁ θεὸς ἀγαπάει ἀποθνήσκει νέος.

I am no Platonist, I am nothing at all; but I would sooner be a Paulician, Manichean, Spinozist, Gentile, Pyrrhonian, Zoroastrian, than one of the seventy-two villainous sects who are tearing each other to pieces for the love of the Lord and hatred of each other. Talk of Galileeism? Show me the effects —are you better, wiser, kinder by your precepts? I will bring you ten Mussulmans shall shame you in all goodwill towards men, prayer to God, and duty to their neighbours. And is there a Talapoin, or a Bonze, who is not superior to a fox-hunting curate? But I will say no more on this endless theme; let me live, well if possible, and die without pain. The rest is with God, who assuredly, had He *come* or *sent*, would have made Himself manifest to nations, and intelligible to all.

I shall rejoice to see you. My present intention is to accept Scrope Davies's invitation; and then, if you accept mine, we shall meet *here* and *there*. Did you know poor Matthews? I shall miss him much at Cambridge.

TO JOHN MURRAY   *Newstead Abbey, Notts., Sept. 5, 1811*

SIR,—The time seems to be past when (as Dr. Johnson said) a man was certain to " hear the truth from his bookseller ", for you have paid me so many compliments, that, if I was not the veriest scribbler on earth, I should feel affronted. As I accept your compliments, it is but fair I should give equal or greater credit to your objections, the more so as I believe them to be well founded. With regard to the political and metaphysical parts, I am afraid I can alter nothing ; but I have high authority for my Errors in that point, for even the *Æneid* was a *political* poem, and written for a *political* purpose ; and as to my unlucky opinions on Subjects of more importance, I am too sincere in them for recantation. On Spanish affairs I have said what I saw, and every day confirms me in that notion of the result formed on the Spot ; and I rather think honest John Bull is beginning to come round again to that Sobriety which Massena's retreat had begun to reel from its centre—the usual consequence of *un*usual success. So you perceive I cannot alter the Sentiments ; but if there are any alterations in the structure of the versification you would wish to be made, I will tag rhymes and turn stanzas as much as you please. As for the " *Orthodox* ", let us hope they will buy, on purpose to abuse—you will forgive the one, if they will do the other. You are aware that any thing from my pen must expect no quarter, on many accounts ; and as the present publication is of a nature very different from the former, we must not be sanguine.

You have given me no answer to my question—tell me fairly, did you show the M.S. to some of your corps?—I sent an introductory stanza to Mr. Dallas, that it might be forwarded to you ; the poem else will open too abruptly. The Stanzas had better be numbered in Roman characters, there is a disquisition on the literature of the modern Greeks, and some smaller poems to come in at the close. These are now at Newstead, but will be sent in time. If Mr. D. has lost the Stanza and note annexed to it, write, and I will send it myself. —You tell me to add two cantos, but I am about to visit my *Collieries* in Lancashire on the 15th instant, which is so *unpoetical* an employment that I need say no more.

I am, sir, your most obedient, etc., etc., BYRON

TO R. C. DALLAS   *Newstead Abbey, September 7, 1811*

As Gifford [1] has been ever my " Magnus Apollo ", any approbation, such as you mention, would, of course, be more welcome than " all Bocara's vaunted gold, than all the gems of Samarcand ". But I am sorry the MS. was shown to him in such a manner, and had written to Murray to say as much, before I was aware that it was too late.

Your objection to the expression " central line " I can only meet by saying that, before Childe Harold left England, it was his full intention to traverse Persia, and return by India, which he could not have done without passing the equinoctial.

The other errors you mention, I must correct in the progress through the press. I feel honoured by the wish of such men that the poem should be continued, but to do that I must return to Greece and Asia; I must have a warm sun, a blue sky; I cannot describe scenes so dear to me by a sea-coal fire. I had projected an additional canto when I was in the Troad and Constantinople, and if I saw them again, it would go on; but under existing circumstances and *sensations*, I have neither harp, " heart, nor voice " to proceed. I feel that *you are all right* as to the metaphysical part; but I also feel that I am sincere, and that if I am only to write " *ad captandum vulgus* ", I might as well edit a magazine at once, or spin canzonettas for Vauxhall.

My work must make its way as well as it can; I know I have every thing against me, angry poets and prejudices; but if the poem is a *poem*, it will surmount these obstacles, and if *not*, it deserves its fate. Your friend's Ode I have read— it is no great compliment to pronounce it far superior to Smythe's on the same subject, or to the merits of the new Chancellor. It is evidently the production of a man of taste, and a poet, though I should not be willing to say it was fully equal to what might be expected from the author of " *Horæ Ionicæ* ". I thank you for it, and that is more than I would do for any other Ode of the present day.

I am very sensible of your good wishes, and, indeed, I have need of them. My whole life has been at variance with propriety, not to say decency; my circumstances are become

[1] William Gifford, editor of the *Quarterly Review* and *Anti-Jacobin*.

involved ; my friends are dead or estranged, and my existence a dreary void. In Matthews I have lost my " guide, philosopher, and friend " ; in Wingfield a friend only, but one whom I could have wished to have preceded in his long journey.

Matthews was indeed an extraordinary man ; it has not entered into the heart of a stranger to conceive such a man : there was the stamp of immortality in all he said or did ;— and now what is he? When we see such men pass away and be no more—men, who seem created to display what the Creator *could make* his creatures, gathered into corruption, before the maturity of minds that might have been the pride of posterity, what are we to conclude? For my own part, I am bewildered. To me he was much, to Hobhouse every thing. My poor Hobhouse doted on Matthews. For me, I did not love quite so much as I honoured him ; I was indeed so sensible of his infinite superiority, that though I did not envy, I stood in awe of it. He, Hobhouse, Davies, and myself, formed a coterie of our own at Cambridge and elsewhere. Davies is a wit and man of the world, and feels as much as such a character can do ; but not as Hobhouse has been affected. Davies, who is not a scribbler, has always beaten us all in the war of words, and by his colloquial powers at once delighted and kept us in order. Hobhouse and myself always had the worst of it with the other two ; and even Matthews yielded to the dashing vivacity of Scrope Davies. But I am talking to you of men, or boys, as if you cared about such beings.

I expect mine agent down on the 14th to proceed to Lancashire, where I hear from all quarters that I have a very valuable property in coals, etc. I then intend to accept an invitation to Cambridge in October, and shall, perhaps, run up to town. I have four invitations—to Wales, Dorset, Cambridge, and Chester ; but I must be a man of business. I am quite alone, as these long letters sadly testify. I perceive, by referring to your letter, that the Ode is from the author ; make my thanks acceptable to him. His muse is worthy a nobler theme. You will write as usual, I hope. I wish you good evening, and am, etc.

TO JOHN CAM HOBHOUSE   *Newstead Abbey,*
                                       September 20th, 1811

My dear H^E,—Our friend Scrope is a pleasant person,
a " facetious companion ", and well " respected by all who
know him " ; he laughs with the living, though he don't weep
with the dead, yet I believe he would do that also, could it
do them good service, but good or bad we must endeavour
to follow his example, and return to the dull routine of business
or pleasure, though I fear the more we see of life, the more we
shall regret those who have ceased to live—we will speak of
them no more.

Demetrius has completed a copious specimen of the Arnaut
dialect, which shall be sent to-morrow ; the print might
perhaps be improved by an elongation of the ὑποκάμισον—
as the drawers don't appear to advantage below it ; altogether
it is very characteristic.

I had a visit lately from Major (Capt.) Leake " *en passant* ".
He talks of returning to Ali Pacha, and says the E[dinburgh]
R[eview] knows nothing of Romaic ; he is grown less taciturn,
better dressed, and more like an (English) man of this world
than he was at Yanina. J^n Claridge is here, improved in
person a good deal, and amiable, but not amusing. Now he
is a good man, a handsome man, an honourable man, a most
inoffensive man, a well informed man, and a—*dull* man, and
this last damned epithet undoes all the rest ; there is Scrope
B. Davies, with perhaps no better intellects, and certainly
not half his sterling qualities, is the life and soul of me, and
everybody else, but my old friend, with the soul of honour and
the zeal of friendship, and a vast variety of insipid virtues,
can't keep me or himself awake.—Alas, " *Motley's the only
wear* ". As for Claridge you can't ever quarrel with him, and
my life is as still as the Lake before the Abbey, till the North
wind disturbs the one, and Fletcher and my learned Thebans
break my pottery, or my tenants, or Mr. Hanson ruffle the
other.

I expect Hanson down daily to proceed to Rochdale,
or nothing will ever be settled.

You are coming out in quarto, but I wish you to be out
first, or at any rate *one* before the other ; I am going to use you

very shabbily, for I fear *that* Note is a " sine quâ non " to " Cᵉ Harold " ; had it been the Horace, you should have had it all to yourself. As it is, you shall have it to extract the essence, long before it is published, and the information will be all the better for being in your own words, and if you are out first (as you must probably will be) I trust we shall answer both our purposes. In my notes to the poem I have assigned your publication as my excuse for saying very little about the Greeks, and referred my readers to *your* work for more interesting particulars of that people. You *must* have six plates at the least, indeed ten or twelve would be better. Of course they are all at your service, and the Romaic MSS. such as they are.

I must contrive to meet you in the spring or summer, and will bring Hodgson or Davies with me. I am invited to Cambridge in Octʳ to meet them and Dr. Clarke. I don't know whether to be glad or sorry that you will not be *there* ; if I am *glad*, you will conceive it is on YOUR account. I shall write with Demetrius' Vocabulary.

Dear H, Yours ever, B.

TO FRANCIS HODGSON *Newstead Abbey, Sept. 25, 1811*

MY DEAR HODGSON,—I fear that before the latest of October or the first of November, I shall hardly be able to make Cambridge. My everlasting agent puts off his coming like the accomplishment of a prophecy. However, finding me growing serious he hath promised to be here on Thursday, and about Monday we shall remove to Rochdale. I have only to give discharges to the tenantry here (it seems the poor creatures must be raised, though I wish it was not necessary), and arrange the receipt of sums, and the liquidation of some debts, and I shall be ready to enter upon new subjects of vexation. I intend to visit you in Granta, and hope to prevail on you to accompany me here or there or anywhere.

I am plucking up my spirits, and have begun to gather my little sensual comforts together. Lucy is extracted from War-wickshire ; some very bad faces have been warned off the premises, and more promising substituted in their stead ;

the partridges are plentiful, hares fairish, pheasants not quite so good, and the Girls on the Manor * * * * Just as I had formed a tolerable establishment my travels commenced, and on my return I find all to do over again; my former flock were all scattered; some married, not before it was needful. As I am a great disciplinarian, I have just issued an edict for the abolition of caps; no hair to be cut on any pretext; stays permitted, but not too low before; full uniform always in the evening; Lucinda to be commander—*vice* the present, about to be wedded (*mem*, she is 35 with a flat face and a squeaking voice), of all the makers and unmakers of beds in the household.

My tortoises (all Athenians), my hedgehog, my mastiff and the other live Greek, are all purely. The tortoises lay eggs, and I have hired a hen to hatch them. I am writing notes for *my* quarto (Murray would have it a *quarto*), and Hobhouse is writing text for *his* quarto; if you call on Murray or Caw-thorn you will hear news of either. I have attacked De Pauw, Thornton, Lord Elgin, Spain, Portugal, the *Edinburgh Review*, travellers, Painters, Antiquarians, and others, so you see what a dish of Sour Crout Controversy I shall prepare for myself. It would not answer for me to give way, now; as I was forced into bitterness at the beginning, I will go through to the last. *Væ Victis!* If I fall, I shall fall gloriously, fighting against a host.

Felicissima Notte a Voss. Signoria, B.

TO R. C. DALLAS　　　　　　　　*Newstead Abbey, Oct. 11, 1811*

I have returned from Lancashire, and ascertained that my property there may be made very valuable, but various circumstances very much circumscribe my exertions at present. I shall be in town on business in the beginning of November, and perhaps at Cambridge before the end of this month; but of my movements you shall be regularly apprised. Your objections I have in part done away by alterations, which I hope will suffice; and I have sent two or three additional stanzas for both "*Fyttes*". I have been again shocked with a *death*, and have lost one very dear to me in happier times;

but " I have almost forgot the taste of grief ", and " supped full of horrors " till I have become callous, nor have I a tear left for an event which, five years ago, would have bowed down my head to the earth. It seems as though I were to experience in my youth the greatest misery of age. My friends fall around me, and I shall be left a lonely tree before I am withered. Other men can always take refuge in their families ; I have no resource but my own reflections, and they present no prospect here or hereafter, except the selfish satisfaction of surviving my betters. I am indeed very wretched, and you will excuse my saying so, as you know I am not apt to cant of sensibility.

Instead of tiring yourself with *my* concerns, I should be glad to hear *your* plans of retirement. I suppose you would not like to be wholly shut out of society? Now I know a large village, or small town, about twelve miles off, where your family would have the advantage of very genteel society, without the hazard of being annoyed by mercantile affluence ; where *you* would meet with men of information and independence ; and where I have friends to whom I should be proud to introduce you. There are, besides, a coffee-room, assemblies, etc., etc., which bring people together. My mother had a house there some years, and I am well acquainted with the economy of Southwell, the name of this little commonwealth. Lastly, you will not be very remote from me ; and though I am the very worst companion for young people in the world, this objection would not apply to *you*, whom I could see frequently. Your expenses, too, would be such as best suit your inclinations, more or less, as you thought proper ; but very little would be requisite to enable you to enter into all the gaieties of a country life. You could be as quiet or bustling as you liked, and certainly as well situated as on the lakes of Cumberland, unless you have a particular wish to be *picturesque*.

Pray, is your Ionian friend in town? You have promised me an introduction. You mention having consulted some friend on the MSS. Is not this contrary to our usual way? Instruct Mr. Murray not to allow his shopman to call the work *Child of Harrow's Pilgrimage* ! ! ! ! ! as he has done to some of my astonished friends, who wrote to inquire after my *sanity* on the occasion, as well they might. I have heard nothing of Murray, whom I scolded heartily. Must I write more notes?

Are there not enough? Cawthorn must be kept back with
the *Hints*. I hope he is getting on with Hobhouse's quarto.
Good evening.

Yours ever, etc.

TO FRANCIS HODGSON   *Newstead Abbey, Oct. 13, 1811*

You will begin to deem me a most liberal correspondent;
but as my letters are free, you will overlook their frequency.
I have sent you answers in prose and verse to all your late
communications; and though I am invading your ease again,
I don't know why, or what to put down that you are not
acquainted with already. I am growing *nervous* (how you will
laugh!)—but it is true,—really, wretchedly, ridiculously,
fine-ladically *nervous*. Your climate kills me; I can neither
read, write, nor amuse myself, or any one else. My days are
listless, and my nights restless; I have very seldom any society,
and when I have, I run out of it. At " this present writing ",
there are in the next room three *ladies*, and I have stolen away
to write this grumbling letter.—I don't know that I sha'n't
end with insanity, for I find a want of method in arranging
my thoughts that perplexes me strangely; but this looks more
like silliness than madness, as Scrope Davies would facetiously
remark in his consoling manner. I must try the hartshorn of
your company; and a session of Parliament would suit me
well,—any thing to cure me of conjugating the accursed verb
" *ennuyer* ".

When shall you be at Cambridge? You have hinted, I
think, that your friend Bland is returned from Holland. I have
always had a great respect for his talents, and for all that I
have heard of his character; but of me, I believe he knows
nothing, except that he heard my sixth form repetitions ten
months together at the average of two lines a morning, and
those never perfect. I remembered him and his *Slaves* as I
passed between Capes Matapan, St. Angelo, and his Isle of
Ceriga, and I always bewailed the absence of the *Anthology*.
I suppose he will now translate Vondel, the Dutch Shakspeare,
and *Gysbert van Amstel* will easily be accommodated to our stage
in its present state; and I presume he saw the Dutch poem,

where the love of Pyramus and Thisbe is compared to the *passion* of *Christ*; also the love of *Lucifer* for Eve, and other varieties of Low Country literature. No doubt you will think me crazed to talk of such things, but they are all in black and white and good repute on the banks of every canal from Amsterdam to Alkmaar.

Yours ever, B.

My poesy is in the hands of its various publishers; but the *Hints from Horace* (to which I have subjoined some savage lines on Methodism, and ferocious notes on the vanity of the triple Editory of the *Edin. Annual Register*), my *Hints*, I say, stand still, and why?—I have not a friend in the world (but you and Drury) who can construe Horace's Latin or my English well enough to adjust them for the press, or to correct the proofs in a grammatical way. So that, unless you have bowels when you return to town (I am too far off to do it for myself), this ineffable work will be lost to the world for—I don't know how many *weeks*.

Childe Harold's Pilgrimage must wait till *Murray's* is finished. He is making a tour in Middlesex, and is to return soon, when high matter may be expected. He wants to have it in quarto, which is a cursed unsaleable size; but it is pestilent long, and one must obey one's bookseller. I trust Murray will pass the Paddington Canal without being seduced by Payne and Mackinlay's example,[1]—I say Payne and Mackinlay, supposing that the partnership held good. Drury, the villain, has not written to me; "I am never (as Mrs. Lumpkin says to Tony) to be gratified with the monster's dear wild notes".

So you are going (going indeed!) into orders. You must make your peace with the Eclectic Reviewers—they accuse you of impiety, I fear, with injustice. Demetrius, the "Sieger of Cities", is here, with "Gilpin Horner". The painter is not necessary, as the portraits he already painted are (by anticipation) very like the new animals.—Write, and send me your "Love Song"—but I want *paulo majora* from you. Make a dash before you are a deacon, and try a *dry* publisher.

Yours always, B.

[1] Mr. Payne of the firm of Payne & Mackinlay, Hodgson's publishers, had committed suicide by drowning in the Paddington Canal.

TO JOHN CAM HOBHOUSE   *Newstead Abbey, October 14th, 1811*

DEAR HOBHOUSE,—In my last I answered your queries, and now I shall acquaint you with my movements, according to your former request. I have been down to Rochdale with Hanson; the property there, if I work the mines myself, will produce about £4000 pr. ann.; but to do this I must lay out at least £10,000 in etceteras, or if I chance to *let* it without incurring such expenditure, it will produce a rental of half the above sum, so we are to work the collieries ourselves, of course. Newstead is to be advanced immediately to £2100 pr. ann., so that my income might be made about £6000 pr. ann. But here comes at least £20,000 of debt, and I must mortgage for that and other expenses, so that altogether my situation is perplexing. I believe the above statement to be nearly correct, and so ends the chapter. If I chose to turn out my old bad tenants, and take monied men, they say Newstead would bear a few hundreds more from its great extent; but this I shall hardly do. It contains 3800 acres, including the Forest land, the Rochdale manor, 8256 acres of Lancashire, which are larger than ours. So there you have my territories on the earth, and in " the waters under the earth "; but I must marry some heiress, or I shall always be involved.

Now for higher matters. My Boke is in yᵉ press, and proceeds leisurely; I have lately been sweating notes, which I don't mean to make very voluminous,—some remarks written at Athens, and the flourish on Romaic which you have seen will constitute most of them. The essence of that " *valuable information* ", as you call it, is at your service, and shall be sent in time for your purpose. I had also by accident detected in Athens a blunder of Thornton, of a ludicrous nature, in the *Turkish language*, of which I mean to make some " pleasaunt mirth ", in return for his abuse of the Greeks. It is the passage about Pouqueville's story of the " Eater of Corrosive Sublimate ". By-the-bye, I rather suspect we shall be at right angles in our opinion of the Greeks; I have not quite made up my mind about them, but you I know are decisively inimical.

I will write to you from Cambridge, or elsewhere. Address to Newstead. Claridge is gone, after a lethargic visit of three perennial weeks. How dull he is! I wish the dog had any *bad* qualities that one might not be ashamed of disliking him.

Adio! D. V. E. Umilissimo Servitore.

B.

TO JOHN CAM HOBHOUSE † *King's College Ce., October 22nd, 1811*

MY DEAR HOBHOUSE,—I write from Scrope's rooms, whom I have just assisted to put to bed in a state of *outrageous* intoxication. I think I never saw him so bad before. We dined at Mr. Caldwell's, of Jesus Coll., where we met Dr. Clarke and others of the gown, and Scrope finished himself as usual. He has been in a similar state every evening since my arrival here a few days ago. We are to dine at Dr. Clarke's on Thursday. I find he knows little of Romaic, so we shall have *that* department entirely to ourselves. I tell you this that you need not fear any competitor, particularly so formidable a one as Dr. Clarke would probably have been. I like him much, though Scrope says *we* talked so bitterly, that he (the said Scrope) lost his listeners.

I proceed hence to town, where I shall enquire after your work, which I am sorry to say stands still for " *want of copy* ", to talk in technicals.

I am very low spirited on many accounts, and wine, which, however, I do not quaff as formerly, has lost its power over me. We all wish you here, and well, wherever you are, but surely better with us. If you don't soon return, Scrope and I mean to visit you in quarters.

The event I mentioned in my last [1] has had an effect on me, I am ashamed to think of. But there is no arguing on these points. I could " have better spared a better being ". Wherever I turn, particularly in this place, the idea goes with me. I say all this at the risk of incurring your contempt; but you cannot despise me more than I do myself. I am indeed very wretched, and like all complaining persons I can't help telling you so.

---

[1] The death of his Cambridge protégé, John Edleston, of whose death during the previous May Byron had recently heard.

The Marquis Sligo is in a great scrape about his kidnapping the seamen; I, who know him, do not think him so culpable as the Navy are determined to make him. He is a good man. I have been in Lancashire, Notts, but all places are alike; I cannot live under my present feelings; I have lost my appetite, my rest, and can neither read, write, or act in comfort. Everybody here is very polite and hospitable, my friend Scrope particularly; I wish to God he would grow sober, as I much fear no constitution can long support his excesses. If I lose him and you, what am I? Hodgson is not here, but expected soon; Newstead is my regular address. Demetrius is here, much pleased with ye place, Lord Sligo is about to send back his Arnaouts. Excuse this dirty paper, it is of Scrope's best. Good night.

Ever yours, BYRON

TO THOMAS MOORE   *Cambridge, October 27, 1811*

SIR,[1]—Your letter followed me from Notts. to this place, which will account for the delay of my reply. Your former letter I never had the honour to receive;—be assured in whatever part of the world it had found me, I should have deemed it my duty to return and answer it in person.

The advertisement you mention, I know nothing of.— At the time of your meeting with Mr. Jeffrey, I had recently entered College, and remember to have heard and read a number of squibs on the occasion; and from the recollection of these I derived all my knowledge on the subject, without the slightest idea of " giving the lie " to an address which I never beheld. When I put my name to the production, which has occasioned this correspondence, I became responsible to all whom it might concern,—to explain where it requires explanation, and, where insufficiently or too sufficiently explicit, at all events to satisfy. My situation leaves me no

---

[1] Moore had taken resentful notice of a joke at his expense in *English Bards*. He had at one moment challenged Byron; but the challenge had miscarried; and by 1811, having during the interval married, he was prepared to adopt a more conciliatory attitude, with results that appear in Byron's letter of November 1st. The party at Samuel Rogers's house helped to launch a life-long friendship.

choice; it rests with the injured and the angry to obtain reparation in their own way.

With regard to the passage in question, *you* were certainly *not* the person towards whom I felt personally hostile. On the contrary, my whole thoughts were engrossed by one, whom I had reason to consider as my worst literary enemy, nor could I foresee that his former antagonist was about to become his champion. You do not specify what you would wish to have done: I can neither retract nor apologise for a charge of falsehood which I never advanced.

In the beginning of the week, I shall be at No. 8, St. James's Street.—Neither the letter nor the friend to whom you stated your intention ever made their appearance.

Your friend, Mr. Rogers, or any other gentleman delegated by you, will find me most ready to adopt any conciliatory proposition which shall not compromise my own honour,— or, failing in that, to make the atonement you deem it necessary to require.

I have the honour to be, Sir,

Your most obedient, humble servant, BYRON

TO THOMAS MOORE   *8, St. James's Street, November 1, 1811*

SIR,—As I should be very sorry to interrupt your Sunday's engagement, if Monday, or any other day of the ensuing week, would be equally convenient to yourself and friend, I will then have the honour of accepting his invitation. Of the professions of esteem with which Mr. Rogers has honoured me, I cannot but feel proud, though undeserving. I should be wanting to myself, if insensible to the praise of such a man; and, should my approaching interview with him and his friend lead to any degree of intimacy with both or either, I shall regard our past correspondence as one of the happiest events of my life. I have the honour to be,

Your very sincere and obedient servant, BYRON

TO JOHN CAM HOBHOUSE   *8, St. James's Street,*
                                              December 9th, 1811

MY DEAR HOBHOUSE,—At length I am your rival in good
fortune.   I, this night, saw *Robert Coates* [1] perform Lothario
at the Haymarket, the house crammed, but bribery (a bank
token) procured an excellent place near the stage.   Before
the curtain drew up, a performer (all gemmen) came forward
and thus addressed the house, Ladies, etc., " A melancholy
accident has happened to the gentleman who undertook the
part of Altamont——" (here a dead stop—then—) " this
accident has *happened* to *his brother*, who fell this afternoon
through a *loop-hole* into the *London Dock*, and was taken up dead,
Altamont has just entered the house, distractedly, is—now
dressing ! ! ! and will appear in five minutes ! ! ! " Such were
verbatim the words of the apologist ; they were followed by a
roar of laughter, and Altamont himself, who did not fall short
of Coates in absurdity.   Damn me, if I ever saw such a scene
in my life ; the play was closed in 3rd act ; after Bob's demise,
nobody would hear a syllable, he was interrupted several
times before, and made speeches, every soul was in hysterics,
and all the actors on his own model.   You can't conceive how
I longed for *you* ; your taste for the ridiculous would have been
gratified to surfeit.   A farce followed in dumb-show, after Bob
had been hooted from the stage, for a bawdy address he
attempted to deliver between play and farce.   " Love à la
mode " was damned, Coates was damned, everything was
damned, and damnable.   His enacting I need not describe,
you have seen him at Bath.   But never did you see the *others*,
never did you hear the *apology*, never did you behold the
" distracted " survivor of a " brother neck-broken through
a *loop-hole* in yᵉ *London Docks* ".   Like George Faulkner these
fellows defied burlesque.   Oh, Captain ! eye hath not seen,
ear hath not heard, nor can the heart of man conceive to-
night's performance.   Baron Geramb was in the stage box,
and Coates in his address *nailed* the *Baron* to the infinite amusement of the audience, and the discomfiture of *Geramb*, who
grew very wroth indeed.

---

[1] " Romeo " Coates, a wealthy and hapless eccentric, fancied himself a great
tragic actor.

I meant to write on other topics, but I must postpone. I can think, and talk, and dream only of these buffoons. " 'Tis done, 'tis numbered with the things that were, would, would it were to come " and you by my side to see it.

Heigh ho! Good-night.

Yours ever, B.

TO WILLIAM HARNESS[1]   *8, St. James's Street, Dec. 15, 1811*

MY DEAREST WILLIAM,—I wrote you an answer to your last, which, on reflection, pleases me as little as it probably has pleased yourself. I shall not wait for your rejoinder; but proceed to tell you, that I had just then been greeted with an epistle of Hodgson's full of his petty grievances, and this at the moment when (from circumstances it is not necessary to enter upon) I was bearing up against recollections to which *his* imaginary sufferings are as a scratch to a cancer. These things combined, put me out of humour with him and all mankind. The latter part of my life has been a perpetual struggle against affections which embittered the earliest portion; and though I flatter myself I have in a great measure conquered them, yet there are moments (and this was one) when I am as foolish as formerly. I never said so much before, nor had I said this now, if I did not suspect myself of having been rather savage in my letter, and wish to inform you this much of the cause. You know I am not one of your dolorous gentlemen: so now let us laugh again.

Yesterday I went with Moore to Sydenham to visit your " costive " Campbell (as you call him). He was not visible. Moore said he was probably within, but " nefariously dirty " and did not like to be seen in so poetical a plight. So we jogged homeward merrily enough. To-morrow I dine with Rogers, and am to hear Coleridge, who is a kind of rage at present. Last night I saw Kemble in Coriolanus;—he *was glorious*, and exerted himself wonderfully. By good luck I got an excellent place in the best part of the house, which was more than overflowing. Clare and Delawarr, who were there on the same speculation, were less fortunate. I saw them by accident,—we were not together. I wished for you, to gratify

---

[1] The Reverend William Harness, " a *Harrow* man ", one of several friends whom Byron at different periods claimed as earliest and dearest.

your dramatic propensities in their fullest extent. Last week I saw an exhibition of a different kind in a Mr. Coates, at the Haymarket, who performed Lothario in a *damned* and damnable manner. * * * So much for these sentimentalites, who console themselves in the stews for the loss—the never to be recovered loss—the despair of the refined attachment of a brace of drabs! When I compare myself with these men, my elders and my betters, I really begin to conceive myself a monument of prudence—a walking statue—without feeling or failing; and yet the world in general hath given me a proud pre-eminence over them in profligacy. Yet I like the men, and, God knows, ought not to condemn their aberrations. But I own I feel provoked when they dignify all this with the name of *love* and deify their common strumpets. Romantic attachments for things marketable at a dollar! Their ladies may be averaged at a token each, I believe they have been bought cheaper.

Dec. 16th.—I have just received your letter;—I feel your kindness very deeply. The foregoing part of my letter, written yesterday, will, I hope, account for the tone of my former, though it cannot excuse it. I do *like* to hear from you—more than *like*. Next to seeing you, I have no greater satisfaction. But you have other duties, and greater pleasures, and I should regret to take a moment from either. Hodgson was to call to-day, but I have not seen him. The circumstance you mention at the close of your letter is another proof in favour of my opinion of mankind. Such you will always find them—selfish and distrustful. I except none. The cause of this is the state of society. In the world, every one is to stir for himself—it is useless, perhaps selfish, to expect any thing from his neighbour. But I do not think we are born of this disposition; for you find *friendship* as a schoolboy, and *love* enough before twenty.

I went to see Hodgson; he keeps me in town, where I don't wish to be at present. He is a good man, but totally without conduct. And now, my dearest William, I must wish you good morrow. Notwithstanding your veto, I must still sign myself "sincerely" but ever most affectionately BYRON

P.S. I shall write the moment I have been able to fix the day. φιλτατε χαιρε.

TO ROBERT RUSHTON   *8, St. James's Street, Jan. 21, 1812*

Though I have no objection to your refusal to carry *letters* to Mealey's, you will take care that the letters are taken by *Spero* at the proper time. I have also to observe, that Susan [1] is to be treated with civility, and not *insulted* by any person over whom I have the smallest control, or, indeed, by any one whatever, while I have the power to protect her. I am truly sorry to have any subject of complaint against *you*; I have too good an opinion of you to think I shall have occasion to repeat it, after the care I have taken of you, and my favourable intentions in your behalf. I see no occasion for any communication whatever between *you* and the *women*, and wish you to occupy yourself in preparing for the situation in which you will be placed. If a common sense of decency cannot prevent you from conducting yourself towards them with rudeness, I should at least hope that your *own interest*, and regard for a master who has *never* treated you with unkindness, will have some weight.

Yours, etc., BYRON

P.S.—I wish you to attend to your arithmetic, to occupy yourself in surveying, measuring, and making yourself acquainted with every particular relative to the *land* of Newstead, and you will *write* to me *one letter every week*, that I may know how you go on.

TO ROBERT RUSHTON   *8, St. James's Street, January 25, 1812*

Your refusal to carry the letter was not a subject of remonstrance: it was not a part of your business; but the language you used to the girl was (as *she* stated it) highly improper.

You say, that you also have something to complain of; then state it to me immediately: it would be very unfair, and very contrary to my disposition, not to hear both sides of the question.

[1] For further information regarding Susan Vaughan, apparently one of the Newstead housemaids whom Byron was inclined to favour, see *To Lord Byron*, by Paston and Quennell (John Murray).

If any thing has passed between you *before* or since my last visit to Newstead, do not be afraid to mention it. I am sure *you* would not deceive me, though *she* would. Whatever it is, *you* shall be forgiven. I have not been without some suspicions on the subject, and am certain that, at your time of life, the blame could not attach to you. You will not *consult* any one as to your answer, but write to me immediately. I shall be more ready to hear what you have to advance, as I do not remember ever to have heard a word from you before *against* any human being, which convinces me you would not maliciously assert an untruth. There is not any one who can do the least injury to you, while you conduct yourself properly. I shall expect your answer immediately.

Yours, etc., BYRON

TO THOMAS MOORE   *January 29, 1812*

MY DEAR MOORE,—I wish very much I could have seen you; I am in a state of ludicrous tribulation. * * *

Why do you say that I dislike your poesy? I have expressed no such opinion, either in *print* or elsewhere. In scribbling myself, it was necessary for me to find fault, and I fixed upon the trite charge of immorality, because I could discover no other, and was so perfectly qualified in the innocence of my heart, to " pluck that mote from my neighbour's eye ".

I feel very, very much obliged by your approbation; but, at *this moment*, praise, even *your* praise, passes by me like " the idle wind ". I meant and mean to send you a copy the moment of publication; but now I can think of nothing but damned, deceitful,—delightful woman, as Mr. Liston says in the *Knight of Snowdon*. Believe me, my dear Moore,

Ever yours, most affectionately, BYRON

TO JOHN CAM HOBHOUSE *   *8 St. James's Street,*
                                      February 10th, 1812

DEAR HOBHOUSE,—I have just recovered from an attack of the *Stone* in the *kidney*, an agreeable disease which promises to be periodically permanent. The very unpromising state of my worldly affairs compels me to recur to a subject upon which I have not often touched, and which I shall now dispatch as quickly as possible. In case of any accident befalling yourself or me, you are aware that I possess no *document, note* or *memorial* of the money transactions between us beyond the mention of the sum in one or two of your letters, and I should, if you have no particular objection, like to have your note of hand for the amount. Of this you will hardly suspect that I shall take any advantage. I wish it merely as an acknowledgment in case of accidents. Now to change the theme—your MSS are found. I have been most painfully ill, cupped on the loin, glystered, purged and vomited secundum artem, and am condemned to the strictest regimen, and the most durable of disorders for the residue of my life. I have been voting for the Catholics. I am about to sell off my furniture etc. at Newstead. I have almost arranged the annuity business with Scrope Davies, who has behaved very well indeed, much better than he has been treated, though that was not my fault. I have dismissed my Seraglio for squabbles and infidelities. Now for you—I regret that your work has met with so many obstructions. I have told Demo to write 150 times, but he either don't or won't understand me; if you were on the spot, all this could be easily arranged; as it is, I see no remedy. Your letters have all been put into his hands. God knows I wish you every success that a man in great bodily pain and mortal uneasiness can wish anything of anybody's. I assure you I have lately suffered very severely from kidneys within and creditors without. My two great *bodily* comfiters are Wm Bankes and Mr. Hanson; one tells me that his Grandfather died of a *Stone*, and the other that his father was killed by the *Gravel*! For my part I am *kilt* (you will understand that phrase by this time) by what a methodist would call a congregation, a bookseller compilation and a quack a complication of disorders.

Yrs. ever, B.

TO FRANCIS HODGSON   *8, St. James's Street, February 16, 1812*

DEAR HODGSON,—I send you a proof. Last week I was
very ill and confined to bed with stone in the kidney, but I
am now quite recovered. The women are gone to their
relatives, after many attempts to explain what was already too
clear. If the stone had got into my heart instead of my kidneys,
it would have been all the better. However, I have quite
recovered *that* also, and only wonder at my folly in excepting
my own strumpets from the general corruption,—albeit a two
months' weakness is better than ten years. I have one request
to make, which is, never mention a woman again in any letter
to me, or even allude to the existence of the sex. I won't
even read a word of the feminine gender ;—it must all be
propria quæ maribus.

In the spring of 1813 I shall leave England for ever. Every
thing in my affairs tends to this, and my inclinations and health
do not discourage it. Neither my habits nor constitution are
improved by your customs or your climate. I shall find employment in making myself a good Oriental scholar. I shall
retain a mansion in one of the fairest islands, and retrace,
at intervals, the most interesting portions of the East. In the
mean time, I am adjusting my concerns, which will (when
arranged) leave me with wealth sufficient even for home, but
enough for a principality in Turkey. At present they are
involved, but I hope, by taking some necessary but unpleasant
steps, to clear every thing. Hobhouse is expected daily in
London : we shall be very glad to see him ; and, perhaps,
you will come up and " drink deep ere he depart ", if not,
" Mahomet must go to the mountain " ;—but Cambridge
will bring sad recollections to him, and worse to me, though
for very different reasons. I believe the only human being,
that ever loved me in truth and entirely, was of, or belonging
to, Cambridge, and, in that, no change can now take place.
There is one consolation in death—where he sets his seal, the
impression can neither be melted nor broken, but endureth for
ever.

Yours always, B.

P.S.—I almost rejoice when one I love dies young, for I
could never bear to see them old or altered.

TO LORD HOLLAND   *8, St. James's Street, February 25, 1812*

My Lord,[1]—With my best thanks, I have the honour to return the Notts. letter to your Lordship. I have read it with attention, but do not think I shall venture to avail myself of its contents, as my view of the question differs in some measure from Mr. Coldham's. I hope I do not wrong him, but *his* objections to the bill appear to me to be founded on certain apprehensions that he and his coadjutors might be mistaken for the "*original advisers*" (to quote him) of the measure. For my own part, I consider the manufacturers as a much injured body of men, sacrificed to the views of certain individuals who have enriched themselves by those practices which have deprived the frame-workers of employment. For instance;—by the adoption of a certain kind of frame, one man performs the work of seven—six are thus thrown out of business. But it is to be observed that the work thus done is far inferior in quality, hardly marketable at home, and hurried over with a view to exportation. Surely, my Lord, however we may rejoice in any improvement in the arts which may be beneficial to mankind, we must not allow mankind to be sacrificed to improvements in mechanism. The maintenance and well-doing of the industrious poor is an object of greater consequence to the community than the enrichment of a few monopolists by any improvement in the implements of trade, which deprives the workman of his bread, and renders the labourer "unworthy of his hire".

My own motive for opposing the bill is founded on its palpable injustice, and its certain inefficacy. I have seen the state of these miserable men, and it is a disgrace to a civilised country. Their excesses may be condemned, but cannot be subject of wonder. The effect of the present bill would be to drive them into actual rebellion. The few words I shall venture to offer on Thursday will be founded upon these opinions formed from my own observations on the spot. By

[1] Lord Holland, the nephew of Charles James Fox, was at this time Recorder of Nottingham. Byron's maiden speech, delivered on February 27th, was an attack on the oppressive Frame-Breaking Bill, introduced by Lord Liverpool. The Holland House coterie had been satirized by Byron in *English Bards*. Anxious to make amends, he presented Lord Holland with an advance copy of *Childe Harold* on March 5th.

previous inquiry, I am convinced these men would have been restored to employment, and the county to tranquillity. It is, perhaps, not yet too late, and is surely worth the trial. It can never be too late to employ force in such circumstances. I believe your Lordship does not coincide with me entirely on this subject, and most cheerfully and sincerely shall I submit to your superior judgment and experience, and take some other line of argument against the bill, or be silent altogether, should you deem it more advisable. Condemning, as every one must condemn, the conduct of these wretches, I believe in the existence of grievances which call rather for pity than punishment. I have the honour to be, with great respect, my Lord, your Lordship's

Most obedient and obliged servant, BYRON

P.S.—I am a little apprehensive that your Lordship will think me too lenient towards these men, and half a *frame-breaker myself*.

TO FRANCIS HODGSON   *8, St. James's Street, March 5, 1812*

MY DEAR HODGSON,—*We* are not answerable for reports of speeches in the papers; they are always given incorrectly, and on this occasion more so than usual, from the debate in the Commons on the same night. The *Morning Post* should have said *eighteen years*. However, you will find the speech, as spoken, in the Parliamentary Register, when it comes out. Lords Holland and Grenville, particularly the latter, paid me some high compliments in the course of their speeches, as you may have seen in the papers, and Lords Eldon and Harrowby answered me. I have had many marvellous eulogies repeated to me since, in person and by proxy, from divers persons *ministerial*—yea, *ministerial!*—as well as oppositionists; of them I shall only mention Sir F. Burdett. *He* says it is the best speech by a *lord* since the " *Lord* knows when ", probably from a fellow-feeling in the sentiments. Lord H. tells me I shall beat them all if I persevere; and Lord G. remarked that the construction of some of my periods are very like *Burke's!!* And so much for vanity. I spoke very violent sentences with a sort of modest impudence, abused every thing and every body, put the Lord Chancellor very much out of humour : and if I may believe what I hear, have not lost any character by the experiment. As to my delivery, loud and fluent enough, perhaps a little theatrical. I could not recognize myself or any one else in the newspapers.

I hire myself unto Griffiths, and my poesy comes out on Saturday. Hobhouse is here ; I shall tell him to write. My stone is gone for the present, but I fear is part of my habit. We *all* talk of a visit to Cambridge.

Yours ever, B.

TO LADY CAROLINE LAMB †   *Sy Evening*

I never supposed you artful : we are all selfish, nature did that for us. But even when you attempt deceit occasionally, you cannot maintain it, which is all the better ; want of success will curb the tendency. Every word you utter, every line you write, proves you to be either *sincere* or a *fool*. Now as I know you are not the one, I must believe you the other. I never knew a woman with greater or more pleasing talents, *general* as in a woman they should be, something of everything, and too much of nothing. But these are unfortunately coupled with a total want of common conduct. For instance, the *note* to your *page*—do you suppose I delivered it? or did you mean that I should? I did not of course. Then your heart, my poor Caro (what a little volcano !), that pours *lava* through your veins ; and yet I cannot wish it a bit colder, to make a *marble slab* of, as you sometimes see (to understand my foolish metaphor) brought in vases, tables, etc., from Vesuvius, when hardened after an eruption. To drop my detestable tropes and figures, you know I have always thought you the cleverest, most agreeable, absurd, amiable, perplexing, dangerous, fascinating little being that lives now, or ought to have lived 2000 years ago. I won't talk to you of beauty ; I am no judge. But our beauties cease to be so when near you, and therefore you have either some, or something better. And now, Caro, this nonsense is the first and last compliment (if it be such) I ever paid you. You have often reproached me as wanting in that respect; but others will make up the deficiency. Come to Lord Grey's; at least do not let me keep you away. All that you so often *say*, I *feel*. Can more be said or felt? This same prudence is tiresome enough; but one *must* maintain it, or what *can* one do to be saved? Keep to it.

[On a covering sheet]

If you write at all, write as usual, but do as you please. Only as I never see you—Basta!

TO LADY CAROLINE LAMB   *May 1st, 1812*

MY DEAR LADY CAROLINE,—I have read over the few poems of Miss Milbank with attention. They display fancy, feeling, and a little practice would very soon induce facility of expression. Though I have an abhorrence of Blank Verse, I like the lines on Dermody so much that I wish they were in rhyme. The lines in the Cave at Seaham have a turn of thought which I cannot sufficiently commend, and here I am at least candid as my own opinions differ upon such subjects. The first stanza is very good indeed, and the others, with a few slight alterations, might be rendered equally excellent. The last are smooth and pretty. But these are all, has she no others? She certainly is a very extraordinary girl; who would imagine so much strength and variety of thought under that placid Countenance? It is not necessary for Miss M. to be an author-ess, indeed I do not think publishing at all creditable either to men or women, and (though you will not believe me) very often feel ashamed of it myself; but I have no hesitation in saying that she has talents which, were it proper or requisite to indulge, would have led to distinction.

A friend of mine (fifty years old, and an author, but not *Rogers*) has just been here. As there is no name to the MSS. I shewed them to him, and he was much more enthusiastic in his praises than I have been. He thinks them beautiful; I shall content myself with observing that they are better, much better, than anything of Miss M.'s protegee [*sic*] Blacket.[1]

[1] Joseph Blackett, " Cobbler Joe ", was a shoe-making bard whom Miss Milbanke had befriended.

You will say as much of this to Miss M. as you think proper.
I say all this very sincerely. I have no desire to be better
acquainted with Miss Milbank; she is too good for a fallen
spirit to know, and I should like her more if she were less
perfect.

Believe me, yours ever most truly, B.

TO THOMAS MOORE   *May 20, 1812*

On Monday, after sitting up all night, I saw Bellingham [1]
launched into eternity, and at three the same day I saw * * *
launched into the country.

I believe, in the beginning of June, I shall be down for a
few days in Notts. If so, I shall beat you up *en passant* with
Hobhouse, who is endeavouring, like you and every body else,
to keep me out of scrapes.

I meant to have written you a long letter, but I find I
cannot. If any thing remarkable occurs, you will hear it from
me—if good; if *bad*, there are plenty to tell it. In the mean
time, do you be happy.

Ever yours, etc.

P.S.—My best wishes and respects to Mrs. Moore;—she
is beautiful. I may say so even to you, for I was never more
struck with a countenance.

TO LORD HOLLAND   *June 25, 1812*

MY DEAR LORD,—I must appear very ungrateful, and
have, indeed, been very negligent, but till last night I was not
apprised of Lady Holland's restoration, and I shall call to-
morrow to have the satisfaction, I trust, of hearing that she is
well.—I hope that neither politics nor gout have assailed your
Lordship since I last saw you, and that you also are " as well
as could be expected ".

----

[1] John Bellingham, a crazy timber-merchant with a grievance, was executed
for the murder of the Prime Minister, Spencer Perceval. The asterisks evidently
stand for Lady Caroline Lamb. The original of this letter has been lost.

The other night, at a ball, I was presented by order to our gracious Regent, who honoured me with some conversation, and professed a predilection for poetry.—I confess it was a most unexpected honour, and I thought of poor Brummell's adventure, with some apprehension of a similar blunder. I have now great hope, in the event of Mr. Pye's decease, of " warbling truth at court ", like Mr. Mallet of indifferent memory.—Consider, one hundred marks a year! besides the wine and the disgrace; but then remorse would make me drown myself in my own butt before the year's end, or the finishing of my first dithyrambic.—So that, after all, I shall not meditate our laureate's death by pen or poison.

Will you present my best respects to Lady Holland? and believe me, hers and yours very sincerely

TO MISS MERCER ELPHINSTONE*   *St. James's Street,*
                                                        29 July 1812

DEAR MISS MERCER,[1]—In compliance with your request, I send the Frank which you will find on the outside; and in compliance with no request at all—but I believe in defiance of the etiquette established between single ladies and all gentlemen whatsoever, plural or singular—I annex a few lines to keep the cover in countenance.

London is very dull, and I am still duller than London. Now I am at a stand still—what shall I say next? I must have recourse to hoping! This then " comes hoping " that you survived the dust of your journey and the fatigue of not dancing at Lady Clonmell's the night before; that Mrs. Lamb bears her widowhood like the Matron of Ephesus, and that all Tunbridge is at this moment waltzing or warbling its best in honour of you both. I hope moreover that you will not gladden the eyes and break the hearts of the Royal Corps of Marines at Plymouth for sometime to come, and that . . . that . . . I am come to an end of all I can say upon nothing.

[1] Miss Margaret Mercer Elphinstone, Baroness Keith in her own right, was a young woman of great wealth and considerable character. She married the Comte de Flahault in 1817. For her correspondence with Byron, see *To Lord Byron*, by Paston and Quennell.

Pray forgive the inside of this for the sake of the *out*, and believe me, if you had done me the honour to require the one, I would never have troubled you with the other. I am (to talk diplomatically) with the very highest consideration, yr sincere and most obed^t serv^t.

B.

P.S.—I am not sure that I have not been guilty of considerable impertinence in sending a word beyond the superscription. If so, let my offence and apology go together with my best respects to Mrs. Lamb and tell her I wish the circuit well over.

TO LADY MELBOURNE* [*Aug. 12th, 1812*]

DEAR LY. M.,—I trust that Ly. C[aroline] has by this time reappeared or that her mother is better acquainted than I am : God knows where she is. If this be the case I hope you will favour me with a line, because in the interim my situation is by no means a *sinecure*, although I did not chuse to add to *your* perplexities this morning by joining in a *duet* with Ly. B.[1] As I am one of the principal performers in this unfortunate drama, I should be glad to know what my part requires next? Mainly I am extremely uneasy on account of Ly. C. and others. As for myself, it is of little consequence. I shall bear and forbear as much as I can. But I must not shrink now from anything.

6 o'clock.

Thus much I had written when I receive yours. Not a word *of* or *from* her. What is the cause of all this—I mean, the *immediate* circumstances which has led to it? I thought everything was well and quiet in the morning till the apparition of Ly. B. If I should hear from her, Ly. B. shall be informed : if *you*, pray tell me. I am apprehensive for her personal safety, for her state of mind. Here I sit alone, and however I might *appear* to you, in the most painful suspense.

Ever yours, B.

[1] Lady Caroline's anxious mother, Lady Bessborough, subsequently nicknamed by Byron " Lady Blarney ". This letter evidently refers to Lady Caroline's famous flight from Melbourne House, when she had temporarily disappeared, much to the confusion of her intimates.

TO LADY CAROLINE LAMB   [*August, 1812?*]

My DEAREST CAROLINE,—If tears which you saw and know
I am not apt to shed,—if the agitation in which I parted from
you,—agitation which you must have perceived through the
whole of this most *nervous* affair, did not commence until the
moment of leaving you approached,—if all I have said and
done, and am still but too ready to say and do, have not
sufficiently proved what my real feelings are, and must ever be
towards you, my love, I have no other proof to offer. God
knows, I wish you happy, and when I quit you, or rather you,
from a sense of duty to your husband and mother, quit me,
you shall acknowledge the truth of what I again promise and
vow, that no other in word or deed, shall ever hold the place
in my affections, which is, and shall be, most sacred to you,
till I am nothing. I never knew till *that moment* the *madness*
of my dearest and most beloved friend; I cannot express
myself; this is no time for words, but I shall have a pride, a
melancholy pleasure, in suffering what you yourself can scarcely
conceive, for you do not know me. I am about to go out with
a heavy heart, because my appearing this evening will stop
any absurd story which the event of the day might give rise
to. Do you think *now* I am *cold* and *stern* and *artful*? Will even
others think so? Will your *mother* ever—that mother to whom
we must indeed sacrifice much, more, much more on my part
than she shall ever know or can imagine? " Promise not to
love you!" ah, Caroline, it is past promising. But I shall
attribute all concessions to the proper motive, and never cease to
feel all that you have already witnessed, and more than can
ever be known but to my own heart,—perhaps to yours.
May God protect, forgive, and bless you. Ever, and even more
than ever,

                    Your most attached, BYRON

P.S.—These taunts which have driven you to this, my
dearest Caroline, were it not for your mother and the kindness
of your connections, is there anything on earth or heaven
that would have made me so happy as to have made you mine
long ago? and not less *now* than *then*, but *more* than ever at
this time. You know I would with pleasure give up all here
and all beyond the grave for you, and in refraining from this,

must my motives be misunderstood? I care not who knows this, what use is made of it,—it is to *you* and to *you* only that they are *yourself* [*sic*]. I was and am yours freely and most entirely, to obey, to honour, love,—and fly with you when, where, and how you yourself *might* and *may* determine.

TO LADY MELBOURNE   *Cheltenham, September 10th, 1812*

DEAR LADY MELBOURNE,—I presume you have heard and will not be sorry to hear *again*, that *they* are safely deposited in Ireland, and that the sea rolls between you and *one* of your torments; the other you see is still at your elbow. Now (if you are as sincere as I sometimes almost dream) you will not regret to hear, that I wish this to end, and it certainly shall not be renewed on my part. It is not that I love another, but loving at all is quite out of my way; I am tired of being a fool, and when I look back on the waste of time, and the destruction of all my plans last winter by this last romance, I am—what I ought to have been long ago. It is true from early habit, one must make love mechanically, as one swims. I was once very fond of both, but now as I never swim, unless I tumble into the water, I don't make love till almost obliged, though I fear *that* is not the shortest way out of the troubled waves with which in such accidents we must struggle. But I will say no more on this topic, as I am not sure of my ground, and you can easily outwit me, as you always hitherto have done.

To-day I have had a letter from Lord Holland, wishing me to write for the opening theatre, but as all Grub Street seems engaged in the contest, I have no ambition to enter the lists, and have thrown my few ideas into the fire. I never risk *rivalry* in anything, you see the very *lowest*, as in this case, discourages me, from a sort of mixed feeling, I don't know if it be *pride*, but *you* will say it certainly is not *modesty*. I suppose your friend Twiss will be *one*. I hear there are five hundred, and I wish him success. I really think he would do it well, but few men who have any character to lose, would risk it in an anonymous scramble, for the sake of their own feelings. I have written to Lord H. to thank him and decline the chance.

Betty [1] is performing here, I fear very ill.   His figure is that of a hippopotamus, his face like the bull and mouth on the panels of a heavy coach, his arms like fins fattened out of shape, his voice the gargling of an alderman with the quinsy, and his acting altogether ought to be natural, for it certainly is like nothing that *Art* has ever yet exhibited on the stage.

Will you honour me with a line at your leisure?   On the most *indifferent* subjects you please, and believe me ever,

Yours very affectionately, B.

TO LADY MELBOURNE   *Cheltenham, September 13th, 1812*

MY DEAR LADY M.,—The end of Lady B[essborough]'s letter shall be the beginning of mine.   " For Heaven's sake do not lose your hold on him."   Pray don't, *I* repeat, and assure you it is a very firm one, " but the yoke is easy, and the burthen is light ", to use one of my scriptural phrases.

So far from being ashamed of being governed like Lord Delacour or any *other Lord* or *master*, I am always but too happy to find one to regulate or misregulate me, and I am as docile as a dromedary, and can bear almost as much.   Will you undertake me?   If you are sincere (which I still a little hesitate in believing), give me but time, let *hers* retain her in Ireland— the " gayer " the better.   I want her just to be sufficiently gay that I may have enough to bear me out on my own part. Grant me but till December, and if I do not disenchant the Dulcinea and Don Quichotte, both, then I must attack the windmills, and leave the land in quest of adventures.   In the meantime I must, and do write the greatest absurdities to keep her " gay ", and the more so because the last epistle informed me that " eight guineas, a mail, and a packet could soon bring her to London ", a threat which immediately called forth a letter worthy of the Grand Cyrus or the Duke of York, or any other hero of Madame Scudery or Mrs. Clarke.[2]

[1] William Henry West Betty, the " Young Roscius ", was an infant prodigy whose accomplishments were widely celebrated.   In 1812, he had come of age. He retired from the theatre, having amassed a large fortune, in 1824.

[2] Mary Anne Clarke, mistress of the Duke of York, while he was Commander-in-Chief.   In 1809 her sale of commissions had provoked a resounding parliamentary scandal.   The Duke of York's love-letters, during the resultant investigation, became public property.

Poor Lady B. ! with her hopes and her fears. In fact it is no jest for her, or indeed any of us. I must let you into one little secret—*her* folly half did this. At the commencement she piqued that " vanity " (which it would be the vainest thing in the world to deny) by telling me she was certain I was not beloved, " that I was only led on for the sake of etc., etc." This raised a devil between us, which now will only be laid, I really do believe, in the *Red* Sea ; I made no answer, but determined, not to *pursue*, for pursuit it was not, but to sit still, and in a week after I was convinced—not that [Caroline] loved me, for I do not believe in the existence of what is called Love—but that any other man in my situation would have believed that he was loved. Now, my dear Lady M., you are all out as to my real sentiments. I was, am, and shall be, I fear, attached to another, one to whom I have never said much, but have never lost sight of, and the whole of this inter-lude has been the result of circumstances which it may be too late to regret. Do you suppose that at my *time* of *life*, were I so very *far* gone, that I should not be in Ireland, or at least have followed into Wales, as it was hinted was *expected*. Now they have crossed the Channel, I feel anything but regret. I told you in my two last, that I did not " like any other, etc., etc." I deceived you and myself in saying so ; there was, and is one whom I wished to marry, had not this affair inter-vened, or had not some occurrences rather discouraged me. When our drama was " rising " (" I'll be d—d if it falls off," I may say with Sir Fretful), in the 5th Act, it was no time to hesitate. I had made up my mind to bear the consequences of my own folly ; honour, pity, and a kind of affection all forbade me to shrink, but now if I can *honorably* be off, if *you* are not de-ceiving me, and if she does not take some accursed step to precipitate her own inevitable fall (if not with me, with some less lucky successor)—if these impossibilities can be got over, all will be well. If not—she will travel.

As I have said so much, I may as well say all. The woman I mean is Miss Milbanke ; I know nothing of her fortune, and I am told that her father is ruined, but my own will, when my Rochdale arrangements are closed, be sufficient for both. My debts are not £25,000, and the deuce is in it, if with R[ochdale] and the surplus of N[ewstead], I could not contrive to be as independent as half the peerage. I know little of her, and have not the most distant reason to suppose that I am at all a favourite in that quarter. But I never saw a woman whom I *esteemed* so much. But that chance is gone, and there's an end. Now, my dear Lady M., I am completely in your power. I have not deceived you as to —— [C. L.]. I hope you will not deem it vanity, when I soberly say that it would have been want of gallantry, though the acme of virtue, if I had played the Scipio on this occasion. If through your means, or any means, I can be free, or at least change my fetters, my regard and admiration would not be increased, but my gratitude would. In the meantime, it is by no means unfelt for what you have already done. To Lady B[ess-borough] I could not say all this, for she would with the best intentions make the most absurd use of it. What a miserable picture does her letter present of this daughter! She seems afraid to know her, and, blind herself, writes in such a manner as to open the eyes of all others.

I am still here in Holland's house, quiet and alone, without any wish to add to my acquaintances. Your departure was, I assure you, much more regretted than that of any of your lineals or collaterals, so do not you go to Ireland, or I shall follow you o'er " flood and fen ", a complete Ignis fatuus— that is *I*, the epithet will not apply to you, so we will divide the expression ; you would be the *light*, and I the *fool*.

I send you back the letter, and this fearful ream of my own. C. is suspicious about our counterplots, and I am obliged to be as treacherous as Talleyrand, but remember *that treachery* is *truth* to you ; I write as rarely as I can, but when I do, I must lie like George Rose. Your name, I never mention when I can help it ; and all my amatory tropes and figures are exhausted. I have a glimmering of hope. I *had* lost it—it is renewed—all depends on it ; her worst enemy could not wish her such a fate as *now* to be thrown back upon me.

Yours ever most truly, B.

P.S.—DEAR LADY M.,—Don't think me careless. My correspondence since I was sixteen has not been of a nature to allow of any trust except to a lock and key, and I have of late been doubly guarded. The few letters of yours, and all others in case of the worst, shall be sent back or burnt. Surely after returning the one with *Mr. L.'s message*, you will hardly suspect me of wishing to take any advantage; *that* was the only important one in behalf of my own interests. Think me bad if you please, but not *meanly* so. Lady B.'s under another cover accompanies this.

TO LADY MELBOURNE   *Cheltenham, September 15th, 1812*

My dear Lady M.,—" If I were looking in your face, entre les deux yeux ", I know not whether I should find " frankness or truth ", but certainly something which looks quite as well if not better than either, and whatever it may be, I would not have it changed for any other expression; as it has defied time, no wonder it should perplex *me*.—" Manage her ! " it is impossible, and as to friendship—no—it must be broken off at once, and all I have left is to take some step which will make her hate me effectually, for she must be in extremes. What you state however is to be dreaded; besides, she presumes upon the weakness and affection of all about her, and the very confidence and kindness which would break or reclaim a good heart, merely lead her own farther from deserving them. Were this but secure, you would find yourself mistaken in me. I speak from experience; except in one solitary instance, three months have ever cured me. Take an example: in the autumn of 1809 in the Mediterranean I was seized with an *everlasting* passion, considerably more violent on my part than this has ever been—everything was settled— and we (the *we* of that day) were to set off for the Friuli : but, lo ! the Peace spoilt everything, by putting this in possession of the French, and some particular occurrences in the interim, determined me to go to Constantinople. However we were to meet next year at a certain time; though I told my *amica* there was no time like the present, and that I could not answer for the future. She trusted to her power, and I at the moment had certainly much greater doubts of her than myself. A year sped, and on my return downwards I found at Smyrna and Athens despatches, requiring the performance of this

" bon billet qu' à la Chatre " [*sic*], and telling me that one of us had returned to the spot on purpose. But things had altered, as I foresaw, and I proceeded very leisurely, not arriving till some months after, pretty sure that in the interim my idol was in no want of worshippers. But she *was* there, and we met at the Palace. The Governor (the most accommodating of all possible chief magistrates) was kind enough to leave us to come to the most diabolical of explanations. It was in the dog-days, during a sirocco (I almost perspire now with the thoughts of it), during the intervals of an intermittent fever (my love had also intermitted with my malady), and I certainly feared the ague and my passion would both return in full force. I however got the better of both, and she sailed up the Adriatic and I down to the Straits. I had, *certes*, a good deal to contend against, for the lady (who was a *select* friend of the Queen of Naples) had something to gain in a few points and nothing to lose in *reputation*, and was a woman perfectly mistress of herself and every art of intrigue, personal or political —not at all in love, but very able to persuade me that she was so, and sure that I should make a most *convenient* and complaisant fellow-traveller. She is now, I am told, writing her memoirs at Vienna, in which I shall cut a very indifferent figure ; and nothing survives of this most ambrosial amour, which made me on one occasion risk my life, and on another almost drove me mad, but a few Duke of York*ish* letters and certain baubles, which I dare swear by this time have decorated the hands of half Hungary and all Bohemia. Cosi finiva la musica.

TO LADY MELBOURNE   *Cheltenham, September 18th, 1812*

MY DEAR LY. MELBOURNE,—I only wish you thought your influence worth a " *boast* ", I should ask, when it is the highest compliment paid to myself. To you it would be none, for (besides the little value of the thing) you have seen enough to convince you how easily I am governed by anyone's *presence*, but *you* would be obeyed even in absence. All persons in this situation are so, from having too much *heart*, or too little head, one or both. Set mine down according to your calculations. You and yours seem to me much the same as the Ottoman family to the faithful; they frequently change their rulers, but never the reigning race. I am perfectly convinced if I fell in love with a woman of Thibet, she would turn out an *emigrée cousine* of some of you.

You ask, " Am I sure of myself? " and I answer no, but *you* are, which I take to be a much better thing. Miss M[ilbanke] I admire because she is a clever woman, an amiable woman, and of high blood, for I have still a few Norman and Scotch inherited prejudices on the last score, were I to marry. As to *love*, that is done in a week (provided the lady has a reasonable share) ; besides, marriage goes on better with esteem and confidence than romance, and she is quite pretty enough to be loved by her husband, without being so glaringly beautiful as to attract too many rivals. She always reminds me of " Emma " in the modern Griselda, and whomever I *may* marry, that is the woman I would wish to *have married*. It is odd enough that my acquaintance with Caroline commenced with a confidence on my part about your niece; C. herself (as I have often told her) was *then* not at all to my taste, nor I (and I may believe her) to hers, and we shall end probably as we began. However, if after all " it is decreed on high ", that, like James the fatalist, I *must* be hers, she shall be *mine* as long as it pleases her, and the circumstances under which she becomes so, will at least make me devote my life to the vain attempt of reconciling her to herself. Wretched as it would render me, she should never know it; the sentence once past, I could never restore that which she had lost, but all the reparation I could make should be made, and the cup drained to the very dregs by myself, so that its bitterness passed from her.

In the meantime, till it *is* irrevocable, I must and may fairly endeavour to extricate both from a situation which, from our total want of all but selfish considerations, has brought us to the brink of the gulf. Before I sink I will at least have a *swim* for it, though I wish with all my heart it was the Hellespont instead, or that I could cross *this* as easily as I did yᵉ other. One reproach I cannot escape. Whatever happens hereafter, *she* will charge it on me, and so shall I, and I fear that

> " The first step or error none e'cr could recall,
> And the woman once fallen for ever must fall ;
> Pursue to the last the career she begun,
> And be *false* unto *many*, as *faithless* to *one*."

Forgive one stanza of my own sad rhymes; you know I never did inflict any upon you before, nor will again. What think you of Lady B.'s last? She is losing those brilliant hopes expressed in the former epistle. I have written three letters to Ireland and cannot compass more, the last to Lady B. herself, in which I never mentioned Lady C.'s name nor yours (if I recollect aright), nor alluded to either. It is an odd thing to say, but I am sure Lady B. will be a little provoked, if *I* am the first to change, for, like the Governor of Tilbury Fort, although " the Countess is resolved ", the mother *intenerisce un poco*, and doubtless will expect her daughter to be adored (like an Irish lease) for a term of 99 years. I say it again, that happy as she must and will be to have it broken off *anyhow*, she will hate me if *I* don't break my heart; now is it not so? Laugh—but answer me truly.

I am not sorry that C. sends you extracts from my epistles. I deserve it for the passage I showed once to you, but remember that was in the *outset*, and when everything said or sung was exculpatory and innocent and what not. Moreover, recollect what absurdities a man must write to his idol, and that " garbled extracts " prove nothing without the context; for my own part I declare that I recollect no such proposal of an *epistolary truce*, and the gambols at divers houses of entertainment with yᵉ express, etc., tend yᵉ rather to confirm my statement. But I cannot be sure, or answerable for all I have said or unsaid, since " Jove " himself (some with Mrs. Malaprop would read *Job*) has forgotten to " laugh at our perjuries ". I am certain that I tremble for the trunkfuls of my contradictions, since, like a minister or a woman, she may one day exhibit them in some magazine or some quartos of villainous memories written in her 7000th love-fit.

Now, dear Lady M., my *paper* spares you.

> Believe me, with great regard, Yours ever, B.

P.S.—In your last you say you are " surrounded by fools " ;
Why then " motley's the only wear " :

> " Oh that I were a fool, a motley fool ;
> I am ambitious of a motley coat."

Well, will you answer, " Thou shalt have one ".

> Chi va piano va sano,
> E chi va sano va lontano.

My progress has been " lontano ", but alas ! yᵉ " sano "
and " piano " are past praying for.

TO LADY MELBOURNE   *September 25th, 1812*

My dear Lady M.,—It would answer no purpose to
write a syllable on any subject whatever, and neither accelerate
nor retard what we wish to prevent. She must be left to chance ;
conjugal affection and the Kilkenny theatricals are equally
in your favour. For my part it is an accursed business, *towards*
nor *from* which I shall not move a single step ; if she throws
herself upon me, " cosi finiva " ; if not, the sooner it is over
the better. From this moment I have done with it ; only
before she returns allow me to know, that I may act accordingly.
But there will be nothing to fear before that time, as if a woman,
and a selfish woman also, would not fill up the vacancy with
the first comer ! As to Annabella, she requires time and all
the cardinal virtues, and in the interim I am a little verging
towards one who demands neither, and saves me besides the
trouble of marrying, by being married already. She besides
does not speak English, and to me nothing but Italian—a great
point, for from certain coincidences the very sound of that
language is music to me, and she has black eyes, and *not* a
very white skin, and reminds me of many in the Archipelago
I wished to forget, and makes me forget what I ought to
remember, all which are against me. I only wish she did not
swallow so much supper—chicken wings, sweetbreads, custards,
peaches and port wine ; a woman should never be seen eating

or drinking, unless it be *lobster salad* and *champagne*, the only truly feminine and becoming viands. I recollect imploring one lady not to eat more than a fowl at a sitting, without effect, and I have never yet made a single proselyte to Pythagoras.

Now a word to yourself—a much more pleasing topic than any of the preceding. I have no very high opinion of your sex, but when I do see a woman superior not only to all her own but to most of ours, I worship her in proportion as I despise the rest. And when I know that men of the first judgment and the most distinguished abilities have entertained and do entertain an opinion which my own humble observation, without any great effort of discernment, has enabled me to confirm on the same subject, you will not blame me for following the example of my elders and betters, and admiring you certainly as much as you ever were admired. My only regret is that the very awkward circumstances in which we are placed prevent and will prevent the improvement of an acquaintance which I now almost regret having made, but recollect, whatever happens, that the loss of it must give me more pain than even the *precious acquisition* (and this is saying *much*) which will occasion that loss.

Ld Jersey has reinvited me to M[iddleton] for the 4th Oct., and I will be there if possible ; in the meantime, whatever step you take to break off this affair has my full concurrence. But *what* you wished me to write, would be a little too indifferent ; and *that* now would be an insult, and I am much more unwilling to hurt her feelings now than ever (not from the mere apprehension of a disclosure in her wrath), but I have always felt that one who has given up much has a claim upon *me* (at least—whatever she deserves from others) for every respect that she may not feel her own degradation, and this is the reason that I have not written at all lately lest some expression might be misconstrued by her. When the lady herself begins the quarrel, and adopts a new " *Cortejo* ", then my conscience is comforted. She has not written to me for some days, which is either a very bad or very good omen.

Y^{rs} ever, B.

TO LADY MELBOURNE   *October 18th, 1812*

My dear Lady M.,—Of A[nnabella] I have little to add, but I do not regret what has passed ; the report alluded to had hurt her feelings, and she has now regained her tranquillity by the refutation to her own satisfaction without disturbing mine.   This was but fair, and was not unexpected by me ; all things considered, perhaps it could not have been better. I think of her nearly as I did.   The specimen ¹ you send me is more favourable to her talents than her discernment, and much *too indulgent* to the subject she has chosen ; in some points the resemblance is very exact, but you have not sent me the whole (I imagine) by the abruptness of both beginning and end. I am glad that your opinion coincides with mine on the subject of her abilities and her excellent qualities; in both these points she is singularly fortunate.   Still there is something of the *woman* about her ; her *preferring* that the letter to you should be sent forward to me, *per essémpio*, appears as if, though she would not encourage, she was not disgusted with being admired.   I also may hazard a conjecture that an *answer* addressed to *herself* might not have been displeasing, but of this you are the best judge from actual observation.   I cannot, however, see the necessity of its being forwarded, unless I was either to admire the composition, or reply to yᵉ contents. *One* I certainly do, the other would merely lead to mutual compliments, very sincere but somewhat *tedious.*

By the bye, what two famous letters *your own* are !   I never saw such traits of discernment, observation of character, knowledge of your *own sex* and sly concealment of your *knowledge* of the *foibles* of *ours*, than [*sic*] in these epistles ;   and so that I preserve you *always* as a friend, and *sometimes* as a correspondent (the oftener the better), believe me, my dear Lᵈʸ M., I shall regret nothing but—the week we passed at Middleton, till I can enjoy such another.

Now for C[aroline].   Your name was never mentioned or hinted at.   The passage was nearly as follows :—" I know

---

¹ In reply to a proposal of marriage, forwarded by her aunt, Annabella Milbanke had not only set forth her views on marriage, but had composed a literary portrait of her suitor.   In this effusion, among other characteristic statements, she observed that Byron's " love of goodness in its chastest form, and his abhorrence of all that degrades human nature, prove the uncorrupted purity of his moral sense ".

from the *best* authority, your *own*, that your time has passed in
a very different manner, nor do I object to it; amuse yourself,
but leave me *quiet*. What would you have? I go nowhere,
I see no one, I mix with no society, I write when it is proper;
these perpetual causeless caprices are equally selfish and
absurd, etc. etc." and so on in answer to her description of
her *lonely lovelorn condition!!!* much in the same sever*er* style.
And now this must end. If she persists I will leave the country.
I shall enter into no explanations, write no epistles, softening
or reverse, nor will I meet her if it can be avoided, and certainly
never but in society. The sooner she is apprised of this the
better; but with one so totally devoid of all conduct it is
difficult to decide. I have no objection to her knowing what
passed about A[nnabella], if it would have any good effect;
nor do I wish it to be concealed, even from others, or the world
in general; my vanity will not be piqued by its development,
and though it was not accepted, I am not at all ashamed of
my admiration of the amiable *Mathematician*.

I did not reproach C. for "*her behaviour*", but the misrepresentation of it, and her suspicions of mine. Why tell me
she was *dying* instead of *dancing*, when I had much rather hear
she was acting, as she in fact acted—viz. like any other person
in good health, tolerable society and high spirits? In short
I am not her lover, and would rather not be her friend, though
I never can, nor will be her enemy. If it can be ended, let
it be without my interference. I will have nothing more to
do with it. Her letters (all but one about *Ld Clare* unanswered,
and the answer to *that* strictly confined to his concerns, except
a hint on vanity at the close) are filled with the most ridiculous
egotism : "*how* the Duke's mob observed her, *how* the boys
followed her, the women caressed and the men admired, and
how many lovers were all sacrificed to this brilliant fit of
constancy ". Who wants it forsooth, or expects it, after
sixteen? Can't she take example from me? Do I embarrass
myself about A.? or the fifty B., C., D., E., F., G., H.'s, etc.
etc., that have preceded her in cruelty, or kindness (the latter
always the greater plague)? Not I; and really, *sans phrase*,
I think *my loss* is the most *considerable*.

I hear L^dy Holland is ill, I hope *not seriously*. Ld O. went
to-day, and I am still here with some idea of proceeding

either to Herefordshire or to Ld Harrowby's, and one notion
of being obliged to go to London to meet my agent.

Pray let me hear from you ; I am so provoked at the thought
that our acquaintance may be interrupted by the old phantasy.
I had and have twenty thousand things to say, and I trust as
many to hear, but somehow our conversations never come to
a clear conclusion.

I thank you again for your efforts with my Princess of
Parallelograms, who has puzzled you more than the Hypo-
thenuse ; in her character she has not forgotten " *Mathematics* ",
wherein I used to praise her cunning. Her proceedings are
quite rectangular, or rather we are two parallel lines prolonged
to infinity side by side, but never to meet. Say what you please
for, or of me, and I will swear it.

Good even, my dear L^{dy} Melbourne,

Ever y^{rs} most affectionately, B.

TO LADY MELBOURNE   *October 24th, 1812*

My dear L^{DY} Melbourne,—I am just setting off through
detestable roads for—[Eywood]. You can make such use of
the incident of our acquaintance as you please with C., only
do not say that I am *there*, because she will possibly write, or
do some absurd thing in that quarter, which will spoil everything, and I think there are enough of persons embroiled
already, without the addition of ——, who has besides enough
to manage already without these additions. This I know also
to be *her* wish, and certainly it is mine. You may say that we
met at C[heltenham] or elsewhere—anything but that we are
now together. By all means confide in L^{dy} " Blarney " or the
" Morning Post ". Seriously, if anything requires a little
hyperbole, let her have it ; I have left off writing entirely, and
will have nothing more to do with it. " If you mention
anything to me " *she* is sure to have it ! How? I have not
written these two months but *twice*, nor was your name mentioned in either. The last was entirely about Ld Clare, between
whom and me she has been intermeddling and conveying
notes from L^{dy} C[lar]e on the subject of a foolish difference

between Clare and myself, in which I believe I am wrong as usual. But that is over. Her last letters to me are full of complaints against *you*, for I know not what disrespectful expressions about the " letter opened." etc. etc. I have not answered them nor shall.

They talk of going to Sicily. On that head I have nothing to say, you and Mr. L[amb] are the best judges; to me it must be a matter of perfect indifference; and though I am written to professedly to be consulted on the subject, what possible answer could I give that would not be impertinent? It would be the *best* place for *her* and the worst for him (in all points of view) on earth, unless he was in some official capacity.

As I have said before, do as you will. In my next I will answer your questions as to the three persons you speak of; at present I have not time, though I am *tempted* by the *theme*. As to A[nnabella] that must take its chance—I mean the *acquaintance*; for it never will be anything more, depend upon it, even if she *revoked*. I have still the same opinion, but I never was *enamoured*; and as I very soon shall be in some other quarter, *Cossi finiva [sic]*.

Do not fear about C[aroline] even if we meet, but allow me to keep out of the way if I can, merely for the sake of peace and quietness. You were never more *groundlessly* alarmed; for I am not what you imagine, in one respect. I have gone through the experiment before; more than once, and I never was separated three months without a perfect *cure*; even though ye acquaintance was renewed. I have even stood as much *violence* as could be brought into the field in ye present occasion. In the first vol. of Marmontel's Memoirs, towards the end, you will find my opinion on the subject of women in *general* in the mouth of Madame de *Tencin*, should you deign to think it worth a moment's notice.

Evers yours most affectionately, B.

P.S.—If you write to Cheltenham my letters will be forwarded. And *do* write. I have very few correspondents, and none but this which give me much pleasure.

TO LADY MELBOURNE   *November 9th, 1812*

My dear L^{DY} M.,—With y^r letter I have received an *Irish* Epistle, foolish, headstrong, and vainly threatening *herself*, etc. etc. To this I shall return no answer; and though it is of very great importance to me to be in London at this time, I shall if possible delay it till I hear from you that there is no chance of any scenes. Mr. D. could hardly avoid guessing but too correctly, for not a servant in the house but was afraid to awaken me, and *he* was called home from a club for that purpose; his first and natural question to the man, was whence he came, from whom, and why? the answer to all which is obvious, but D. ought not to have mentioned it, and so I shall tell him.

Why he placed me in Notts at this moment I cannot say, except that he knew no better. Mr. C[laughton] [1] may repent of his bargain for aught I know to the contrary, but he has paid part of the money. If he fails, the Law will decide between us; and if he acts in an ungentlemanly manner, the remedy is still more simple.

With regard to L^{dy} B[essborough] and L^{dy} C[aroline], I have little more to say, and I hope nothing to do.—She has hurt and disgusted me by her latter conduct beyond expression, and even if I did not love another, I would never speak to her again while I existed, and this you have my full consent to state to those whom it may concern. I have passed my time since her departure *always* quietly and partly delightfully, nor will I submit to caprice and injustice. This *was* to *be* broken off—it is broken off. I had neither the hope nor the inclination to satisfy L^{dy} B[essborough] on all points; if it is unfair to comply with her own express wishes, let her complain till she is tired, but I trust a little reflection will convince even her that she is wrong to be dissatisfied. C. threatens to revenge herself upon *herself*, by all kinds of perverseness; this is her concern. All I desire is to have nothing more to do with them—no explanations, no interviews; in short I neither can nor will bear it any longer. As long as there was a necessity for supporting her I did not *shrink* from any consequences,

---

[1] A prospective purchaser of Newstead, who eventually failed to complete his bargain.

but when all was adjusted and you agreed to overlook the past, in the hope of the future, my resolution was taken, and to that I have adhered, and will adhere. I cannot exist without some object of love. I have found one with whom I am perfectly satisfied, and who as far as I can judge is no less so with me; our mutual wish is *quiet*, and for this reason I find a double pleasure (after all the ridiculous display of last season) in repose. I have engaged myself too far to recede, nor do I regret it. Are *you* at least satisfied with what I have done to comply with your wishes, if L^dy B[essborough] is not? If L^dy C[aroline] wishes any interview pray explain for me that *I* WILL NOT meet her; if she has either pride or feeling this will be sufficient. All letters, etc. etc., may be easily destroyed without it.

TO JOHN MURRAY *Eywood, Presteign, January 8, 1813*

DEAR SIR,—You have been imposed upon by a letter forged in my name to obtain the picture left in your possession. This I know by the confession of the culprit, and as she is a woman (and of rank), with whom I have unfortunately been too much connected, you will for the present say very little about it; but if you have the letter *retain* it—write to me the particulars. You will also be more cautious in future, and not allow anything of mine to pass from your hands without my *Seal* as well as Signature.

I have not been in town, nor have written to you since I left it. So I presume the forgery was a skilful performance. —I shall endeavour to get back the picture by fair means, if possible.

Yours ever, BYRON

P.S.—Keep the letter if you have it. I did not receive your parcel, and it is now too late to send it on, as I shall be in town on the 17th. The *delinquent* is one of the first families in this kingdom; but, as Dogberry says, this is " flat burglary ". Favour me with an answer. I hear I am scolded in the *Quarterly*; but you and it are already forgiven. I suppose that made you bashful about sending it.

TO LADY CAROLINE LAMB* *January [?], 1813*
[This letter was found enclosed in a letter to Lady Melbourne of Jan. 10th, 1813.]

You should answer the note for the writer seems unhappy. And when we are so a slight is doubly felt.

I shall go at 12; but you must send me a ticket, which I shall religiously pay for. I shall not call because I do not see that we are at all improved by it. Why did you send your boy? I was out, and am always so occupied in a morning that I could not have seen him as I wished had I been at home. I have seen Moore's wife, who is beautiful, with the darkest eyes. They have left town. M. is in great distress about us, and indeed people talk as if there were no other pair of absurdities in London. It is hard to bear all this without cause,

but worse to give cause for it. Our folly has had the effect
of a fault. I conformed and could conform, if you would lend
your aid, but I can't bear to see you look unhappy, and am
always on the watch to observe if you are trying to make me
so. We must make an effort. This dream, this delirium of
two months must pass away. We in fact do not know one
another. A month's absence would make us rational. You
do not think so. I know it. We have both had 1000 previous
fancies of the same kind, and shall get the better of this and
be ashamed of it according to the maxim of Rochefoucault.
But it is better that I should leave town than you, and I will
make a turn [?], or go to Cambridge or Edinburgh. Now
don't abuse me, or think me altered. It is because I am not,
cannot alter, that I shall do this, and cease to make fools talk,
friends grieve, and the wise pity.

> Ever most affectionately and truly Yrs, B.

TO JOHN CAM HOBHOUSE*   *January 17th, 1813*

DEAR H.,—I am on my way to town, writing from my
sordid Inn. Many thanks for your successful diplomacy with
Ma-Mee. And now " Grant him one favour and he'll ask you
two "—I have written to Batt for rooms. Would it hurt your
dignity to order me some at any other hotel (by a note) in
case he should not have them?—for I have no opportunity of
receiving your or his answer before I reach London, and if
he has not any to spare and I arrive late I shall be as bewildered as Whittington.

I rejoice in your good understanding with Murray. Through
him you will become a " *staple author* ". D. is a *damned* nincom.
assuredly. He has bored me into getting young Fox to recommend his further *damnation* to the Manager Whitbread. God
(and the Gods) knows and know what will become of his " 25
acts and some odd scenes ".

I am at Ledbury. Ly. O. and famille I left at Hereford,
as I hate travelling with Children unless they have gotten a
Stranguary. However I wait here for her tomorrow like a
dutiful Cortejo. O[xford] has been in town these ten days.
Car. L. has been *forging letters* in my name and hath thereby

pilfered the best picture of *me*, the Newstead Miniature!!!
Murray was the imposed upon. The Devil, and Medea, and
her Dragons to boot, are possessed of that little maniac. Bankes
is gone or going to tourify. I gave him a few letters.

I expect and hope you will have a marvellous run and
trust you have not forgotten "*monogamy* my dr. boy". If
the " learned world are not in arms against your paradoxes "
I shall despise these coster-monger days when Merit availeth
not.

Excuse my buffoonery, for I write under the influence of
a solitary nipperkin of Grog, such as the Salsette afforded " us
youth " in the Arches [?]

Ever yrs. dr. H., B.

TO FRANCIS HODGSON   *February 3, 1813*

MY DEAR HODGSON,—I will join you in any bond for the
money you require, be it that or a larger sum. With regard
to security, as Newstead is in a sort of abeyance between sale
and purchase, and my Lancashire property very unsettled,
I do not know how far I can give more than personal security,
but what I can I will. At any rate you can try, and as the sum
is not very considerable, the chances are favourable. I hear
nothing of my own concerns, but expect a letter daily. Let
me hear from you where you are and will be this month.
I am a great admirer of the *R.A.* [*Rejected Addresses*], though
I have had so great a share in the cause of their publication,
and I like the *C.H.* [*Childe Harold*] imitation one of the best.
Lady Oxford has heard me talk much of you as a relative of the
Cokes, etc., and desires me to say she would be happy to have
the pleasure of your acquaintance. You must come and see
me at K[insham].¹ I am sure you would like *all* here if you
knew them.

The " Agnus " is furious. You can have no idea of the
horrible and absurd things she has said and done since (really
from the best motives) I withdrew my homage. " Great
pleasure " is, certes, my object, but " *why brief*, Mr. Wild? "

¹ Kinsham Court, a dower house belonging to Lord Oxford, of which Byron
was for a time the tenant.

I cannot answer for the future, but the past is pretty secure; and in it I can number the last two months as worthy of the gods in *Lucretius*. I cannot review in the " *Monthly* " ; in fact I can just now do nothing, at least with a pen ; and I really think the days of Authorship are over with me altogether. I hear and rejoice in Bland's and Merivale's intentions. Murray has grown great, and has got him new premises in the fashionable part of the town. We live here so shut out of the *monde* that I have nothing of general import to communicate, and fill this up with a " happy new year ", and drink to you and Drury.

Ever yours, dear H., B.

I have no intention of continuing " *Childe Harold* ". There are a few additions in the " body of the book " of description, which will merely add to the number of pages in the next edition. I have taken Kinsham Court. The business of last summer I broke off, and now the amusement of the gentle fair is writing letters literally threatening my life, and much in the style of " Miss Mathews " in " *Amelia* ", or " Lucy " in the " *Beggar's Opera* ". Such is the reward of restoring a woman to her family, who are treating her with the greatest kindness, and with whom I am on good terms. I am still in *palatia Circes*, and, being no Ulysses, cannot tell into what animal I may be converted ; as you are aware of the turn of both parties, your conjectures will be very correct, I daresay, and, seriously, I am very much *attached*. She has had her share of the denunciations of the brilliant Phryne, and regards them as much as I do. I hope you will visit me at K. which will not be ready before spring, and I am very sure you would like my neighbours if you knew them. If you come down now to Kington, pray come and see me.

TO THE HON. AUGUSTA LEIGH   *4, Bennet Street, St. James's,
March 26th, 1813*

MY DEAREST AUGUSTA,—I did not answer your letter, because I could not answer as I wished, but expected that every week would bring me some tidings that might enable me to reply better than by apologies. But Claughton has not, will not, and, I think, cannot pay his money, and though, luckily, it was stipulated that he should never have possession till the whole was paid, the estate is still on my hands, and your brother consequently not less embarrassed than ever. This is the truth, and is all the excuse I can offer for inability, but not unwillingness, to serve you.

I am going abroad again in June,[1] but should wish to see you before my departure. You have perhaps heard that I have been fooling away my time with different " *regnantes* " ; but what better can be expected from me? I have but one *relative*, and her I never see. I have no connections to domesticate with, and for marriage I have neither the talent nor the inclination. I cannot fortune-hunt, nor afford to marry without a fortune. My parliamentary schemes are not much to my taste—I spoke twice last Session, and was told it was well enough ; but I hate the thing altogether, and have no intention to " strut another hour " on that stage. I am thus wasting the best part of life, daily repenting and never amending.

On Sunday, I set off for a fortnight for Eywood, near Presteign, in Herefordshire—with the *Oxfords*. I see you put on a *demure* look at the name, which is very becoming and matronly in you ; but you won't be sorry to hear that I am quite out of a more serious scrape with another singular personage which threatened me last year, and trouble enough I had to steer clear of it I assure you. I hope all my nieces are well, and increasing in growth and number ; but I wish you were not always buried in that bleak common near Newmarket.

I am very well in health, but not happy, nor even comfortable ; but I will not bore you with complaints. I am a fool, and deserve all the ills I have met, or may meet with, but nevertheless very *sensibly*, dearest Augusta,

Your most affectionate brother, BYRON

TO THE HON. AUGUSTA LEIGH   4, *Bennet Street,*
June 26ᵗʰ, 1813

MY DEAREST AUGUSTA,—Let me know when you arrive, and when, and where, and how, you would like to see me,

Byron planned at this moment to go abroad with the Oxfords.

—any where in short but at *dinner*. I have put off going into
ye country on purpose to *waylay* you.

Ever yours, B^N

TO THE HON. AUGUSTA LEIGH   [*June, 1813*]

My dearest Augusta,—And if you knew *whom* I had put
off besides my journey—you would think me grown strangely
fraternal. However I won't overwhelm you with my *own
praises*.

Between one and two be it—I shall, in course, prefer
seeing you all to myself without the incumbrance of third
persons, even of *your* (for I won't own the relationship) fair
cousin of *eleven page* memory, who, by the bye, makes one of
the finest busts I have seen in the Exhibition, or out of it.
Good night !

Ever yours, Byron

P.S.—Your writing is grown like my Attorney's, and gave
me a qualm, till I found the remedy in your signature.

TO LADY MELBOURNE   *July 6th, 1813*

Dear L^y M,—Since I wrote ye enclosed I have heard a
strange story of C.'s scratching herself with glass, and I know
not what besides ; of all this I was ignorant till this evening.
What I did, or said to provoke her I know not. I told her
it was better to *waltz* ; " because she danced well, and it
would be imputed to *me*, if she did not "—but I see nothing
in this to produce cutting and maiming ; besides, before
supper I saw her, and though she said, and did even then
a foolish thing, I could not suppose her so frantic as to be in
earnest. She took hold of my hand as I passed, and pressed
it against some sharp instrument, and said, " I mean to use
this ". I answered, " Against me, I presume ? " and passed
on with L^y R[ancliffe], trembling lest Ld Y. or L^y R. should
overhear her ; though not believing it possible that this was

more than one of her, not uncommon, *bravadoes*, for *real feeling* does not disclose its intentions, and always shuns display.   I thought little more of this, and leaving the table in search of her would have appeared more particular than proper—though, of course, had I guessed her to be serious, or had I been conscious of offending I should have done everything to pacify or prevent her.   I know not what to say, or do. I am quite unaware of what I did to displease ; and useless regret is all I can feel on the subject.   Can she be in her senses? Yet I would rather think myself to blame—than that she were so silly without cause.

I really remained at L^y H[eathcote's] till 5, totally ignorant of all that passed.   Nor do I now know where this cursed scarification took place, nor when—I mean the room—and the hour.

TO LADY MELBOURNE   *July 6th, 1813*

My dear Lady M.,—God knows what has happened, but at four in the morning L^y Ossulstone looking angry (and at that moment, ugly), delivered to me a confused kind of message from you of some scene—this is all I know, except that with laudable logic she drew the usual feminine deduction that I " *must* have behaved very ill ".   If L^y C. is offended, it really must be anger at my *not* affronting her—for one of the few things I said, was a request to know her will and pleasure, if there was anything I could say, do, or not do to give her the least gratification.   She walked away without answering, and after leaving me in this not very dignified situation, and showing her independence to twenty people near, I only saw her dancing and in the doorway for a moment, where she said something so very violent that I was in distress lest Ld Y. or L^y Rancliffe overheard her.   I went to supper, and saw and heard no more till L^y Ossulstone told me your words and her own opinion, and here I am in stupid innocence and ignorance of my offence or her proceedings.   If I am to be haunted with hysterics wherever I go, and whatever I do, I think she is not the only person to be pitied.   I should have returned to her after her *doorway whisper*, but I could not with any kind of politeness leave L^y Rancliffe to drown herself in wine and water, or be suffocated in a jelly dish, without a spoon, or a hand to help her; besides if there was, and I foresaw there would be something ridiculous, surely I was better absent than present.

This is really insanity, and everybody seems inoculated with the same distemper. L^y W[estmoreland] says, "You must have done something; you know between people in your situation, a word or a look goes a great way", etc. etc. So it seems indeed—but I never knew that *neither* words nor looks—in short down-right, innocent, vacant, undefinable *nothing*, had the same precious power of producing this perpetual worry.

I wait to hear from you, in case I have to answer you. I trust nothing has occurred to spoil your breakfast, for which the Regent has got a fine day.

TO THOMAS MOORE   *4, Benedictine Street, St. James's,*
July 8, 1813

I presume by your silence that I have blundered into something noxious in my reply to your letter, for the which I beg leave to send beforehand a sweeping apology which you may apply to any, or all, parts of that unfortunate epistle. If I err in my conjecture, I expect the like from you in putting our correspondence so long in quarantine. God he knows what I have said; but he also knows (if he is not as indifferent to mortals as the *nonchalant* deities of Lucretius), that you are the last person I want to offend. So, if I have,—why the devil don't you say it at once, and expectorate your spleen?

Rogers is out of town with Madame de Stael,[1] who hath published an Essay against Suicide, which, I presume, will make somebody shoot himself;—as a sermon by Blenkinsop, in *proof* of Christianity, sent a hitherto most orthodox acquaintance of mine out of a chapel of ease a perfect atheist. Have you found or founded a residence yet? and have you begun

[1] Madame de Staël had recently arrived in London, accompanied by her eldest son, her daughter and her unacknowledged second husband, M. de Rocca.

or finished a poem? If you won't tell me what *I* have done, pray say what you have done, or left undone, yourself. I am still in equipment for voyaging, and anxious to hear from, or of, you *before* I go, which anxiety you should remove more readily, as you think I sha'n't cogitate about you afterwards. I shall give the lie to that calumny by fifty foreign letters, particularly from any place where the plague is rife,—without a drop of vinegar or a whiff of sulphur to save you from infection.

The Oxfords have sailed almost a fortnight, and my sister is in town, which is a great comfort,—for, never having been much together, we are naturally more attached to each other. I presume the illuminations have conflagrated to Derby (or wherever you are) by this time. We are just recovering from tumult and train oil, and transparent fripperies, and all the noise and nonsense of victory. Drury Lane had a large *M.W.*, which some thought was Marshal Wellington; others, that it might be translated into Manager Whitbread; while the ladies of the vicinity of the saloon conceived the last letter to be complimentary to themselves. I leave this to the commentators to illustrate. If you don't answer this, I sha'n't say what *you* deserve, but I think *I* deserve a reply. Do you conceive there is no Post-Bag but the Twopenny? Sunburn me, if you are not too bad.

TO THOMAS MOORE *July 13, 1813*

Your letter set me at ease; for I really thought (as I hear of your susceptibility) that I had said—I know not what— something I should have been very sorry for, had it, or I, offended you;—though I don't see how a man with a beautiful wife—*his own* children,—quiet—fame—competency and friends, (I will vouch for a thousand, which is more than I will for a unit in my own behalf,) can be offended with any thing.

Do you know, Moore, I am amazingly inclined—remember I say but *inclined*—to be seriously enamoured with Lady A[delaide] F[orbes]—but this * * has ruined all my prospects. However, you know her; is she *clever*, or sensible, or good-tempered? either *would* do—I scratch out the *will*. I don't ask as to her beauty—that I see; but my circumstances are mending, and were not my other prospects blackening, I would take a wife, and that should be the woman, had I a chance. I do not yet know her much, but better than I did.

I want to get away, but find difficulty in compassing a passage in a ship of war. They had better let me go; if I cannot, patriotism is the word—" nay, an they'll mouth, I'll rant as well as they ". Now, what are you doing?—writing, we all hope, for own sakes. Remember you must edit my posthumous works, with a Life of the Author, for which I will send you Confessions, dated " Lazaretto ", Smyrna, Malta, or Palermo—one can die any where.

There is to be a thing on Tuesday ycleped a national fête. The Regent and * * * are to be there, and every body else, who has shillings enough for what was once a guinea. Vauxhall is the scene—there are six tickets issued for the modest women, and it is supposed there will be three to spare. The passports for the lax are beyond my arithmetic.

P.S.—The Stael last night attacked me most furiously— said that I had " no right to make love—that I had used * * barbarously—that I had no feeling, and was totally *in*sensible to *la belle passion*, and *had* been all my life ". I am very glad to hear it, but did not know it before. Let me hear from you anon.

TO THOMAS MOORE   *July 25, 1813*

I am not well versed enough in the ways of single woman to make much matrimonial progress.

I have been dining like the dragon of Wantley for this last week. My head aches with the vintage of various cellars, and my brains are muddled as their dregs. I met your friends the Daltons :—she sang one of your best songs so well, that, but for the appearance of affectation, I could have cried; he reminds me of Hunt, but handsomer, and more musical in soul, perhaps. I wish to God he may conquer his horrible anomalous complaint. The upper part of her face is beautiful, and she seems much attached to her husband. He is right, nevertheless, in leaving this nauseous town. The first winter would infallibly destroy her complexion,—and the second, very probably, every thing else.

I must tell you a story. Morris (of indifferent memory) was dining out the other day, and complaining of the Prince's coldness to his old wassailers. D'Israeli (a learned Jew) bored him with questions—why this? and why that? "Why did the Prince act thus? "—"Why, sir, on account of Lord * *, who ought to be ashamed of himself."—"And why ought Lord * * to be ashamed of himself? "—"Because the Prince, sir, * * * * * * * *."—"And why, sir, did the Prince cut *you*? "—"Because, G—d d—mme, sir, I stuck to my principles."—"And *why* did you stick to your principles? "

Is not this last question the best that was ever put, when you consider to whom? It nearly killed Morris. Perhaps you may think it stupid, but, as Goldsmith said about the peas, it was a very good joke when I heard it—as I did from an ear-witness—and is only spoilt in my narration.

The season has closed with a dandy ball;—but I have dinners with the Harrowbys, Rogers, and Frere and Mackintosh, where I shall drink your health in a silent bumper, and regret your absence till " too much canaries " wash away my memory, or render it superfluous by a vision of you at the opposite side of the table. Canning has disbanded his party by a speech from his * * * *—the true throne of a Tory. Conceive his turning them off in a formal harangue, and bidding them think for themselves. " I have led my ragamuffins where they are well peppered. There are but three of the 150 left alive ", and they are for the *Townsend* (*query*, might not Falstaff mean the Bow Street officer? I dare say Malone's posthumous edition will have it so) for life.

Since I wrote last, I have been into the country. I journeyed by night—no incident, or accident, but an alarm on the part of my valet on the outside, who, in crossing Epping Forest, actually, I believe, flung down his purse before a mile-stone, with a glow-worm in the second figure of number XIX—mistaking it for a footpad and dark lantern. I can only attribute his fears to a pair of new pistols wherewith I had armed him ; and he thought it necessary to display his vigilance by calling out to me whenever we passed any thing—no matter whether moving or stationary. Conceive ten miles, with a tremor every furlong. I have scribbled you a fearfully long letter. This sheet must be blank, and is merely a wrapper, to preclude the tabellarians of the post from peeping. You once complained of my *not* writing;—I will " heap coals of fire upon your head " by *not* complaining of your *not* reading. Ever, my dear Moore, your'n (isn't that the Staffordshire termination?),

BYRON

TO THOMAS MOORE　　　　　　*Bennet Street, August 22, 1813*

As our late—I might say, deceased—correspondence had too much of the town-life leaven in it, we will now, *paulo majora*, prattle a little of literature in all its branches; and first of the first—criticism. The Prince is at Brighton, and Jackson, the boxer, gone to Margate, having, I believe, de- coyed Yarmouth to see a milling in that polite neighbourhood. Made de Stael Holstein has lost one of her young barons, who has been carbonadoed by a vile Teutonic adjutant,— kilt and killed in a coffee-house at Scrawsenhawsen. Corinne is, of course, what all mothers must be,—but will, I venture to prophesy, do what few mothers could—write an Essay upon it. She cannot exist without a grievance—and somebody to see, or read, how much grief becomes her. I have not seen her since the event; but merely judge (not very charitably) from prior observation.

In a " mail-coach copy " of the *Edinburgh*, I perceive *The Giaour* is second article. The numbers are still in the Leith smack—*pray which way is the wind?* The said article is so very mild and sentimental, that it must be written by Jeffrey *in love*;—you know he is gone to America to marry some fair one, of whom he has been, for several *quarters, éperdument amoureux*. Seriously—as Winifred Jenkins says of Lismahago —Mr. Jeffrey (or his deputy) " has done the handsome thing by me ", and I say *nothing*. But this I will say, if you and I had knocked one another on the head in this quarrel, how he would have laughed, and what a mighty bad figure we should have cut in our posthumous works. By the by, I was call'd *in* the other day to mediate between two gentlemen bent upon carnage, and—after a long struggle between the natural desire of destroying one's fellow-creatures, and the dislike of seeing men play the fool for nothing,—I got one to make an apology, and the other to take it, and left them to live happy ever after. One was a peer, the other a friend untitled, and both fond of high play;—and one, I can swear for, though very mild, " not fearful ", and so dead a shot, that, though the other is the thinnest of men, he would have split him like a cane. They both conducted themselves very well, and I put them out of *pain* as soon as I could.

There is an American *Life* of G. F. Cooke, *Scurra* deceased, lately published. Such a book!—I believe, since *Drunken Barnaby's Journal*, nothing like it has drenched the press. All green-room and tap-room—drams and the drama—brandy, whisky-punch, and, *latterly*, toddy, overflow every page. Two things are rather marvellous,—first, that a man should live so long drunk, and, next, that he should have found a sober biographer. There are some very laughable things in it, nevertheless;—but the pints he swallowed, and the parts he performed, are too regularly registered.

All this time you wonder I am not gone; so do I; but the accounts of the plague are very perplexing—not so much for the thing itself as the quarantine established in all ports, and from all places, even from England. It is true, the forty or sixty days would, in all probability, be as foolishly spent on shore as in the ship; but one likes to have one's choice, nevertheless. Town is awfully empty; but not the worse for that. I am really puzzled with my perfect ignorance of what I mean to do;—not stay, if I can help it, but where to go? Sligo is for the North;—a pleasant place, Petersburgh, in September, with one's ears and nose in a muff, or else tumbling into one's neckcloth or pocket-handkerchief! If the winter treated Buonaparte with so little ceremony, what would it inflict upon your solitary traveller?—Give me a *sun*, I care not how hot, and sherbet, I care not how cool, and *my* Heaven is as easily made as your Persian's. *The Giaour* is now a thousand and odd lines. " Lord Fanny spins a thousand such a day ", eh, Moore?—thou wilt needs be a wag, but I forgive it.

Yours ever, BYRON

P.S.—I perceive I have written a flippant and rather cold-hearted letter! let it go, however. I have said nothing, either, of the brilliant sex; but the fact is, I am at this moment in a far more serious, and entirely new, scrape than any of the last twelve months,—and that is saying a good deal. It is unlucky we can neither live with nor without these women.

I am now thinking of regretting that, just as I have left Newstead, you reside near it. Did you ever see it? *do*—but don't tell me that you like it. If I had known of such intellectual neighbourhood, I don't think I should have quitted it. You could have come over so often, as a bachelor,—for it was a thorough bachelor's mansion—plenty of wine and such sordid sensualities—with books enough, room enough, and an air of antiquity about all (except the lasses) that would have suited you, when pensive, and served you to laugh at when in glee. I had built myself a bath and a *vault*—and now I sha'n't even be buried in it. It is odd that we can't even be certain of a *grave*, at least a particular one. I remember, when about fifteen, reading your poems there, which I can repeat almost now,—and asking all kinds of questions about the author, when I heard that he was not dead according to the preface; wondering if I should ever see him—and though, at that time, without the smallest poetical propensity myself, very much taken, as you may imagine, with that volume. Adieu—I commit you to the care of the gods—Hindoo, Scandinavian, and Hellenic!

P.S. 2d.—There is an excellent review of Grimm's *Correspondence* and Made de Stael in this No of the *E[dinburgh] R[eview]*. Jeffrey, himself, was my critic last year; but this is, I believe, by another hand. I hope you are going on with your *grand coup*—pray do—or that damned Lucien Buonaparte will beat us all. I have seen much of his poem in MS., and he really surpasses every thing beneath Tasso. Hodgson is translating him *against* another bard. You and (I believe Rogers,) Scott, Gifford, and myself, are to be referred to as judges between the twain,—that is, if you accept the office. Conceive our different opinions! I think we, most of us (I am talking very impudently, you will think—*us*, indeed!) have a way of our own,—at least, you and Scott certainly have.

TO LADY MELBOURNE   *September 5th, 1813.*

DEAR LADY MELBOURNE,—I return you the plan of
A[nnabella]'s spouse elect,[1] of which I shall say nothing
because I do not understand it ; though I dare say it is exactly
what it ought to be. Neither do I know why I am writing this
note, as I mean to call on you, unless it be to try your " new
patent pens " which delight me infinitely with their colours.
I have pitched upon a yellow one to begin with. Very likely
you will be out, and I must return all the annexed epistles.
I would rather have seen your answer. She seems to have been
spoiled—not as children usually are—but systematically
Clarissa Harlowed into an awkward kind of correctness, with
a dependence upon her own infallibility which will or may lead
her into some egregious blunder. I don't mean the usual
error of young gentlewomen, but she will find exactly what
she wants, and then discover that it is much more dignified
than entertaining. [*The second page of this letter has been torn
off.*]

TO MISS MILBANKE [EXTRACT]   *Sep^{tr} 6th, 1813*

I look upon myself as a very facetious personage and may
appeal to most of my acquaintance (L^y M. for instance) in
proof of my assertion. Nobody laughs more, and though
your friend Joanna Baillie says somewhere that " Laughter
is the child of misery ", I do not believe her (unless indeed in a
hysteric), tho' I think it is sometimes the parent. Nothing
could do me more honor than the acquaintance of that Lady,
who does not possess a more enthusiastic admirer than myself.
She is our only dramatist since Otway and Southerne ; I don't
except Home. With all my presumed prejudice against your
sex, or rather the perversion of manners and principle in many,
which you admit in some circles, I think the worst woman
that ever existed would have made a man of very passable
reputation. They are all better than us, and their faults,
such as they are, must originate with ourselves. Your sweeping

---

[1] Besides her sketch of Byron's character, Annabella Milbanke had produced
an imaginary portrait of her ideal husband.

sentence " on the circles where we have met " amuses me much when I recollect some of those who constituted that society. After all, bad as it is, it has its *agrémens*. The great object of life is sensation—to feel that we exist, even though in pain. It is this " craving void " which drives us to gaming —to battle—to travel—to intemperate, but keenly felt pursuits of any description, whose principal attraction is the agitation inseparable from their accomplishment. I am but an awkward dissembler; as my friend you will bear with my faults. I shall have the less constraint in what I say to you—firstly because I may derive some benefit from your observations—and next because I am very sure you can never be perverted by any paradoxes of mine. You have said a good deal and very well too on the subject of Benevolence systematically exerted; two lines of Pope will explain mine (if I have any) and that of half mankind—

" Perhaps prosperity becalmed his breast,
  Perhaps the Wind just shifted from the East ".

By the bye you are a *bard* also—have you quite given up that pursuit? Is your friend Pratt one of your critics? or merely one of your systematic benevolents? You were very kind to poor Blackett which he requited by falling in love, rather presumptuously to be sure—like Metastasio with the Empress Maria Theresa. When you can spare an instant, I shall of course be delighted to hear from you—but do not let me encroach a moment on better avocations—— Adieu.

Ever yours, B.

TO THE HON. AUGUSTA LEIGH   [*Wednesday*],
                                    Septr 15th, 1813

My dear Augusta,—I joined my friend Scrope about 8, and before eleven we had swallowed six bottles of his burgundy and Claret, which left him very unwell and me rather feverish; we were *tête à tête*. I remained with him next day and set off last night for London, which I reached at three in the morning.

Tonight I shall leave it again, perhaps for Aston or Newstead. I have not yet determined, nor does it much matter. As you perhaps care more on the subject than I do, I will tell you when I know myself.

When my departure is arranged, and I can get this long-evaded passage, you will be able to tell me whether I am to expect a visit or not, and I can come for or meet you as you think best. If you write, address to Bennet Street.

Yours very truly, B.

TO LADY MELBOURNE †   *Aston Hall, Rotherham,*
September 21st, 1813

My dear L^y M^e,—My stay at Cambridge was very short, but feeling feverish and restless in town I flew off, and here I am on a visit to my friend Webster, now married, and (according to ye Duke of Buckingham's curse) " settled in ye country ". His bride, Lady Frances, is a pretty, pleasing woman, but in delicate health, and, I fear, going—if not gone—into a decline. Stanhope and his wife—pretty and pleasant too, but not at all consumptive—left us to-day, leaving only ye family, another single gentleman, and your slave. The sister, L^y Catherine, is here too, and looks very pale from a *cross* in her love for Lord Bury (Ld Alb[emarl]e's son) ; in short, we are a society of happy wives and unfortunate maidens. The place is very well, and quiet, and the children only scream in a low voice, so that I am not much disturbed, and shall stay a few days in tolerable repose. W[ebster] don't want sense, nor good nature, but both are occasionally obscured by his suspicions, and absurdities of all descriptions ; he is passionately fond of having his wife admired, and at the same time jealous to jaundice of everything and everybody. I have hit upon the medium of praising her to him perpetually behind her back, and never looking at her before his face ; as for her, I believe she is disposed to be very faithful, and I don't think anyone now here is inclined to put her to the test. W[ebster] himself is, with all his jealousy and admiration, a little tired ; he has been lately at Newstead, and wants to go again. I suspected this sudden

penchant, and soon discovered that a foolish nymph of the
Abbey, about whom fortunately I care not, was the attraction.
Now if I wanted to make mischief I could extract much good
perplexity from a proper management of such events; but I
am grown so good, or so indolent, that I shall not avail myself
of so pleasant an opportunity of tormenting mine host, though
he deserves it for poaching. I believe he has hitherto been
unsuccessful, or rather it is too astonishing to be believed.
He proposed to me, with great gravity, to carry him over
there, and I replied with equal candour, that *he* might set
out when he pleased, but that I should remain here to take
care of his household in the interim—a proposition which I
thought very much to the purpose, but which did not seem at
all to his satisfaction. By way of opiate he preached me a
sermon on his wife's good qualities, concluding by an assertion
that in all moral and mortal qualities, she was very like
" Christ ! ! ! " I think the Virgin Mary would have been a more
appropriate typification; but it was the first comparison of
the kind I ever heard, and made me laugh till he was angry,
and then I got out of humour too, which pacified him, and
shortened the panegyric.

Ld Petersham is coming here in a day or two, who will
certainly flirt furiously with L^y F[rances], and I shall have
some comic Iagoism with our little Othello. I should have no
chance with his Desdemona myself, but a more lively and better
dressed and formed personage might, in an innocent way, for
I really believe the girl is a very good, well-disposed wife, and
will do very well if she lives, and he himself don't tease her
into some dislike of her lawful owner.

I passed through Hatfield the night of your *ball*. Suppose
we had jostled at a turnpike ! ! At Bugden I blundered on a
Bishop; the Bishop put me in mind of ye Government—the
Government of the Governed—and the governed of their
indifference towards their governors, which you must have
remarked as to all *parties*. These reflections expectorated as
follows—you know I *never* send you my scribblings—and when
you read these, you will wish I never may:

" 'Tis said *Indifference* marks the present time,
    Then hear the reason—though 'tis told in rhyme—

A king who *can't*, a Prince of Wales who *don't*,
Patriots who *sha'n't*, and Ministers who *won't*,
What matters who are *in* or *out* of place,
The *Mad*, the *Bad*, the *Useless*, or the *Base*? "

You may read the 2nd couplet *so*, if you like,

" A King who *cannot*, and a Prince who don't,
Patriots who would not, ministers who won't."

I am asked to stay for the Doncaster races, but I am not in plight, and am a miserable beau at the best of times; so I shall even return to town, or elsewhere; and in the meantime ever am

Yours, dear Lʸ Mᵉ, B.

P.S.—If you write, address to B[*enne*]*t Street*; were I once gone, I should not wish my letters to travel *here* after me, for fear of *accidents*.

There is a delightful epitaph on Voltaire in Grimm. I read it coming down. The French I should probably misspell, so take it only in bad English—" Here lies the spoilt child of the a world which he spoiled ". This is good, short and true.

TO LADY MELBOURNE   *[London] October 1st, 1813*

MY DEAR Lʸ M.,—You will have received two letters of mine, to atone for my late portentous silence, and this is intended as a further expiation. I have just been dining at Holland House. The Queen is grown thin and gracious, both of which become her royalty. I met Curran [1] there, who electrified me with his imagination, and delighted me with his humour. He is a man of a million. The Irish *when* good are perfect; the little I have seen of him has less *leaven* than any mortal compound I have lately looked into.

---

[1] John Philpot Curran, the Irish patriot, one of the most accomplished orators of his time and a brilliant frequenter of the Holland House coterie. For further impressions of Curran, see *Detached Thoughts*.

To-day I heard from my friend W[ebster] again; his *Countess* is, he says, " inexorable ". What a lucky fellow— happy in his obstacles. In his case I should think them very pleasant; but I don't lay this down as a general proposition. All my prospect of amusement is clouded, for Petersham has sent an excuse; and there will be no one to make him jealous of but the curate and the butler—and I have no thoughts of setting up for myself. I am not exactly cut out for the lady of the mansion; but I think a stray dandy would have a chance of preferment. She evidently expects to be attacked, and seems prepared for a brilliant defence; my character as a roué has gone before me, and my careless and quiet behaviour astonished her so much that I believe she began to think herself ugly, or me blind—if not worse. They seemed surprised at my declining the races in particular; but for this I had good reasons; firstly: I wanted to go elsewhere; secondly: if I had gone, I must have paid some attention to some of them; which is troublesome, unless one has something in memory, or hope to induce it; and then mine host is so marvellous green-eyed that he might have included me in his calenture —which I don't deserve—and probably should not like it a bit better if I did.

I have also reasons for returning there on Sunday, with which they have nothing to do; but if C. takes a suspicious twist that way, let her—it will keep her in darkness; but I hope, however, she won't take a fit of scribbling, as she did to L^y Oxford last year—though Webster's face on the occasion would be quite a comet, and delight me infinitely more than O[xford]'s, which was comic enough.

Friday morn.—Yours arrived. I will answer on the next page.

So—L^dy H[olland] says I am *fattening*, and you say I talk " *nonsense* ". Well—I must fast and unfool again, if possible. But, as Curran told me last night that he had been assured upon oath by half the Court, that " the Prince was *not* at all *corpulent*, that he was stout certainly, but by no means pro-tuberant, or obese ", " there's comfort yet ". As to folly, that's incurable.

" See C. ! *if* I should see C. ! " I hope not, though I am not sure a visit would be so disagreeable as it ought to be.

" I pique myself on constancy ", but it is but a sensitive plant ,and thrives best by itself. Then there is the story of L^y B[essborough]'s novelty, which I am sure she longs to unravel. How your passage on " the kneeling in the *middle* of the room " made me laugh this morning; it certainly was not the centre of gravity—pardon a wretched quibble which I don't often hazard. I did not kneel in the middle of the room; but the first time I saw her this year, she thought proper to fix herself there and turn away her head: and, as one does not kneel exactly for one's own convenience, my genuflexions would have been all lost upon her if she did not perceive them.

To return to the W[ebster]s. I am glad they amaze you; anything that confirms, or extends one's observations on life and character delights me, even when I don't know people—for this reason I would give the world to pass a month with Sheridan, or any lady or gentleman of the old school, and hear them talk every day, and all day of themselves, and acquaintance, and all they have heard and seen in their lives. W[ebster] seems in no present peril. I believe the woman is mercenary; and I happen to know that he can't at present bribe her. I told him that it would be known, and that he must expect reprisals—and what do you think was his answer? " I think any woman fair game, because I can *depend* upon L^y F.'s principles—she can't go wrong, and therefore I may." " Then, why are you jealous of her? " " Because—because—zounds! I am not jealous. Why the devil do you suppose I am? " I then enumerated some very gross symptoms which he had displayed, even before her face, and his servants, which he could not deny; but persisted in his determination to add to his " bonnes fortunes ";—it is a strange being! When I came home in 1811, he was always saying, " B., do marry— it is the happiest ", etc. The first thing he said on my arrival at A[ston] was, " B., whatever you do, *don't marry* "; which, considering he had an unmarried sister-in-law in the house, was a very *un*necessary precaution.

Every now and then he has a fit of fondness, and kisses her hand before his guests; which she receives with the most lifeless indifference, which struck me more than if she had appeared pleased, or annoyed. Her brother told me last year that she married to get rid of her family (who are ill-tempered), and had not been *out* two months; so that, to use a fox-hunting phrase, she was "killed in covert".

You have enough of them, and me for ye present.

Y^{rs} ever, B.

P.S. I do not wish to know ye person's name, but to whom is the likeness—to *me* or to *her*?

TO THOMAS MOORE   *October 2, 1813*

You have not answered some six letters of mine. This, therefore, is my penultimate. I will write to you once more, but, after that—I swear by all the saints—I am silent and supercilious. I have met Curran at Holland House—he beats every body;—his imagination is beyond human, and his humour (it is difficult to define what is wit) perfect. Then he has fifty faces, and twice as many voices, when he mimics—I never met his equal. Now, were I a woman, and eke a virgin, that is the man I should make my Scamander. He is quite fascinating. Remember, I have met him but once; and you, who have known him long, may probably deduct from my panegyric. I almost fear to meet him again, lest the impression should be lowered. He talked a great deal about you—a theme never tiresome to me, nor any body else that I know. What a variety of expression he conjures into that naturally not very fine countenance of his! He absolutely changes it entirely. I have done—for I can't describe him, and you know him. On Sunday I return to Aston, where I shall not be far from you. Perhaps I shall hear from you in the mean time. Good night.

Saturday morn.—Your letter has cancelled all my anxieties. I did *not suspect* you in *earnest*. Modest again! Because I don't do a very shabby thing, it seems, I "don't fear your competition". If it were reduced to an alternative of preference, I *should* dread you, as much as Satan does Michael. But is there not room enough in our respective regions? Go on—it will soon be my turn to forgive. To-day I dine with Mackintosh and Mrs. *Stale*—as John Bull may be pleased to

denominate Corinne—whom I saw last night, at Covent
Garden, yawning over the humour of Falstaff.

The reputation of "gloom", if one's friends are not included in the *reputants*, is of great service; as it saves one from
a legion of impertinents, in the shape of common-place acquaintance. But thou know'st I can be a right merry and
conceited fellow, and rarely *larmoyant*. Murray shall reinstate
your line forthwith. I believe the blunder in the motto was
mine;—and yet I have, in general, a memory for *you*, and am
sure it was rightly printed at first.

I do "blush" very often, if I may believe Ladies H. and
M.;—but luckily, at present, no one sees me. Adieu.

TO LADY MELBOURNE   *Aston Hall, Rotherham,*
                                     October 5th, 1813

MY DEAR L^Y M.,—W. has lost his Countess, his time and
his temper (I would advise anyone who finds the *last* to return
it immediately; it is of no use to any but the owner). L^y
F[rances] has lost Petersham, for the present at least; the
other sister, as I have said before, has lost Ld Bury; and I
have nobody to lose—*here*, at least—and am not very anxious
to find one. Here be two friends of the family, besides your
slave: a Mr. Westcombe—very handsome, but silly—and a
Mr. Agar—frightful, but facetious. The whole party are out
in carriages—a species of amusement from which I always
avert; and, consequently, declined it to-day; it is very well
with two, but not beyond a *duet*. I think, being bumped
about between two or more of one's acquaintance intolerable.
W[ebster] grows rather intolerable, too. He is out of humour
with my *Italian* books (Dante and Alfieri, and some others as
harmless as ever wrote), and requests that sa femme may not
see them, because, forsooth, it is a language which doth
infinite damage!! and because I enquired after the Stanhopes,
our mutual acquaintance, he *answers* me by another *question*,
"Pray, do you enquire after *my* wife of others in the same way?"
so that you see my Virtue is its own reward—for never, in
word or deed, did I speculate upon his spouse; nor did I ever

see much in her to encourage either hope, or much fulfilment of hope, supposing I had any. She is pretty, but not surpassing —too thin, and not very animated; but good-tempered— and a something interesting enough in her manner and figure; but I never should think of her, nor anyone else, if left to my own cogitations, as I have neither the patience nor presumption to advance till met half-way. The other two pay her ten times more attention, and, of course, are more attended to. I really believe he is bilious, and suspects something extra- ordinary from my nonchalance; at all events, he has hit upon the wrong person. I can't help laughing to you, but he will soon make me very serious with him, and then he will come to his senses again. The oddest thing is, that he wants me to stay with him some time; which I am not much inclined to do, unless the gentleman transfers his fretfulness to someone else. I have written to you so much lately, you will be glad to be spared from any further account of the " Blunderhead family ".

Ever y^{rs}, my dear L^y M^e, B.

TO LADY MELBOURNE   *October 8th, 1813*

My dear L^y M.,—I have volumes, but neither time nor space. I have already trusted too deeply to hesitate now; besides, for certain reasons, you will not be sorry to hear that I am anything but what I was. Well then, to begin, and first, a word of mine host.—He has lately been talking *at*, rather than *to*, me before the party (with the exception of the women) in a tone, which as I never use it myself, I am not particularly disposed to tolerate in others. What *he* may do with impunity, it seems, but not suffer, till at last I told him that the whole of his argument involved the interesting contradiction that " he might love where he liked, but that no one else might like what he ever thought proper to love ", a doctrine which, as the learned Partridge observed, contains a " non sequitur " from which I, for one, begged leave as a general proposition to dissent. This nearly produced a scene with me, as well as another guest, who seemed to admire my sophistry the most of the two; and as it was after dinner, and debating time, might have ended in more than wineshed, but that the devil, for some wise purpose of his own, thought proper to restore good humour, which has not as yet been further infringed.

In these last few days I have had a good deal of conversation with an amiable person, whom (as we deal in *letters* and initials only) we will denominate *Ph.*[1] Well, these things are dull in detail. Take it once, I have made love, and if I am to believe mere *words* (for there we have hitherto stopped), it is returned. I must tell you the place of declaration, however, a billiard room. I did not, as C. says: " kneel in the middle of the room ", but, like Corporal Trim to the Nun, " I made a speech ", which, as you might not listen to it with the same patience, I shall not transcribe. We were before on very amicable terms, and I remembered being asked an odd question, " how a woman who liked a man could inform him of it when he did not perceive it ". I also observed that we went on with our game (of billiards) without *counting the hazards*; and supposed that, as mine certainly were not, the thoughts of the other party also were not exactly occupied by what was our ostensible pursuit. Not quite, though pretty well satisfied with my progress, I took a very imprudent step with pen and paper, in tender and tolerably turned *prose* periods (no poetry even when in earnest). Here were risks, certainly: first, how to convey, then how would it be received? It was received, however, and deposited not very far from the heart which I wished it to reach when, who should enter the room but the person who ought at that moment to have been in the Red Sea, if Satan had any civility. But *she* kept her countenance, and the paper; and I my composure as well as I could. It was a risk, and *all* had been lost by failure; but then recollect how much more I had to gain by the reception, if not declined, and how much one always hazards to obtain anything worth having. My billet prospered, it did more, it even (I am this moment interrupted by the *Marito*, and write this before him, he has brought me a political pamphlet in MS. to decypher and applaud, I shall content myself with the last; oh, he is gone again), my billet produced an *answer*, a very unequivocal one too, but a little too much about virtue, and indulgence of attachment in some sort of

[1] Lady Frances Webster.

etherial process, in which the soul is principally concerned, which I don't very well understand, being a bad metaphysician ; but one generally *ends* and *begins* with platonism, and, as my proselyte is only twenty, there is time enough to materialize. I hope nevertheless this spiritual system won't last long, and at any rate must make the experiment. I remember my last case was the reverse, as Major O'Flaherty recommends, " we fought first and explained afterwards ".

This is the present state of things : much mutual profession, a good deal of melancholy, which, I am sorry to say, was remarked by " the Moor ", and as much love as could well be made, considering the time, place and circumstances.

I need not say that the folly and petulance of [Webster] has tended to all this. If a man is not contented with a pretty woman, and not only runs after any little country girl he meets with, but absolutely boasts of it ; he must not be surprised if others admire that which he knows not how to value. Besides, he literally provoked, and goaded me into it, by something not unlike bullying, *indirect* to be sure, but tolerably obvious : " he *would* do this, and he would do that ", " if any man ", etc., etc., and *he* thought that every " woman " was *his* lawful prize, nevertheless. Oons ! who is this strange monopolist? It is odd enough, but on other subjects he is like other people, on this he seems infatuated. If he had been rational, and not prated of his pursuits, I should have gone on very well, as I did at Middleton. Even now, I shan't quarrel with him if I can help it ; but one or two of his speeches have blackened the blood about my heart, and curdled the milk of kindness. If put to the proof, I shall behave like other people, I presume.

I have heard from A[nnabella], but her letter to me is *melancholy*, about her old friend Miss My's departure, etc., etc. I wonder who will have her at last ; her letter to you is *gay* you say ; that to me must have been written at the same time ; the little demure nonjuror !

I wrote to C[aroline] the other day, for I was afraid she might repeat last year's epistle, and make it *circular* among my friends.

Good evening, I am now going to *billiards*.

Ever y^{rs}, B.

P.S. 6 o'clock.—This business is growing serious, and I think *Platonism* in some peril. There has been very nearly a scene, almost an *hysteric*, and really without cause, for I was conducting myself with (to me) very irksome decorum. Her expressions astonish me, so young and cold as she appeared. But these professions must end as usual, and *would* I think *now*, had " l'occasion " been *not* wanting. Had anyone come in during the *tears*, and consequent consolation, all had been spoiled; we must be more cautious, or less larmoyante.

P.S. second, 10 o'clock.—I write to you, just escaped from claret and vocification on G—d knows what paper. My landlord is a rare gentleman. He has just proposed to me a bet that *he*, for a certain sum, " wins any given *woman*, against any given *homme* including *all friends* present ", which I declined with becoming deference to him, and the rest of the company. Is not this, at the moment, a perfect comedy? I forgot to mention that on his entrance yesterday during the letter scene, it reminded me so much of an awkward passage in " The Way to Keep Him " between Lovemore, Sir Bashful, and my Lady, that, embarrassing as it was, I could hardly help laughing. I hear his voice in the passage; he wants me to go to a ball at Sheffield, and is talking to me as I write. Good night. I am in the act of praising his pamphlet.

I don't half like your story of *Corinne*, some day I will tell you why, if I can, but at present, good night.

TO LADY MELBOURNE   *Newstead Abbey, October 10th, 1813*

MY DEAR L^Y M.,—I write to you from the melancholy mansion of my fathers, where I am dull as the longest deceased of my progenitors. I hate reflection on irrevocable things, and won't now turn sentimentalist. W[ebster] alone accompanied me here (I return to-morrow to [Aston]). He is now sitting opposite; and between us are red and white Cham-[pagn]e, Burgundy, two sorts of Claret, and lighter vintages, the relics of my youthful cellar, which is yet in formidable number and famous order. But I leave the wine to him, and prefer conversing soberly with you.

Ah! if you knew what a quiet Mussulman life (except in wine) I led here for a few years. But no matter.

Yesterday I sent you a long letter, and must recur to the same subject which is uppermost in my thoughts. I am as much astonished, but I hope not so much mistaken, as Lord Ogleby at the dénouement or rather commencement of the last week. It has changed my views, my wishes, my hopes, my everything, and will furnish you with additional proof of my weakness. Mine guest (late host) has just been congratulating himself on possessing a partner without *passion*. I don't know, and cannot yet speak with certainty, but I never yet saw more decisive preliminary symptoms.

As I am apt to take people at their word, on receiving my answer, that whatever the weakness of her heart might be, I should never derive further proof of it than the confession, instead of pressing the point, I told her that I was willing to be hers on her own terms, and should never attempt to infringe upon the conditions. I said this without pique, and believing her perfectly in earnest for the time; but in the midst of our mutual professions, or, to use her own expression, " more than mutual ", she bursts into an agony of crying, and at such a time, and in such a place, as rendered such a scene particularly perilous to both—her sister in the next room, and —— not far off. Of course I said and did almost everything proper on the occasion, and fortunately we restored sunshine in time to prevent anyone from perceiving the cloud that had darkened our horizon. She says she is convinced that my own declaration was produced solely because I perceived her previous penchant, which by-the-bye, as I think I said to you before, I neither perceived nor expected. I really did not suspect her of a predilection for anyone, and even now in public, with the exception of those little indirect, yet mutually understood—I don't know how and it is unnecessary to name, or describe them—her conduct is as coldly correct as her still, fair, Mrs. L[amb]-like[1] aspect. She, however, managed to give me a note and to receive another, and a ring before [Webster]'s very face, and yet she is a thorough devotee, and takes prayers, morning and evening, besides being measured for a new Bible once a quarter.

[1] Mrs. George Lamb, Lady Caroline's sister-in-law.

The only alarming thing is that [Webster] complains of her aversion from being beneficial to population and posterity. If this is an invariable maxim, I shall lose my labour. Be this as it may, she owns to more than I ever heard from any woman within the time, and I shan't take [Webster]'s word any more for her feelings than I did for that celestial comparison, which I once mentioned. I think her eye, her change of colour, and the trembling of her hand, and above all her devotion, tell a different tale.

Good night. We return to-morrow, and now I drink your health; you are my only correspondent, and I believe friend.

Ever yours, B.

TO LADY MELBOURNE   *[Aston] October 11th, 1813*

MY DEAR L^{DY} M.,—C[aroline] is angry with me for having written by the *post* not a *very cold* letter, but below (it seems) her freezing point; pray say something—anything to prevent any of the old absurdities. Her letter arrived during my absence at N[ewstead] with a never sufficiently to be confounded seal, with C. at full length on the malignant wax; this must have been to answer the purpose it effected; at any rate, the person who opened the *bag* was the last I wished to see the *impression*, and it is not yet *effaced*, but it shall be—this is not to be endured. That my " chienne of a star ", as Captain Raggado says, should have produced such an incident, and at such a time!

I have written to you so much, and so frequently, that you must be sick of the sight of my scrawls. I believe all the *stars* are no better than they should be. [Webster] is on the verge of a precious scrape, his quondam *tutor!* and ally, who has done him some not very reputable services since his marriage, writing, I believe his billets, and assisting him to those to whom they were addressed, being now discarded, threatens a development, etc. [Webster] consults me on the subject! Of this I shall take no advantage in another quarter, however convenient; if I gain my point it shall be as fairly as such things will admit. It is odd enough that his name has never hitherto been taken in vain by her or me. I have told him that if the discovery is inevitable, his best way is to anticipate it, and sue for an act of indemnity : if she likes him she will forgive, and if she don't like him, it don't matter whether she does or no.

From me she shall never hear of it.

It is three in the morning, and I cannot rest, but I must try. I have been at N[ewstead] and between that and this my mind is in a state of chaotic inaction ; but you won't pity me, and I don't deserve it. Was there ever such a slave to impulse.

As y^{rs} ever, B.

Monday Afternoon

I am better to-day, but not much advanced. I began the week so well that I thought the conclusion would have been more decisive. But the topography of this house is not the most favourable. I wonder how my father managed ; but he had it not till L^y Carmarthen [1] came with it too. We shall be at Newstead again, the whole party for a week, in a few days, and there the genii of the place will be perhaps more propitious. *He* haunts me—here he is again, and here are a party of purple stockings come to dine. Oh, that accursed pamphlet ! I have not read it ; what shall I say to the author, now in the room? Thank the stars which I yesterday abused, he is diverted by the mirror opposite, and is now surveying with great complacency himself—he is gone !

Your letter has arrived, but it is evidently written before my last three have been delivered. Adieu, for the present. I must dress, and have got to *sheer* one of those precious curls on which you say I set so high a value ; and I cannot, and *would* not, play the same pass you may laughingly remember on a similar occasion with C. My proselyte is so young a beginner that you won't wonder at these exchanges and mummeries. You are right, she is " very pretty ", and not so inanimate as I imagined, and must at least be allowed an excellent taste ! !

---

[1] Captain John Byron's first wife. Divorced by Lord Carmarthen, she married Captain Byron and became the mother of Augusta.

10 o'clock

Nearly a scene (always *nearly*) at dinner. There is a Lady Sitwell, a wit and blue; and, what is more to the purpose, a dark, tall, fierce-looking, conversable personage. As it is usual to separate the women at table, I was under the necessity of placing myself between her and the sister, and was seated, and in the agonies of conjecture whether the dish before me required carving, when my little Platonist exclaimed, " Ld Byron, *this* is your place ". I stared, and before I had time to reply, she repeated, looking like C. when *gentle* (for she is very unlike that fair creature when angry), " Ld Byron, change places with Catherine ". I did, and very willingly, though awkwardly; but " the Moor " (mine host) roared out, " B[yron], that is the most ungallant thing I ever beheld ". Lady Catherine by way of mending matters, answered, " Did you not hear Frances ask him? " *He* has looked like the Board of *Green* Cloth ever since, and is now mustering wine and spirits for a lecture to her, and a squabble with me; he had better let it alone, for I am in a pestilent humour at this present writing, and shall certainly disparage his eternal " *pamphlet* ".

Good even. I solicit your good wishes in all good deeds, and your occasional remembrance.

TO LADY MELBOURNE   *October 13th, 1813*

My dear L^y M.,—You must pardon the quantity of my letters, and much of the *quality* also, but I have really no other *confidential* correspondent on earth, and much to say which may call forth the advice which has so often been to me of essential service. Anything, you will allow, is better than the *last*; and I cannot exist without some object of attachment. You will laugh at my perpetual *changes*, but recollect, the circumstances which have broken off the last three and don't exactly attribute their conclusion to caprice. I think you will at least admit, whatever C[aroline] may assert, that I did not use her ill, though I find *her own* story, even in this part of the world, to be the *genuine* narrative; as to L^y O[xford], that I did to please you, and luckily, finding it pleasant to myself also, and very useful to C., it might have lasted longer, but for the voyage. I spare you the third.

I am so spoilt by intellectual *drams* that I begin to believe that *danger* and *difficulty* render these things more piquant to my taste. As far as the *former* goes, C. might have suited me very well, but though we may admire *drams*, nobody is particularly fond of aqua fortis; at least, I should have liked it a *little diluted*, the liquid I believe which is now slowly mingling in my cup. In the meantime, let us laugh while we can, for I see no reason why you should be tormented with sentimental or solid sorrows of your acquaintance. I think you will allow that I have as little of that affectation as any person of similar pursuits.

I mentioned to you yesterday a laughable occurrence at dinner. This morning *he* burst forth with a homily upon the subject to the *two* and myself, instead of taking us separately (like the last of the *Horatii* with the *Curiatii*). You will easily suppose with such odds he had the worst of it, and the satisfaction of being laughed at into the bargain. Serious as I am—or seem,—I really cannot frequently keep my countenance : yesterday, *before my face*, they disputed about their apartments at N[ewstead], *she* insisting that her sister should share her room, and he very properly, but heinously out of place, maintaining, and proving to his own satisfaction, that none but husbands have any legal claim to divide their spouse's pillow. You may suppose, notwithstanding the ludicrous effect of the scene, I felt and looked a little uncomfortable ; this she must have seen—for, of course, I said not a word—and turning round at the close of the dialogue, she whispered, " N'importe, this is all nothing ", an ambiguous sentence which I am puzzled to translate ; but, as it was meant to console me, I was very glad to hear it, though quite unintelligible.

As far as I can pretend to judge of her disposition and character—I will say, of course, I am partial—she is, you know, very handsome, and very gentle, though sometimes decisive ; fearfully romantic, and singularly warm in her *affections* ; but I should think of a *cold* temperament, yet I have my doubts on that point, too ; accomplished (as all decently educated women are), and clever, though her style a little too *German* ;

no dashing nor desperate talker, but never—and I have watched in *mixed* conversation—saying a silly thing (*duet dialogues* in course between young and Platonic people must be varied with a little chequered absurdity); good tempered (always excepting L^y O[xford], which was, outwardly, the *best* I ever beheld), and jealous as *myself*—the ne plus ultra of green-eyed monstrosity; seldom abusing other people, but listening to it with great patience. These qualifications, with an unassuming and sweet voice, and very soft manner, constitute the *bust* (all I can yet pretend to model) of my present idol.

You, who know me and my weakness so well, will not be surprised when I say that I am totally absorbed in this passion —that I am even ready to take a *flight* if necessary, and as she says, " We cannot part ", it is no impossible dénouement— though as yet *one* of us at least does not think of it. W. will probably want to cut my throat, which would not be a difficult task, for I trust I should not return the fire of a man I had injured, though I could not refuse him the pleasure of trying me as a target. But I am not sure I shall not have more work in that way. There is a friend in the house who looks a little suspicious; he can only conjecture, but if he *Iagonizes*, or finds, or makes mischief, let him look to it. To W[ebster] I am decidedly wrong, yet he almost provoked me into it—*he* loves other women; at least he follows them; *she* evidently did not love him, even before. I came here with no plan, no intention of the kind as my former letters will prove to *you* (the only person to whom I care about proving it) and have not yet been here *ten* days—a week yesterday, on recollection: you cannot be more astonished than I am how, and why all this has happened.

All my correspondences, and every other business, are at a standstill; I have not answered A., no, nor B., nor C., nor any *initial* except your own, you will wish me to be less troublesome to *that one*, and I shall now begin to draw at longer dates upon y^r patience.

Ever yours, B.

P.S.—*always P.S.* I begged you to pacify C[aroline], who is pettish about what she calls a *cold* letter; it was not so, but she evidently has been too long quiet; she threatens me with grow-

ing very bad, and says that if so, " I am the sole cause ". This I
should regret, but she is in no danger ; no one in his senses will
run the risk, till her late exploits are forgotten. Her last I
shall not answer ; it was very silly in me to write at all ; but
I did it with the best intention, like the Wiseacre in " The
Rovers ",—" Let us by a song conceal our purposes ", you
remember in the " Anti-Jacobin ". I have gone through a
catechism about her, without abusing or betraying her ; this
is not exactly the way to recommend myself ; I have generally
found that the *successor* likes to hear both of the last regnante.
But I really did not, notwithstanding the temptation.

TO LADY MELBOURNE   *October 14th, 1813*

But this is " le premier pas ", my dear L^y M., at least I
think so, and perhaps you will be of my opinion when you
consider the *age*, the *country*, and the short time since such *pas*
became probable ; I believe little but " l'occasion manque ",
and to that many things are tending. He [Webster] is a little
indirect blusterer who neither knows what he would have, nor
what he deserves. To-day at breakfast (I was too late for the
scene) he attacked *both* the girls in such a manner, no one
knew why, or wherefore, that one had left the room, and the
other had half a mind to leave the house ; this too before
servants, and the other guest! On my appearance the storm
blew over, but the narrative was detailed to me subsequently
by one of the sufferers. You may be sure that I shall not
" consider *self* ", nor create a squabble while it can be avoided ;
on the contrary I have been endeavouring to serve him essentially (except on the *one* point, and there I was goaded into
it by his own absurdities), and to extricate him from some
difficulties of various descriptions. Of course all obligations
are cancelled between two persons in our circumstances, but
that I shall not dwell upon ; of the other I shall try to make an
" affaire réglée " ; if that don't succeed we shall probably go
off together ; but *she* only shall make me resign the hope. As
for him he may convert his antlers into *powder-horns* and
welcome, and such he has announced as his intention when

" *any* man at *any* time, etc. etc. ", " he would not give *him* a chance, but exterminate *him* without suffering defence ". Do you know I was fool enough to lose my temper at this circuitous specimen of Bobadil jealousy, and tell him and the other (there are a brace, lion and jackal) that *I*, not their roundabout *he*, desired no better than to put these " epithets of war ", with which their sentences were " horribly stuffed ", to the proof. This was silly and suspicious, but my liver could bear it no longer. My poor little *Helen* tells me that there never was such a *temper* and *talents*, that the marriage was *not* one of attachment, that—in short, *my* descriptions fade before hers, all foolish fellows are alike, but this has a patent for his cap and bells.

The scene between Sir B. and Lovemore I remember, but the one I alluded to was the letter of Lovemore to L^y Constant —there is no comedy after all like real life. We have progressively improved into a less spiritual species of tenderness, but the seal is not yet fixed, though the wax is preparing for the impression. There *ought* to be an excellent *occasion* to-morrow; but who can command circumstances? The most we can do is to avail ourselves of them.

Publicly I have been cautious enough, and actually declined a dinner where they went, because I thought something *intelligible* might be seen or suspected. I regretted, but regret it less, for I hear one of the Fosters was there, and they be cousins and gossips of our good friends the D.'s. Good-night. Do *you fear* to write to *me*? Are *these* epistles, or your answers in any peril *here*? I must remember, however, the advice of a sage personage to me while abroad—take it in their English— " Remember, milor, that *delicaci* ensure every succès."

Y^rs ever, B.

TO LADY MELBOURNE *Newstead Abbey, October 17th, 1813*

MY DEAR LADY M.,—The whole party are here—and now to my narrative. But first I must tell you that I am rather unwell, owing to a folly of last night. About midnight, after deep and drowsy potations, I took it into my head to empty my *skull cup*, which holds rather better than a bottle of claret, at *one draught*, and nearly died the death of Alexander—which I shall be content to do when I have achieved his conquests. I had just sense enough left to feel that I was not fit to join the ladies, and went to bed, where, my valet tells me, that I was first convulsed, and afterwards so motionless, that he thought, " Good night to Marmion ". I don't know how I came to do so very silly a thing ; but I believe my guests were boasting, and " company, villainous company, hath been the spoil of me ". I detest drinking in general, and beg your pardon for this excess. I *can't* do so any more.

To my theme. You were right. I have been a little too sanguine as to the *conclusion*—but hear. One day, left entirely to ourselves, was nearly fatal—another such *victory*, and with Pyrrhus we were lost—it came to this. " I am entirely at your *mercy*. I own it. I give myself up to you. I am not *cold*— whatever I seem to others ; but I know that I cannot bear the reflection hereafter. Do not imagine that these are mere words. I tell you the truth—now act as you will." Was I wrong? I spared her. There was a something so very peculiar in her manner—a kind of mild decision—no scene—not even a struggle ; but still I know not what, that convinced me that she was serious. It was not the mere " *No* ", which one has heard forty times before, and always with the same accent ; but the *tone*, and the aspect—yet I sacrificed much—the hour *two* in the morning—away—the Devil whispering that it was mere *verbiage*, etc. And yet I know not whether I can regret it—she seems so very thankful for my forbearance—a proof, at least, that she was not playing merely the usual decorous reluctance, which is sometimes so tiresome on these occasions.

You ask if I am prepared to go " all lengths ". If you mean by " all lengths " anything including duel, or divorce? I answer, *Yes*. I love her. If I did not, and much too, I should have been more selfish on the occasion before mentioned. I have offered to go away with her, and her answer, whether sincere or not, is " that on *my account* she declines it ". In the meantime we are all as wretched as possible ; he scolding on *account* of *unaccountable* melancholy ; the sister very suspicious, but rather amused—the friend very suspicious too (why I know not), not at all amused—il Marito something like Lord

Chesterfield in De Grammont, putting on a martial physiog-
nomy, prating with his worthy ally; swearing at servants,
sermonizing both sisters; and buying sheep; but never
quitting her side now; so that we are in despair. *I* am very
feverish, restless, and silent, as indeed seems to be the tacit
agreement of everyone else. In short I can foresee nothing—
it may end in nothing; but here are half a dozen persons very
much occupied, and two, if not three, in great perplexity;
and, as far as I can judge, so we must continue.

She *don't* and *won't* live with him, and they have been so
far separate for a long time; therefore I have nothing to answer
for on that point. Poor thing—she is either the most *artful* or
artless of her age (20) I ever encountered. She *owns* to so
much, and perpetually says, " Rather than you should be
angry ", or " Rather than you should like anyone else, I will
do whatever you please "; " I won't speak to this, that, or the
other if you dislike it ", and throws, or seems to throw, herself
so entirely upon my discretion in every respect, that it disarms
me quite; but I am really wretched with the perpetual conflict with myself. Her health is so very delicate; she is so thin
and pale, and seems to have lost her appetite so entirely, that I
doubt her living much longer. This is also her own opinion.
But these fancies are common to all who are not very happy;
if she were once my wife, or likely to be so, a warm climate
should be the first resort, nevertheless, for her recovery.

The most perplexing—and yet I can't prevail upon myself
to give it up—is the caressing system. In her it appears perfectly childish, and I do think innocent; but it really puzzles
all the Scipio about me to confine myself to the laudable
portion of these endearments.

What a cursed situation I have thrust myself into! Potiphar
(it used to be O[xford]'s name) putting some stupid question
to me the other day, I told him that I rather admired the
sister, and what does he? but tell her this; and his *wife* too,
who a little too hastily asked him " if he was mad? " which
put him to demonstration that a man ought not to be asked if
he was mad, for relating that a friend thought his wife's sister
a pretty woman. Upon this topic he held forth with great
fervour for a customary period. I wish he had a quinsey.

Tell L[or]d H[ollan]d that Clarke is the name, and Craven

Street (No. forgotten) the residence—may be heard of at
Trin. Coll.—excellent man—able physician—shot a friend in
a duel (about his sister) and I believe killed him professionally
afterwards. Ld H. may have him for self or friends. I don't
know where I am going—my mind is a chaos. I always am
setting all upon single stakes, and this is one. Your story of the
Frenchman Matta, in " Grammont," and the Marquis.
Heigh ho ! Good night. Address to Aston.

                                                    Ever yrs., B.

P.S.—My stay is quite uncertain—a moment may overturn
everything; but you shall hear—happen what may—nothing
or something.

TO LADY MELBOURNE   *Northampton, October 19th, 1813*

MY DEAR LADY M.,—[Webster] and I are thus far on our
way to town—he was seized with a sudden fit of friendship, and
would accompany me—or rather, finding that some business
could not conveniently be done without me, he thought proper
to assume ye appearance of it. He is not exactly the companion
I wished to take ; it is really laughable when you think of the
other—a kind of pig in a poke. Nothing but squabbles between
them for the last three days, and at last he rose up with a solemn
and mysterious air, and spake, " L^y [Frances], you have at
last rendered an explanation necessary between me and Ld.
B[yron], which must take place ". I stared, and knowing that
it is the custom of country gentlemen (if Farquhar is correct)
to apprize their moieties of such intentions, and being also a
little out of humour and conscience, I thought a crisis must
ensue, and answered very quietly that " he would find me in
such a room at his leisure ready to hear, and reply ". " Oh ! "
says he, " I shall choose my own time." I wondered that he
did not choose his *own* house, too, but walked away, and
waited for him. All this mighty prelude led only to what he
called an explanation for *my satisfaction*, that whatever appearances were, *he* and *she* were on the very best terms, that she
loved him so much, and he her, it was impossible not to dis-
agree upon *tender* points, and for fear a man who, etc., etc.,

should suppose that marriage was not the happiest of all possible estates, he had taken this resolution of never quarrelling without letting me know that he was the best husband, and most fortunate person in existence. I told him he had fully convinced me, that it was utterly impossible people who liked each other could behave with more interesting suavity—and so on. Yesterday morning, on our going (I pass over the scene, which shook me, I assure you), " B.," quoth he, " I owe to you the most unhappy moments of my life ". I begged him to tell me how, that I might either sympathize, or put him out of his pain. " Don't you see how the poor girl *doats* on me " (he replied) ; " when I quit her but for a week, as you perceive, she is absolutely overwhelmed, and you stayed so long, and I necessarily for you, that she is in a worse state than I ever saw her in before, even before we married ! "

Here we are—I could not return to A[ston] unless he had asked me—it is true he did, but in such a manner as I should not accept. What will be the end, I know not. I have left everything to *her*, and would have rendered all further *plots* superfluous by the most conclusive step ; but she wavered, and escaped. Perhaps so have I—at least it is as well to think so— yet it is not over.

Whatever I may feel, you know me too well to think I shall plague my friends with long faces or elegies.

My dear Lady M., Ever Yours, B.

TO LADY MELBOURNE   *October 21st, 1813*

MY DEAR L^Y M.,—You may well be surprised, but I had more reasons than one or two. Either [Webster] had taken it into his notable head, or wished to put it into mine, aye, and worse still, into ye girls, also ; that I was a pretendant to the *hand* of the sister of " the Lady " whom I had nearly—but no matter—(to continue Archer's speech with the variation of one word) " 'tis a cursed *fortnight's* piece of work, and there's an end ". This brilliant notion, besides widening ye breach between him and me, did not add to the harmony of the two females ; at least my idol was not pleased with the prospect of any transfer of incense to another altar. She was so unguarded, after telling me too fifty times to " take care of Catherine ", " that she could conceal nothing, etc., etc.", as to give me a very unequivocal proof of her own imprudence, in a carriage —(dusk to be sure) before her face—and yet with all this, and much more, she was the most tenacious personage either from fear, or weakness, or delicate health, or G—d knows what, that with the vigilance of no less than three Arguses in addition, it was utterly impossible, save once, to be decisive—and then— tears and tremors and prayers, which I am not yet old enough to find piquant in such cases, prevented me from making her wretched.   I do detest everything which is not perfectly mutual, and any subsequent reproaches (as I know by one former long ago bitter experience) would heap coals of fire upon my head. Do you remember what Rousseau says to somebody, " If you would know that you are beloved, watch your lover when he leaves you "—to me the most pleasing moments have generally been, when there is nothing more to be required ; in short, the subsequent repose without satiety— which Lewis never dreamed of in that poem of his, " Desire and Pleasure "—when you are secure of the past, yet without regret or disappointment ; of this there was no prospect with her, she had so much more dread of the d—l, than gratitude for his kindness ; and I am not yet sufficiently in his good graces to indulge my own passions at the certain misery of another. Perhaps after all, I was her dupe—if so—I am the dupe also of the few good feelings I could ever boast of, but here perhaps I am my own dupe too, in attributing to a good motive what may be quite otherwise.

[Webster] is a most extraordinary person ; he has just left me, and a snuff-box with a flaming inscription, after squabbling with me for these last ten days ! and I too, have been of some real service to *him*,[1] which I merely mention to mark the in-consistency of human nature. I have brought off a variety of foolish trophies (foolish indeed without victory), such as epistles, and lockets, which look as if she were in earnest ; but she would not go off *now*, nor render going off unnecessary. Am I not candid to own my want of success, when I might have assumed the airs of an " aimable Vainqueur "? but that

---

[1] Byron had lent Webster £1000.

is so paltry and so common—without cause, too; and what I hear, and see every day, that I would not, even to gain the point I have missed. I assure you no one knows but you one particle of this business, and you always must know everything concerning me. It is hard if I may not have one friend. Believe me, none will ever be so valued, and none ever was so trusted, by

Yours ever, B.

TO LADY MELBOURNE   *November 22nd, 1813*

My dear L^y M.,—C[aroline] has at last done a very good-natured thing; she sent me Holmes's picture for a *friend leaving England*, to which friend it is now making the best of its way. You do not go to M[iddleton] till 28th, and I shall procrastinate accordingly. Yesterday the Lady Ossulstone sent for me to complain of you *all*. We had met at Ld Holland's the night before, and she asserted that the " extreme gravity of my countenance " made her and Ld O. believe that I had some whim about that slip of the pen-*knife* of *C.'s* and the consequent rumours, etc., etc., and some resentment about her in particular; to all of which I pleaded ignorance and innocence. She says Lady Blarney is a very noxious person, and hates her, and that none of you have taken the least notice of her since; that she is the most *discreet* of women, to prove which she produced an epistle of L^y Somebody's, *wondering* (it was but *three* hours after) she had not *already* written a full and true account of it to her!! I thought I should have laughed in her pretty black face—and, in short, we are all very repulsive sort of persons, and have not behaved well to her, nor anybody else. Remember all *this* (like all our *this*-es) is *entre nous*; and so there is an end of the matter. We had had a kind of squabble at the Argyle, which I could not help tormenting her a little by reminding her, not of *that*, but that evening, when we were all wrong-paired. *She* wanted to sit by Mildmay at supper, and I wanted to have been next that Kashmeer Butterfly of the " Blues "—Lady Charlemont—or in short, anybody but a person who had serious concerns to think of. Everybody else was coupled much in the same way; in short, Noah's ark *upset* had been but a type of the *pairing* of our supper-table. L^y Holland and I go on very well; her *unqualified* praises of you, proving their *sincerity!* She is the first woman I ever heard praise another *entirely*. L^y B[essborough] had better let us remain undisturbed, for if L^y H[olland] thinks that it annoys her there will be no end to ye intimacy. I have taken the half-weeks (3 days in each) of Lord Salisbury's box at Covent Garden, and there, when C. is in town, we can always talk for an hour on emergency.

The occasional oddity of Ph.'s letters has amused me much. The simplicity of her cunning, and her exquisite reasons. She vindicates her treachery to [Webster] thus : after condemning deceit in general, and hers in particular, she says : " but then remember it is to deceive ' un marito ', and to prevent all the unpleasant consequences, etc., etc."; and she says this in perfect persuasion that she has a full conception of the " fitness of things ", and the " beauty of virtue ", and " the social compact ", as Philosopher Square has it. Again, she desires me to write to *him kindly*, for she believes he cares for nobody but *me!* Besides, she will then hear *of* when she can't hear *from* me. Is not all this a comedy? Next to Ld Ossulstone's *voucher* for her discretion, it has enlivened my ethical studies on the human mind beyond 50 volumes. How admirably we accommodate our reasons to our wishes !

She concludes by denominating that respectable man *Argus*, a very irreverent appellation. If we can both hold out till spring, perhaps he may have occasion for his optics. After all " it is to deceive un marito ". Does not this expression convey to you the strongest mixture of right and wrong? A really guilty person could not have used it, or rather they would, *but* in different words. I find she has not the *but*, and that makes much difference if you consider it. The experienced would have said it is " *only* deceiving *him* ", thinking of themselves. She makes a *merit* of it on his account and mine.

The Dutch have taken Holland, and got Bernadotte and Orange, the Stork and King Log at once, in their froggery.[1]

Ever y^rs, B.

[1] In 1813 the Dutch revolted against Napoleon and declared their independence, electing the Prince of Orange as their constitutional sovereign. Bernadotte, King of Sweden, also joined the allies.

I must quote to you correctly—" How easily mankind are deceived. *May he be always deceived!* and I, alas, am the base instrument of deception ; but in this instance *concealment* is not a *crime*, for it preserves the Peace of ' d'un marito ' : the contrary would ", etc. I have been arguing on wrong premises ; but no matter, the *marked* lines are quite as good.

TO LADY MELBOURNE   *Monday Even.* [*Nov. 1813*]

A " person of the least consequence " ! You wrong yourself there, my dear L^dy M.—and so far she is right—you know very well, and so do I, that you can make me do whatever you please without reluctance—I am sure there exists no one to whom I feel half so much obliged—and for whom (gratitude apart) I entertain a greater regard. With regard to her, I certainly love—and in that case it has always been my lot to be entirely at the disposal of " la regnante " ; their caprices I cannot reason upon—and only obey them. In favour of my acquaintance with you there is however a special clause, and nothing shall make me cancel it, I promise you. I meant to have paid you a visit on Saturday in your box—but I thought it possible C[aroline] might be there—from her I find two epistles—in the last the old story of the interview, to which if she still harps upon it I have no objection—she desires me not to go to L^dy Ossulstone's—I was not asked—she was there, I presume, for she talks of going away if I came. But I can't help laughing at the coincidence of objections in the late and present to my going there—both unnecessary—for the presence of the one or the absence of the other would operate sufficiently as a dissuasive. I am just returned from Harrow, where I managed to get a headache, which that I may not communicate I will close this sheet—ever, L^dy M.,

Yours most truly, B.

P.S.—C.'s letter is half in rhyme—an additional proof that she is not in earnest—at least I know from experience one may begin with it—or end—when the subject is dead or changed and indifferent, but during the meridian it is improbable—all is happiness and nonsense.

TO THOMAS MOORE   *November 30, 1813*

Since I last wrote to you, much has occurred, good, bad, and indifferent,—not to make me forget you, but to prevent me from reminding you of one who, nevertheless, has often thought of you, and to whom *your* thoughts, in many a measure, have frequently been a consolation. We were once very near neighbours this autumn; and a good and bad neighbourhood it has proved to me. Suffice it to say, that your French quotation was confoundedly to the purpose,—though very *unexpectedly* pertinent, as you may imagine by what I *said* before, and my silence since. However, " Richard's himself again ", and except all night and some part of the morning, I don't think very much about the matter.

All convulsions end with me in rhyme; and to solace my midnights, I have scribbled another Turkish story—not a Fragment—which you will receive soon after this. It does not trench upon your kingdom in the least, and if it did, you would soon reduce me to my proper boundaries. You will think, and justly, that I run some risk of losing the little I have gained in fame, by this further experiment on public patience; but I have really ceased to care on that head. I have written this, and published it, for the sake of the *employment*,—to wring my thoughts from reality, and take refuge in " imaginings ", however " horrible "; 'and, as to success! those who succeed will console me for a failure—excepting yourself and one or two more, whom luckily I love too well to wish one leaf of their laurels a tint yellower. This is the work of a week, and will be the reading of an hour to you, or even less,—and so, let it go * * * *.

P.S.—Ward and I *talk* of going to Holland. I want to see how a Dutch canal looks after the Bosphorus. Pray respond.

TO THOMAS MOORE   *December 8, 1813*

Your letter, like all the best, and even kindest things in this world, is both painful and pleasing. But, first, to what sits nearest. Do you know I was actually about to dedicate to you,—not in a formal inscription, as to one's *elders*,—but through a short prefatory letter, in which I boasted myself your intimate, and held forth the prospect of *your* poem; when, lo! the recollection of your strict injunctions of secrecy as to the said poem, more than *once* repeated by word and letter, flashed upon me, and marred my intents. I could have no motive for repressing my own desire of alluding to you (and not a day passes that I do not think and talk of you), but an idea that you might, yourself, dislike it. You cannot doubt my sincere admiration, waving personal friendship for the present, which, by the by, is not less sincere and deep rooted. I have you by rote and by heart; of which *ecce signum!* When I was at Aston, on my first visit, I have a habit, in passing my time a good deal alone, of—I won't call it singing, for that I never attempt except to myself—but of uttering, to what I think tunes, your " Oh breathe not ", " When the last glimpse ", and " When he who adores thee ", with others of the same minstrel;—they are my matins and vespers. I assuredly did not intend them to be overheard, but, one morning, in comes, not *La Donna*, but *Il Marito*, with a very grave face, saying, " Byron, I must request you won't sing any more, at least of *those* songs ". I stared, and said, " Certainly, but why? "— " To tell you the truth," quoth he, " they make my wife *cry*, and so melancholy, that I wish her to hear no more of them."

Now, my dear M., the effect must have been from your words, and certainly not my music. I merely mention this foolish story to show you how much I am indebted to you for even my pastimes. A man may praise and praise, but no one recollects but that which pleases—at least, in composition. Though I think no one equal to you in that department, or in satire,—and surely no one was ever so popular in both,—I certainly am of opinion that you have not yet done all *you* can do, though more than enough for any one else. I want, and the world expects, a longer work from you; and I see in you what I never saw in poet before, a strange diffidence of your own powers, which I cannot account for, and which must be unaccountable, when a *Cossac* like me can appal a *cuirassier*. Your story I did not, could not, know,—I thought only of a Peri. I wish you had confided in me, not for your sake, but mine, and to prevent the world from losing a much better poem than my own, but which, I yet hope, this *clashing* will not even now deprive them of. Mine is the work of a week, written, *why* I have partly told you, and partly I cannot tell you by letter—some day I will.

Go on—I shall really be very unhappy if I at all interfere with you. The success of mine is yet problematical; though the public will probably purchase a certain quantity, on the presumption of their own propensity for *The Giaour* and such " horrid mysteries ". The only advantage I have is being on the spot; and that merely amounts to saving me the trouble of turning over books which I had better read again. If *your chamber* was furnished in the same way, you have no need to *go there* to describe—I mean only as to *accuracy*—because I drew it from recollection.

This last thing of mine *may* have the same fate, and I assure you I have great doubts about it. But, even if not, its little day will be over before you are ready and willing. Come out— " screw your courage to the sticking-place ". Except the *Post Bag* (and surely you cannot complain of a want of success there), you have not been *regularly* out for some years. No man stands higher,—whatever you may think on a rainy day, in your provincial retreat. " Aucun homme, dans aucune langue, n'a été, peut-être, plus complètement le poëte du cœur et le poëte des femmes. Les critiques lui reprochent de n'avoir représenté le monde ni tel qu'il est, ni tel qu'il doit être ; *mais les femmes répondent qu'il l'a représenté tel qu'elles le désirent*."—I should have thought Sismondi had written this for you instead of Metastasio.

Write to me, and tell me of *yourself*. Do you remember what Rousseau said to some one—" Have we quarrelled? you have talked to me often, and never once mentioned yourself ".

P.S.—The last sentence is an indirect apology for my egotism,—but I believe in letters it is allowed. I wish it was *mutual*. I have met with an odd reflection in Grimm ; it shall not—at least the bad part—be applied to you or me, though *one* of us has certainly an indifferent name—but this it is :— " Many people have the reputation of being wicked, with whom we should be too happy to pass our lives ". I need not add it is a woman's saying—a Mademoiselle de Sommery's.

TO E. D. CLARKE   *Decr. 15th, 1813*

My DEAR SIR,[1]—Your very kind letter is the more agreeable because, setting aside talents, judgement and the " laudari a laudato " &c, *you* have been on the spot. *You* have seen and described more of the East than any of your predecessors— I need not say how ably and successfully—and (excuse the *Bathos*) *you* are of the very few who can pronounce how far my *costume* (to use an affected but expressive word) is correct. As to poesy, *that* is, as " Men, Gods and Columns " please to decide upon it; but I am sure that I am anxious to have an observer's, particularly a *famous* observer's, testimony on the fidelity of my *manners* and *dresses*; and as far as memory and an Oriental twist in my imagination have permitted, it has been my endeavour to present to the Franks a sketch of that with which you *have* and will present them a complete picture [*sic*]. It was with this notion that I felt compelled to make my hero and heroine *relatives*, as you well know that none else could *there* obtain that degree of intercourse leading to genuine affection. I had nearly made them rather too much akin to each other; and, though the wild passions of the East, and some great examples in Alfieri, Ford and Schiller (to stop short of Antiquity) might have pleaded in favour of a copyist, yet the times and the *North* (*not* Frederic but our climate) inclined me to alter their consanguinity and confine them to cousinship. I also wished to try my hand on a female character in Zuleika, and have endeavoured, as far as the grossness of our masculine ideas will allow, to preserve her purity without impairing the ardour of her attachment. As to *criticism*, I have been reviewed about 150 times, praised and abused. I will not say that I am become indifferent to either eulogy or condemnation; but for some years at least I have felt grateful for the former and have never attempted to answer the latter. For success equal to the first efforts I had and have no hope. The novelty was over, and the " Bride ", like all other brides, must suffer or rejoice for and with her husband. By the bye, I have used Bride

[1] Edward Daniel Clarke, Professor of Mineralogy at Cambridge and well-known traveller. He was the author of *Travels in Various Countries of Europe, Asia and Africa*, in six volumes. Byron had met and discussed Greece with him during 1811. The poem to which Byron refers is *The Bride of Abydos*.

Turkishly as *affianced,* not married; and so far it is an English *bull,* which I trust will be at least a comfort to all Hibernians not bigotted to monopoly. You are good enough to mention your *quotations* in your 3rd vol. I shall not only be indebted to it for the renewal of the high gratification received from the 2 first but for presenting my relics embalmed in your own spices, and ensuring me readers to whom I could not otherwise have aspired.

I called on you as bounden by duty and inclination when last in your neighbourhood; but I shall always take my *chance* —you surely would not have me inflict upon a formal annunciation. I am proud of your friendship, but not so proud as to break in upon your better avocations.

I trust that Mrs. Clarke is well. I have never had the honour of presentation; but I have heard so much of her in many quarters that any notice she is pleased to take of my productions is not less gratifying than my thanks are sincere both to her and you. By all accounts I may safely congratulate you on the possession of a " Bride " whose personal and mental accomplishments are more than poetical.

Ever yrs. mostly truly, BYRON.

P.S.—Murray has sent, or will send, a double copy of the Bride and Giaour. In the last are some lengthy additions. Pray accept these according to old custom " from the Author " to one of his better brethren. Your *Persian* or any memorial will be a most agreeable, and it is my fault if not a useful, present.

JOURNAL: NOVEMBER 14, 1813–APRIL 19, 1814

IF this had been begun ten years ago, and faithfully kept ! ! !— heigho ! there are too many things I wish never to have remembered, as it is. Well,—I have had my share of what are called the pleasures of this life, and have seen more of the European and Asiatic world than I have made a good use of. They say " Virtue is its own reward ",—it certainly should be paid well for its trouble. At five-and-twenty, when the better part of life is over, one should be *something* ;—and what am I? nothing but five-and-twenty—and the odd months. What have I seen? the same man all over the world,—ay, and woman too. Give *me* a Mussulman who never asks questions, and a she of the same race who saves one the trouble of putting them. But for this same plague—yellow fever—and Newstead delay, I should have been by this time a second time close to the Euxine. If I can overcome the last, I don't so much mind your pestilence ; and, at any rate, the spring shall see me there, —provided I neither marry myself, nor unmarry any one else in the interval. I wish one was—I don't know what I wish. It is odd I never set myself seriously to wishing without attaining it—and repenting. I begin to believe with the good old Magi, that one should only pray for the nation, and not for the individual ;—but, on my principle, this would not be very patriotic.

No more reflections.—Let me see—last night I finished " Zuleika ",[1] my second Turkish Tale. I believe the composition of it kept me alive—for it was written to drive my thoughts from the recollection of—

" Dear sacred name, rest ever unreveal'd."

At least, even here, my hand would tremble to write it. This afternoon I have burnt the scenes of my commenced comedy. I have some idea of expectorating a romance, or rather a tale in prose ;—but what romance could equal the events—

" quæque ipse . . . . . . vidi,
Et quorum pars magna fui."

To-day Henry Byron called on me with my little cousin Eliza. She will grow up a beauty and a plague ; but, in the mean time, it is the prettiest child ! dark eyes and eyelashes, black and long as the wing of a raven. I think she is prettier even than my niece, Georgina,—yet I don't like to think so neither : and though older, she is not so clever.

Dallas called before I was up, so we did not meet. Lewis, too,—who seems out of humour with every thing. What can

---

[1] *The Bride of Abydos*, Byron's first Turkish Tale being *The Giaour*.

be the matter? he is not married—has he lost his own mistress or any other person's wife? Hodgson, too, came. He is going to be married, and he is the kind of man who will be the happier. He has talent, cheerfulness, every thing that can make him a pleasing companion ; and his intended is handsome and young, and all that. But I never see any one much improved by matrimony. All my coupled contemporaries are bald and discontented. W[ordsworth] and S[outhey] have both lost their hair and good humour ; and the last of the two had a good deal to lose. But it don't much signify what falls *off* a man's temples in that state.

Mem. I must get a toy to-morrow for Eliza, and send the device for the seals of myself and * * * * * Mem. too, to call on the Stael and Lady Holland to-morrow, and on * *, who has advised me (without seeing it, by the by) not to publish " Zuleika " ; I believe he is right, but experience might have taught him that not to print is *physically* impossible. No one has seen it but Hodgson and Mr. Gifford. I never in my life *read* a composition, save to Hodgson, as he pays me in kind. It is a horrible thing to do too frequently ;—better print, and they who like may read, and if they don't like, you have the satisfaction of knowing that they have, at least, *purchased* the right of saying so.

I have declined presenting the Debtors' Petition, being sick of parliamentary mummeries. I have spoken thrice ; but I doubt my ever becoming an orator. My first was liked ; the second and third—I don't know whether they succeeded or not. I have never yet set to it *con amore* ;—one must have some excuse to one's self for laziness, or inability, or both, and this is mine. " Company, villanous company, hath been the spoil of me " ;—and then, I have drunk medicines ", not to make me love others, but certainly enough to hate myself.

Two nights ago I saw the tigers sup at Exeter 'Change. Except Veli Pacha's lion in the Morea,—who followed the Arab keeper like a dog,—the fondness of the hyæna for her keeper amused me most. Such a conversazione !—There was a " hippopotamus ", like Lord Liverpool in the face ; and the " Ursine Sloth " had the very voice and manner of my valet— but the tiger talked too much. The elephant took and gave me my money again—took off my hat—opened a door—

trunked a whip—and behaved so well, that I wish he was my butler. The handsomest animal on earth is one of the panthers; but the poor antelopes were dead. I should hate to see one *here*:—the sight of the *camel* made me pine again for Asia Minor. " *Oh quando te aspiciam?* "

November 16

Went last night with Lewis [1] to see the first of *Antony and Cleopatra*. It was admirably got up, and well acted—a salad of Shakspeare and Dryden. Cleopatra strikes me as the epitome of her sex—fond, lively, sad, tender, teasing, humble, haughty, beautiful, the devil!—coquettish to the last, as well with the " asp " as with Antony. After doing all she can to persuade him that—but why do they abuse him for cutting off that poltroon Cicero's head? Did not Tully tell Brutus it was a pity to have spared Antony? and did he not speak the Philippics? and are not " *words things* "? and such " *words* " very pestilent " *things* " too? If he had had a hundred heads, they deserved (from Antony) a rostrum (his was stuck up there) apiece—though, after all, he might as well have pardoned him, for the credit of the thing. But to resume—Cleopatra, after securing him, says, " yet go—it is your interest ", etc.—how like the sex! and the questions about Octavia—it is woman all over.

To-day received Lord Jersey's invitation to Middleton—to travel sixty miles to meet Madame De Stael! I once travelled three thousand to get among silent people; and this same lady writes octavos, and *talks* folios. I have read her books—like most of them, and delight in the last; so I won't hear it, as well as read.

Read Burns to-day. What would he have been, if a patrician? We should have had more polish—less force—just as much verse, but no immortality—a divorce and a duel or two, the which had he survived, as his potations must have been less spirituous, he might have lived as long as Sheridan, and outlived as much as poor Brinsley. What a wreck is that man! and all from bad pilotage; for no one had ever better gales, though now and then a little too squally. Poor dear Sherry!

[1] Matthew Gregory (" Monk ") Lewis, frequenter of Holland House and celebrated author of macabre and sadistic tales: elsewhere voted by Byron " a damned bore ".

I shall never forget the day he and Rogers and Moore and I passed together; when *he* talked, and *we* listened, without one yawn, from six till one in the morning.

Got my seals * * * * * *. Have again forgot a plaything for *ma petite cousine* Eliza; but I must send for it to-morrow. I hope Harry will bring her to me. I sent Lord Holland the proofs of the last " *Giaour* ", and " *The Bride of Abydos* ". He won't like the latter, and I don't think that I shall long. It was written in four nights to distract my dreams from * *. Were it not thus, it had never been composed; and had I not done something at that time, I must have gone mad, by eating my own heart,—bitter diet;—Hodgson likes it better than " *The Giaour* ", but nobody else will,—and he never liked the Fragment. I am sure, had it not been for Murray, *that* would never have been published, though the circumstances which are the ground-work make it * * * heigh-ho!

To-night I saw both the sisters of * *; my God! the youngest so like! I thought I should have sprung across the house, and am so glad no one was with me in Lady H.'s box. I hate those likenesses—the mock-bird, but not the nightingale —so like as to remind, so different as to be painful. One quarrels equally with the points of resemblance and of distinction.

Nov. 17

No letter from * *; but I must not complain. The respectable Job says, " Why should a *living man* complain? " I really don't know, except it be that a *dead man* can't; and he, the said patriarch, *did* complain, nevertheless, till his friends were tired and his wife recommended that pious prologue, " Curse—and die " ; the only time, I suppose, when but little relief is to be found in swearing. I have had a most kind letter from Lord Holland on " *The Bride of Abydos* ", which he likes, and so does Lady H. This is very good-natured in both, from whom I don't deserve any quarter. Yet I *did* think, at the time, that my cause of enmity proceeded from Holland House, and am glad I was wrong, and wish I had not been in such a hurry with that confounded satire, of which I would suppress even the memory;—but people, now they can't get it, make a fuss, I verily believe, out of contradiction.

George Ellis and Murray have been talking something about Scott and me, George *pro Scoto*,—and very right too. If they want to depose him, I only wish they would not set me up as a competitor. Even if I had my choice, I would rather be the Earl of Warwick than all the *kings* he ever made! Jeffrey and Gifford I take to be the monarch-makers in poetry and prose. The *British Critic*, in their Rokeby Review, have pre-supposed a comparison which I am sure my friends never thought of, and W. Scott's subjects are injudicious in descending to. I like the man—and admire his works to what Mr. Braham calls *Entusymusy*. All such stuff can only vex him, and do me no good. Many hate his politics—(I hate all politics); and, here, a man's politics are like the Greek *soul*—an εἴδωλον, besides God knows what *other soul*; but their estimate of the two generally go together.

Harry has not brought *ma petite cousine*. I want us to go to the play together;—she has been but once. Another short note from Jersey, inviting Rogers and me on the 23d. I must see my agent to-night. I wonder when that Newstead business will be finished. It cost me more than words to part with it—and to *have* parted with it! What matters it what I do? or what becomes of me?—but let me remember Job's saying, and console myself with being " a living man ".

I wish I could settle to reading again,—my life is monoton-ous, and yet desultory. I take up books, and fling them down again. I began a comedy, and burnt it because the scene ran into *reality*;—a novel, for the same reason. In rhyme, I can keep more away from facts; but the thought always runs through, through . . . yes, yes, through. I have had a letter from Lady Melbourne—the best friend I ever had in my life, and the cleverest of women.

Not a word from * * [Lady F. W. Webster]. Have they set out from * *? or has my last precious epistle fallen into the lion's jaws? If so—and this silence looks suspicious—I must clap on my " musty morion " and " hold out my iron ". I am out of practice—but I won't begin again at Manton's now. Besides, I would not return his shot. I was once a famous wafer-splitter; but then the bullies of society made it necessary. Ever since I began to feel that I had a bad cause to support, I have left off the exercise.

What strange tidings from that Anakim of anarchy— Buonaparte! Ever since I defended my bust of him at Harrow against the rascally time-servers, when the war broke out in 1803, he has been a *Héros de Roman* of mine—on the Continent; I don't want him here. But I don't like those same flights— leaving of armies, etc., etc. I am sure when I fought for his bust at school, I did not think he would run away from himself. But I should not wonder if he banged them yet. To be beat by men would be something; but by three stupid, legitimate- old-dynasty boobies of regular-bred sovereigns—O-hone-a-rie! —O-hone-a-rie! It must be, as Cobbett says, his marriage with the thick-lipped and thick-headed *Autrichienne* brood. He had better have kept to her who was kept by Barras. I never knew any good come of your young wife, and legal espousals, to any but your " sober-blooded boy " who " eats fish " and drinketh " no sack ". Had he not the whole opera? all Paris? all France? But a mistress is just as perplexing—that is, *one*— two or more are manageable by division.

I have begun, or had begun, a song, and flung it into the fire. It was in remembrance of Mary Duff,[1] my first of flames, before most people begin to burn. I wonder what the devil is the matter with me! I can do nothing, and—fortunately there is nothing to do. It has lately been in my power to make two persons (and their connections) comfortable, *pro tempore*, and one happy, *ex tempore*,—I rejoice in the last particularly, as it is an excellent man. I wish there had been more inconvenience and less gratification to my self-love in it, for then there had been more merit. We are all selfish—and I believe, ye gods of Epicurus! I believe in Rochefoucault about *men*, and in Lucretius (not Busby's translation) about yourselves. Your bard has made you very *nonchalant* and blest; but as he has excused *us* from damnation, I don't envy you your blessedness *much*—a little, to be sure. I remember, last year, * * [Lady Oxford] said to me, at * * [Eywood], " Have we not passed our last month like the gods of Lucretius? " And so we had. She is an adept in the text of the original (which I like too) ; and when that booby Bus. sent his translating prospectus, she subscribed. But, the devil prompting him to add a specimen, she transmitted him a subsequent answer, saying, that " after

---

[1] A distant cousin whom Byron had loved in childhood.

perusing it, her conscience would not permit her to allow her name to remain on the list of subscribblers ". Last night, at Lord H.'s—Mackintosh, the Ossulstones, Puységur, etc., there—I was trying to recollect a quotation (as *I* think) of Stael's, from some Teutonic sophist about architecture. " Architecture ", says this Macoronico Tedescho, " reminds me of frozen music." It is somewhere—but where?—the demon of perplexity must know and won't tell. I asked M., and he said it was not in her : but Puységur said it must be *hers*, it was so *like*. H. laughed, as he does at all " *De l'Allemagne* " —in which, however, I think he goes a little too far. B., I hear, contemns it too. But there are fine passages ;—and, after all, what is a work—any—or every work—but a desert with fountains, and, perhaps, a grove or two, every day's journey? To be sure, in Madame, what we often mistake, and " pant for ", as the " cooling stream ", turns out to be the " *mirage* " (criticè *verbiage*) ; but we do, at last, get to something like the temple of Jove Ammon, and then the waste we have passed is only remembered to gladden the contrast.

Called on C * *, to explain * * *. She is very beautiful, to my taste, at least; for on coming home from abroad, I recollect being unable to look at any woman but her—they were so fair, and unmeaning, and *blonde*. The darkness and regularity of her features reminded me of my " Jannat al Aden ". But this impression wore off; and now I can look at a fair woman, without longing for a Houri. She was very good-tempered, and every thing was explained.

To-day, great news—" the Dutch have taken Holland ", —which, I suppose, will be succeeded by the actual explosion of the Thames. Five provinces have declared for young Stadt, and there will be inundation, conflagration, constupration, consternation, and every sort of nation and nations, fighting away, up to their knees, in the damnable quags of this will-o'-the-wisp abode of Boors. It is said Bernadotte is amongst them, too ; and, as Orange will be there soon, they will have (Crown) Prince Stork and King Log in their Loggery at the same time. Two to one on the new dynasty !

Mr. Murray has offered me one thousand guineas for *The Giaour* and *The Bride of Abydos*. I won't—it is too much, though I am strongly tempted, merely for the *say* of it. No bad price for a fortnight's (a week each) what?—the gods know—it was intended to be called poetry.

I have dined regularly to-day, for the first time since Sunday last—this being Sabbath, too. All the rest, tea and dry biscuits —six *per diem*. I wish to God I had not dined now!—It kills me with heaviness, stupor, and horrible dreams; and yet it was but a pint of Bucellas, and fish. Meat I never touch,— nor much vegetable diet. I wish I were in the country, to take exercise,—instead of being obliged to *cool* by abstinence, in lieu of it. I should not so much mind a little accession of flesh, —my bones can well bear it. But the worst is, the devil always came with it,—till I starved him out,—and I will *not* be the slave of *any* appetite. If I do err, it shall be my heart, at least, that heralds the way. Oh, my head—how it aches?—the horrors of digestion! I wonder how Buonaparte's dinner agrees with him?

Mem. I must write to-morrow to " Master Shallow, who owes me a thousand pounds ", and seems, in his letter, afraid I should ask him for it;—as if I would!—I don't want it (just now, at least,) to begin with; and though I have often wanted that sum I never asked for the repayment of 10*l.* in my life— from a friend. His bond is not due this year, and I told him when it was, I should not enforce it. How often must he make me say the same thing?

I am wrong—I did once ask * * * to repay me. But it was under circumstances that excused me *to him*, and would to any one. I took no interest, nor required security. He paid me soon,—at least, his *padre*. My head! I believe it was given me to ache with. Good even.

Nov. 22, 1813

" Orange Boven! " So the bees have expelled the bear that broke open their hive. Well,—if we are to have new De Witts and De Ruyters, God speed the little republic! I should like to see the Hague and the village of Brock, where they have such primitive habits. Yet, I don't know,—their canals would cut a poor figure by the memory of the Bosphorus; and the Zuyder Zee look awkwardly after " Ak-Denizi ". No matter, —the bluff burghers, puffing freedom out of their short tobacco- pipes, might be worth seeing; though I prefer a cigar or a hooka, with the rose-leaf mixed with the milder herb of the Levant. I don't know what liberty means,—never having seen it,—but wealth is power all over the world; and as a shilling performs the duty of a pound (besides sun and sky and beauty for nothing) in the East,—*that* is the country. How I envy Herodes Atticus!—more than Pomponius. And yet a little *tumult*, now and then, is an agreeable quickener of sensation; such as a revolution, a battle, or an *aventure* of any lively description. I think I rather would have been Bonneval, Ripperda, Alberoni, Hayreddin, or Horuc Barbarossa, or even Wortley Montague, than Mahomet himself.

Rogers will be in town soon?—the 23d is fixed for our Middleton visit. Shall I go? umph!—In this island, where one can't ride out without overtaking the sea, it don't much matter where one goes.

I remember the effect of the *first Edinburgh Review* on me. I heard of it six weeks before,—read it the day of its denunciation,—dined and drank three bottles of claret, (with S. B. Davies, I think,) neither ate nor slept the less, but, nevertheless, was not easy till I had vented my wrath and my rhyme, in the same pages, against every thing and every body. Like George in the *Vicar of Wakefield*, " the fate of my paradoxes " would allow me to perceive no merit in another. I remembered only the maxim of my boxing-master, which, in my youth, was found useful in all general riots,—" Whoever is not for you is against you—*mill* away right and left," and so I did;—like Ishmael, my hand was against all men, and all men's anent me. I did wonder, to be sure, at my own success—

" And marvels so much wit is all his own ",

as Hobhouse sarcastically says of somebody (not unlikely myself, as we are old friends);—but were it to come over again, I would *not*. I have since redde the cause of my couplets, and it is not adequate to the effect. C * * told me that it was believed I alluded to poor Lord Carlisle's nervous disorder in one of the lines.[1] I thank Heaven I did not know

---

[1] " Roscommon! Sheffield! with your spirits fled
No future laurels deck a noble head;
No Muse will cheer, with renovating smile,
The paralytic puling of Carlisle."

it—and would not, could not, if I had. I must naturally be the last person to be pointed on defects or maladies.

Rogers is silent,—and, it is said, severe. When he does talk, he talks well; and, on all subjects of taste, his delicacy of expression is pure as his poetry. If you enter his house—his drawing-room—his library—you of yourself say, this is not the dwelling of a common mind. There is not a gem, a coin, a book thrown aside on his chimney-piece, his sofa, his table, that does not bespeak an almost fastidious elegance in the possessor. But this very delicacy must be the misery of his existence. Oh the jarrings his disposition must have encountered through life!

Southey, I have not seen much of. His appearance is *Epic*; and he is the only existing entire man of letters. All the others have some pursuit annexed to their authorship. His manners are mild, but not those of a man of the world, and his talents of the first order. His prose is perfect. Of his poetry there are various opinions: there is, perhaps, too much of it for the present generation; posterity will probably select. He has *passages* equal to any thing. At present, he has *a party*, but no *public*—except for his prose writings. The life of Nelson is beautiful.

Sotheby[1] is a *Littérateur*, the Oracle of the Coteries, of the * * s, Lydia White (Sydney Smith's " Tory Virgin "), Mrs. Wilmot (she, at least, is a swan, and might frequent a purer stream), Lady Beaumont, and all the Blues, with Lady Charlemont at their head—but I say nothing of *her*—" look in her face and you forget them all ", and every thing else. Oh that face!—by *te, Diva potens Cypri*, I would, to be beloved by that woman, build and burn another Troy.

Moore has a peculiarity of talent, or rather talents,— poetry, music, voice, all his own; and an expression in each, which never was, nor will be, possessed by another. But he is capable of still higher flights in poetry. By the by, what humour, what—every thing, in the " *Post-Bag!* " There is nothing Moore may not do, if he will but seriously set about it. In society, he is gentlemanly, gentle, and, altogether, more pleasing than any individual with whom I am acquainted.

---

[1] William Sotheby, cavalry officer turned man of letters. See also *Detached Thoughts* : " A good man; rhymes well (if not wisely), but is a bore ".

For his honour, principle, and independence, his conduct to
* * * * speaks " trumpet-tongued ". He has but one fault—
and that one I daily regret—he is not *here*.

Nov. 23

Ward [1]—I like Ward. By Mahomet! I begin to think I like
every body ;—a disposition not to be encouraged ;—a sort of
social gluttony that swallows every thing set before it. But I
like Ward. He is *piquant*; and, in my opinion, will stand *very*
high in the House, and every where else, if he applies *regularly*.
By the by, I dine with him to-morrow, which may have some
influence on my opinion. It is as well not to trust one's gratitude *after* dinner. I have heard many a host libelled by his
guests, with his burgundy yet reeking on their rascally lips.

I have taken Lord Salisbury's box at Covent Garden for
the season ; and now I must go and prepare to join Lady
Holland and party, in theirs, at Drury Lane, *questa sera*.

Holland doesn't think the man *is Junius*; but that the yet
unpublished journal throws great light on the obscurities of
that part of George the Second's reign.—What is this to
George the Third's? I don't know what to think. Why
should Junius be yet dead? If suddenly apoplexed, would he
rest in his grave without sending his εἰδωλον to shout in the
ears of posterity, " Junius was X. Y. Z., Esq., buried in the
parish of * * *. Repair his monument, ye churchwardens!
Print a new edition of his Letters, ye booksellers ! " Impossible,
—the man must be alive, and will never die without the disclosure. I like him ;—he was a good hater.

Came home unwell and went to bed,—not so sleepy as
might be desirable.

Tuesday morning

I awoke from a dream !—well ! and have not others
dreamed?—Such a dream !—but she did not overtake me. I
wish the dead would rest, however. Ugh ! how my blood
chilled,—and I could not wake—and—and—heigho !

" Shadows to-night
Have struck more terror to the soul of Richard,
Than could the substance of ten thousand * * s,
Arm'd all in proof, and led by shallow * *."

[1] The Hon. John William Ward, afterwards Lord Dudley, journalist and orator.

I do not like this dream,—I hate its " foregone conclusion ".
And am I to be shaken by shadows? Ay, when they remind
us of—no matter—but, if I dream thus again, I will try
whether *all* sleep has the like visions. Since I rose, I've been
in considerable bodily pain also ; but it is gone, and now, like
Lord Ogleby, I am wound up for the day.

A note from Mountnorris—I dine with Ward ;—Canning
is to be there, Frere [1] and Sharpe,[2] perhaps Gifford. I am to be
one of " the five " (or rather six), as Lady * * said a little
sneeringly yesterday. They are all good to meet, particularly
Canning, and—Ward, when he likes. I wish I may be well
enough to listen to these intellectuals.

No letters to-day ;—so much the better,—there are no
answers. I must not dream again ;—it spoils even reality. I
will go out of doors, and see what the fog will do for me.
Jackson has been here : the boxing world much as usual ;—
but the club increases. I shall dine at Crib's [3] to-morrow. I
like energy—even animal energy—of all kinds ; and I have
need of both mental and corporeal. I have not dined out, nor,
indeed, *at all*, lately : have heard no music—have seen nobody.
Now for a *plunge*—high life and low life. *Amant* alterna
Camœnæ!

I have burnt my *Roman*—as I did the first scenes and sketch
of my comedy—and, for aught I see, the pleasure of burning is
quite as great as that of printing. These two last would not
have done. I ran into *realities* more than ever ; and some would
have been recognised and others guessed at.

Redde the *Ruminator*—a collection of Essays, by a strange,
but able, old man (Sir Egerton Brydges), and a half-wild young
one, author of a poem on the Highlands, called *Childe Alarique*.
The word " sensibility " (always my aversion) occurs a thousand
times in these Essays ; and, it seems, is to be an excuse for all
kinds of discontent. This young man can know nothing of
life ; and, if he cherishes the disposition which runs through his
papers, will become useless, and, perhaps, not even a poet,

[1] John Hookham Frere, a distinguished member of the Holland House
circle.
[2] Richard (" Conversation ") Sharp, the wealthy Radical, another ornament
of Holland House parties.
[3] Tom Cribb, the retired pugilist, who kept a public house in Duke Street,
St. James's.

after all, which he seems determined to be. God help him! no one should be a rhymer who could be any thing better. And this is what annoys one, to see Scott and Moore, and Campbell and Rogers, who might have all been agents and leaders, now mere spectators. For, though they may have other ostensible avocations, these last are reduced to a secondary consideration. * *, too, frittering away his time among dowagers and unmarried girls. If it advanced any *serious* affair, it were some excuse; but, with the unmarried, that is a hazardous speculation, and tiresome enough, too; and, with the veterans, it is not much worth trying, unless, perhaps, one in a thousand.

If I had any views in this country, they would probably be parliamentary. But I have no ambition; at least, if any, it would be *aut Cæsar aut nihil.* My hopes are limited to the arrangement of my affairs, and settling either in Italy or the East (rather the last), and drinking deep of the languages and literature of both. Past events have unnerved me; and all I can now do is to make life an amusement, and look on while others play. After all, even the highest game of crowns and sceptres, what is it? *Vide* Napoleon's last twelvemonth. It has completely upset my system of fatalism. I thought, if crushed, he would have fallen, when *fractus illabitur orbis*, and not have been pared away to gradual insignificance; that all this was not a mere *jeu* of the gods, but a prelude to greater changes and mightier events. But men never advance beyond a certain point; and here we are, retrograding, to the dull, stupid old system,—balance of Europe—poising straws upon kings' noses, instead of wringing them off! Give me a republic, or a despotism of one, rather than the mixed government of one, two, three. A republic!—look in the history of the Earth—Rome, Greece, Venice, France, Holland, America, our short (*eheu!*) Commonwealth, and compare it with what they did under masters. The Asiatics are not qualified to be republicans, but they have the liberty of demolishing despots, which is the next thing to it. To be the first man—not the Dictator—not the Sylla, but the Washington or the Aristides— the leader in talent and truth—is next to the Divinity! Franklin, Penn, and, next to these, either Brutus or Cassius—even Mirabeau—or St. Just. I shall never be any thing, or rather

always be nothing. The most I can hope is, that some will say,
" He might, perhaps, if he would ".

12, midnight

Here are two confounded proofs from the printer. I have
looked at the one, but for the soul of me, I can't look over that
Giaour again,—at least, just now, and at this hour—and yet
there is no moon.

Ward talks of going to Holland, and we have partly discussed an *ensemble* expedition. It must be in ten days, if at all,
if we wish to be in at the Revolution. And why not? * * is
distant, and will be at * *, still more distant, till spring. No
one else, except Augusta, cares for me; no ties—no trammels
—*andiamo dunque—se torniamo, bene—se non, ch' importa?* Old
William of Orange talked of dying in " the last ditch " of his
dingy country. It is lucky I can swim, or I suppose I should
not well weather the first. But let us see. I have heard
hyænas and jackalls in the ruins of Asia; and bull-frogs in
the marshes; besides wolves and angry Mussulmans. Now,
I should like to listen to the shout of a free Dutchman.

Alla! Viva! For ever! Hourra! Huzza!—which is
the most rational or musical of these cries? " Orange Boven ",
according to the *Morning Post*.

Wednesday, 24

No dreams last night of the dead, nor the living; so—I
am " firm as the marble, founded as the rock ", till the next
earthquake.

Ward's dinner went off well. There was not a disagreeable
person there—unless *I* offended any body, which I am sure I
could not by contradiction, for I said little, and opposed
nothing. Sharpe (a man of elegant mind, and who has lived
much with the best—Fox, Horne Tooke, Windham, Fitz-
patrick, and all the agitators of other times and tongues,) told
us the particulars of his last interview with Windham, a few
days before the fatal operation which sent " that gallant spirit
to aspire the skies ". Windham,—the first in one department
of oratory and talent, whose only fault was his refinement
beyond the intellect of half his hearers,—Windham, half his
life an active participator in the events of the earth, and one of
those who governed nations,—*he* regretted,—and dwelt much

on that regret, that " he had not entirely devoted himself to literature and science ! ! ! " His mind certainly would have carried him to eminence there, as elsewhere ;—but I cannot comprehend what debility of that mind could suggest such a wish. I, who have heard him, cannot regret any thing but that I shall never hear him again. What ! would he have been a plodder? a metaphysician?—perhaps a rhymer? a scribbler? Such an exchange must have been suggested by illness. But he is gone, and Time " shall not look upon his like again ".

I am tremendously in arrear with my letters,—except to * *, and to her my thoughts overpower me :—my words never compass them. To Lady Melbourne I write with most pleasure —and her answers, so sensible, so *tactique*—I never met with half her talent. If she had been a few years younger, what a fool she would have made of me, had she thought it worth her while,—and I should have lost a valuable and most agreeable *friend*. Mem.—a mistress never is nor can be a friend. While you agree, you are lovers ; and, when it is over, any thing but friends.

I have not answered W. Scott's last letter,—but I will. I regret to hear from others, that he has lately been unfortunate in pecuniary involvements. He is undoubtedly the Monarch of Parnassus, and the most *English* of bards. I should place Rogers next in the living list (I value him more as the last of the *best* school)—Moore and Campbell both *third*—Southey and Wordsworth and Coleridge—the rest, οἱ πολλοι—thus :— There is a triangular *Gradus ad Parnassum* !—the names are too numerous for the base of the triangle. Poor Thurlow has gone wild about the poetry of Queen Bess's reign—*c'est dommage*. I have ranked the names upon my triangle more upon what I believe popular opinion, than any decided opinion of my own. For, to me, some of Moore's last *Erin* sparks—" As a beam o'er the face of the waters "—" When he who adores thee "— " Oh blame not "—and " Oh breathe not his name "—are worth all the Epics that ever were composed.

Rogers thinks the *Quarterly* will attack me next. Let them. I have been " peppered so highly " in my time, *both* ways, that it must be cayenne or aloes to make me taste. I can sincerely say, that I am not very much alive *now* to criticism. But—in tracing this—I rather believe that it proceeds from my not attaching that importance to authorship which many do, and which, when young, I did also. " One gets tired of every thing, my angel ", says Valmont. The " angels " are the only things of which I am not a little sick—but I do think the preference of *writers* to *agents*—the mighty stir made about scribbling and scribes, by themselves and others—a sign of

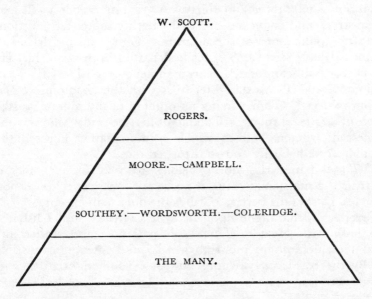

W. SCOTT.

ROGERS.

MOORE.—CAMPBELL.

SOUTHEY.—WORDSWORTH.—COLERIDGE.

THE MANY.

effeminacy, degeneracy, and weakness. Who would write, who had any thing better to do? " Action—action—action " —said Demosthenes: " Action*s*—action*s* ", I say, and not writing,—least of all, rhyme. Look at the querulous and monotonous lives of the " genus " ;—except Cervantes, Tasso, Dante, Ariosto, Kleist (who were brave and active citizens), Æschylus, Sophocles, and some other of the antiques also— what a worthless, idle brood it is !

12, Mezza Notte

Just returned from dinner with Jackson (the Emperor of Pugilism) and another of the select, at Crib's,[1] the champion's. I drank more than I like, and have brought away some three

---

[1] Tom Cribb had won his championship by defeating Molineaux, the coloured boxer, in 1810 and 1811.

bottles of very fair claret—for I have no headach. We had
Tom Crib up after dinner;—very facetious, though somewhat
prolix. He don't like his situation—wants to fight again—pray
Pollux (or Castor, if he was the *miller*) he may! Tom has been
a sailor—a coal-heaver—and some other genteel profession,
before he took to the cestus. Tom has been in action at sea,
and is now only three-and-thirty. A great man! has a wife and
a mistress, and conversations well—bating some sad omissions
and misapplications of the aspirate. Tom is an old friend of
mine; I have seen some of his best battles in my nonage. He
is now a publican, and, I fear, a sinner;—for Mrs. Crib is on
alimony, and Tom's daughter lives with the champion. *This*
Tom told me,—Tom, having an opinion of my morals, passed
her off as a legal spouse. Talking of her, he said, " she was the
truest of women "—from which I immediately inferred she
could *not* be his wife, and so it turned out.

These panegyrics don't belong to matrimony;—for, if
" true ", a man don't think it necessary to say so; and if not,
the less he says the better. Crib is the only man except * * * *,
I ever heard harangue upon his wife's virtue; and I listened
to both with great credence and patience, and stuffed my
handkerchief into my mouth, when I found yawning irresistible
—By the by, I am yawning now—so, good night to thee.—
Μπαῖρων.

Thursday, November 26

Awoke a little feverish, but no headach—no dreams
neither, thanks to stupor! Two letters; one from [? Frances
Webster], the other from Lady Melbourne—both excellent in
their respective styles. [? Frances Webster]'s contained also a
very pretty lyric on " concealed griefs "; if not her own, yet
very like her. Why did she not say that the stanzas were, or
were not, of her own composition? I do not know whether
to wish them *hers* or not. I have no great esteem for poetical
persons, particularly women; they have so much of the " ideal "
in *practics*, as well as *ethics*.

I have been thinking lately a good deal of Mary Duff.[1]

---

[1] Hobhouse declined to accept Moore's account of this precocious passion,
remarking in his pencil notes on a copy of the *Life* that he was " acquainted with
a singular fact, scarcely fit for narration but much less romantic and more satisfactory than the amour with Mary Duff ".

How very odd that I should have been so utterly, devotedly fond of that girl, at an age when I could neither feel passion, nor know the meaning of the word. And the effect! My mother used always to rally me about this childish amour; and, at last, many years after, when I was sixteen, she told me one day, " Oh, Byron, I have had a letter from Edinburgh, from Miss Abercromby, and your old sweetheart Mary Duff is married to a Mr. Co^e ". And what was my answer? I really cannot explain or account for my feelings at that moment; but they nearly threw me into convulsions, and alarmed my mother so much, that after I grew better, she generally avoided the subject—to *me*—and contented herself with telling it to all her acquaintance. Now, what could this be? I had never seen her since her mother's *faux pas* at Aberdeen had been the cause of her removal to her grandmother's at Banff; we were both the merest children. I had and have been attached fifty times since that period; yet I recollect all we said to each other, all our caresses, her features, my restlessness, sleeplessness, my tormenting my mother's maid to write for me to her, which she at last did, to quiet me. Poor Nancy thought I was wild, and, as I could not write for myself, became my secretary. I remember, too, our walks, and the happiness of sitting by Mary, in the children's apartment, at their house not far from the Plain-stanes at Aberdeen, while her lesser sister Helen played with the doll, and we sat gravely making love, in our way.

How the deuce did all this occur so early? where could it originate? I certainly had no sexual ideas for years afterwards; and yet my misery, my love for that girl were so violent, that I sometimes doubt if I have ever been really attached since. Be that as it may, hearing of her marriage several years after was like a thunder-stroke—it nearly choked me—to the horror of my mother and the astonishment and almost incredulity of every body. And it is a phenomenon in my existence (for I was not eight years old) which has puzzled, and will puzzle me to the latest hour of it; and lately, I know not why, the *recollection* (*not* the attachment) has recurred as forcibly as ever. I wonder if she can have the least remembrance of it or me? or remember pitying her sister Helen for not having an admirer too? How very pretty is the perfect image of her in my memory —her brown, dark hair, and hazel eyes; her very dress! I should be quite grieved to see *her now*; the reality, however beautiful, would destroy, or at least confuse, the features of the lovely Peri which then existed in her, and still lives in my imagination, at the distance of more than sixteen years. I am now twenty-five and odd months. . . .

I think my mother told the circumstances (on my hearing of her marriage) to the Parkynses, and certainly to the Pigot family, and probably mentioned it in her answer to Miss A., who was well acquainted with my childish *penchant*, and had sent the news on purpose for *me*,—and thanks to her!

Next to the beginning, the conclusion has often occupied my reflections, in the way of investigation. That the facts are thus, others know as well as I, and my memory yet tells me so, in more than a whisper. But, the more I reflect, the more I am bewildered to assign any cause for this precocity of affection.

Lord Holland invited me to dinner to-day; but three days' dining would destroy me. So, without eating at all since yesterday, I went to my box at Covent Garden.

Saw * * * * looking very pretty, though quite a different style of beauty from the other two. She has the finest eyes in the world, out of which she pretends *not* to see, and the longest eyelashes I ever saw, since Leila's and Phannio's Moslem curtains of the light. She has much beauty,—just enough,—but is, I think, *méchante*.

I have been pondering on the miseries of separation, that—oh how seldom we see those we love! yet we live ages in moments, *when met*. The only thing that consoles me during absence is the reflection that no mental or personal estrangement, from ennui or disagreement, can take place; and when people meet hereafter, even though many changes may have taken place, in the mean time, still, unless they are *tired* of each other, they are ready to reunite, and do not blame each other for the circumstances that severed them.

Saturday 27—(I believe or rather am in *doubt*, which
is the *ne plus ultra* of mortal faith)

I have missed a day; and, as the Irishman said, or Joe Miller says for him, " have gained a loss ", or *by* the loss. Every thing is settled for Holland, and nothing but a cough, or

a caprice of my fellow-traveller's, can stop us.   Carriage
ordered, funds prepared, and, probably, a gale of wind into
the bargain. *N'importe*—I believe, with Clym o' the Clow, or
Robin Hood, "By our Mary, (dear name!) thou art both
Mother and May, I think it never was a man's lot to die before
his day". Heigh for Helvoetsluys, and so forth!

To-night I went with young Henry Fox[1] to see *Nourjahad*,
a drama, which the *Morning Post* hath laid to my charge, but
of which I cannot even guess the author. I wonder what they
will next inflict upon me. They cannot well sink below a
melodrama; but that is better than a satire, (at least, a personal
one,) with which I stand truly arraigned, and in atonement of
which I am resolved to bear silently all criticisms, abuses, and
even praises, for bad pantomimes never composed by me,
without even a contradictory aspect. I suppose the root of
this report is my loan to the manager of my Turkish drawings
for his dresses, to which he was more welcome than to my
name. I suppose the real author will soon own it, as it has
succeeded; if not, Job be my model, and Lethe my beverage!

* * * * has received the portrait safe; and, in answer, the
only remark she makes upon it is, "indeed it is like"—and
again, "indeed it is like". With her the likeness "covered a
multitude of sins"; for I happen to know that this portrait
was not a flatterer, but dark and stern,—even black as the mood
in which my mind was scorching last July, when I sat for it.
All the others of me, like most portraits whatsoever, are, of
course, more agreeable than nature.

Redde the *Edinburgh Review* of Rogers. He is ranked
highly; but where he should be. There is a summary view of
us all—*Moore* and *me* among the rest; and both (the *first*
justly) praised—though, by implication (justly again) placed
beneath our memorable friend. Mackintosh is the writer, and
also of the critique on the Stael. His grand essay on Burke, I
hear, is for the next number. But I know nothing of the
Edinburgh, or of any other *Review*, but from rumour; and I
have long ceased; indeed, I could not, in justice, complain of

---

[1] Lord and Lady Holland's eldest legitimate son. Byron had a particular
sympathy for him since he, too, was lame. Fox subsequently became the author
of an interesting journal, and one of Byron's numerous successors in the affections
of the Countess Guiccioli.

any, even though I were to rate poetry, in general, and my rhymes in particular, more highly than I really do. To withdraw *myself* from *myself* (oh that cursed selfishness!) has ever been my sole, my entire, my sincere motive in scribbling at all; and publishing is also the continuance of the same object, by the action it affords to the mind, which else recoils upon itself. If I valued fame, I should flatter received opinions, which have gathered strength by time, and will yet wear longer than any living works to the contrary. But, for the soul of me, I cannot and will not give the lie to my own thoughts and doubts, come what may. If I am a fool, it is, at least, a doubting one; and I envy no one the certainty of his self-approved wisdom.

All are inclined to believe what they covet, from a lottery-ticket up to a passport to Paradise,—in which, from the description, I see nothing very tempting. My restlessness tells me I have something " within that passeth show ". It is for Him, who made it, to prolong that spark of celestial fire which illuminates, yet burns, this frail tenement; but I see no such horror in a " dreamless sleep ", and I have no conception of any existence which duration would not render tiresome. How else " fell the angels ", even according to your creed? They were immortal, heavenly, and happy, as their *apostate Abdiel* is now by his treachery. Time must decide; and eternity won't be the less agreeable or more horrible because one did not expect it. In the mean time, I am grateful for some good, and tolerably patient under certain evils—*grace à Dieu et mon bon tempérament.*

Tuesday, 30th

Two days missed in my log-book;—*hiatus* haud *deflendus*. They were as little worth recollection as the rest; and, luckily, laziness or society prevented me from *notching* them.

Sunday, I dined with the Lord Holland in St. James's Square. Large party—among them Sir S. Romilly and Lady R^y—General Sir Somebody Bentham, a man of science and talent, I am told—Horner—*the* Horner, an Edinburgh Reviewer, an excellent speaker in the " Honourable House ", very pleasing, too, and gentlemanly in company, as far as I have seen—Sharpe—Philips of Lancashire—Lord John Russell, and others, " good men and true ". Holland's society is very good ; you always see some one or other in it worth knowing. Stuffed myself with sturgeon, and exceeded in champagne and wine in general, but not to confusion of head. When I *do* dine, I gorge like an Arab or a Boa snake, on fish and vegetables, but no meat. I am always better, however, on my tea and biscuit than any other regimen, and even *that* sparingly.

Why does Lady H. always have that damned screen between the whole room and the fire ? I, who bear cold no better than an antelope, and never yet found a sun quite *done* to my taste, was absolutely petrified, and could not even shiver. All the rest, too, looked as if they were just unpacked, like salmon from an ice-basket, and set down to table for that day only. When she retired, I watched their looks as I dismissed the screen, and every cheek thawed, and every nose reddened with the anticipated glow.

Saturday, I went with Harry Fox to *Nourjahad*; and, I believe, convinced him, by incessant yawning, that it was not mine. I wish the precious author would own it, and release me from his fame. The dresses are pretty, but not in costume ; —Mrs. Horn's, all but the turban, and the want of a small dagger (if she is a sultana), *perfect*. I never saw a Turkish woman with a turban in my life—nor did any one else. The sultanas have a small poniard at the waist. The dialogue is drowsy—the action heavy—the scenery fine—the actors tolerable. I can't say much for their seraglio—Teresa, Phannio, or * * * *, were worth them all.

Sunday, a very handsome note from Mackintosh, who is a rare instance of the union of very transcendent talent and great good nature. To-day (Tuesday) a very pretty billet from M. la Baronne de Stael Holstein. She is pleased to be much pleased with my mention of her and her last work in my notes. I spoke as I thought. Her works are my delight, and so is she herself, for—half an hour. I don't like her politics—at least, her *having changed* them ; had she been *qualis ab incepto*, it were nothing. But she is a woman by herself, and has done more than all the rest of them together, intellectually ;—she ought to have been a man. She *flatters* me very prettily in her note ;— but I *know* it. The reason that adulation is not displeasing is, that, though untrue, it shows one to be of consequence enough, in one way or other, to induce people to lie, to make us their friend :—that is their concern.

* * is, I hear, thriving on the repute of a *pun* which was *mine* (at Mackintosh's dinner some time back), on Ward, who was asking, " how much it would take to *re-whig* him? " I answered that, probably, " he must first, before he was *re-whigged*, be re-*warded* ". This foolish quibble, before the Stael and Mackintosh, and a number of conversationers, has been mouthed about, and at last settled on the head of * *, where long may it remain !

George[1] is returned from afloat to get a new ship. He looks thin, but better than I expected. I like George much more than most people like their heirs. He is a fine fellow, and every nch a sailor. I would do any thing, *but apostatise*, to get him on n his profession.

Lewis called. It is a good and good-humoured man, but pestilently prolix and paradoxical and *personal*. If he would but talk half, and reduce his visits to an hour, he would add to his popularity. As an author he is very good, and his vanity is *uverte*, like Erskine's, and yet not offending.

Yesterday, a very pretty letter from Annabella, which I answered. What an odd situation and friendship is ours !—without one spark of love on either side, and produced by circumstances which in general lead to coldness on one side, and aversion on the other. She is a very superior woman, and very little spoiled, which is strange in an heiress—a girl of twenty—a peeress that is to be, in her own right—an only child, and a *savante*, who has always had her own way. She is a poetess—a mathematician—a metaphysician, and yet, withal, very kind, generous, and gentle, with very little pretension. Any other head would be turned with half her acquisitions, and a tenth of her advantages.

Wednesday, December 1, 1813

To-day responded to La Baronne de Stael Holstein, and sent to Leigh Hunt[2] (an acquisition to my acquaintance—

[1] The poet's cousin and heir presumptive, who succeeded him as the seventh Lord Byron in 1824.

[2] Leigh Hunt and his brother had been fined and sentenced to two years' imprisonment for a savage personal attack on the Prince Regent in the *Examiner* of March 1812.

through Moore—of last summer) a copy of the two Turkish tales. Hunt is an extraordinary character, and not exactly of the present age. He reminds me more of the Pym and Hampden times—much talent, great independence of spirit, and an austere, yet not repulsive, aspect. If he goes on *qualis ab incepto*, I know few men who will deserve more praise or obtain it. I must go and see him again;—the rapid succession of adventure, since last summer, added to some serious uneasiness and business, have interrupted our acquaintance; but he is a man worth knowing; and though, for his own sake, I wish him out of prison, I like to study character in such situations. He has been unshaken, and will continue so. I don't think him deeply versed in life;—he is the bigot of virtue (not religion), and enamoured of the beauty of that " empty name ", as the last breath of Brutus pronounced, and every day proves it. He is, perhaps, a little opinionated, as all men who are the *centre* of *circles*, wide or narrow—the Sir Oracles, in whose name two or three are gathered together—must be, and as even Johnson was; but, withal, a valuable man, and less vain than success and even the consciousness of preferring " the right to the expedient " might excuse.

To-morrow there is a party of *purple* at the " blue " Miss Berry's. Shall I go? um!—I don't much affect your bluebottles;—but one ought to be civil. There will be, " I guess now " (as the Americans say), the Staels and Mackintoshes— good—the * * * s and * * * s—not so good—the * * * s, etc., etc.—good for nothing. Perhaps that blue-winged Kashmirian butterfly of book-learning, Lady Charlemont, will be there. I hope so; it is a pleasure to look upon that most beautiful of faces.

Wrote to H.:—he has been telling that I —— I am sure, at least, *I* did not mention it, and I wish he had not. He is a good fellow, and I obliged myself ten times more by being of use than I did him,—and there's an end on't.

Baldwin is boring me to present their King's Bench petition. I presented Cartwright's last year; and Stanhope and I stood against the whole House, and mouthed it valiantly—and had some fun and a little abuse for our opposition. But " I am not i' th' vein " for this business. Now, had * * been here, she would have *made* me do it. *There* is a woman, who, amid all her fascination, always urged a man to usefulness or glory. Had she remained, she had been my tutelar genius.

Baldwin is very importunate—but, poor fellow, " I can't get out, I can't get out—said the starling ". Ah, I am as bad as that dog Sterne, who preferred whining over " a dead ass to relieving a living mother "—villain—hypocrite—slave—sycophant! but *I* am no better. Here I cannot stimulate myself to a speech for the sake of these unfortunates, and three words and half a smile of * * had she been here to urge it (and urge it she infallibly would—at least she always pressed me on senatorial duties, and particularly in the cause of weakness) would have made me an advocate, if not an orator. Curse on Rochefoucault for being always right! In him a lie were virtue,— or, at least, a comfort to his readers.

George Byron has not called to-day ; I hope he will be an admiral, and, perhaps, Lord Byron into the bargain. If he would but marry, I would engage never to marry myself, or cut him out of the heirship. He would be happier, and I should like nephews better than sons.

I shall soon be six-and-twenty (January 22d, 1814). Is there any thing in the future that can possibly console us for not being always *twenty-five* ?

" Oh Gioventu !
Oh Primavera ! gioventu dell' anno.
Oh Gioventu ! primavera della vita."

Sunday, December 5

Dallas's nephew (son to the American Attorney-general) is arrived in this country, and tells Dallas that my rhymes are very popular in the United States. These are the first tidings that have ever sounded like *Fame* to my ears—to be redde on the banks of the Ohio ! The greatest pleasure I ever derived, of this kind, was from an extract, in Cooke the actor's life, from his journal, stating that in the reading-room at Albany, near Washington, he perused *English Bards, and Scotch Reviewers*. To be popular in a rising and far country has a kind of *posthumous feel*, very different from the ephemeral *éclat* and fête-ing, buzzing and party-ing compliments of the well-dressed multitude. I can safely say that, during my *reign* in the spring of

1812, I regretted nothing but its duration of six weeks instead of a fortnight, and was heartily glad to resign.

Last night I supped with Lewis; and, as usual, though I neither exceeded in solids nor fluids, have been half dead ever since. My stomach is entirely destroyed by long abstinence, and the rest will probably follow. Let it—I only wish the *pain* over. The "leap in the dark" is the least to be dreaded.

The Duke of * * called. I have told them forty times that, except to half-a-dozen old and specified acquaintances, I am invisible. His Grace is a good, noble, ducal person; but I am content to think so at a distance, and so—I was not at home.

Galt [1] called.—Mem.—to ask some one to speak to Raymond in favour of his play. We are old fellow-travellers, and, with all his eccentricities, he has much strong sense, experience of the world, and is, as far as I have seen, a good-natured philosophical fellow. I showed him Sligo's letter on the reports of the Turkish girl's *aventure* at Athens soon after it happened. He and Lord Holland, Lewis, and Moore, and Rogers, and Lady Melbourne have seen it. Murray has a copy. I thought it had been *unknown*, and wish it were; but Sligo arrived only some days after, and the *rumours* are the subject of his letter. That I shall preserve,—*it is as well*. Lewis and Galt were both *horrified*; and L. wondered I did not introduce the situation into *The Giaour*. He *may* wonder;—he might wonder more at that production's being written at all. But to describe the *feelings* of *that situation* were impossible—it is *icy* even to recollect them.

The *Bride of Abydos* was published on Thursday the second of December; but how it is liked or disliked, I know not. Whether it succeeds or not is no fault of the public, against whom I can have no complaint. But I am much more indebted to the tale than I can ever be to the most partial reader; as it wrung my thoughts from reality to imagination—from selfish regrets to vivid recollections—and recalled me to a country replete with the *brightest* and *darkest*, but always most *lively* colours of my memory. Sharpe called, but was not let in, which I regret.

---

[1] John Galt, author of *The Annals of the Parish*, met Byron at Gibraltar during the year 1809 and afterwards travelled with him from Gibraltar to Malta. His impressions of that journey are the most interesting part of his fragmentary *Life of Byron*.

Saw [Rogers] yesterday. I have not kept my appointment at Middleton, which has not pleased him, perhaps; and my projected voyage with [Ward] will, perhaps, please him less. But I wish to keep well with both. They are instruments that don't do in concert; but, surely, their separate tones are very musical, and I won't give up either.

It is well if I don't jar between these great discords. At present I stand tolerably well with all, but I cannot adopt their *dislikes*;—so many *sets*. Holland's is the first;—every thing *distingué* is welcome there, and certainly the *ton* of his society is the best. Then there is Madame de Stael's—there I never go, though I might, had I courted it. It is composed of the * * s and the * * family, with a strange sprinkling,—orators, dandies, and all kinds of *Blue*, from the regular Grub Street uniform, down to the azure jacket of the *Littérateur*. To see * * and * * sitting together, at dinner, always reminds me of the grave, where all distinctions of friend and foe are levelled; and they —the Reviewer and the Reviewée—the Rhinoceros and Elephant—the Mammoth and Megalonyx—all will lie quietly together. They now *sit* together, as silent, but not so quiet, as if they were already immured.

I did not go to the Berrys' the other night. The elder is a woman of much talent, and both are handsome, and must have been beautiful. To-night asked to Lord H.'s—shall I go? um !—perhaps.

Morning, two o'clock

Went to Lord H.'s—party numerous—*mi*lady in perfect good humour, and consequently *perfect*. No one more agreeable, or perhaps so much so, when she will. Asked for Wednesday to dine and meet the Stael—asked particularly, I believe, out of mischief to see the first interview after the *note*, with which Corinne professes herself to be so much taken. I don't much like it; she always talks of *my*self or *her*self, and I am not (except in soliloquy, as now,) much enamoured of either subject—especially one's works. What the devil shall I say about *De l'Allemagne*? I like it prodigiously; but unless I can twist my admiration into some fantastical expression, she won't believe me; and I know, by experience, I shall be overwhelmed with fine things about rhyme, etc., etc. The lover,

Mr. * * [Rocca], was there to-night, and C * * said " it was the only proof *he* had seen of her good taste ". Monsieur L'Amant is remarkably handsome ; but *I* don't think more so than her book.

C * * [Campbell] looks well,—seems pleased, and dressed to *sprucery*. A blue coat becomes him,—so does his new wig. He really looked as if Apollo had sent him a birthday suit, or a wedding-garment, and was witty and lively. He abused Corinne's book, which I regret ; because, firstly, he understands German, and is consequently a fair judge ; and, secondly, he is *first-rate*, and, consequently, the best of judges. I reverence and admire him ; but I won't give up my opinion—why should I ? I read *her* again and again, and there can be no affectation in this. I cannot be mistaken (except in taste) in a book I read and lay down, and take up again ; and no book can be totally bad which finds *one*, even *one* reader, who can say as much sincerely.

Campbell talks of lecturing next spring ; his last lectures were eminently successful. Moore thought of it, but gave it up,—I don't know why. * * had been prating *dignity* to him, and such stuff ; as if a man disgraced himself by instructing and pleasing at the same time.

Introduced to Marquis Buckingham—saw Lord Gower— he is going to Holland ; Sir J. and Lady Mackintosh and Horner, G. Lamb, with I know not how many (Richard Wellesley, one—a clever man), grouped about the room. Little Henry Fox, a very fine boy, and very promising in mind and manner,—he went away to bed, before I had time to talk to him. I am sure I had rather hear him than all the *savans*.

Monday, Dec. 6

Murray tells me that Croker asked him why the thing was called the *Bride* of Abydos ? It is a cursed awkward question, being unanswerable. *She* is not a *bride*, only about to be one ; but for, etc., etc., etc.

I don't wonder at his finding out the *Bull* ; but the detection * * * is too late to do any good. I was a great fool to make it, and am ashamed of not being an Irishman.

Campbell last night seemed a little nettled at something or

other—I know not what. We were standing in the ante-saloon, when Lord H. brought out of the other room a vessel of some composition similar to that which is used in Catholic churches, and, seeing us, he exclaimed, " Here is some *incense* for you ". Campbell answered—" Carry it to Lord Byron, *he is used to it* ".

Now, this comes of " bearing no brother near the throne ". I, who have no throne, nor wish to have one *now*, whatever I may have done, am at perfect peace with all the poetical fraternity; or, at least, if I dislike any, it is not *poetically*, but *personally*. Surely the field of thought is infinite; what does it signify who is before or behind in a race where there is no *goal*? The temple of fame is like that of the Persians, the universe; our altar, the tops of mountains. I should be equally content with Mount Caucasus, or Mount Anything; and those who like it, may have Mount Blanc or Chimborazo, without my envy of their elevation.

I think I may *now* speak thus; for I have just published a poem, and am quite ignorant whether it is *likely* to be *liked* or not. I have hitherto heard little in its commendation, and no one can *downright* abuse it to one's face, except in print. It can't be good, or I should not have stumbled over the threshold, and blundered in my very title. But I began it with my heart full of * * *, and my head of oriental*ities* (I can't call them *isms*), and wrote on rapidly.

This journal is a relief. When I am tired—as I generally am—out comes this, and down goes every thing. But I can't read it over; and God knows what contradictions it may contain. If I am sincere with myself (but I fear one lies more to one's self than to any one else), every page should confute, refute, and utterly abjure its predecessor.

Another scribble from Martin Baldwin the petitioner; I have neither head nor nerves to present it. That confounded supper at Lewis's has spoiled my digestion and my philanthropy. I have no more charity than a cruet of vinegar. Would I were an ostrich, and dieted on fire-irons,—or any thing that my gizzard could get the better of.

To-day saw Ward. His uncle is dying, and W. don't much affect our Dutch determinations. I dine with him on Thursday, provided *l'oncle* is not dined upon, or peremptorily bespoke by

the posthumous epicures before that day. I wish he may
recover—not for *our* dinner's sake, but to disappoint the under-
taker, and the rascally reptiles that may well wait, since they
will dine at last.

Gell called—he of Troy—after I was out. Mem.—to
return his visit. But my Mems. are the very landmarks of
forgetfulness;—something like a light-house, with a ship
wrecked under the nose of its lantern. I never look at a Mem.
without seeing that I have remembered to forget. Mem.—
I have forgotten to pay Pitt's taxes, and suppose I shall be
surcharged. "An I do not turn rebel when thou art king"—
oons! I believe my very biscuit is leavened with that impostor's
imposts.

Lady Melbourne returns from Jersey's to-morrow;—I must
call. A Mr. Thomson has sent a song, which I must applaud.
I hate annoying them with censure or silence;—and yet I hate
lettering.

Saw Lord Glenbervie and his Prospectus, at Murray's,
of a new Treatise on Timber. Now here is a man more useful
than all the historians and rhymers ever planted. For, by
preserving our woods and forests, he furnishes materials for all
the history of Britain worth reading, and all the odes worth
nothing.

Redde a good deal, but desultorily. My head is crammed
with the most useless lumber. It is odd that when I do read,
I can only bear the chicken broth of—*any thing* but Novels. It
is many a year since I looked into one, (though they are sometimes ordered, by way of experiment, but never taken,) till I
looked yesterday at the worst parts of the *Monk*. These descriptions ought to have been written by Tiberius at Caprea—
they are forced—the *philtered* ideas of a jaded voluptuary. It is
to me inconceivable how they could have been composed by a
man of only twenty—his age when he wrote them. They
have no nature—all the sour cream of cantharides. I should
have suspected Buffon of writing them on the death-bed of his
detestable dotage. I had never redde this edition, and merely
looked at them from curiosity and recollection of the noise they
made, and the name they had left to Lewis. But they could do
no harm, except * * * *.

Called this evening on my agent—my business as usual.

Our strange adventures are the only inheritances of our family that have not diminished.

I shall now smoke two cigars, and get me to bed. The cigars don't keep well here. They get as old as a *donna di quaranti anni* in the sun of Africa. The Havannah are the best; —but neither are so pleasant as a hooka or chiboque. The Turkish tobacco is mild, and their horses entire—two things as they should be. I am so far obliged to this Journal, that it preserves me from verse,—at least from keeping it. I have just thrown a poem into the fire (which it has relighted to my great comfort), and have smoked out of my head the plan of another. I wish I could as easily get rid of thinking, or, at least, the confusion of thought.

Tuesday, December 7

Went to bed, and slept dreamlessly, but not refreshingly. Awoke, and up an hour before being called; but dawdled three hours in dressing. When one subtracts from life infancy (which is vegetation),—sleep, eating, and swilling—buttoning and unbuttoning—how much remains of downright existence? The summer of a dormouse.

Redde the papers and *tea*-ed and soda-watered, and found out that the fire was badly lighted. Lord Glenbervie wants me to go to Brighton—um!

This morning, a very pretty billet from the Stael about meeting her at Ld. H.'s to-morrow. She has written, I dare say, twenty such this morning to different people, all equally flattering to each. So much the better for her and those who believe all she wishes them, or they wish to believe. She has been pleased to be pleased with my slight eulogy in the note annexed to *The Bride*. This is to be accounted for in several ways,—firstly, all women like all, or any, praise; secondly, this was unexpected, because I have never courted her; and, thirdly, as Scrub says, those who have been all their lives regularly praised, by regular critics, like a little variety, and are glad when any one goes out of his way to say a civil thing; and, fourthly, she is a very good-natured creature, which is the best reason, after all, and, perhaps, the only one.

A knock—knocks single and double. Bland called. He says Dutch society (he has been in Holland) is second-hand

French; but the women are like women every where else. This is a bore: I should like to see them a little *unlike*; but that can't be expected.

Went out—came home—this, that, and the other—and " all is vanity, saith the preacher ", and so say I, as part of his congregation. Talking of vanity, whose praise do I prefer? Why, Mrs. Inchbald's, and that of the Americans. The first, because her *Simple Story* and *Nature and Art* are, to me, *true* to their *titles*; and, consequently, her short note to Rogers about *The Giaour* delighted me more than any thing, except the *Edinburgh Review*. I like the Americans, because *I* happened to be in *Asia*, while the *English Bards, and Scotch Reviewers* were redde in *America*. If I could have had a speech against the *Slave Trade in Africa*, and an epitaph on a dog in *Europe* (i.e. in the *Morning Post*), my *vertex sublimis* would certainly have displaced stars enough to overthrow the Newtonian system.

Friday, December 10, 1813

I am *ennuyé* beyond my usual tense of that yawning verb, which I am always conjugating; and I don't find that society much mends the matter. I am too lazy to shoot myself—and it would annoy Augusta, and perhaps * *; but it would be a good thing for George, on the other side, and no bad one for me; but I won't be tempted.

I have had the kindest letter from Moore. I *do* think that man is the best-hearted, the only *hearted* being I ever encountered; and, then, his talents are equal to his feelings.

Dined on Wednesday at Lord H.'s—the Staffords, Staels, Cowpers, Ossulstones, Melbournes, Mackintoshes, etc., etc.— and was introduced to the Marquis and Marchioness of Stafford, —an unexpected event. My quarrel with Lord Carlisle (their or his brother-in-law) having rendered it improper, I suppose, brought it about. But, if it was to happen at all, I wonder it did not occur before. She is handsome, and must have been beautiful—and her manners are *princessly*.

The Stael was at the other end of the table, and less loquacious than heretofore. We are now very good friends; though she asked Lady Melbourne whether I had really any *bon-hommie*. She might as well have asked that question before she told C. L. "*c'est un démon*". True enough, but rather premature, for *she* could not have found it out, and so—she wants me to dine there next Sunday.

Murray prospers, as far as circulation. For my part, I adhere (in liking) to my Fragment. It is no wonder that I wrote one—my mind is a fragment.

Saw Lord Gower, Tierney, etc., in the square. Took leave of Lord Gower, who is going to Holland and Germany. He tells me that he carries with him a parcel of *Harolds* and *Giaours*, etc., for the readers of Berlin, who, it seems, read English, and have taken a caprice for mine. Um!—have I been *German* all this time, when I thought myself *Oriental*?

Lent Tierney my box for to-morrow; and received a new comedy sent by Lady C. A.—but *not hers*. I must read it, and endeavour not to displease the author. I hate annoying them with cavil; but a comedy I take to be the most difficult of compositions, more so than tragedy.

Galt says there is a coincidence between the first part of *The Bride* and some story of his—whether published or not, I know not, never having seen it. He is almost the last person on whom any one would commit literary larceny, and I am not conscious of any *witting* thefts on any of the genus. As to originality, all pretensions are ludicrous,—" there is nothing new under the sun ".

Went last night to the play. Invited out to a party, but did not go;—right. Refused to go to Lady * *'s on Monday;—right again. If I must fritter away my life, I would rather do it alone. I was much tempted;—C * * looked so Turkish with her red turban, and her regular, dark, and clear features. Not that *she* and *I* ever were, or could be, any thing; but I love any aspect that reminds me of the " children of the sun ".

To dine to-day with Rogers and Sharpe, for which I have some appetite, not having tasted food for the preceding forty-eight hours. I wish I could leave off eating altogether.

————

Saturday, December 11

————

Sunday, December 12

By Galt's answer, I find it is some story in *real life*, and not any work with which my late composition coincides. It is still more singular, for mine is drawn from *existence* also.

I have sent an excuse to Madame de Stael. I do not feel sociable enough for dinner to-day ;—and I will not go to Sheridan's on Wednesday. Not that I do not admire and prefer his unequalled conversation ; but—that "*but*" must only be intelligible to thoughts I cannot write. Sheridan was in good talk at Rogers's the other night, but I only stayed till *nine*. All the world are to be at the Stael's to-night, and I am not sorry to escape any part of it. I only go out to get me a fresh appetite for being alone. Went out—did not go to the Stael's but to Ld. Holland's. Party numerous—conversation general. Stayed late—made a blunder—got over it—came home and went to bed, not having eaten. Rather empty, but *fresco*, which is the great point with me.

Monday, December 13, 1813

Called at three places—read, and got ready to leave town to-morrow. Murray has had a letter from his brother bibliopole of Edinburgh, who says, " he is lucky in having such a *poet* "— something as if one was a pack-horse, or " ass, or any thing that is his " ; or, like Mrs. Packwood, who replied to some inquiry after the Odes on Razors,—" Laws, sir, we keeps a poet ". The same illustrious Edinburgh bookseller once sent an order for books, poesy, and cookery, with this agreeable postscript—" The *Harold* and *Cookery* are much wanted ". Such is fame, and, after all, quite as good as any other " life in others' breath ". 'Tis much the same to divide purchasers with Hannah Glasse [1] or Hannah More.

Some editor of some magazine has *announced* to Murray his intention of abusing the thing " *without reading it* ". So much the better ; if he redde it first, he would abuse it more.

Allen [2] (Lord Holland's Allen—the best informed and one of the ablest men I know—a perfect Magliabecchi—a devourer,

---

[1] Authoress of *The Art of Cookery Made Easy.*

[2] John Allen was for many years the Hollands's librarian, confidential friend and general *factotum.*

a *Helluo* of books, and an observer of men,) has lent me a quantity of Burns's unpublished and never-to-be-published Letters. They are full of oaths and obscene songs. What an antithetical mind !—tenderness, roughness—delicacy, coarseness—sentiment, sensuality—soaring and grovelling, dirt and deity—all mixed up in that one compound of inspired clay !

It seems strange ; a true voluptuary will never abandon his mind to the grossness of reality. It is by exalting the earthly, the material, the *physique* of our pleasures, by veiling these ideas, by forgetting them altogether, or, at least, never naming them hardly to one's self, that we alone can prevent them from disgusting.

December 14, 15, 16

Much done, but nothing to record. It is quite enough to set down my thoughts,—my actions will rarely bear retrospection.

December 17, 18

Lord Holland told me a curious piece of sentimentality in Sheridan. The other night we were all delivering our respective and various opinions on him and other *hommes marquans*, and mine was this :—" Whatever Sheridan has done or chosen to do has been, *par excellence*, always the *best* of its kind. He has written the *best* comedy (*School for Scandal*), the *best* drama (in my mind, far before that St. Giles's lampoon, the *Beggar's Opera*), the best farce (the *Critic*—it is only too good for a farce), and the best Address (Monologue on Garrick), and, to crown all, delivered the very best Oration (the famous Begum Speech) ever conceived or heard in this country." Somebody told S. this the next day, and on hearing it he burst into tears !

Poor Brinsley ! if they were tears of pleasure, I would rather have said these few, but most sincere, words than have written the Iliad or made his own celebrated Philippic. Nay, his own comedy never gratified me more than to hear that he had derived a moment's gratification from any praise of mine, humble as it must appear to " my elders and my betters ".

Went to my box at Covent Garden to-night ; and my delicacy felt a little shocked at seeing S * * *'s mistress (who, to my certain knowledge, was actually educated, from her birth, for her profession) sitting with her mother, " a three-piled b——d, b——d-Major to the army ", in a private box opposite. I felt rather indignant ; but, casting my eyes round the house, in the next box to me, and the next, and the next, were the most distinguished old and young Babylonians of quality ;—so I burst out a laughing. It was really odd ; Lady * * *divorced*—Lady * * and her daughter, Lady * *, both *divorceable*—Mrs. * *, in the next the *like*, and still nearer * * * * * * ! What an assemblage to *me*, who know all their histories. It was as if the house had been divided between your public and your *understood* courtesans ;—but the intriguantes much outnumbered the regular mercenaries. On the other side were only Pauline and *her* mother, and, next box to her, three of inferior note. Now, where lay the difference between *her* and *mamma*, and Lady * * and daughter? except that the two last may enter Carleton and any *other house*, and the two first are limited to the opera and b—— house. How I do delight in observing life as it really is !—and myself, after all, the worst of any. But no matter—I must avoid egotism, which, just now, would be no vanity.

I have lately written a wild, rambling, unfinished rhapsody, called " *The Devil's Drive* ", the notion of which I took from Porson's " *Devil's Walk* ".

Redde some Italian, and wrote two Sonnets on * * *. I never wrote but one sonnet before, and that was not in earnest, and many years ago, as an exercise—and I will never write another. They are the most puling, petrifying, stupidly platonic compositions. I detest the Petrarch so much, that I would not be the man even to have obtained his Laura, which the metaphysical, whining dotard never could.

January 16, 1814

To-morrow I leave town for a few days. I saw Lewis to-day, who is just returned from Oatlands, where he has been squabbling with Mad. de Stael about himself, Clarissa Harlowe, Mackintosh, and me. My homage has never been paid in that quarter, or we would have agreed still worse. I don't talk—I can't flatter, and won't listen, except to a pretty or a foolish woman. She bored Lewis with praises of himself till he sickened —found out that Clarissa was perfection, and Mackintosh the first man in England. There I agree, at least *one* of the first— but Lewis did not. As to Clarissa, I leave to those who can read it to judge and dispute. I could not do the one, and am, consequently, not qualified for the other. She told Lewis wisely, he being my friend, that I was affected, in the first place ; and that, in the next place, I committed the heinous offence of sitting at dinner with my *eyes* shut, or half shut. I wonder if I really have this trick. I must cure myself of it, if true. One insensibly acquires awkward habits, which should be broken in time. If this is one, I wish I had been told of it before. It would not so much signify if one was always to be checkmated by a plain woman, but one may as well see some of one's neighbours, as well as the plate upon the table.

I should like, of all things, to have heard the Amabæan eclogue between her and Lewis—both obstinate, clever, odd, garrulous, and shrill. In fact, one could have heard nothing else. But they fell out, alas !—and now they will never quarrel again. Could not one reconcile them for the " nonce "? Poor Corinne—she will find that some of her fine sayings won't suit our fine ladies and gentlemen.

I am getting rather into admiration of [Lady C. Annesley] the youngest sister of [Lady F. Webster]. A wife would be my salvation. I am sure the wives of my acquaintances have hitherto done me little good. Catherine is beautiful, but very young, and, I think, a fool. But I have not seen enough to judge ; besides, I hate an *esprit* in petticoats. That she won't love me is very probable, nor shall I love her. But, on my system, and the modern system in general, that don't signify. The business (if it came to business) would probably be arranged between papa and me. She would have her own way ;

I am good-humoured to women, and docile ; and, if I did not fall in love with her, which I should try to prevent, we should be a very comfortable couple. As to conduct, *that* she must look to. But *if* I love, I shall be jealous ;—and for that reason I will not be in love. Though, after all, I doubt my temper, and fear I should not be so patient as becomes the *bienséance* of a married man in my station. Divorce ruins the poor *femme*, and damages are a paltry compensation. I do fear my temper would lead me into some of our oriental tricks of vengeance, or, at any rate, into a summary appeal to the court of twelve paces. So " I'll none on't ", but e'en remain single and solitary ;— though I should like to have somebody now and then to yawn with one.

Ward, and, after him, * *, has stolen one of my buffooneries about Mde de Stael's Metaphysics and the Fog, and passed it, by speech and letter, as their own. As Gibbet says, " they are the most of a gentleman of any on the road ". W. is in sad enmity with the Whigs about this Review of Fox (if he *did* review him) ;—all the epigrammatists and essayists are at him. I hate *odds*, and wish he may beat them. As for me, by the blessing of indifference, I have simplified my politics into an utter detestation of all existing governments ; and, as it is the shortest and most agreeable and summary feeling imaginable, the first moment of an universal republic would convert me into an advocate for single and uncontradicted despotism. The fact is, riches are power, and poverty is slavery all over the earth, and one sort of establishment is no better nor worse for a *people* than another. I shall adhere to my party, because it would not be honourable to act otherwise ; but, as to *opinions*, I don't think politics *worth* an *opinion*. *Conduct* is another thing : —if you begin with a party, go on with them. I have no consistency, except in politics ; and *that* probably arises from my indifference on the subject altogether.

Feb. 18

Better than a month since I last journalised :—most of it out of London and at Notts., but a busy one and a pleasant, at least three weeks of it. On my return, I find all the news-papers in hysterics, and town in an uproar, on the avowal and republication of two stanzas on Princess Charlotte's weeping

at Regency's speech to Lauderdale in 1812.[1] They are daily
at it still;—some of the abuse good, all of it hearty. They talk
of a motion in our House upon it—be it so.

Got up—redde the *Morning Post* containing the battle of
Buonaparte, the destruction of the Custom-house, and a paragraph on me as long as my pedigree, and vituperative, as usual.

Hobhouse is returned to England. He is my best friend,
the most lively, and a man of the most sterling talents extant.

The Corsair has been conceived, written, published, etc.,
since I last took up this journal. They tell me it has great
success;—it was written *con amore*, and much from *existence*.
Murray is satisfied with its progress; and if the public are
equally so with the perusal, there's an end of the matter.

Nine o' clock

Been to Hanson's on business. Saw Rogers, and had a
note from Lady Melbourne, who says, it is said I am " much
out of spirits ". I wonder if I really am or not? I have
certainly enough of " that perilous stuff which weighs upon the
heart ", and it is better they should believe it to be the result of
these attacks than of the real cause; but—ay, ay, always *but*,
to the end of the chapter.

Hobhouse has told me ten thousand anecdotes of Napoleon,
all good and true. My friend H. is the most entertaining of
companions, and a fine fellow to boot.

Redde a little—wrote notes and letters, and am alone,
which Locke says is bad company. " Be not solitary, be not
idle."—Um!—the idleness is troublesome; but I can't see so
much to regret in the solitude. The more I see of men, the less
I like them. If I could but say so of women too, all would be
well. Why can't I? I am now six-and-twenty; my passions
have had enough to cool them; my affections more than
enough to wither them,—and yet—and yet—always *yet* and
but—" Excellent well, you are a fishmonger—get thee to a
nunnery ". " They fool me to the top of my bent."

[1] Byron's *Stanzas to a Lady Weeping*—occasioned by the report that Princess
Charlotte had burst into tears at a Carlton House banquet on hearing her father,
the Prince Regent, attack his former friends, the Whigs—had originally appeared
anonymously in the *Morning Chronicle* during March 1812. Byron's avowal of
authorship caused a considerable commotion.

Midnight

Began a letter, which I threw into the fire. Redde—but to little purpose. Did not visit Hobhouse, as I promised and ought. No matter, the loss is mine. Smoked cigars.

Napoleon!—this week will decide his fate. All seems against him; but I believe and hope he will win—at least, beat back the invaders. What right have we to prescribe sovereigns to France? Oh for a Republic! " Brutus, thou sleepest." Hobhouse abounds in continental anecdotes of this extraordinary man; all in favour of his intellect and courage, but against his *bonhommie*. No wonder;—how should he, who knows mankind well, do other than despise and abhor them?

The greater the equality, the more impartially evil is distributed, and becomes lighter by the division among so many— therefore, a Republic!

More notes from Madame de Stael unanswered—and so they shall remain. I admire her abilities, but really her society is overwhelming—an avalanche that buries one in glittering nonsense—all snow and sophistry.

Shall I go to Mackintosh's on Tuesday? um!—I did not go to Marquis Lansdowne's nor to Miss Berry's, though both are pleasant. So is Sir James's,—but I don't know—I believe one is not the better for parties; at least, unless some *regnante* is there.

I wonder how the deuce any body could make such a world; for what purpose dandies, for instance, were ordained —and kings—and fellows of colleges—and women of " a certain age "—and many men of any age—and myself, most of all!

> " Divesne prisco natus ab Inacho
>   Nil interest, an pauper et infimâ
>   De gente, sub dio [*sic*] moreris,
>   Victima nil miserantis Orci.
>   Omnes eodem cogimur ", etc.

Is there any thing beyond?—*who* knows? *He* that can't tell. Who tells that there *is*? He who don't know. And when shall he know? perhaps, when he don't expect, and generally when he don't wish it. In this last respect, however, all are not alike: it depends a good deal upon education,—something upon nerves and habits—but most upon digestion.

Saturday, Feb. 19

Just returned from seeing Kean in Richard. By Jove, he is a soul! Life—nature—truth without exaggeration or diminution. Kemble's Hamlet is perfect; but Hamlet is not Nature. Richard is a man; and Kean is Richard. Now to my own concerns.

Went to Waite's. Teeth are all right and white; but he says that I grind them in my sleep and chip the edges. That same sleep is no friend of mine, though I court him sometimes for half the twenty-four.

February 20

Got up and tore out two leaves of this Journal—I don't know why. Hodgson just called and gone. He has much *bonhommie* with his other good qualities, and more talent than he has yet had credit for beyond his circle.

An invitation to dine at Holland House to meet Kean. He is worth meeting; and I hope, by getting into good society, he will be prevented from falling like Cooke. He is greater now on the stage, and off he should never be less. There is a stupid and underrating criticism upon him in one of the newspapers. I thought that, last night, though great, he rather under-acted more than the first time. This may be the effect of these cavils; but I hope he has more sense than to mind them. He cannot expect to maintain his present eminence, or to advance still higher, without the envy of his green-room fellows, and the nibbling of their admirers. But, if he don't beat them all, why then—merit hath no purchase in " these coster-monger days ".

I wish that I had a talent for the drama; I would write a tragedy *now*. But no,—it is gone. Hodgson talks of one,—he will do it well;—and I think M—e [Moore] should try. He has wonderful powers, and much variety; besides, he has lived and felt. To write so as to bring home to the heart, the heart must have been tried,—but, perhaps, ceased to be so. While you are under the influence of passions, you only feel, but cannot describe them,—any more than, when in action, you could turn round and tell the story to your next neighbour! When all is over,—all, all, and irrevocable,—trust to memory— she is then but too faithful.

·Went out, and answered some letters, yawned now and then, and redde the *Robbers*. Fine,—but *Fiesco* is better ; and Alfieri, and Monti's *Aristodemo best*. They are more equal than the Tedeschi dramatists.

Answered—or rather acknowledged—the receipt of young Reynolds's poem, *Safie*. The lad is clever, but much of his thoughts are borrowed,—*whence*, the Reviewers may find out. I hate discouraging a young one ; and I think,—though wild and more oriental than he would be, had he seen the scenes where he has placed his tale,—that he has much talent, and, certainly fire enough.

Received a very singular epistle ; and the mode of its conveyance, through Lord H.'s hands, as curious as the letter itself. But it was gratifying and pretty.

Sunday, February 27

Here I am, alone, instead of dining at Lord H.'s, where I was asked,—but not inclined to go any where. Hobhouse says I am growing a *loup garou*,—a solitary hobgoblin. True ;—" I am myself alone ". The last week has been passed in reading —seeing plays—now and then visitors—sometimes yawning and sometimes sighing, but no writing,—save of letters. If I could always read, I should never feel the want of society. Do I regret it?—um !—" Man delights not me ", and only one woman—at a time.

There is something to me very softening in the presence of a woman,—some strange influence, even if one is not in love with them—which I cannot at all account for, having no very high opinion of the sex. But yet,—I always feel in better humour with myself and every thing else, if there is a woman within ken. Even Mrs. Mule, my firelighter,—the most ancient and withered of her kind,—and (except to myself) not the best-tempered—always makes me laugh,—no difficult task when I am " i' the vein ".

Heigho ! I would I were in mine island !—I am not well ; and yet I look in good health. At times I fear, " I am not in my perfect mind " ;—and yet my heart and head have stood many a crash, and what should ail them now? They prey upon themselves, and I am sick—sick—" Prithee, undo this button—why should a cat, a rat, a dog have life—and *thou*

no life at all? "   Six-and-twenty years, as they call them, why,
I might and should have been a Pasha by this time.   " I 'gin
to be a-weary of the sun."

Buonaparte is not yet beaten; but has rebutted Blucher,
and repiqued Schwartzenburg. This it is to have a head. If
he again wins, *Væ victis!*

Sunday, March 6

On Tuesday last dined with Rogers,—Madame de Staël,
Mackintosh, Sheridan, Erskine, and Payne Knight, Lady
Donegal, and Miss R. there. Sheridan told a very good story
of himself and Madame de Recamier's handkerchief; Erskine
a few stories of himself only. *She* is going to write a big book
about England, she says;—I believe her. Asked by her how I
liked Miss Edgeworth's thing, called *Patronage*, and answered
(very sincerely) that I thought it very bad for *her*, and worse
than any of the others. Afterwards thought it possible Lady
Donegal, being Irish, might be a patroness of Miss Edgeworth,
and was rather sorry for my opinion, as I hate putting people
into fusses, either with themselves or their favourites; it looks
as if one did it on purpose. The party went off very well, and
the fish was very much to my gusto. But we got up too soon
after the women; and Mrs. Corinne always lingers so long
after dinner that we wish her in—the drawing-room.

To-day Campbell called, and while sitting here in came
Merivale. During our colloquy, C. (ignorant that Merivale
was the writer) abused the " mawkishness of the *Quarterly
Review* of Grimm's *Correspondence* ". I (knowing the secret)
changed the conversation as soon as I could; and C. went
away, quite convinced of having made the most favourable
impression on his new acquaintance. Merivale is luckily a
very good-natured fellow, or God he knows what might have
been engendered from such a malaprop. I did not look at him
while this was going on, but I felt like a coal—for I like Merivale, as well as the article in question.

Asked to Lady Keith's to-morrow evening—I think I will go;
but it is the first party invitation I have accepted this " season ",
as the learned Fletcher called it, when that youngest brat of
Lady * *'s cut my eye and cheek open with a misdirected
pebble—" Never mind, my Lord, the scar will be gone before the
season "; as if one's eye was of no importance in the mean time.

Lord Erskine called, and gave me his famous pamphlet,[1] with a marginal note and corrections in his handwriting. Sent it to be bound superbly, and shall treasure it.

Sent my fine print of Napoleon to be framed. It *is* framed; and the Emperor becomes his robes as if he had been hatched in them.

March 7

Rose at seven—ready by half-past eight—went to Mr. Hanson's, Bloomsbury Square—went to church with his eldest daughter, Mary Anne (a good girl), and gave her away to the Earl of Portsmouth.[2] Saw her fairly a countess—congratulated the family and groom (bride)—drank a bumper of wine (wholesome sherris) to their felicity, and all that—and came home. Asked to stay to dinner, but could not. At three sat to Phillips for faces. Called on Lady M. [Melbourne]—I like her so well, that I always stay too long. (Mem.—to mend of that.)

Passed the evening with Hobhouse, who has begun a poem, which promises highly;—wish he would go on with it. Heard some curious extracts from a life of Morosini, the blundering Venetian, who blew up the Acropolis at Athens with a bomb, and be damned to him! Waxed sleepy—just come home—must go to bed, and am engaged to meet Sheridan to-morrow at Rogers's.

Queer ceremony that same of marriage—saw many abroad, Greek and Catholic—one, at *home*, many years ago. There be some strange phrases in the prologue (the exhortation), which made me turn away, not to laugh in the face of the surpliceman. Made one blunder, when I joined the hands of the happy—rammed their left hands, by mistake, into one another. Corrected it—bustled back to the altar-rail, and said " Amen ". Portsmouth responded as if he had got the whole by heart; and, if any thing, was rather before the priest. It is now midnight and * * *.

March 10, Thor's Day

On Tuesday dined with Rogers,—Mackintosh, Sheridan, Sharpe,—much talk, and good,—all, except my own little

---

[1] Lord Erskine, Lord Chancellor in 1806, was a Whig and sympathizer with the principles of the French Revolution. The pamphlet to which Byron alludes was published in 1797, *On the Causes and Consequences of the War with France.*

[2] Mary Anne Hanson's marriage to Lord Portsmouth eventually led to an embittered law-suit, during which the bridegroom's sanity at the time of their marriage was called in question.

prattlement. Much of old times—Horne Tooke—the Trials—evidence of Sheridan, and anecdotes of those times, when *I*, alas! was an infant. If I had been a man, I would have made an English Lord Edward Fitzgerald.

Set down Sheridan at Brookes's,—where, by the by, he could not have well set down himself, as he and I were the only drinkers. Sherry means to stand for Westminster, as Cochrane (the stock-jobbing hoaxer) must vacate. Brougham is a candidate. I fear for poor dear Sherry. Both have talents of the highest order, but the youngster has *yet* a character. We shall see, if he lives to Sherry's age, how he will pass over the redhot ploughshares of public life. I don't know why, but I hate to see the *old* ones lose; particularly Sheridan, notwithstanding all his *méchanceté*.

Received many, and the kindest, thanks from Lady Portsmouth, *père* and *mère*, for my match-making. I don't regret it, as she looks the countess well, and is a very good girl. It is odd how well she carries her new honours. She looks a different woman, and high-bred, too. I had no idea that I could make so good a peeress.

Went to the play with Hobhouse. Mrs. Jordan superlative in Hoyden, and Jones well enough in Foppington. *What plays!* what wit!—*hélas!* Congreve and Vanbrugh are your only comedy. Our society is too insipid now for the like copy. Would *not* go to Lady Keith's. Hobhouse thought it odd. I wonder *he* should like parties. If one is in love, and wants to break a commandment and covet any thing that is there, they do very well. But to go out amongst the mere herd, without a motive, pleasure, or pursuit—'sdeath! " I'll none of it." He told me an odd report,—that *I* am the actual Conrad, the veritable Corsair, and that part of my travels are supposed to have passed in privacy. Um!—people sometimes hit near the truth; but never the whole truth. H. don't know what I was about the year after he left the Levant; nor does any one—nor —— nor —— nor —— however, it is a lie—but, " I doubt the equivocation of the fiend that lies like truth! "

I shall have letters of importance to-morrow. Which, * *, * *, or * *? heigho!—* * is in my heart, * * in my head, * * in my eye, and the *single* one, Heaven knows where. All write, and will be answered. " Since I have crept in favour with

myself, I must maintain it "; but I never " mistook my person ",
though I think others have.

* * called to-day in great despair about his mistress, who
has taken a freak of * * *. He began a letter to her, but was
obliged to stop short—I finished it for him, and he copied and
sent it. If *he* holds out, and keeps to my instructions of affected
indifference, she will lower her colours. If she don't, he will,
at least, get rid of her, and she don't seem much worth keeping.
But the poor lad is in love—if that is the case, she will win.
When they once discover their power, *finita è la musica*.

Sleepy, and must go to bed.

Tuesday, March 15

Dined yesterday with Rogers, Mackintosh, and Sharpe.
Sheridan could not come. Sharpe told several very amusing
anecdotes of Henderson, the actor. Stayed till late, and came
home, having drunk so much *tea*, that I did not get to sleep till
six this morning. R. says I am to be in *this Quarterly*—cut up,
I presume, as they " hate us youth ". *N'importe*. As Sharpe
was passing by the doors of some debating society (the Westminster Forum), in his way to dinner, he saw rubricked on the
wall *Scott's* name and *mine*—" Which the best poet? " being
the question of the evening; and I suppose all the Templars
and *would-bes* took our rhymes in vain in the course of the
controversy. Which had the greater show of hands, I neither
know nor care; but I feel the coupling of the names as a
compliment—though I think Scott deserves better company.

Wedderburn Webster called—Lord Erskine, Lord Holland,
etc., etc. Wrote to * * *The Corsair* report. She says she don't
wonder, since " Conrad is so *like* ". It is odd that one, who
knows me so thoroughly, should tell me this to my face. However, if she don't know, nobody can.

Mackintosh is, it seems, the writer of the defensive letter in
the *Morning Chronicle*. If so, it is very kind, and more than I
did for myself.

Told Murray to secure for me Bandello's Italian Novels at
the sale to-morrow. To me they will be *nuts*. Redde a satire
on myself, called " Anti-Byron ", and told Murray to publish
it if he liked. The object of the author is to prove me an
atheist and a systematic conspirator against law and govern-

ment. Some of the verse is good; the prose I don't quite understand. He asserts that my " deleterious works " have had " an effect upon civil society, which requires ", etc., etc., etc., and his own poetry. It is a lengthy poem, and a long preface, with an harmonious title-page. Like the fly in the fable, I seem to have got upon a wheel which makes much dust; but, unlike the said fly, I do not take it all for my own raising.

A letter from *Bella*, which I answered. I shall be in love with her again if I don't take care.

I shall begin a more regular system of reading soon.

Thursday, March 17

I have been sparring with Jackson for exercise this morning; and mean to continue and renew my acquaintance with the muffles. My chest, and arms, and wind are in very good plight, and I am not in flesh. I used to be a hard hitter, and my arms are very long for my height (5 feet 8½ inches). At any rate, exercise is good, and this the severest of all; fencing and the broadsword never fatigued me half so much.

Redde the *Quarrels of Authors* (another sort of *sparring*)—a new work, by that most entertaining and researching writer, Israeli. They seem to be an irritable set, and I wish myself well out of it. " I'll not march through Coventry with them, that's flat." What the devil had I to do with scribbling? It is too late to inquire, and all regret is useless. But, an it were to do again,—I should write again, I suppose. Such is human nature, at least my share of it;—though I shall think better of myself, if I have sense to stop now. If I have a wife, and that wife has a son—by any body—I will bring up mine heir in the most anti-poetical way—make him a lawyer, or a pirate, or—any thing. But, if he writes too, I shall be sure he is none of mine, and cut him off with a Bank token. Must write a letter—three o'clock.

Sunday, March 20

I intended to go to Lady Hardwicke's, but won't. I always begin the day with a bias towards going to parties; but, as the evening advances, my stimulus fails, and I hardly ever go out—and, when I do, always regret it. This might have been a pleasant one ;—at least, the hostess is a very superior woman. Lady Lansdowne's to-morrow—Lady Heathcote's Wednesday. Um !—I must spur myself into going to some of them, or it will look like rudeness, and it is better to do as other people do— confound them !

Redde Machiavel, parts of Chardin, and Sismondi, and Bandello—by starts. Redde the *Edinburgh*, 44, just come out. In the beginning of the article on Edgeworth's *Patronage*, I have gotten a high compliment, I perceive. Whether this is creditable to me, I know not ; but it does honour to the editor, because he once abused me. Many a man will retract praise ; none but a high-spirited mind will revoke its censure, or *can* praise the man it has once attacked. I have often, since my return to England, heard Jeffrey most highly commended by those who know him for things independent of his talents. I admire him for *this*—not because he has *praised me* (I have been so praised elsewhere and abused, alternately, that mere habit has rendered me as indifferent to both as a man at twenty-six can be to any thing), but because he is, perhaps, the *only man* who, under the relations in which he and I stand, or stood, with regard to each other, would have had the liberality to act thus ; none but a great soul dared hazard it. The height on which he stands has not made him giddy ;—a little scribbler would have gone on cavilling to the end of the chapter. As to the justice of his panegyric, that is matter of taste. There are plenty to question it, and glad, too, of the opportunity.

Lord Erskine called to-day. He means to carry down his reflections on the war—or rather wars—to the present day. I trust that he will. Must send to Mr. Murray to get the binding of my copy of his pamphlet finished, as Lord E. has promised me to correct it, and add some marginal notes to it. Any thing in his handwriting will be a treasure, which will gather compound interest from years. Erskine has high expectations of Mackintosh's promised History. Undoubtedly it must be a classic, when finished.

Sparred with Jackson again yesterday morning, and shall to-morrow. I feel all the better for it, in spirits, though my arms and shoulders are very stiff from it. Mem.—to attend the pugilistic dinner :—Marquess Huntley is in the chair.

Lord Erskine thinks that ministers must be in peril of going out. So much the better for him. To me it is the same who are in or out;—we want something more than a change of ministers, and someday we will have it.

I remember, in riding from Chrisso to Castri (Delphos), along the sides of Parnassus, I saw six eagles in the air. It is uncommon to see so many together; and it was the number—not the species, which is common enough—that excited my attention.

The last bird I ever fired at was an *eaglet*, on the shore of the Gulf of Lepanto, near Vostitza. It was only wounded, and I tried to save it, the eye was so bright; but it pined, and died in a few days; and I never did since, and never will, attempt the death of another bird. I wonder what put these two things into my head just now? I have been reading Sismondi, and there is nothing there that could induce the recollection.

I am mightily taken with Braccio di Montone, Giovanni Galeazzo, and Eccelino. But the last is *not* Bracciaferro (of the same name), Count of Ravenna, whose history I want to trace. There is a fine engraving in Lavater, from a picture by Fuseli, of *that* Ezzelin, over the body of Meduna, punished by him for a *hitch* in her constancy during his absence in the Crusades. He was right—but I want to know the story.

Tuesday, March 22

Last night, *party* at Lansdowne House. To-night, *party* at Lady Charlotte Greville's—deplorable waste of time, and something of temper. Nothing imparted—nothing acquired—talking without ideas:—if any thing like *thought* in my mind, it was not on the subjects on which we were gabbling. Heigho! —and in this way half London pass what is called life. To-morrow there is Lady Heathcote's—shall I go? yes—to punish myself for not having a pursuit.

Let me see—what did I see? The only person who much struck me was Lady S[taffor]d's eldest daughter, Lady C[harlotte] L[eveson]. They say she is *not* pretty. I don't know—every thing is pretty that pleases; but there is an air of *soul* about her—and her colour changes—and there is that shyness of the antelope (which I delight in) in her manner so much, that I observed her more than I did any other woman in the rooms, and only looked at any thing else when I thought she might perceive and feel embarrassed by my scrutiny. After all, there may be something of association in this. She is a friend of Augusta's, and whatever she loves I can't help liking.

Her mother, the Marchioness, talked to me a little; and I was twenty times on the point of asking her to introduce me to *sa fille*, but I stopped short. This comes of that affray with the Carlisles.

Earl Grey told me laughingly of a paragraph in the last *Moniteur*, which has stated, among other symptoms of rebellion, some particulars of the *sensation* occasioned in all our government gazettes by the "tear" lines,—*only* amplifying, in its re-statement, an epigram (by the by, no epigram except in the *Greek* acceptation of the word) into a *roman*. I wonder the *Couriers*, etc., etc., have not translated that part of the *Moniteur*, with additional comments.

The Princess of Wales has requested Fuseli to paint from *The Corsair*—leaving to him the choice of any passage for the subject: so Mr. Locke tells me. Tired, jaded, selfish, and supine—must go to bed.

Roman, at least *Romance*, means a song sometimes, as in the Spanish. I suppose this is the *Moniteur's* meaning, unless he has confused it with *The Corsair*.

Albany, March 28

This night got into my new apartments, rented of Lord Althorpe, on a lease of seven years. Spacious, and room for my books and sabres. *In* the *house*, too, another advantage. The last few days, or whole week, have been very abstemious, regular in exercise, and yet very *un*well.

Yesterday, dined *tête-à-tête* at the Cocoa with Scrope Davies—sat from six till midnight—drank between us one bottle of champagne and six of claret, neither of which wines ever affect me. Offered to take Scrope home in my carriage; but he was tipsy and pious, and I was obliged to leave him on his knees praying to I know not what purpose or pagod. No headach, nor sickness, that night nor to-day. Got up, if any thing, earlier than usual—sparred with Jackson *ad sudorem*, and

have been much better in health than for many days. I have
heard nothing more from Scrope. Yesterday paid him four
thousand eight hundred pounds, a debt of some standing, and
which I wished to have paid before. My mind is much re-
lieved by the removal of that *debit*.

Augusta wants me to make it up with Carlisle. I have
refused *every* body else, but I can't deny her any thing;—so I
must e'en do it, though I had as lief " drink up Eisel—eat a
crocodile ". Let me see—Ward, the Hollands, the Lambs,
Rogers, etc., etc.,—every body, more or less, have been trying
for the last two years to accommodate this *couplet* quarrel, to no
purpose. I shall laugh if Augusta succeeds.

Redde a little of many things—shall get in all my books
to-morrow. Luckily this room will hold them—with " ample
room and verge, etc., the characters of hell to trace ". I must
set about some employment soon; my heart begins to eat
itself again.

April 8

Out of town six days. On my return, found my poor little
pagod, Napoleon, pushed off his pedestal;—the thieves are in
Paris. It is his own fault. Like Milo, he would rend the oak;
but it closed again, wedged his hands, and now the beasts—
lion, bear, down to the dirtiest jackal—may all tear him. That
Muscovite winter *wedged* his arms;—ever since, he has fought
with his feet and teeth. The last may still leave their marks;
and " I guess now " (as the Yankees say) that he will yet play
them a pass. He is in their rear—between them and their
homes. Query—will they ever reach them?

Saturday, April 9, 1814

I mark this day!

Napoleon Buonaparte has abdicated the throne of the world.
" Excellent well." Methinks Sylla did better; for he revenged
and resigned in the height of his sway, red with the slaughter
of his foes—the finest instance of glorious contempt of the
rascals upon record. Dioclesian did well too—Amurath not
amiss, had he become aught except a dervise—Charles the
Fifth but so so—but Napoleon, worst of all. What! wait till
they were in his capital, and then talk of his readiness to give

up what is already gone ! !   " What whining monk art thou—
what holy cheat? "   'Sdeath !—Dionysius at Corinth was yet a
king to this. The " Isle of Elba " to retire to !—Well—if it had
been Caprea, I should have marvelled less.   " I see men's
minds are but a parcel of their fortunes."   I am utterly bewildered and confounded.

I don't know—but I think *I*, even *I* (an insect compared
with this creature), have set my life on casts not a millionth
part of this man's. But, after all, a crown may be not worth
dying for. Yet, to outlive *Lodi* for this ! ! ! Oh that Juvenal or
Johnson could rise from the dead ! *Expende—quot libras in duce
summo invenies?* I knew they were light in the balance of
mortality ; but I thought their living dust weighed more
carats. Alas ! this imperial diamond hath a flaw in it, and is now
hardly fit to stick in a glazier's pencil :—the pen of the historian
won't rate it worth a ducat.

Psha ! " something too much of this ". But I won't give
him up even now ; though all his admirers have, " like the
thanes, fallen from him ".

April 10

I do not know that I am happiest when alone ; but this I
am sure of, that I never am long in the society even of *her* I
love, (God knows too well, and the devil probably too,) without
a yearning for the company of my lamp and my utterly confused and tumbled-over library. Even in the day, I send away
my carriage oftener than I use or abuse it. *Per esempio,*—I have
not stirred out of these rooms for these four days past : but I
have sparred for exercise (windows open) with Jackson an hour
daily, to attenuate and keep up the ethereal part of me. The
more violent the fatigue, the better my spirits for the rest of the
day ; and then, my evenings have that calm nothingness of
languor, which I most delight in. To-day I have boxed an
hour—written an ode to Napoleon Buonaparte—copied it—
eaten six biscuits—drunk four bottles of soda water—redde
away the rest of my time—besides giving poor [? Webster] a
world of advice about this mistress of his, who is plaguing him
into a phthisic and intolerable tediousness. I am a pretty
fellow truly to lecture about " the sect ". No matter, my
counsels are all thrown away.

April 19, 1814

There is ice at both poles, north and south—all extremes are the same—misery belongs to the highest and the lowest only, to the emperor and the beggar, when unsixpenced and unthroned. There is, to be sure, a damned insipid medium— an equinoctial line—no one knows where, except upon maps and measurement.

> " And all our *yesterdays* have lighted fools
> The way to dusty death."

I will keep no further journal of that same hesternal torch-light; and, to prevent me from returning, like a dog, to the vomit of memory, I tear out the remaining leaves of this volume, and write, in *Ipecacuanha,*—" that the Bourbons are re-stored!!!"—" Hang up philosophy." To be sure, I have long despised myself and man, but I never spat in the face of my species before—" O fool! I shall go mad ".

TO THOMAS MOORE   *January 6, 1814*

I have got a devil of a long story in the press, entitled
" *The Corsair* ", in the regular heroic measure. It is a pirate's
isle, peopled with my own creatures, and you may easily
suppose they do a world of mischief through the three cantos.
Now for your dedication—if you will accept it. This is positively my last experiment on public *literary* opinion, till I turn
my thirtieth year,—if so be I flourish until that downhill period.
I have a confidence for you—a perplexing one to me, and, just
at present, in a state of abeyance in itself. * * * * * * However, we shall see. In the mean time, you may amuse yourself
with my suspense, and put all the justices of peace in requisition, in case I come into your county with " hackbut bent ".

Seriously, whether I am to hear from her or him, it is a
pause, which I shall fill up with as few thoughts of my own as I
can borrow from other people. Any thing is better than
stagnation ; and now, in the interregnum of my autumn and
a strange summer adventure, which I don't like to think of,
(I don't mean * *'s, however, which is laughable only), the
antithetical state of my lucubrations makes me alive, and
Macbeth can " sleep no more " :—he was lucky in getting rid
of the drowsy sensation of waking again.

Pray write to me. I must send you a copy of the letter of
dedication. When do you come out? I am sure we don't
clash this time, for I am all at sea, and in action,—and a wife,
and a mistress, etc.

Thomas, thou art a happy fellow ; but if you wish us to
be so, you must come up to town, as you did last year ; and
we shall have a world to say, and to see, and to hear. Let me
hear from you.

P.S.—Of course you will keep my secret, and don't even
talk in your sleep of it. Happen what may, your dedication is
ensured, being already written ; and I shall copy it out fair to-
night, in case business or amusement—*Amant alterna Camœnæ.*

TO LADY MELBOURNE   *January 8th, 1814*

My dear Lʸ Mᴱ,—I have had too much in my head to
write ; but don't think my silence capricious.

C. is quite out—in yᵉ first place *she* [1] was not under the same roof, but first with my old friends the H[arrowby]'s in B[erkele]y Square, and afterwards at her friends the V[illiers]'s, nearer me. The separation and the express are utterly false, and without even a shadow of foundation; so you see her spies are ill paid, or badly informed. But if she had been in yᵉ same house, it is less singular than C.'s *coming* to it; the house was a very decent house, till that illustrious person thought proper to render it otherwise.

As to Mᵉ de Staël, I never go near her; her books are very delightful, but in society I see nothing but a plain woman forcing one to listen, and look at her, with her pen behind her ear, and her mouth full of ink—so much for her.

Now for a confidence—my old love of all loves—Mrs. ——[2] (whom somebody told you knew nothing about me) has written to me *twice*—no *love*, but she wants to see me; and though it will be a melancholy interview, I shall go; we have hardly met, and never been on any intimate terms since her marriage. *He* has been playing the Devil with all kinds of vulgar mistresses; and behaving ill enough, in every respect. I enclose you the *last*, which pray return immediately with your *opinion*, whether I *ought* to see her, or not—you see she is unhappy; she was a spoilt heiress; but has seen little or nothing of the world—very pretty, and once simple in character, and clever, but with no peculiar accomplishments, but endeared to me by a thousand childish, and singular recollections—you know her estate joined mine; and we were as children very much together; but no matter; *this* was a love match, they are *separated*.

I have heard from Ph.[3] who seems embarrassed with constancy. Her *date* is the *Grampian* hills, to be sure. With that latitude, and her precious *époux*, it must be a shuddering kind of existence.

C. may do as she pleases, thanks to your good-nature, rather than my merits, or prudence; there is little to dread from her love, and I forgive her hatred.

[1] Augusta Leigh. Caroline Lamb, " C.", had recently made an incursion into Byron's lodgings.

[2] Mary Anne Chaworth, the object of Byron's schoolboy passion, had married John Musters in 1805.

[3] Lady Frances Webster.

L^y H.'s second son is in Notts, and *she* has been guessing, and asking about Mrs. C. ; no matter ; so that I keep her from all other conjectures. I wrote to you in a tone which nothing but hurry can excuse. Don't think me impertinent, or peevish, but merely confused ; *consider* one moment *all things*, and do not wonder. By-the-bye, I lately passed my time very *happily*.

By-the-bye, this letter will prove to you that we were at least friends, and that the mother-in-law erred when she told you that it was quite a *dream*. You will believe me another time. Adieu, ever y^rs Pray write and believe me

Most affect^y y^rs, B.

TO LADY MELBOURNE   *January 13th, 1814*

M^Y DEAR L^Y M^E,—I do not see how you could well have said less, and that I am not angry may be proved by my saying a word more on ye subject.

You are quite mistaken, however, as to *her*, and it must be from some misrepresentation of mine, that you throw the blame so completely on the side least deserving, and least able to bear it. I dare say I made the best of my own story, as one always does from natural selfishness without intending it, but it was not her fault, but my own *folly* (give it what name may suit it better) and her weakness, for the intentions of both were very different, and for some time adhered to, and when not, it was entirely my own—in short, I know no name for my conduct. Pray do not speak so harshly of her to me—the cause of all.

I wrote to you yesterday on other subjects, and particularly C. As to *manner*, mine is the same to anyone I know and like, and I am almost sure less marked to her than to *you*, besides any constraint, or reserve would appear much more extraordinary than the reverse, until something more than manner is ascertainable. Nevertheless, I heartily wish Me de Staël at the devil with her observations. I am certain I did not see her, and she might as well have had something else to do with her eyes than to observe people at so respectful a distance.

So " *Ph.* is out of my thoughts "—in the first place, if she were out of them, she had probably not found a place in my words, and in the next, she has no *claim*. If people will stop at the first tense of the verb " aimer ", they must not be surprised if one finishes the conjugation with somebody else—" How soon I get the better of—" in the name of St. Francis and his wife of snow, and Pygmalion and his statue—what was there here to get the better of? A few kisses, for which she was no worse, and I no better. Had the event been different, so would my subsequent resolutions, and feelings—for I am neither un-grateful, nor at all disposed to be disappointed; on the contrary, I do firmly believe that I have often begun to *love*, at the very time I have heard people say that some dispositions become indifferent. Besides, her fool of a husband, and my own recent good resolutions, and a mixture of different piques and mental stimulants, together with something not unlike encouragement on her part, led me into that foolish business, out of which the way is quite easy; and I really do not see that I have much to reproach myself with on her account. If you think differently pray say so.

As to Mrs. C[haworth-Musters], I will go; but I don't see any good that can result from it, certainly none to me—but I have no right to consider myself. When I say this, I merely allude to uncomfortable *feelings*, for there is neither chance, nor fear of anything else; for she is a very good girl, and I am too much dispirited to rise, even to admiration. I do verily believe *you* hope otherwise, as a means of improving me; but I am sunk in my own estimation, and care of course very little for that of others.

As to *Ph.* she will end as all women in her situation do. It is impossible she can care about a man who acted so weakly as I did, with regard to herself.

What a fool I am—I have been interrupted by a visitor who is just gone, and have been laughing this half hour at a thousand absurdities, as if I had nothing serious to think about.

Y^{rs} ever, B.

P.S.—Another epistle from M[ary]. My answer must be under cover to " dear friend ", who is doing or suffering a folly —what can *she*, *Miss R[adford]*, be about?—the only thing that could make it look ill, is *mystery*. I wrote to her and *franked*, thinking there was no need of concealment; and indeed conceiving the affectation of it in an impertinence—but she desires me not—and I obey. I suspect R[adford] of wishing to make a scene between *him* and *me*, out of dislike to both, but that shall not prevent me from going, a moment.

I shall leave town on Sunday.

FRAGMENT OF A LETTER TO LADY MELBOURNE

[Undated]

. . . pantomime. I don't think I laughed once, save in soliloquy, for ten days, which *you*, who know me, won't believe (everyone else thinks me the most gloomy of existences). We used to sit and look at one another, except in *duetto*, and then even our serious nonsense was not fluent; to be sure our gestures were rather more sensible. The most amusing part was the interchange of notes, for we sat up all night scribbling to each other, and came down like ghosts in the morning. I shall never forget the quiet manner in which she would pass her epistles in a music-book, or any book, looking in [Webster's] face with great tranquillity the whole time, and taking mine in the same way. One she offered me as I was leading her to dinner at N[ewstead], all the servants before, and W[ebster] and sister close behind. To take it was impossible, and how she was to retain it, without *pockets*, was equally perplexing. I had the cover of a letter from Claughton in mine, and gave it to her, saying, " There is the frank for L^y Water^d you asked for "; she returned it with the note beneath, with " it is dated wrong, alter it to-morrow ", and W[ebster] complaining that women did nothing but scribble—wondered how people could have the patience to frank and alter franks, and then happily digressed to the day of the month—fish sauce—good wine— and bad weather.

Your " matrimonial ladder " wants but one more descending step—" d—nation ". I wonder how the carpenter omitted it—it concerned me much. I wish I were married, and don't care about beauty, nor *subsequent* virtue—nor much about fortune. I have made up my mind to share the decorations of

my betters—but I should like—let me see—liveliness, gentleness, cleanliness, and something of comeliness—and *my own*
first born. Was ever man more moderate? what do you think
of my " Bachelor's wife "? What a letter have I written !

TO LADY MELBOURNE   *January 16th, 1814*

My DEAR LADY M[ELBOURN]E,—Lewis is just returned from
Oatlands, where he has been quarrelling with Stael about
everything and everybody. She has not even let poor quiet
me alone, but has discovered, first, that I am affected ; and
2ndly, that I " *shut* my *eyes* during dinner ! " What this last
can mean I don't know, unless *she* is opposite. If I then do, she
is very much obliged to me ; and if at the same time I could
contrive to shut my ears, she would be still more so. If I really
have so ludicrous a habit, will *you* tell me so—and I will try
and break myself of it. In the meantime, I think the charge
will amuse you. I have worse faults to find with *her* than
" *shutting* her eyes "—one of which is opening her mouth too
frequently.

Do not you think people are very naught[y]? What do
you think I have this very day heard said of poor M[ary].? It
provoked me beyond anything, as *he* was named as authority—
why the abominable stories they circulate about Lady *W.*, of
which I can say no more. All this is owing to " dear friend " ;
and yet, as far as it regards " dear friend ", I must say I have
·very sufficing suspicions for believing them totally false ; at
least, she must have altered strangely within these nine years—
but this is the age of revolutions. Her ascendancy always
appeared to me that of a cunning mind over a weak one. But
—but—why the woman is a fright, which, after all, is the best
reason for not believing it.

I still mean to set off to-morrow, unless this snow adds so
much to the impracticability of the roads as to render it useless.
I don't mind anything but delay ; and I might as well be in
London as at a sordid inn, waiting for a thaw, or the subsiding
of a flood and the clearing of snow. I wonder what *your*
answer will be on *Ph.'s letter*. I am growing rather partial to

her younger sister; who is very pretty, but fearfully young—
and I think a *fool*. A wife, you say, would be my salvation.
Now I could have but one motive for marrying into that family
—and even *that* might possibly only produce a scene, and spoil
everything; but at all events it would in some degree be a
revenge, and in the very face of your compliment (*ironical*, I
believe) on the want of *selfishness*, I must say that I never can
quite get over the "*not*" of last summer—no—though it were
to become "yea" to-morrow.

I do believe that to marry would be my wisest step—but
whom? I might manage *this* easily with "le Père", but I
don't admire the connection—and I have not committed myself by any attentions hitherto. But all wives would be much
the same. I have no *heart* to spare and expect none in return;
but, as Moore says, "A pretty wife is something for the fastidious vanity of a roué to *retire* upon". And mine might do
as she pleased, so that she had a fair temper, and a *quiet* way of
conducting herself, leaving me the same liberty of conscience.
What I want is a companion—a friend rather than a sentimentalist. I have seen enough of love matches—and of all
matches—to make up my mind to the common lot of happy
couples. The only misery would be if I fell in love afterwards—
which is not unlikely, for habit has a strange power over my
affections. In that case I should be jealous, and then you do
not know what a devil any bad passion makes me. I should
very likely *do* all that *C. threatens* in her paroxysms; and I have
more reasons than you are aware of, for mistrusting myself on
this point.

Heigh-ho! Good night.

Ever y^{rs} most truly, B.

P.S.—The enclosed was written last night, and I am just
setting off. You shall hear from Newstead—if one ever gets
there in a coach really as large as the cabin of a "74", and, I
believe, meant for the Atlantic instead of the Continent.

1,000 thanks for yours of this morn; "never loved so
before". Well, then, I hope never to be loved *so* again—for
what is it to the *purpose*? You wonder how I answered it?
To tell you the *truth* (which I could not tell *her*), I have not
answered it at all—nor *shall*. I feel so much inclined to believe

her sincere, that I cannot sit down and coolly repay her truth with fifty falsehoods. I do not believe her for the same *reason* you *believe*, but because by writing she *commits* herself—and that is seldom done unless in earnest.

I shall be delighted to hear your *defence* against my insinuations, but you will make nothing of it—and he *is* very much to be envied. But you mistake me, for I do not mean in *general*; on the contrary, I coincide with him in taste but upon *one* instance.

C. was right about the poem. I have scribbled a longer one than either of the last, and it is in the press, but you know I never hold forth to you on such topics—why should I? Now you will think this a piece of conceit, but, really, it is a relief to the fever of my mind to *write*; and as at present I am what they call popular as an author—it enables me to serve one or two people without embarrassing anything but my brains— for I never have, nor shall avail myself of the *lucre*. And yet it would be folly merely to make presents to a bookseller, whose accounts *to* me last year are just 1,500 guineas, *without* including C[hild]e H[arol]d. Now the odd part is, that if I were a regular stipendiary, and wanted it, probably I should not be offered *one half*. But such are mankind—always offering or denying in the wrong place. But I have written more than enough already; and this is my last experiment on *public* patience—and just at present I won't try *yours* any further.

Ever, my dear L^{dy} M^e, etc., B.

TO LADY MELBOURNE *Newark, February 6th, 1814*

MY DEAR L^Y M^E,—I am thus far on my return to town, and having passed the Trent (which threatens a flood on ye first opportunity), I hope to reach town in tolerable plight.

Mr. Claughton has been with us during the last two days at N[ewstea]d, and this day set off for Cheshire, and I for the south, to prepare for a final and amicable arrangement.

M[ary Chaworth] I have not seen. Business and the weather, and badness of roads, and partly a late slight illness of her own, have interfered to prevent our meeting for the

present, but I have heard a good deal from and of her. Him
I have not heard from nor of; nor have I seen him; nor do I
know exactly where he is; but somewhere in the country, I
believe. You will very probably say that I ought to have gone
over at all events, and Augusta has also been trying her rhetoric
to the same purpose, and urging me repeatedly to call before I
left the county. But I have been one day too busy, and another
too lazy, and altogether so sluggish upon the subject, that I
am thus far on my return without making this important visit
on my way. She seems in her letters very undecided whether to
return to —— or no, and I have always avoided both sides of
the topic, or, if I touched on it at all, it was on the *rational*
bearing of the question.

I have written to you two long letters from the Abbey, and,
as I hope to see you soon, I will not try your eye-glass and
patience further at present.

Ever yʳˢ, B.

FRAGMENT OF A LETTER TO LADY MELBOURNE

[Undated]

. . . prospect. I never shall. One of my great induce-
ments to that brilliant negociation with the Princess of Parallelograms, was the vision of our *family party*, and the quantity of
domestic lectures I should faithfully detail, without mutual
comments thereupon.

You seem to think I am in some scrape at present by my
unequal spirits. Perhaps I am, but you shan't be shocked, so
you shan't. I won't draw further upon you for sympathy.
You will be in town so soon, and I have scribbled so much,
that you will be glad to see a letter shorter than usual.

I wish you would *lengthen* yours.

Ever my dear Lʸ Mᵉ, B.

TO LADY MELBOURNE   *February 11th, 1814*

MY DEAR LADY M.,—On my arrival in town on Wednesday,
I found myself in what the learned call a dilemma, and the

vulgar a scrape.[1] Such a clash of paragraphs, and a conflict of newspapers, lampoons of all description, some good, and all hearty, the Regent (as reported) wroth; Ld Carlisle in a fury; the *Morning Post* in hysterics; and the *Courier* in convulsions of criticism and contention. To complete the farce, the Morning Papers this day announce the intention of some zealous Rosencrantz or Guildenstern to " play upon this pipe " in our house of hereditaries. This last seems a little too ludicrous to be true, but, even if so—and nothing is too ridiculous for some of them to attempt—all the motions, censures, sayings, doings and ordinances of that august body, shall never make me even endeavour to explain, or soften a syllable of the twenty words which have excited, *what* I really do not yet exactly know, as the accounts are contradictory, but be it what it may, " as the wine is tapped it shall be drunk to the lees ". You tell me not to be " violent ", and not to " answer ". I *have not* and shall *not* answer, and although the consequences may be, for aught I know to the contrary, exclusion from society, and all sorts of disagreeables, the " Demon whom I still have served, has not yet cowed my better part of man " ; and whatever I may, and have, or shall feel, I have that within me, that bounds against opposition. I have *quick feelings*, and not very *good nerves*; but somehow they have more than once served me pretty well, when I most wanted them, and may again. At any rate I shall try.

Did you ever know anything like this? At a time when peace and war, and Emperors and Napoleons, and the destinies of the things they have made of mankind, are trembling in the balance, the Government Gazettes can devote half their attention and columns, day after day, to 8 *lines*, written two years ago and now *republished only* (by an individual), and suggest them for the consideration of Parliament, probably about the same period with the treaty of peace.

I really begin to think myself a most important personage; what would poor Pope have given to have brought down this upon his " epistle to Augustus "?

I think you must allow, considering all things, public and private, that mine has been an odd destiny. But I prate, and will spare you.

[1] Caused by Byron's acknowledgment of *Stanzas to a Lady Weeping*, which had appeared bound up with *The Corsair*.

Pray when are you most visible? or will any of your " pre-dilections " interfere between you and me?

How is C[aroline].? It is a considerable compensation for all other disturbances, that she has left us in peace, and I do not think you will ever be further troubled with her anniversary scenes. I am glad you like the Corsair, and was afraid he might be too larmoyant a gentleman for your favour. But all these externals are nothing to *that within*, on a subject to which I have not alluded.

Ever y^{rs} most affec^{ly}, B.

P.S.—Murray took fright and shuffled in my absence, as you say, but I made him instantly replace the lines as before. It was not time to shrink now, and if it were otherwise, they should never be expunged and never shall. All the edicts on earth could not suppress their circulation, after the foolish fuss of these journalists who merely extend the demands of curiosity by the importance they attach to two " doggerel stanzas ", as they repeatedly call them.

TO MISS ANNE ISABELLA MILBANKE   *Fy. 12th, 1814*

I am just returned to London after a month's absence and am indeed sorry to hear that your own will be so much longer—and the cause is not of a description to reconcile your friends to it entirely, although the benefit you will derive to your health will prevent us from regretting anything but the time—if the effect is accomplished. All expressions of my good wishes to you and for you would be superfluous.

Mr. Ward postponed our Dutch expedition ; but as I have now nearly arranged my domestic concerns—or at least have put them in train—and the Newstead business is set at rest in my favour, " the world is all before me " and all parts of it as much a country to me as it was to Adam—perhaps more so ; for Eve as an atonement for tempting him out of one habita-tion might probably assist him in selecting another, and persuade him into some " Valley of Sweet Waters " on the banks of Euphrates.

In thanking you for your letter will you allow me to say

that there is one sentence I do not understand. As you may have forgotten it I will copy it. . . .

This I believe is word for word from your letter now before me. I do not see in what you have deceived yourself; and you have certainly never been otherwise than candid with me —and I have endeavoured to act accordingly. In regard to your kind observations on my adoption of my conduct to your wishes—I trust I should have been able to do so even without your suggestion. The moment I sunk into your friend, I tried to regard you in no other light. Our affections are not in our own power; but it would seem strange indeed because you could not like me that I should repine at the better fortune of another. If I had ever possessed a preference, the case would have been altered—and I might not have been so patient in resigning my pretensions. But you never did— never for an instant—trifle with me nor amuse me with what is called encouragement—a thing, by-the-bye, which men are continually supposing they receive without sufficient grounds ; but of which I am no great judge—as except in this instance I never had an opportunity. When I say " this instance ", I mean of course any advance on my part towards that con- nexion which requires duty as well as attachment; and I begin to entertain an opinion that though they do not always go together, their separate existence is very precarious. I have lately seen a singular instance of ill-fortune. You have perhaps heard that in my childhood I was extremely intimate with the family of my nearest neighbours—an inheritor of the estate of a very old house and her mother. She is two years older than me; and consequently at so early a period any proposal on my part was out of the question—although from the continuity of our lands and other circumstances of no great importance, it was supposed that our union was within the probabilities of human life. I never did propose to her, and if I had it would have answered very little purpose—for she married another. From that period we met rarely—and I do not know very well why—but when we did meet, it was with coldness on both sides. To cut short a tale which is growing tedious : eight years have now elapsed, and she is separated from her husband at last after frequent dissensions arising entirely from *his* neglect, and (I fear) injuries still more serious.

At eight-and-twenty, still in the prime of life, beautiful (at least she was so), with a large fortune, of an ancient family, unimpeached and unimpeachable in her own conduct—this woman's destiny is bitter. For the first time for many years I heard from her desiring to see me. There could be nothing improper in this request. I was the friend of her youth; and I have every reason to believe—to be certain—that a being of better principle never breathed. But she was once deep in my heart; and though she had long ceased to be so, and I had no doubts of her, yet I had many of myself—at least of my own feelings if revived rather than of any consequence that might arise from them; and as we had not met since I was 21 . . . to be brief, I did not see her. There is the whole history of circumstances to which you may have possibly heard some allusion from those who knew me in the earlier part of my life. I *confide* them to you, and shall dwell upon them no further except to state that they bear no relation whatever to what I hinted at in a former letter as having occurred to prevent my reviving the topic discussed between us—at least with a view to renewal.

I have to ask for an answer, when you have leisure, and to thank you for your description, which brings the scene fully before me. Are you aware of an amplified coincidence of thought with Burns?

> " Or like the snowflake on the river
> A moment shines—then melts forever."

The verses are very graceful and pleasing. My opinion of your powers in that way I long ago mentioned to another person—who perhaps transmitted it to you. I am glad you like *The Corsair*, which they tell me is popular. God bless you. Ever yours

B.

P.S.—I am not perhaps an impartial judge of Lady M.— as amongst other obligations I am indebted to her for my acquaintance with yourself; but she is doubtless in talent a superior—a *supreme* woman—and her heart I know to be of the kindest, in the best sense of the word. Her defects I never could perceive—as her society makes me forget them and everything else for the time. I do love that woman (*filially or fraternally*) better than any being on earth; and you see that I am therefore unqualified to give an opinion.

TO THOMAS MOORE   *March 3, 1814*

MY DEAR FRIEND,—I have a great mind to tell you that I *am* " uncomfortable ", if only to make you come to town; where no one ever more delighted in seeing you, nor is there any one to whom I would sooner turn for consolation in my most vapourish moments. The truth is, I have " no lack of argument " to ponder upon of the most gloomy description, but this arises from *other* causes. Some day or other, when we are *veterans*, I may tell you a tale of present and past times; and it is not from want of confidence that I do not now,—but—but— always a *but* to the end of the chapter.

There is nothing, however, upon the *spot* either to love or hate;—but I certainly have subjects for both at no very great distance, and am besides embarrassed between *three* whom I know, and one (whose name, at least) I do not know. All this would be very well if I had no heart; but, unluckily, I have found that there is such a thing still about me, though in no very good repair, and, also, that it has a habit of attaching itself to *one* whether I will or no. *Divide et impera*, I begin to think, will only do for politics.

If I discover the " toad ", as you call him, I shall " tread ", —and put spikes in my shoes to do it more effectually. The effect of all these fine things I do not inquire much nor perceive. I believe * * felt them more than either of us. People are civil enough, and I have had no dearth of invitations,—none of which, however, I have accepted. I went out very little last year, and mean to go about still less. I have no passion for circles, and have long regretted that I ever gave way to what is called a town life;—which, of all the lives I ever saw (and they are nearly as many as Plutarch's), seems to me to leave the least for the past and future.

How proceeds the poem? Do not neglect it, and I have no fears. I need not say to you that your fame is dear to me,—

I really might say *dearer* than my own ; for I have lately begun to think my things have been strangely over-rated ; and, at any rate, whether or not, I have done with them for ever. I may say to you what I would not say to every body, that the last two were written, *The Bride* in four, and *The Corsair* in ten days,—which I take to be a most humiliating confession, as it proves my own want of judgment in publishing, and the public's in reading things, which cannot have stamina for permanent attention. " So much for Buckingham."

I have no dread of your being too hasty, and I have still less of your failing. But I think a *year* a very fair allotment of time to a composition which is not to be Epic ; and even Horace's " *Nonum prematur* " must have been intended for the Millennium, or some longer-lived generation than ours. I wonder how much we should have had of *him*, had he observed his own doctrines to the letter. Peace be with you ! Remember that I am always and most truly yours, etc.

P.S.—I never heard the " report " you mention, nor, I dare say, many others. But, in course, you, as well as others, have " damned good-natured friends ", who do their duty in the usual way. One thing will make you laugh. * * * *

TO LADY MELBOURNE   *April 8th, 1814*

I have been out of town since Saturday, and only returned last night from my visit to Augusta.

I swallowed the D—l in ye shape of a collar of brawn one evening for supper (after an enormous dinner, too), and it required all kinds of brandies, and I don't know what besides, to put me again in health and good humour ; but I am now quite restored, and it is to avoid your congratulations upon *fatness* (which I abhor and you always inflict upon me after a return from the country) that I don't pay my respects to you to-day. Besides which, I dislike to see L^d M^e standing by the chimney-piece, all horror and astonishment at my appearance while C. is within reach of the twopenny postman. To-day I have been very sulky ; but an hour's exercise with Mr. Jackson, of pugilistic memory, has given me spirits, and fatigued me into that state of languid laziness, which I prefer to all other.

I left all my relations—at least my niece and her mamma—very well. L[eigh] was in Yorkshire; and I regret not having seen him of course very much. My intention was to have joined a party at Cambridge; but somehow I overstaid my time, and the inclination to visit the University went off, and here I am alone, and not overpleased with being so.

You don't think the " Q[uarterly] R[eview] so very complimentary "; most people do. I have no great opinion on the subject, and (except in the E[dinburg]h) am not much interested in any criticisms, favourable or otherwise. I have had my day, have done with all that stuff; and must try something new—politics—or rebellion—or Methodism—or gaming. Of the two last I have serious thoughts, as one can't travel till we see how long Paris is to be the quarter of the Allies. I can't help suspecting that my little Pagod will play them some trick still. If Wellington, or one hero had beaten another, it would be nothing; but to be worried by brutes, and conquered by recruiting sergeants—why there is not a *character* amongst them.

Ever yrs. most affect^{ly}, B.

TO THOMAS MOORE *2, Albany, April 9, 1814*

Viscount Althorpe is about to be married, and I have gotten his spacious bachelor apartments in Albany, to which you will, I hope, address a speedy answer to this mine epistle.

I am but just returned to town, from which you may infer that I have been out of it; and I have been boxing, for exercise, with Jackson for this last month daily. I have also been drinking, and, on one occasion, with three other friends at the Cocoa Tree, from six till four, yea, unto five in the matin. We clareted and champagned till two—then supped, and finished with a kind of regency punch composed of madeira, brandy, and *green* tea, no *real* water being admitted therein. There was a night for you! without once quitting the table, except to ambulate home, which I did alone, and in utter contempt of a hackney-coach and my own *vis*, both of which were deemed necessary for our conveyance. And so,—I am very well, and they say it will hurt my constitution.

I have also, more or less, been breaking a few of the favourite commandments; but I mean to pull up and marry, if any one will have me. In the mean time, the other day I nearly killed myself with a collar of brawn, which I swallowed for supper, and *in*digested for I don't know how long; but that is by the by. All this gourmandise was in honour of Lent; for I am forbidden meat all the rest of the year, but it is strictly enjoined me during your solemn fast. I have been, and am, in very tolerable love; but of that hereafter as it may be.

My dear Moore, say what you will in your preface; and quiz any thing or any body,—me if you like it. Oons! dost thou think me of the *old*, or rather *elderly* school? If one can't jest with one's friends, with whom can we be facetious? You have nothing to fear from * *, whom I have not seen, being out of town when he called. He will be very correct, smooth, and all that, but I doubt whether there will be any " grace beyond the reach of art ";—and, whether there is or not, how long will you be so damned modest? As for Jeffrey, it is a very handsome thing of him to speak well of an old antagonist,— and what a mean mind dared not do. Any one will revoke praise; but—were it not partly my own case—I should say that very few have strength of mind to unsay their censure, or follow it up with praise of other things.

What think you of the review of *Levis*?[1] It beats the *Bag* and my hand-grenade hollow, as an invective, and hath thrown the Court into hysterics, as I hear from very good authority. Have you heard from * * * * * *

No more rhyme for—or rather, *from*—me. I have taken my leave of that stage, and henceforth will mountebank it no longer. I have had my day, and there's an end. The utmost I expect, or even wish, is to have it said in the *Biographia Britannica*, that I might perhaps have been a poet, had I gone on and amended. My great comfort is, that the temporary celebrity I have wrung from the world has been in the very teeth of all opinions and prejudices. I have flattered no ruling

---

[1] A criticism of *Souvenirs et portraits, par M. de Levis* had recently appeared in the *Edinburgh Review*.

powers; I have never concealed a single thought that tempted me. They can't say I have truckled to the times, nor to popular topics, (as Johnson, or somebody, said of Cleveland,) and whatever I have gained has been at the expenditure of as much *personal* favour as possible; for I do believe never was a bard more unpopular, *quoad homo*, than myself. And now I have done;—*ludite nunc alios*. Every body may be damned, as they seem fond of it, and resolve to stickle lustily for endless brimstone.

Oh—by the by, I had nearly forgot. There is a long poem, an *Anti-Byron*, coming out, to prove that I have formed a conspiracy to overthrow, by *rhyme*, all religion and government, and have already made great progress! It is not very scurrilous, but serious and ethereal. I never felt myself important, till I saw and heard of my being such a little Voltaire as to induce such a production. Murray would not publish it, for which he was a fool, and so I told him; but some one else will, doubtless. "Something too much of this."

Your French scheme is good, but let it be *Italian*; all the Angles will be at Paris. Let it be Rome, Milan, Naples, Florence, Turin, Venice, or Switzerland, and "egad!" (as Bayes saith,) I will connubiate and join you; and we will write a new *Inferno* in our Paradise. Pray think of this—and I will really buy a wife and a ring, and say the ceremony, and settle near you in a summer-house upon the Arno, or the Po, or the Adriatic.

Ah! my poor little pagod, Napoleon, has walked off his pedestal. He has abdicated, they say. This would draw molten brass from the eyes of Zatanai. What! "kiss the ground before young Malcolm's feet and then be baited by the rabble's curse!" I cannot bear such a crouching catastrophe. I must stick to Sylla, for my modern favourites don't do,— their resignations are of a different kind. All health and prosperity, my dear Moore. Excuse this lengthy letter.

Ever, etc.

P.S.—The *Quarterly* quotes you frequently in an article on America; and every body I know asks perpetually after you and yours. When will you answer them in person?

MY DEAR L^Y M^E,—Thanks as to C—— though the task will be difficult; if she is to determine as to kindness or unkindness, the best way will be to avoid each other *without appearing* to do so, or if we jostle, at any rate *not to bite*.

Oh! but it is " worth while ", I can't tell you why, and it is *not* an " *Ape* ", and if it is, that must be my fault; however, I will positively reform. You must however allow that it is utterly impossible I can ever be half so well liked elsewhere, and I have been all my life trying to make someone love me, and never got the sort that I preferred before. But positively she and I will grow good and all that, and so we are *now* and shall be these three weeks and more too.

Yesterday I dined at the Princess's,[1] where I deported myself like a white stick; till, as the Devil would have it, a man with a flute played a solemn and somewhat tedious piece of music. Well, I got through that, but down sate Lady Anne H. to give evidence at the pianoforte with a Miss Somebody (the " privy purse ", in a pair of spectacles—dark green) these, and the flute man, and the " damnable faces " (as Hamlet says) of the whole party, threw me into a convulsion of uncourtly laughter, which Gell and Lady Crewe encouraged; at least the *last* joined in it so heartily that the hooping-cough would have been an Æolian harp in comparison to us both. At last I half strangled it, and myself, with my kerchief; and here I am grave and sedate again.

You will be sorry to hear that I have got a physician just in time for an old complaint, " troublesome, but not dangerous ", like Lord Stair and L^y Stair's, of which I am promised an eventual removal. It is very odd; he is a staid grave man, and puts so many questions to me about *my mind*, and the state of it, that I begin to think he half suspects my senses. He asked me how I felt " when anything weighed upon my mind? " and I answered him by a question, why he should suppose that anything did? I was laughing and sitting quietly in my chair the whole time of his visits, and yet he thinks me horribly restless and irritable, and talks about my having lived *excessively* " out of all compass " some time or other; which has no more to do

---

[1] The Princess of Wales.

with the malady he has to deal with than I have with the Wisdom of Solomon.

To-morrow I go to the Berrys; on Wednesday to the Jerseys; on Thursday I dine at Ld Grey's, and there is L^y Hard[wick]e in the evening; and on Friday I am asked to a Lady Charleville's, whom I don't know, and where I shan't go. We shall meet, I hope, at one or two of these places.

I don't often bore you with rhyme—but as a wrapper ¹ to this note I send you some upon a *brunette*, which I have shown to no one else. If you think them not much beneath the common places you may give them to any of your " album " acquaintances.

Ever y^rs most truly, B.

TO LADY MELBOURNE   *April 29th, 1814*

I delivered " mamma's message " with anatomical precision; ² the *knee* was the refractory limb was it not? Injured I presume at prayers, for I cannot conjecture by what other possible attitude a female knee could become so perverse. Having given an account of my embassy, I enclose you a note which will only repeat what you already know, but to obviate a possible *Pharisaical* charge, I must observe that the first part of her epistle alludes to an answer of mine, in which, talking about that eternal Liturgy, I said that I had no great opinions one way or the other, assuredly no decided unbelief, and that the *clamour* had wrung from me many of the objectionable passages in the pure quintessence of the spirit of contradiction, etc., etc. She talks of " talking " over the same metaphysics. To shorten the conversation, I shall propose the Litany— " from the crafts and assau——" aye, that will do very well; what comes next, " deliver us ", an't it? Seriously, if she imagines that I particularly delight in canvassing the creed of St. Athanasius, or prattling of rhyme, I think she will be mistaken; but *you* know best. I don't suspect myself of often talking about poets, or clergymen, of rhyme or the rubrick; but very likely I am wrong; for assuredly no one knows *itself*, and for aught I know, I may for these last two years have

¹ Not preserved with the original letter.
² Byron was now in sentimental correspondence with Lady Melbourne's niece, Annabella Milbanke.

inflicted upon you a world of theology, and the greater part of Walker's rhyming dictionary.

I don't know what to say or do about going. Sometimes I wish it, at other times I think it foolish, as assuredly my design will be imputed to a motive, which, by-the-bye, if once fairly there, is very likely to come into my head, and *failing*, to put me into no very good humour with myself. I am not now in love with her; but I can't at all foresee that I should not be so, if it came " a warm June " (as Falstaff observes), and, seriously, I do admire her as a very superior woman, a little encumbered with Virtue, though perhaps your opinion and mine, from the laughing turn of " our philosophy ", may be less exalted upon her merits than that of the more zealous, though in fact less benevolent advocates, of charity schools and Lying-in Hospitals.

By the close of her note you will perceive that she has been " frowning " occasionally, and has written some pretty lines upon it to a friend (he or she is not said). As for rhyme I am naturally no fair judge, and can like it no better than a grocer does figs.

I am quite irresolute and undecided. If I were sure of *myself* (not of her) I would go; but I am not, and never can be, and what is still worse, I have no judgement and less common sense than an infant. This is *not affected* humility; with *you* I have no affectation; with the world I have a part to play; to be diffident there, is to wear a drag-chain, and luckily I do so thoroughly despise half the people in it, that my insolence is almost natural.

I enclose you also a letter written some time ago, and of which I do not remember the precise contents; most likely they contradict every syllable of this, no matter. Don't plague yourself to write; we shall meet at Mrs. Hope's I trust.

Ever yours, B.

TO LADY MELBOURNE   *April, 30th, 1814*

MY DEAR LADY M^E,—*You*—or rather *I*—have done *my* A[1] much injustice. The expression which you recollect as

---

[1] Augusta Leigh, so called to distinguish her from " *your* A ", Annabella Milbanke.

objectionable meant only " loving " in the *senseless* sense of that wide word, and it must be some selfish stupidity of mine in telling my own story, but really and truly—as I hope mercy and happiness for her—by that God who made me for my own misery, and not much for the good of others, *she* was not to blame, one thousandth part in comparison.   She was not aware of her own peril till it was too late, and I can only account for her subsequent " *abandon* " by an observation which I think is not unjust, that women are much more *attached* than men if they are treated with anything like fairness or tenderness.

As for *your* A, I don't know what to make of her.   I enclose her last but one, and *my* A's last but one, from which you may form your own conclusions on *both*.   I think you will allow *mine* to be a very extraordinary person in point of *talent*, but I won't say more, only do not allow your good nature to lean to my side of *this* question ;   on all others I shall be glad to avail myself of your partiality.

Now for *common* life.   There *is* a party at Lady J[erse]y's on Monday and on Wednesday.   I am asked to both, and excused myself out of Tuesday's dinner because I want to see Kean in Richard again.   Pray *why* did you say I am getting into a *scrape* with R.'s moiety? [1]   One must talk to somebody.   I always give you the preference when you are disposed to listen, and when you seem fidgetted, as you do now and then (and no wonder, for latterly I do but repeat), I turn to anyone, and she was the first that I stumbled upon.   As for anything more, I have not even advanced to the tip of her little finger, and never shall unless she gives it.   You won't believe me, and won't care if you do, but I really believe that I have more true regard and affection for yourself than for any other existence.   As for my A, my feelings towards her are a mixture of good and diabolical. I hardly know one passion which has not some share in them, but I won't run into the subject.

Your niece has committed herself perhaps, but it can be of no consequence ;   if I pursued and succeeded in that quarter, of course I must give up all other pursuits, and the fact is that my wife, if she had common sense, would have more power over me than any other whatsoever, for my heart always

_____
[1] Probably Milbanke.

alights on the nearest *perch*—if it is withdrawn it goes God knows where—but one must like something.

Ever yrs., B.

TO LADY MELBOURNE   *April—May 1st, 1814*

My dear Lady Mᴱ,—She says " if la tante " ; neither did she imagine nor did I assert that you did have an opinion of what Philosopher Square calls " the fitness of things ".

You are very kind in allowing us the few merits we can claim : *she* surely is very clever, and not only so but in some things of good judgement : her expressions about Aᵃ are exactly your *own*, and these most certainly without being aware of the coincidence, and excepting our one *tremendous* fault. I know her to be in point of temper and goodness of heart almost unequalled ; now grant me this, that she is in truth a very *loveable* woman and I will try and not love any longer. If you don't believe me, ask those who know her *better*. I say *better*, for a man in love is blind as that deity.

You yourself soften a little in the P.S., and say the letters " make you melancholy ". It is indeed a very triste and extraordinary business, and what is to become of us I know not, and I won't think just now.

Did you observe that she says, " *if* la tante approved she should "? She is little aware how much " la tante " has to *dis*approve, but you perceive that, without intending it, she pays me a compliment by supposing you to be my friend and a sincere one, whose *approval* could alter even *her* opinions.

To-morrow I am asked to Lady Jersey's in the evening, and on Wednesday again. Tuesday I go to Kean and dine after the play with Lord Rancliffe, and on Friday there is Mrs. Hope's : we shall clash at some of them.

What on earth can plague you? I won't ask, but am very sorry for it, it is very hard that one who feels so much for others should suffer pain herself. God bless you. Good night.

Ever yours most truly, B.

P.S.—A thousand loves and excuses to Mrs. Damer with whom I weep *not* to dine.

P.S. *ad.*—It, indeed, puzzles me to account for ——: it is true she married a fool, but she *would* have him ; they agreed, and agree very well, and I never heard a complaint, but many vindications, of him. As for me, brought up as I was, and sent into the world as I was, both physically and morally, nothing better could be expected, and it is odd that I always had a foreboding and I remember when a child reading the Roman history about a *marriage* I will tell you of when we meet, asking ma mère why I should not marry **X**.

Since writing this I have received yᵉ enclosed. I will not trouble you with another, but *this* will, I think, enable you to appreciate *her* better. She seems very triste, and I need hardly add that the reflection does not enliven me.

TO MISS MERCER ELPHINSTONE*   *2 Albany, May 3ᵈ, 1814*

I send you the Arnaout garments which will make an admirable costume for a Dutch Dragoon. The Camesa or Kilt (to speak Scottishly) you will find very long. It is the custom with the Beys, and a sign of rank, to wear it to the ancle—I know not why, but it is so. The million shorten it to the knee, which is more antique—and becoming, at least to those who have legs and a propensity to show them. I have sent but one camesa, the other I will dispatch when it has undergone the Musselman process of ablution.

There are greaves for the legs—2 waistcoats, one beneath, one over the Jacket—the cloak—a sash—a short shawl and cap —and a pair of garters (something of the Highland order) with an Ataghan wherewithal to cut your fingers if you don't take care. Over the sash there is a small leather girdle with a buckle in the centre.

It is put off and on in a few minutes. If you like the dress, keep it. I shall be very glad to get rid of it, as it reminds me of one or two things I don't wish to remember. To make it more acceptable, I have worn this very little and never in England except for half an hour at Phillips, I had more of the same description but parted with them when my Arnaouts went

back to Tepalen and I returned to England. It will do for a
masquerade.

One word about " caprice ".   I know you were merely in
jest and that my *caprices*, supposing such to exist, must be a
subject of laughter or indifference ; but I am not unconscious
of something not unlike them in the course of our acquaintance. Yet you must recollect that from your situation you can
never be *sure* you have a friend (as somebody has said of
Sovereigns I believe) and that any apparent anxiety on my part
to cultivate your acquaintance might have appeared to yourself like importunity, and—as I happen to know—would have
been attributed by others to a motive *not* very creditable to me
and agreeable to neither.

This is quite enough, and more than I have a right to
trouble you with on this or any other subject.

Ever yrs very sincerely, B.

TO THOMAS MOORE   *May 4, 1814*

" Last night we supp'd at R—fe's board ", etc.
* * * * * * * I wish people would not shirk their *dinners*—
ought it not to have been a dinner?—and that damned
anchovy sandwich !

That plaguy voice of yours made me sentimental, and almost
fall in love with a girl who was recommending herself, during
your song, by *hating* music. But the song is past, and my
passion can wait, till the *pucelle* is more harmonious.

Do you go to Lady Jersey's to-night? It is a large party,
and you won't be bored into " softening rocks ", and all that.
Othello is to-morrow and Saturday too. Which day shall we
go? When shall I see you? If you call, let it be after three,
and as near four as you please.

Ever, etc.

TO THOMAS MOORE   *May 5, 1814*

Do you go to the Lady Cahir's this even? If you do go—
and whenever we are bound to the same follies let us embark

in the same *Shippe of Fooles*. I have been up till five, and up at nine; and feel heavy with only winking for the last three or four nights.

I lost my party and place at supper trying to keep out of the way of * * * *. I would have gone away altogether, but that would have appeared a worse affectation than t'other. You are of course engaged to dinner, or we may go quietly together to my box at Covent Garden, and afterwards to this assemblage. Why did you go away so soon?

Ever, etc.

P.S.—*Ought not* Rancliffe's supper to have been a dinner? Jackson is here, and I must fatigue myself into spirits.

TO LADY MELBOURNE   *May 16th, 1814*

MY DEAR Lᵞ Mᴇ,—Your letter is not without effect when I tell you that I have *not written* to-day and shall weigh my words when I write to —— to-morrow. I *do* thank you, and as some-body says—I hope *not* Iago—" I think you know I love you well ".

As for C., we both know her for a foolish wicked woman. I am sorry to hear that she is still fermenting her weak head and cold heart to an *ice cream* which will only sicken everyone about her: as I heard a girl say the other night at *Othello*, when I asked her how she liked it, " I shall like it much better when that woman (a bad actress in Desdemona) is fairly smothered ". So—if C. were fairly shut up, and bread and watered into common sense and some regard to truth, no one would be the worse, and she herself much the better for the process.

By-the-bye (*entre nous*, remember) she has sent for Moore on some mysterious concern, which he will tell me probably, at least if it regards the old eternal, and never sufficiently to be bored with, story.

I dine at Lord Jersey's to-morrow—that is, I am asked, and (to please you) I am trying to fall in love, which I suppose will end in falling *out* with somebody, for I am perplexed about two and would rather have both. I don't see any use in one without a chance at least of the other.

But all this is nonsense. I won't say a word more about your grievance, though I cannot at all conceive what there can be more *now* than ever to plague you anywhere, particularly as C. has nothing to do with it.

Horace Twiss has sent me his melodies, which I perceive are inscribed to you; don't you think yourself lucky to have escaped one of *my* dedications? I am going to dine at Wm. Spencer's to-day. I believe I told you the *claret* story at Mrs. Hope's last ball but one.

Ever yours most affectionately, B.

P.S. I am just elected into Watier's. Shall I resume *play*? That will be a change, and for the better.

TO LADY MELBOURNE   *May 28th, 1814*

DEAR LADY M^E,—I have just received a wrathful epistle from C[aroline] demanding letters, pictures, and all kinds of gifts which I never requested, and am ready to resign as soon as they can be gathered together; at the same signal it might be as well for her to restore *my* letters, as everybody has read them by this time, and they can no longer be of use to herself and her five hundred sympathizing friends. She also complains of some barbarous usage, of which I know nothing, except that I was told of an *inroad* which occurred when I was fortunately out; and am not at all disposed to regret the circumstance of my absence, either for her sake or my own. I am also menaced in her letter with immediate *marriage*, of which I am equally unconscious; at least *I* have not proposed to anybody, and if anyone has to me I have quite forgotten it. If she alludes to L[ad]y A[delaide] F[orbes] she has made a sad mistake; for not a syllable of love ever passed between us, but a good deal of heraldry, and mutual hatred of music; the merits of Mr. Kean, and the excellence of white soup and plovers' eggs for a light supper. Besides, Lady R., who is good authority, says that *I* do not care about L^y A., nor L^y A. about me, and that if such an impossibility did occur, she could not possibly approve of it, nor anyone else; in all which I quite acquiesce with yᵉ said Lady R., with whom, however, I never had a moment's conversation on the subject; but hear this from a friend, who is in very bad humour with her, and not much better with me; why, I can't divine, being as innocent and ill-used as C. herself in her very best story. If you can *pare* her down to good humour, do. I am really at this moment thinking as little of the person with whom she commits me to matrimony, as of herself; and I mean to leave London next week if I can. In the meantime, I hope we shall meet at Lady Grey's, or Clare's this evening.

Ever yʳˢ, most affectionately, B.

TO HENRIETTA D'USSIÈRES[1] *   *June 8th, 1814*

Excepting your compliments (which are only excusable because you don't know me) you write like a clever woman, for which reason I hope you *look* as *un*like one as possible. I never knew but one of your country—Mᵉ de Stael—and she is frightful as a precipice. As it seems impracticable my visiting you, cannot you contrive to visit me? telling me the time previously that I may be in yᵉ way—and if this same interview leads to the " leap into the Serpentine " you mention, we can take the jump together, and shall be very good company, for I swim like a Duck (one of the few things I can do well) and you say that your Sire taught you the same useful acquirement. I like your education of all things. It in some degree resembles my own, for the first ten years of my life were passed much amongst mountains, and I had also a tender and peremptory parent who indulged me sometimes with holidays and now and then with a box on the ear. If you will become acquainted with me, I will promise not to make love to you unless you like it—and even if I did there is no occasion for you to receive more of it than you please. You must, however, do me two favours—the first is not to mistake me for S., who is an excellent

---

[1] A young woman of Swiss descent, domiciled in London, who had written to Byron, claiming advice and sympathy. For further information on this unsolicited correspondent, see *To Lord Byron*, by Paston and Quennell.

man, but to whom I have not the honour to bear the smallest
(I won't say *slightest*, for he has the circumference of an Alderman) resemblance; and the next is to recollect that as " no
man is a hero to his Valet " so I am a hero to no person whatsoever, and not treat me with such outrageous respect and awe,
which makes me feel as if I was in a strait waistcoat. You
shall be a *heroine*, however, if you prefer it and I will be and
am y^r very humble Servt

B.

P.S.—" Surprized " oh! no!—I am surprized at nothing,
except at your taking so much trouble about one who is not
worth it. . . .

You say—what would " my servants think "? 1^{stly} they
seldom think at all. 2^{ndly} they are generally out of the way—
particularly when most wanted. 3^{rdly} *I* do not know you—and
I humbly imagine that they are no wiser than their Master.

TO SAMUEL ROGERS   *June 9, 1814*

I am always obliged to trouble you with my awkwardnesses,
and now I have a fresh one. Mr. W.[1] called on me several
times, and I have missed the honour of making his acquaintance, which I regret, but which *you*, who know my desultory
and uncertain habits, will not wonder at, and will, I am sure,
attribute to any thing but a wish to offend a person who has
shown me much kindness, and possesses character and talents
entitled to general respect. My mornings are late, and passed
in fencing and boxing, and a variety of most unpoetical
exercises, very wholesome, etc., but would be very disagreeable
to my friends, whom I am obliged to exclude during their
operation. I never go out till the evening, and I have not
been fortunate enough to meet Mr. W. at Lord Lansdowne's
or Lord Jersey's, where I had hoped to pay him my respects.

I would have written to him, but a few words from you will
go further than all the apologetical sesquipedalities I could
muster on the occasion. It is only to say that, without intend-

[1] Francis Wrangham, cleric and man of letters.

ing it, I contrive to behave very ill to every body, and am very sorry for it.

Ever, dear R., etc.

TO LADY MELBOURNE *June 10th, 1814*

DEAR LADY M^E,—I don't remember one syllable of such a request; but the truth is that I do not always read ye letters through. She has no more variety than my maccaw; and her note is not much more musical. Judge then, whether (being also in ye delectable situation which winds up the moral of your note) I can attend the ye same tones if there is a nightingale, or a canary bird to be got by love, or money.

All you say is exceeding true; but who ever said, or supposed that you were not shocked, and all that? You *have* done everything in your power; and more than any other person breathing would have done for *me*, to make me act rationally; but there is an old saying (excuse the Latin, which I won't quote, but translate), "Whom the gods wish to destroy they first madden". I am as mad as C. on a different topic, and in a different way; for I never break out into scenes, but am not a whit more in my senses. I will, however, not persuade *her* into any *fugitive* piece of absurdity, but more I cannot promise. I love no one else (in a proper manner), and, whatever you may imagine, I cannot, or at least do not, put myself in the way of—let me see—Annabella is the most prudish and correct person I know, so I refer you to the last emphatic substantive, in her last letter to you.

There is that little Lady R. tells me that C. has taken a sudden fancy to *her*—what can that be for? C. has also taken some offence at Lady G. Sloane's frigid appearance; and supposes that Augusta, who never troubles her head about her, has said something or other on my authority—*this* I remember is in *C.'s* last letter—one of her twaddling questions I presume— she seems puzzled about me, and not at all near the truth. The Devil, who ought to be civil on such occasions, will probably keep her from it still; if he should not, I must invent some flirtation, to lead her from approaching it.

I am sorry to hear of your *tristesse*, and conceive that I have at last guessed or perceived the real cause; it won't trouble you long; besides, what is it or anything else compared with our melodrame? *Take* comfort, you very often give it.

Ever y^{rs}, B.

TO SAMUEL ROGERS   *Tuesday*

My DEAR ROGERS,—Sheridan was yesterday, at first, too sober to remember your invitation, but in the dregs of the third bottle he fished up his memory, and found that he had a party at home. I left and leave any other day to him and you, save Monday, and some yet undefined dinner at Burdett's. Do you go to-night to Lord Eardley's, and if you do, shall I call for you (anywhere)? it will give me great pleasure.

Ever yours entire, B.

P.S.—The Staël out-talked Whitbread, overwhelmed his spouse, was *ironed* by Sheridan, confounded Sir Humphry, and utterly perplexed your slave. The rest (great names in the Red-book, nevertheless,) were mere segments of the circle. Ma'mselle danced a Russ saraband with great vigour, grace, and expression.

TO THOMAS MOORE   *June 14, 1814*

I *could* be very sentimental now, but I won't. The truth is, that I have been all my life trying to harden my heart, and have not yet quite succeeded—though there are great hopes—and you do not know how it sunk with your departure. What adds to my regret is having seen so little of you during your stay in this crowded desert, where one ought to be able to bear thirst like a camel,—the springs are so few, and most of them so muddy.

The newspapers will tell you all that is to be told of emperors,[1]

[1] The Allied sovereigns, headed by the Emperor of Russia, visited London in state during June 1814.

etc. They have dined, and supped, and shown their flat faces in all thoroughfares, and several saloons. Their uniforms are very becoming, but rather short in the skirts; and their conversation is a catechism, for which and the answers I refer you to those who have heard it.

I think of leaving town for Newstead soon. If so, I shall not be remote from your recess, and (unless Mrs. M. detains you at home over the caudle-cup and a new cradle) we will meet. You shall come to me, or I to you, as you like it;—but *meet* we will. An invitation from Aston has reached me, but I do not think I shall go. I have also heard of * * *—I should like to see her again, for I have not met her for years; and though " the light that ne'er can shine again " is set, I do not know that " one dear smile like those of old " might not make me for a moment forget the " dulness " of " life's stream ".

I am going to R[ancliffe]'s to-night—to one of those suppers which " *ought* to be dinners ". I have hardly seen her, and never *him*, since you set out. I told you, you were the last link of that chain. As for * *, we have not syllabled one another's names since. The post will not permit me to continue my scrawl. More anon.

Ever, dear Moore, etc.

P.S.—Keep the Journal; I care not what becomes of it; and if it has amused you, I am glad that I kept it. *Lara* is finished, and I am copying him for my third vol., now collecting;—but *no separate* publication.

TO THE HON. AUGUSTA LEIGH *June 18th, 1814*

DEAREST A.,—Well, I *can* " judge for myself ", and a pretty piece of judgement it is! You shall hear. Last night at Earl Grey's, or rather this *morning* (about 2 by the account of the said Aurora), in one of the cooler rooms, sitting in the corner of a great chair wherein was deposited Lady M., *she* talking Platonics and listening to a different doctrine, I observed Mr. Rogers not far off colloquizing with your friend.[1] Presently he came up and interrupted our duet, and, after different remarks, began upon her and her's. What seized me I know not, but I

[1] Lady Charlotte Leveson-Gower.

desired him to introduce me, at which he expressed much good humour.

I stopped him, and said he had better ask her first, and in the mean time, to give her entire option, I walked away to another part of the room separated by a great Screen, so that she had the best opportunity of getting off without the awkwardness of being overheard or seen, etc., etc.; all which I duly considered.

My Goddess of the Arm-chair in the mean time was left to a soliloquy, as she afterwards told me, wondering what Rogers and I were about.　To my astonishment, in a minute up comes R. with *your* che at the *pas de charge* of introduction; the bow was made, the curtsey returned, and so far " excellent well ", all except the disappearance of the said Rogers, who immediately marched off, leaving us in the middle of a huge apartment with about 20 scattered pairs all employed in their own concerns.　While I was thinking of a *nothing* to say, the Lady began—" a friend of mine,—a great friend of yours ", and stopped.　Wondering what the Devil was coming next, I said, " perhaps you mean a relation "—" Oh yes—a relation ——" and stopped *again*.　Finding this would never do, and being myself beginning to break down into shyness,—she too confused,—I uttered your respectable name, and prattled I know not what syllables, and so on for about 3 minutes; and then how we parted I know not, for never did two people seem to know less what they said or did.　Well! we met again 2 or 3 times in passages, etc., where I endeavoured to improve this dialogue into something like sense, still taking you and people she knew (and the dead Marquis of Granby, I believe) for the topics.　In this interval she lost her party, and seemed in an agony.　" Shall I get your shawl? "　" I have got it " (they were going; by the bye, *La Mère* was not there).　" Is it your brother that you want? he is not gone."　" No—but have you seen Lady or Mrs. Somebody?　Oh! there she is "—and away she went!

She is shy as an Antelope, and unluckily as pretty, or we should not remark it.　By the bye, I must say that it looked more like *dislike* than shyness; and I do not much wonder— for her first confusion in calling you a *friend*, forgetting the relationship, set me off—not laughing—but in one of our *glows* and stammers, and then all I had heard from you and others of *her* diffidence brought our own similar malady upon me in a double degree.

The only thing is that she might have not been introduced, unless she had liked, as I did not stand near as people usually do, so that the introdu*cee* can't get off, but was out of sight and hearing. Then I must say that *till* the first sentence, there was a deal of valour on both sides; but after that—Oh Dear! this is all your fault. The Duchess of Somerset also, to mend matters, insisted on presenting me to a Princess *Biron*, Duchess of Hohen—God-know's-what, and another person to her two isters, Birons too. But I flew off, and *would* not, saying I had enough of introductions for that night at least.

Devonshire asked me *twice* (last night) to come to Chiswick on Sunday!—is not *that* a little odd? I have seen Blucher, etc., etc., and was surprized into an introduction, after all, to a Prince Radzivil, a Pole and a Potentate, a good and great man but very like a Butler. God bless you, my dear.

Ever yours most affectionately, BYRON.

TO LADY MELBOURNE   *June 21st*, 1814

Since I wrote last night I have received the two enclosed. What shall I do about Ph. and her epistles? since by her own account they run great hazard in their way to her. I am willing to give them up, but she says not a syllable about mine; no matter.

The other is from A., and prim and pretty as usual. Somebody or other has been seized with a fit of amazement at her correspondence with so naughty a personage, and this has naturally given a fillup of contradiction in my favour which was much wanted.

Ever y^{rs}, B.

TO LADY MELBOURNE   *June 26th*, 1814

MY DEAR L^Y M^E,—To continue the conversation which Lord C^r has broken off by falling asleep (and his wife by keeping awake) I know nothing of C.'s last night adventures;

to prove it there is her letter which I have not read through, nor answered nor written these two months, and then only by *desire* to keep her quiet.

You talked to me about keeping her out. It is impossible; she comes at all times, at any time, and the moment the door is open in she walks. I can't throw her out of the window: as to getting rid of her, that is rational and probable, but *I* will not receive her.

The Bessboroughs may take her if they please—or any steps they please; I have no hesitation in saying that I have made up my mind as to the alternative, and would sooner, much sooner, be with the dead in purgatory, than with her, *Caroline* (I put the name at length as I am not jesting), upon earth. She may hunt me down—it is the power of any mad or bad woman to do so by any man—but *snare* me she shall not: torment me she may; how am I to bar myself from her! I am already almost a prisoner; she has no shame, no feeling, no one estimable or redeemable quality. These are strong words, but I know what I am writing; they will avail nothing but to convince you of my own determination. My first object in such a dilemma would be to take —— with me; that might fail, so much the better, but even if it did—I would lose a hundred souls rather than be bound to C. If there is one human being whom I do utterly *detest* and *abhor* it is she, and, all things considered, I feel to myself justified in so doing. She has been an adder in my path ever since my return to this country; she has often belied and sometimes betrayed me; she has crossed me everywhere; she has watched and worried and *guessed* and been a curse to me and mine.

You may show *her* this if you please—or to anyone you please; if these were the last words I were to write upon earth I would not revoke one letter except to make it more legible.

Ever yours most sincerely, BYRON.

TO LADY MELBOURNE   *July 2nd, 1814*

DEAR LADY M.,—I leave town to-morrow for two or three days, and as I shall probably be occupied at Cambridge, I

may as well " say my say " with regard to C. " Conquer."
Oh no—*crush*—if you please, and not unlikely whether she goes
or stays. She perplexed me very much with questions and
guesses—and as I verily believe her growing actually and
seriously disordered in her intellects, there is no conjecturing
what she may assert or do, as far as I can judge from observation, not less towards myself than others (though in a different
way to the last), she cannot be in her senses.[1] I was obliged to
talk to her, for she laid hold of Hobhouse, and passed before
where another person and myself were discussing points of
Platonism, so frequently and remarkably, as to make us
anticipate a scene ; and as she was masked, and dominoed,
and it was daylight, there could be little harm, and there was
at least a probability of more quiet. Not all I could say could
prevent her from displaying her green *pantaloons* every now and
then ; though I scolded like her grandfather upon these very
uncalled for, and unnecessary gesticulations. Why do you say
that I was mistaken about another mask with you? I never
even pretended to guess at so pious a person, nor supposed
they were in so profane an assembly, and now I am convinced
they were not there at all ; since you tell me of the illness of the
little boy, who so happily recovered, by the timely devotion of
her staying away to take care of him.

　　To be sure, I thought I saw somebody very like ; but there
is no trusting to likenesses, and it is not easy to unmask anybody,
even without their pasteboard.

　　I don't wonder at your dislike to C., etc., and whatever
absurdity, or enormity, her madness may plunge me into, I
do think you have already done at least tenfold more than
anyone on earth would have done ; and if you were to do more,
I should conceive you no less mad than herself. I thank you
for the past, for the thousandth time, and as to the present and
future I shall parry her off as well as I can, and if foiled, I
must abide by the consequence : so there's an end. After all,
it is not much your concern (except as far as good nature went),
and rests between me and the Blarneys, whom I regard not.
To *yourself* I own that I am anxious to appear as having done

---

[1] The events to which Byron refers took place at the celebrated Watier's
Masquerade, held by the members of Watier's Club in honour of the return of the
Duke of Wellington

all that could be done to second your wishes in breaking off
the connection, which would have been effectual with any, or
every other person.

I am glad you were amused with ——'s correspondent.
—— is very much astonished, but in very good humour, and
I too—on account of my *theory*, of which, by-the-bye, I
despaired very much at first in the present instance. I think
I should make a good Tartuffe; it was by paring down my
demeanour to a very quiet and hesitating deportment, which
however my natural shyness (though that goes off at times)
helped to forward, that I ensured the three days' recollection
of ——'s amiable ally.

Good-bye, for the present. I am still sadly sleepy with the
wear and tear of the last two nights, and have had nothing
for my trouble. I wanted very much to talk to you, but you
preferred Robinson. The next time he breaks a leg I shall be
less sorry, and send you to nurse him.

I am in amity (the purest, and of course most insipid) with
a person; and one condition is, that I am to tell her her faults
without reserve. How long do you think such a treaty, fully
observed, would endure? I will tell you—five minutes. I
was assailed by a Mask for some time, teazing enough, but with
a sweet voice, and someone of whom all I could learn was that
" I had said of her, she *had been* very beautiful ". This quite
cured my desire of discovery, as such a speech could never be
forgiven, so I told her, and got away.

Good-bye again.

Ever most affectionately, your servitor, B.

TO THOMAS MOORE   *Hastings, August 3, 1814*

By the time this reaches your dwelling, I shall (God wot)
be in town again probably. I have been here renewing my
acquaintance with my old friend Ocean; and I find his bosom
as pleasant a pillow for an hour in the morning as his daughters
of Paphos could be in the twilight. I have been swimming and
eating turbot, and smuggling neat brandies and silk handker-
chiefs,—and listening to my friend Hodgson's raptures about
a pretty wife-elect of his,—and walking on cliffs, and tumbling

down hills and making the most of the *dolce far-niente* for the last fortnight. I met a son of Lord Erskine's, who says he has been married a year, and is the " happiest of men " ; and I have met the aforesaid H., who is also the " happiest of men " ; so, it is worth while being here, if only to witness the superlative felicity of these foxes, who have cut off their tails, and would persuade the rest to part with their brushes to keep them in countenance.

It rejoiceth me that you like *Lara*. Jeffrey is out with his 45th Number, which I suppose you have got. He is only too kind to me, in my share of it, and I begin to fancy myself a golden pheasant, upon the strength of the plumage wherewith he hath bedecked me. But then, " *surgit amari* ", etc.—the gentlemen of the *Champion*, and Perry, have got hold (I know not how) of the condolatory address to Lady Jersey on the picture-abduction by our Regent, and have published them—with my name, too, smack—without even asking leave, or inquiring whether or no! Damn their impudence, and damn every thing. It has put me out of patience, and so, I shall say no more about it.

You shall have *Lara* and *Jacque* ¹ (both with some additions) when out; but I am still demurring and delaying, and in a fuss, and so is Rogers in his way.

Newstead is to be mine again. Claughton forfeits twenty-five thousand pounds; but that don't prevent me from being very prettily ruined. I mean to bury myself there—and let my beard grow—and hate you all.

Oh! I have had the most amusing letter from Hogg, the Ettrick minstrel and shepherd. He wants me to recommend him to Murray; and, speaking of his present bookseller, whose " bills " are never " lifted ", he adds, *totidem verbis*, " God damn him and them both ". I laughed, and so would you too, at the way in which this execration is introduced. The said Hogg is a strange being, but of great, though uncouth, powers. I think very highly of him, as a poet; but he, and half of these Scotch and Lake troubadours, are spoilt by living in little circles and petty societies. London and the world is the only place to take the conceit out of a man—in the milling phrase.

¹ Rogers' poem, *Jacqueline*, was first circulated in combination with Byron's *Lara*.

Scott, he says, is gone to the Orkneys in a gale of wind ;—during which wind, he affirms, the said Scott, " he is sure, is not at his ease,—to say the best of it ". Lord, Lord, if these home-keeping minstrels had crossed your Atlantic or my Mediterranean, and tasted a little open boating in a white squall—or a gale in " the Gut "—or the " Bay of Biscay ", with no gale at all—how it would enliven and introduce them to a few of the sensations !—to say nothing of an illicit amour or two upon shore, in the way of essay upon the Passions, beginning with simple adultery, and compounding it as they went along.

I have forwarded your letter to Murray,—by the way, you had addressed it to *Miller*. Pray write to me, and say what art thou doing? " Not finished? "—Oons ! how is this?—these " flaws and starts " must be " authorised by your grandam ", and are unbecoming of any other author. I was sorry to hear of your discrepancy with the * * s, or rather your abjuration of agreement. I don't want to be impertinent, or buffoon on a serious subject, and am therefore at a loss what to say.

I hope nothing will induce you to abate from the proper price of your poem, as long as there is a prospect of getting it. For my own part, I have *seriously* and *not whiningly* (for that is not my way—at least, it used not to be) neither hopes, nor prospects, and scarcely even wishes. I am, in some respects, happy, but not in a manner that can or ought to last,—but enough of that. The worst of it is, I feel quite enervated and indifferent. I really do not know, if Jupiter were to offer me my choice of the contents of his benevolent cask, what I would pick out of it. If I was born, as the nurses say, with a " silver spoon in my mouth ", it has stuck in my throat, and spoiled my palate, so that nothing put into it is swallowed with much relish,—unless it be cayenne. However, I have grievances enough to occupy me that way too ;—but for fear of adding to yours by this pestilent long diatribe, I postpone the reading of them, *sine die*.

Ever, dear M., yours, etc.

P.S.—Don't forget my godson. You could not have fixed on a fitter porter for his sins than me, being used to carry double without inconvenience. * * *

TO MISS ANNE ISABELLA MILBANKE   *August 10th, 1814*

I will answer your question as openly as I can. I did—do —and always shall love you; and as this feeling is not exactly an act of will, I know no remedy, and at all events should never find one in the sacrifice of your comfort. When our acquaintance commenced, it appeared to me from all that I saw and heard that you were the woman most adapted to render any man (who was neither inveterately foolish nor wicked) happy; but I was informed that you were attached, if not engaged—and very luckily—to a person for whose success all the females of the family where I received my intelligence were much interested. Before such powerful interest—and your supposed inclinations—I had too much humility or pride to hazard importunity or even attention; till I at last learned— almost by accident—that I was misinformed as to the engagement. The rest you know; and I will not trouble you with " a twice told tale ", " signifying nothing ".

What your own feelings and objections were and are I have not the right and scarcely the wish to enquire. It is enough for me that they exist; they excite neither astonishment nor displeasure. It would be a very hard case if a woman were obliged to account for her repugnance. You would probably like me if you could; and as you cannot I am not quite coxcomb enough to be surprised at a very natural occurrence. You ask me how far my peace is, or may be, affected by those feelings towards you. I do not know—not quite enough to invade yours, or request from your pity what I cannot owe to your affection.

I am interrupted—perhaps it is as well upon such a subject.

TO THOMAS MOORE   *August 12, 1814*

I was *not* alone, nor will be while I can help it. Newstead is not yet decided. Claughton is to make a grand effort by Saturday week to complete,—if not, he must give up twenty-five thousand pounds and the estate, with expenses, etc., etc. If I resume the Abbacy, you shall have due notice, and a cell set apart for your reception, with a pious welcome. Rogers I have not seen, but Larry and Jacky came out a few days ago. Of their effect I know nothing. * * *

There is something very amusing in *your* being an *Edinburgh Reviewer*. You know, I suppose, that Thurlow is none of the placidest, and may possibly enact some tragedy on being told that he is only a fool. If, now, Jeffrey were to be slain on account of an article of yours, there would be a fine conclusion. For my part, as Mrs. Winifred Jenkins says, " he has done the handsome thing by me ", particularly in his last number; so, he is the best of men and the ablest of critics, and I won't have him killed—though I dare say many wish he were, for being so good-humoured.

Before I left Hastings I got in a passion with an ink-bottle, which I flung out of the window one night with a vengeance ;— and what then? Why, next morning I was horrified by seeing that it had struck, and split upon, the petticoat of Euterpe's graven image in the garden, and grimed her as if it were on purpose. Only think of my distress,—and the epigrams that might be engendered on the Muse and her misadventure.

I had an adventure almost as ridiculous, at some private theatricals near Cambridge—though of a different description —since I saw you last. I quarrelled with a man in the dark for asking me who I was (insolently enough to be sure), and followed him into the green-room (a *stable*) in a rage, amongst a set of people I never saw before. He turned out to be a low comedian, engaged to act with the amateurs, and to be a civil-spoken man enough, when he found out that nothing very pleasant was to be got by rudeness. But you would have been amused with the row, and the dialogue, and the dress— or rather the undress—of the party, where I had introduced myself in a devil of a hurry, and the astonishment that ensued. I had gone out of the theatre, for coolness, into the garden ;— there I had tumbled over some dogs, and, coming away from them in very ill humour, encountered the man in a worse, which produced all this confusion.

Well—and why don't you " launch "?—Now is your time. The people are tolerably tired with me, and not very much enamoured of Wordsworth, who has just spawned a quarto of metaphysical blank verse, which is nevertheless only a part of a poem.

Murray talks of divorcing Larry and Jacky—a bad sign for the authors, who, I suppose, will be divorced too, and throw the blame upon one another. Seriously, I don't care a cigar about it, and I don't see why Sam should.

Let me hear from and of you and my godson. If a daughter, the name will do quite as well.

Ever, etc.

TO LADY MELBOURNE   *Newstead Abbey,*
                              [Sunday] September 18th, 1814

MY DEAR LADY M^E,—Miss Milbanke has accepted me; and her answer was accompanied by a very kind letter from your brother. May I hope for your consent, too? Without it I should be unhappy, even were it not for many reasons important in other points of view; and with it I shall have nothing to require, except your good wishes now, and your friendship always.

I lose no time in telling you how things are at present. Many circumstances may doubtless occur in this, as in other cases, to prevent its completion, but I will hope otherwise. I shall be in town by Thursday, and beg one line to Albany, to say you will see me at your own day, hour, and place.

In course I mean to reform most thoroughly, and become " a good man and true ", in all the various senses of these respective and respectable appellations. Seriously, I will endeavour to make your niece happy; not by " my deserts, but what I will deserve ". Of my deportment you may reasonably doubt; of her merits you can have none. I need not say that this must be a *secret*. Do let me find a few words from you in Albany, and believe me ever

Most affec^{tly} y^{rs}, B.

TO MISS ANNE ISABELLA MILBANKE   *Septr. 18th 1814*

Your letter has given me a new existence [1]—it was unexpected—I need not say welcome—but *that* is a poor word to express my present feelings—and yet equal to any other—for express them adequately I cannot. I have ever regarded you

[1] Byron refers to Miss Milbanke's letter, finally accepting his proposal of marriage.

as one of the first of human beings—not merely from my own observation but that of others—as one whom it was as difficult *not* to love—as scarcely possible to deserve; —I know your worth—and revere your virtues as I love yourself and if every proof in my power of my full sense of what is due to you will contribute to *your* happiness—I shall have secured my own.— It *is* in your power to render me happy—you have made me so already.—I wish to answer your letter immediately—but am at present scarcely collected enough to do it rationally—I was upon the point of leaving England without hope without fear —almost without feeling—but wished to make one effort to discover—not if I could pretend to your present affections—for to those I had given over all presumption—but whether time —and my most sincere endeavour to adopt any mode of conduct that might lead you to think well of me—might not eventually in securing your approbation awaken your regard.— These hopes are now dearer to me than ever; dear as they have ever been; —from the moment I became acquainted my attachment has been increasing and the very follies—give them a harsher name—with which I was beset and bewildered the conduct to which I had recourse for forgetfulness only made recollection more lively and bitter by the comparisons it forced on me in spite of Pride—and of Passions—which might have destroyed but never deceived me.—

I am going to London on some business which once over— I hope to be permitted to visit Seaham; your father I will answer immediately and in the mean time beg you will present my best thanks and respects to him and Lady Milbanke. Will you write to me? and permit me to assure you how faithfully I shall ever be

yr. most attached and obliged Sert.[1]

TO THOMAS MOORE   *Newstead Abbey, Sept. 20, 1814*

> Here's to her who long
>   Hath waked the poet's sigh!
> The girl who gave to song
>   What gold could never buy.

---

[1] In this letter the characteristically wild punctuation is left unchanged, since it well conveys his agitation.

My dear Moore,—I am going to be married—that is, I am accepted, and one usually hopes the rest will follow. My mother of the Gracchi (that *are* to be), *you* think too strait-laced for me, although the paragon of only children, and invested with " golden opinions of all sorts of men ", and full of " most blest conditions " as Desdemona herself. Miss Milbanke is the lady, and I have her father's invitation to proceed there in my elect capacity,—which, however, I cannot do till I have settled some business in London, and got a blue coat.

She is said to be an heiress, but of that I really know nothing certainly, and shall not enquire. But I do know, that she has talents and excellent qualities ; and you will not deny her judgment, after having refused six suitors and taken me.

Now, if you have anything to say against this, pray do ; my mind's made up, positively fixed, determined, and therefore I will listen to reason, because now it can do no harm. Things may occur to break it off, but I will hope not. In the mean time, I tell you (a *secret*, by the by,—at least, till I know she wishes it to be public) that I have proposed and am accepted. You need not be in a hurry to wish me joy, for one mayn't be married for months. I am going to town to-morrow : but expect to be here, on my way there, within a fortnight.

If this had not happened, I should have gone to Italy. In my way down, perhaps, you will meet me at Nottingham, and come over with me here. I need not say that nothing will give me greater pleasure. I must, of course, reform thoroughly ; and, seriously, if I can contribute to her happiness, I shall secure my own. She is so good a person, that—that—in short, I wish I was a better.

Ever, etc.

TO MISS MILBANKE [FRAGMENT]   *14 Oct^{tr} 1814*

I have not seen the paragraph you mention ; but it cannot speak more humbly of me in the comparison than I think. This is one of the lesser evils to which notoriety and a carelessness of fame,—in the only good sense of the word,—has rendered me liable,—a carelessness which I do not now feel since I have obtained something worth caring for. The truth is that could I have foreseen that your life was to be linked to mine,—had I even possessed a distinct hope however distant,— I would have been a different and better being. As it is, I have sometimes doubts, even if I should not disappoint the future nor act hereafter unworthily of you, whether the past ought not to make you still regret me—even that portion of it with which you are not unacquainted.

I did not believe such a woman existed—at least for me,— and I sometimes fear I ought to wish that she had not. I must turn from the subject.

My love, do forgive me if I have written in a spirit that renders you uncomfortable. I cannot embody my feelings in words. I have nothing to desire—nothing I would see altered in *you*—but so much in myself. I can conceive no misery equal to mine, if I failed in making you happy,—and yet how can I hope to do justice to those merits from whose praise there is not a dissentient voice?

TO THOMAS MOORE   *October 14, 1814*

An there were any thing in marriage that would make a difference between my friends and me, particularly in your case, I would "none on't". My agent sets off for Durham next week, and I shall follow him, taking Newstead and you in my way. I certainly did not address Miss Milbanke with these views, but it is likely she may prove a considerable *parti*. All her father can give, or leave her, he will; and from her childless uncle, Lord Wentworth, whose barony, it is supposed, will devolve on Ly. Milbanke (*his* sister), she has expectations. But these will depend upon his own disposition, which seems very partial towards her. She is an only child, and Sir R.'s estates, though dipped by electioneering, are considerable. Part of them are settled on her; but whether *that* will be *dowered* now, I do not know,—though, from what has been intimated to me, it probably will. The lawyers are to settle this among them, and I am getting my property into matrimonial array, and myself ready for the journey to Seaham, which I must make in a week or ten days.

I certainly did not dream that she was attached to me, which it seems she has been for some time. I also thought her of a very cold disposition, in which I was also mistaken—it is a long story, and I won't trouble you with it. As to her virtues etc., etc., you will hear enough of them (for she is a kind of *pattern* in the north), without my running into a display on the subject. It is well that *one* of us is of such fame, since there is sad deficit in the *morale* of that article upon my part,—all owing to my " bitch of a star ", as Captain Tranchemont says of his planet.

Don't think you have not said enough of me in your article on T[hurlow] ; what more could or need be said?

* * Your long-delayed and expected work—I suppose you will take fright at *The Lord of the Isles* and Scott now. You must do as you like,—I have said my say. You ought to fear comparison with none, and any one would stare, who heard you were so tremulous,—though, after all, I believe it is the surest sign of talent. Good morning. I hope we shall meet soon, but I will write again, and perhaps you will meet me at Nottingham. Pray say so.

P.S.—If this union is productive, you shall name the first fruits.

TO JOHN CAM HOBHOUSE *October 17th, 1814*

MY DEAR HOBHOUSE,—If I have not answered your very kind letter immediately, do not impute it to neglect. I have expected you would be in town or near it, and waited to thank you in person. Believe me, no change of time or circumstance short of insanity, can make any difference in my feelings, and I hope, in my conduct towards you. I have known you too long, and tried you too deeply ; a new mistress is nothing to an old friend, the latter can't be replaced in this world, nor, I very much fear, in the next, and neither in this nor the other

could I meet with one so deserving of my respect and regard.
Well, H.—I am engaged, and we wait only for settlements
" and all that " to be married. My intended, it seems, has
liked me very well for a long time, which, I am sure, her
encouragement gave me no reason to suspect; but so it is, according to her account. The circumstances which led to the
renewal of my proposal I will acquaint you with when we
meet, if you think such material concerns worth your enquiry.
Hanson is going down next week to Durham, to confabulate
with Sir R.'s agents on the score of temporalities, and I suppose
I must soon follow to my sire-in-law's that is to be. I confess
that the character of wooer in this regular way does not sit
easy upon me. I wish I could wake some morning, and find
myself fairly married. I do hate (out of Turkey) all fuss, and
bustle, and ceremony so much; and one can't be married,
according to what I hear, without *some*. I wish, whenever this
same form is muttered over us, that you could make it convenient to be present. I will give you due notice:—if you
would but take a wife and be coupled then also, like people
electrified in company through the same chain, it would be
still further comfort.
    Good even.

                                    Ever yours most truly, B.

TO MISS MILBANKE [FRAGMENT]   *20th Octr 1814*

    I have been so much amused with your " extracts ", though
I had no idea what an evil spirit I then appeared in your eyes.
You were quite right however, as far as appearances, but that
was not my natural character. I was just returned from a far
country where everything was different, and felt bewildered
and not very happy in my own, which I had left without
regret and returned to without interest. I found myself, I did
not very well know why, an object of curiosity which I never
wished to excite—and about a poem which I had no conception was to make such a fuss. My mind and my feelings were
moreover occupied with considerations which had nothing in
common with the circle where I was whirling, so that no

wonder I was repulsive and cold. I never could conquer my disposition to be both in a crowd from which I was always wishing myself away.

Those who know me most intimately can tell you that I am if anything too *childish*, with a greater turn for the ridiculous than for anything serious,—and, I could hope, not very ill natured *off the stage*, and, if angry, never loud. I can't say much for these qualifications, but I have such a regard for yours, that I am sure we shall be a very happy couple. I wish you had a greater passion for governing, for I don't shine in conducting myself, and am very docile with a gentle guide.

TO LADY MELBOURNE   *Seaham, November 4th, 1814*

MY DEAR LADY Mᴱ,—I have been here these two days; but waited to observe before I imparted to you—" my confidential counsel ", as Master Hoar would say—my remarks.

Your brother pleases me much. To be sure his stories are long; but I believe he has told most of them, and he is to my mind the perfect gentleman; but I don't like Lady M[ilbanke] at all. I can't tell why, for we don't differ, but so it is; she seems to be everything here, which is all very well; and I am, and mean to be, very conformable, and dutiful, but nevertheless I wish she and mine aunt could change places, as far as regards me and mine. A[nnabella]'s meeting and mine made a kind of scene; though there was no acting, nor even speaking, but the pantomime was very expressive. She seems to have more feeling than we imagined; but is the most *silent* woman I ever encountered; which perplexes me extremely. I like them to talk, because then they *think* less. Much cogitation will not be in my favour; besides, I can form my judgments better, since, unless the countenance is flexible, it is difficult to steer by mere looks. I am studying her, but can't boast of my progress in getting at her disposition; and if the conversation is to be all on one side I fear committing myself; and those who only listen, must have their thoughts so much about them as to seize any weak point at once. However, the die is cast; neither party can recede; the lawyers are here—mine and all—and I presume, the parchment once scribbled, I shall become Lord Annabella.

I can't yet tell whether we are to be happy or not. I have every disposition to do her all possible justice, but I fear she won't govern me; and if she don't it will not do at all; but perhaps she may mend of that fault. I have always thought— first, that she did not like me at all; and next, that her supposed after-liking was *imagination*. This last I conceive that my presence would—perhaps has removed—if so, I shall soon discover it, but mean to take it with great philosophy, and to behave attentively and well, though I never could love but that which *loves*; and this I must say for myself, that my attachment always increases in due proportion to the return it meets with, and never changes in the presence of its object; to be sure, like Mrs. Damer, I have " an opinion of absence ".

Pray write. I think you need not fear that the *answer* to *this* will run any of the risks you apprehend. It will be a great comfort to me, in all events, to call you aunt, and to know that you are sure of my being

Ever y^{rs}, B.

TO MISS ANNE ISABELLA MILBANKE   *Novr. 23rd 1814*

My Love—While I write this letter I have desired my very old and kind friend Mr. Hodgson to send you a note, which I will enclose, as it contains a piece of information that will come better from him than me—and yet not give you less pleasure. I think of setting off for London to-morrow— where I will write again. I am quite confused and bewildered here with the voting and the fuss and the crowd—to say nothing of yesterday's dinner and meeting all one's old acquaintances, the consequence of which is that infallible next-day's headache ever attendant upon sincere Friendship. Here are Hobhouse and our cousin George Lamb—who called on me ; and we have all voted the same way, but they say nevertheless our man won't win—but have many votes howbeit. To-day I dine with Clarke the traveller—one of the best and most goodnatured of souls—and uniformly kind to me. When we meet I think and hope I shall make you laugh at the scene I went through—or rather which went through me; for I was quite unprepared, and am not at the best of times sufficiently master of " the family shyness " to acquit myself otherwise than awkwardly on such an occasion.

Well but—sweet Heart—do write and love me—and regard me as thine

ever and most

P.S.—Love to parents.   I have not and am not to see H's note, so I hope it is all very correct.

3
Marriage

January 1815 to October 1816

Byron had not been averse from the prospect of marriage; but, when the prospect began to materialize, he had shown many signs of hesitation. *Never was lover less in haste,* observed Hobhouse, noting the lack of enthusiasm with which he prepared to join the Milbankes. Almost from the first day the marriage was unfortunate: Byron was in one of his darkest moods; and his attitude towards the young woman he had married, even allowing for his love of exaggeration and an element of romantic bravado, was neither kindly nor considerate. After an over-clouded honeymoon, the married couple returned to London and took up residence at an expensive house in Piccadilly Terrace. Byron's creditors, excited by the report that he had married an heiress, became extremely troublesome; and incessant financial difficulties added to the depression of spirits from which he was already suffering. Nor was the anxious solemnity with which Lady Byron watched her husband's movements calculated to soothe him. She did not approve of his choice of friends, who encouraged him, she believed, to sit up drinking brandy, and she mistrusted his connection with Drury Lane Theatre, where Byron and Douglas Kinnaird both served on the Committee. Despite the intervention of Augusta Leigh, who did what she could to comfort her sister-in-law and calm her brother's tantrums, the relationship between Byron and his wife became rapidly more painful. It was not improved by the birth of their only child, Augusta Ada Byron, on December 10th, 1815. During January bailiffs entered the house; and on the 15th, at Byron's request, Annabella and her child set out from London and took refuge with her parents. En route *she* wrote him an affectionate message; but, during the first week of February 1816, Sir Ralph Milbanke informed the poet that Lady Byron's parents " could not feel themselves justified in permitting her return ", and proposed a separation. Byron

refused indignantly, but eventually agreed, though he professed
that he still could not understand why his wife should wish to
leave him. On April 25th, 1816, he sailed from England for
the last time and, having travelled across the Low Countries
with Dr. Polidori, his personal physician, settled beside the Lake
of Geneva at the Villa Diodati. There his associates were Percy
Bysshe Shelley (a connection much regretted by Mrs. Leigh and
by her confidant, Byron's old acquaintance, the Reverend Francis
Hodgson), Shelley's youthful mistress, Mary Godwin, and her
turbulent step-sister, Claire Clairmont, who had previously
encountered Byron in London and who after a time returned to
England to give birth to his natural child, Allegra.

TO LADY MELBOURNE *Halnaby, January 3rd, 1815*

MY DEAREST AUNT,—We were married yesterday at ten
upon yᵉ clock, so there's an end of that matter, and the beginning of many others. Bell has gone through all the ceremonies with great fortitude, and I am much as usual, and your
dutiful nephew. All those who are disposed to make presents
may as well send them forthwith, and pray let them be handsome, and we wait your congrats besides, as I am sure your
benediction is very essential to all our undertakings.

Lady M[ilbanke] was a little hysterical, and fine-feeling;
and the kneeling was rather tedious, and the cushions hard;
but upon the whole it did vastly well. The drawing-room at
Seaham was the scene of our conjunction, and then we set off,
according to approved custom, to be shut up by ourselves.

You would think we had been married these fifty years.
Bell is fast asleep on a corner of the sopha, and I am keeping
myself awake with this epistle—she desires her love, and mine
you have had ever since we were acquainted. Pray, how
many of our new relations (at least, of mine) mean to own us?
I reckon upon George and you, and Lord M[elbourne] and

the Countess and Count of the Holy Roman Empire; as for *Caro* and Caro George, and *William,* I don't know what to think, do you?

I shall write to you again anon; at present, receive this as an apology for that silence of which you were kind enough to complain; and believe me ever most affectionately thine,

BYRON

P.S.—I enclose you an order for the box; it was not at liberty before. The week after next will be mine, and so on alternately. I have lent it, for the present week only, to another person; the next is yours.

TO THOMAS MOORE   *January 19, 1815*

Egad! I don't think he is " down "; and my prophecy—like most auguries, sacred and profane—is not annulled, but inverted. * * *

To your question about the " dog " — Umph! — my " mother ", I won't say any thing against—that is, about her: but how long a " mistress " or friend may recollect paramours or competitors (lust and thirst being the two great and only bonds between the amatory or the amicable), I can't say,—or, rather, you know, as well as I could tell you. But as for canine recollections, as far as I could judge by a cur of mine own, (always bating Boatswain, the dearest, and, alas! the maddest of dogs,) I had one (half a *wolf* by the she side) that doted on me at ten years old, and very nearly ate me at twenty. When I thought he was going to enact Argus, he bit away the backside of my breeches, and never would consent to any kind of recognition, in despite of all kinds of bones which I offered him. So, let Southey blush and Homer too, as far as I can decide upon quadruped memories.

I humbly take it, the mother knows the son that pays her jointure—a mistress her mate, till he * * and refuses salary—a friend his fellow, till he loses cash and character—and a dog his master, till he changes him.

So, you want to know about milady and me? But let me not, as Roderick Random says, " profane the chaste mysteries of Hymen "—damn the word, I had nearly spelt it with a small *h*. I like Bell as well as you do (or did, you villain !) Bessy—and that is (or was) saying a great deal.

Address your next to Seaham, Stockton-on-Tees, where we are going on Saturday (a bore, by the way,) to see father-in-law, Sir Jacob, and my lady's lady-mother. Write—and write more at length—both to the public and

Yours ever most affectionately, B.

TO THOMAS MOORE   *Seaham, Stockton-on-Tees, February 2, 1815*

I have heard from London that you have left Chatsworth and all the women full of " entusymusy " about you, personally and poetically; and, in particular, that " When first I met thee " has been quite overwhelming in its effect. I told you it was one of the best things you ever wrote, though that dog Power wanted you to omit part of it. They are all regretting your absence at Chatsworth, according to my informant— " all the ladies quite ", etc., etc., etc. Stap my vitals !

Well, now you have got home again—which I dare say is as agreeable as a " draught of cool small beer to the scorched palate of a waking sot "—now you have got home again, I say, probably I shall hear from you. Since I wrote last, I have been transferred to my father-in-law's, with my lady and my lady's maid, etc., etc., etc., and the treacle-moon is over, and I am awake, and find myself married. My spouse and I agree to—and in—admiration. Swift says " no *wise* man ever married " ; but, for a fool, I think it the most ambrosial of all possible future states. I still think one ought to marry upon *lease*; but am very sure I should renew mine at the expiration, though next term were for ninety and nine years.

I wish you would respond, for I am here *oblitusque meorum obliviscendus et illis*. Pray tell me what is going on in the way of intriguery, and how the w——s and rogues of the upper Beggar's Opera go on—or rather go off—in or after marriage; or who are going to break any particular commandment. Upon this dreary coast, we have nothing but county meetings and shipwrecks : and I have this day dined upon fish, which probably dined upon the crews of several colliers lost in the late gales. But I saw the sea once more in all the glories of surf and foam,—almost equal to the Bay of Biscay, and the interesting white squalls and short seas of Archipelago memory.

My papa, Sir Ralpho, hath recently made a speech at a Durham tax-meeting; and not only at Durham, but here, several times since after dinner. He is now, I believe, speaking it to himself (I left him in the middle) over various decanters, which can neither interrupt him nor fall asleep,—as might possibly have been the case with some of his audience.

Ever thine, B.

I must go to tea—damn tea. I wish it was Kinnaird's brandy, and with you to lecture me about it.

TO LADY MELBOURNE *Seaham, February 2nd, 1815*

MY DEAR AUNT,—Sans letter paper, I have co-opted awkwardly enough a sheet of foolscap whereupon to answer your epistle. I cannot " laugh " at anything which gave you pain, and therefore will say nothing about your nervous headache, except that I am glad that it is gone; one may see a " double face " without being *delirious* though; but I must cease talking of your complaint for fear of growing as sentimental as Bob Adair, your larmoyant admirer. Had you seen Lord Stair? If so the disorder, as far as the *ache* (the face is too dull to be double) is accounted for.

It rejoices me to hear of Moore's success; he is an excellent companion as well as poet, though I cannot recollect that I " wept " at the song you mention. I ought to have done so; but whether I did or not, it is one of the most beautiful and touching compositions that ever he penned, and much better than ever was compounded by anyone else.

The *moon* is over; but Bell and I are as lunatic as heretofore; she does as she likes, and don't bore me, and we may win the Dunmow flitch of bacon for anything I know. Mamma and Sir Ralph are also very good, but I wish the last would not speak his speech at the Durham meeting above once a week after its first delivery.

I won't betray you, if you will only write me something worth betraying. I suppose your " C— noir " is **X**, but if **X** were a raven, or a griffin, I must still take omens from her flight.

I can't help loving her, though I have quite enough at home to prevent me from loving anyone essentially for some time to come.

We have two visitors here, a Mrs. and Miss Somebody; the latter plain, and both humdrum, they have made me so sleepy that I must say Good night.

Ever yours most nepotically, B.

TO THOMAS MOORE   *July 7, 1815*

Grata superveniet, etc., etc. I had written to you again, but burnt the letter, because I began to think you seriously hurt at my indolence, and did not know how the buffoonery it contained might be taken. In the mean time, I have yours, and all is well.

I had given over all hopes of yours. By-the-by, my *grata superveniet* should be in this present tense; for I perceive it looks now as if it applied to this present scrawl reaching you, whereas it is to the receipt of thy Kilkenny epistle that I have tacked that venerable sentiment.

Poor Whitbread died yesterday morning,—a sudden and severe loss. His health had been wavering, but so fatal an attack was not apprehended. He dropped down, and I believe never spoke afterwards. I perceive Perry attributes his death to Drury Lane,—a consolatory encouragement to the new Committee. I have no doubt that * *, who is of a plethoric habit, will be bled immediately; as I have, since my marriage, lost much of my paleness, and—*horresco referens* (for I hate even *moderate* fat)—that happy slenderness, to which when I first knew you, I had attained, I by no means sit easy under this dispensation of the *Morning Chronicle*. Every one must regret the loss of Whitbread; he was surely a great and very good man.

Paris is taken for the second time. I presume it, for the future, will have an anniversary capture. In the late battles, like all the world, I have lost a connexion,—poor Frederic Howard, the best of his race. I had little intercourse, of late years, with his family, but I never saw or heard but good of him. Hobhouse's brother is killed. In short, the havoc has not left a family out of its tender mercies.

Every hope of a republic is over, and we must go on under the old system. But I am sick at heart of politics and slaughters; and the luck which Providence is pleased to lavish on Lord Castlereagh is only a proof of the little value the gods set upon prosperity, when they permit such * * * s as he and that drunken corporal, old Blucher, to bully their betters. From this, however, Wellington should be excepted. He *is* a man,— and the Scipio of our Hannibal. However, he may thank the Russian frosts, which destroyed the *real élite* of the French army, for the successes of Waterloo.

La! Moore—how you blasphemes about " Parnassus " and " Moses! " I am ashamed for you. Won't you do any thing for the drama? We beseech an Opera. Kinnaird's blunder was partly mine. I wanted you of all things in the Committee, and so did he. But we are now glad you were wiser; for it is, I doubt, a bitter business.

When shall we see you in England? Sir Ralph Noel (*late* Milbanke—he don't promise to be *late* Noel in a hurry), finding that one man can't inhabit two houses, has given his place in the north to me for a habitation; and there Lady B. threatens to be brought to bed in November. Sir R. and my Lady Mother are to quarter at Kirby—Lord Wentworth's that was. Perhaps you and Mrs. Moore will pay us a visit at Seaham in the course of the autumn. If so, you and I (*without* our *wives*) will take a *lark* to Edinburgh and embrace Jeffrey. It is not much above one hundred miles from us. But all this, and other high matters, we will discuss at meeting, which I hope will be on your return. We don't leave town till August.

Ever yours, etc., B.

TO S. T. COLERIDGE *   *13 Terrace, Piccadilly, October 18th, 1815*

DEAR SIR,—Your letter I have just received. I will willingly do whatever you direct about the volumes in question—the sooner the better : it shall not be for want of endeavour on my part, as a negotiator with the " Trade " (to talk technically) that you are not enabled to do yourself justice. Last spring I saw Wr. Scott. He repeated to me a considerable portion of an unpublished poem of yours—the wildest and finest I ever heard in that kind of composition. The title he did not mention, but I think the heroine's name was Geraldine. At all events, the " toothless mastiff bitch " and the " witch Lady ", the description of the hall, the lamp suspended from the image, and more particularly of the girl herself as she went forth in the evening—all took a hold on my imagination which I never shall wish to shake off. I mention this, not for the sake of boring you with compliments, but as a prelude to the hope that this poem is or is to be in the volumes you are now about to publish. I do not know that even " Love " or the " Antient Mariner " are so impressive—and to me there are few things in our tongue beyond these two productions.

Wr. Scott is a staunch and sturdy admirer of yours, and with a just appreciation of your capacity deplored to me the want of inclination and exertion which prevented you from giving full scope to your mind. I will answer your question as to the " Beggar's Bush " tomorrow or next day. I shall see Rae and Dibdin (the acting Mrs.) tonight for that purpose.

Oh—your tragedy—I do not wish to hurry you, but I am indeed very anxious to have it under consideration. It is a field in which there are none living to contend against you and in which I should take a pride and pleasure in seeing you compared with the dead. I say this *not* disinterestedly, but as a *Committee*man. We have nothing even tolerable, except a tragedy of Sotheby's, which shall not interfere with yours when ready. You can have no idea what trash there is in the four hundred *fallow* dramas now lying on the shelves of D[rury] L[ane]. I never thought so highly of good writers as lately, since I have had an opportunity of comparing them with the bad.

Ever yours truly,

BYRON

TO LEIGH HUNT   *13, Terrace, Piccadilly,*
                                 September—October 30, 1815

MY DEAR HUNT,—Many thanks for your books, of which you already know my opinion. Their external splendour should not disturb you as inappropriate—they have still more within than without. I take leave to differ with you on Wordsworth, as freely as I once agreed with you; at that time I gave him credit for a promise, which is unfulfilled. I still think his capacity warrants all you say of *it* only, but that his performances since *Lyrical Ballads* are miserably inadequate to the ability which lurks within him : there is undoubtedly much natural talent spilt over the *Excursion*; but it is rain upon rocks—where it stands and stagnates, or rain upon sands —where it falls without fertilizing. Who can understand him? Let those who do, make him intelligible. Jacob Behmen, Swedenborg, and Joanna Southcote, are mere types of this arch-apostle of mystery and mysticism. But I have done,— no, I have not done, for I have two petty, and perhaps unworthy objections in small matters to make to him, which, with his pretensions to accurate observation, and fury against Pope's false translation of " the Moonlight scene in Homer ", I wonder he should have fallen into ;—these be they :—He says of Greece in the body of his book—that it is a land of

> " *Rivers, fertile plains,* and *sounding* shores,
> Under a cope of *variegated* sky ".

The rivers are dry half the year, the plains are barren, and the shores *still* and *tideless* as the Mediterranean can make them ; the sky is any thing but variegated, being for months and months but " darkly, deeply, beautifully blue ".—The next is in his notes, where he talks of our " Monuments crowded together in the busy, etc., of a large town ", as compared with the " still seclusion of a Turkish cemetery in some *remote* place ". This is pure stuff; for *one* monument in our church-yards there are *ten* in the Turkish, and so crowded, that you cannot walk between them ; that is, divided merely by a path or road ; and as to " *remote* places ", men never take the trouble in a barbarous country, to carry their dead very far ; they must have lived near to where they were buried. There are no cemeteries in " remote places ", except such as have the cypress and the tombstone still left, where the olive and the habitation of the living have perished. . . .

These things I was struck with, as coming peculiarly in my own way; and in both of these he is wrong; yet I should have noticed neither, but for his attack on Pope for a like blunder, and a peevish affectation about him of despising a popularity which he will never obtain. I write in great haste, and, I doubt, *not* much to the purpose; but you have it hot and hot, just as it comes, and so let it go. By-the-way, both he and you go too far against Pope's " So when the moon ", etc.; it is no translation, I know; but it is not such false description as asserted. I have read it on the spot; there is a burst, and a lightness, and a glow about the night in the Troad, which makes the " planets vivid ", and the " pole glowing ". The moon is—at least the sky is, clearness itself; and I know no more appropriate expression for the expansion of such a heaven —o'er the scene—the plain—the sky—Ida—the—Hellespont —Simois—Scamander—and the Isles—than that of a " flood of glory ". I am getting horribly lengthy, and must stop: to the whole of your letter " I say ditto to Mr. Burke ", as the Bristol candidate cried by way of electioneering harangue. You need not speak of morbid feelings and vexations to me; I have plenty; but I must blame partly the times, and chiefly myself: but let us forget them. *I* shall be very apt to do so when I see you next. Will you come to the theatre and see our new management? You shall cut it up to your heart's content, root and branch, afterwards, if you like; but come and see it! If not, I must come and see you.

Ever yours, very truly and affectionately, BYRON

P.S.—Not a word from Moore for these two months. Pray let me have the rest of *Rimini*. You have two excellent points in that poem—originality and Italianism. I will back you as a bard against half the fellows on whom you have thrown away much good criticism and eulogy; but don't let your bookseller publish in *quarto*; it is the worst size possible for circulation. I say this on bibliopolical authority.

Again, yours ever, B.

TO THOMAS MOORE   *Terrace, Piccadilly, October 31, 1815*

I have not been able to ascertain precisely the time of duration of the stock market; but I believe it is a good time for selling out, and I hope so. First, because I shall see you; and, next, because I shall receive certain monies on behalf of Lady B., the which will materially conduce to my comfort,— I wanting (as the duns say) " to make up a sum ".

Yesterday, I dined out with a large-ish party, where were Sheridan and Colman,[1] Harry Harris of C[ovent] G[arden], and his brother, Sir Gilbert Heathcote, Douglas Kinnaird, and others, of note and notoriety. Like other parties of the kind, it was first silent, then talky, then argumentative, then disputatious, then unintelligible, then altogethery, then inarticulate, and then drunk. When we had reached the last step of this glorious ladder, it was difficult to get down again without stumbling; and, to crown all, Kinnaird and I had to conduct Sheridan down a damned corkscrew staircase, which had certainly been constructed before the discovery of fermented liquors, and to which no legs, however crooked, could possibly accommodate themselves. We deposited him safe at home, where his man, evidently used to the business, waited to receive him in the hall.

Both he and Colman were, as usual, very good; but I carried away much wine, and the wine had previously carried away my memory; so that all was hiccup and happiness for the last hour or so, and I am not impregnated with any of the conversation. Perhaps you heard of a late answer of Sheridan to the watchman who found him bereft of that " divine particle of air ", called reason, * * *. He, the watchman, who found Sherry in the street, fuddled and bewildered, and almost insensible, " Who are *you*, sir? "—no answer. " What's your name? "—a hiccup. " What's your name? "—Answer, in a slow, deliberate, and impassive tone—" Wilberforce ! ! ! " Is not that Sherry all over?—and, to my mind, excellent. Poor fellow, *his* very dregs are better than the " first sprightly runnings " of others.

My paper is full, and I have a grievous head-ach.

[1] George Colman the Younger, the popular dramatist, a favourite at Drury Lane, where Byron, somewhat to his wife's distress, served on the Committee.

P.S.—Lady B. is in full progress. Next month will bring
to light (with the aid of " Juno Lucina, *fer opem* ", or rather
opes, for the last are most wanted,) the tenth wonder of the
world—Gil Blas being the eighth, and he (my son's father)
the ninth.

TO THOMAS MOORE   *January 5, 1816*

I hope Mrs. M. is quite re-established. The little girl was born on the 10th of December last; her name is Augusta *Ada* (the second a very antique family name,—I believe not used since the reign of King John). She was, and is, very flourishing and fat, and reckoned very large for her days—squalls and sucks incessantly. Are you answered? Her mother is doing very well, and up again.

I have now been married a year on the second of this month—heigh-ho! I have seen nobody lately much worth noting, except Sebastiani and another general of the Gauls once or twice at dinners out of doors. Sebastiani is a fine, foreign, villanous-looking, intelligent, and very agreeable man; his compatriot is more of the *petit-maître* and younger, but I should think not at all of the same intellectual calibre with the Corsican—which Sebastiani, you know, is, and a cousin of Napoleon's.

Are you never to be expected in town again? To be sure, there is no one here of the fifteen hundred fillers of hot rooms, called the fashionable world. My approaching papa-ship detained us for advice, etc., etc., though I would as soon be here as any where else on this side of the Straits of Gibraltar.

I would gladly—or, rather, sorrowfully—comply with your request of a dirge for the poor girl you mention. But how can I write on one I have never seen or known? Besides, you will do it much better yourself. I could not write upon any thing, without some personal experience and foundation: far less on a theme so peculiar. Now, you have both in this case; and, if you had neither, you have more imagination, and would never fail.

This is but a dull scrawl, and I am but a dull fellow. Just at present, I am absorbed in 500 contradictory contemplations, though with but one object in view—which will probably end in nothing, as most things we wish do. But never mind,—as somebody says, " for the blue sky bends over all ". I only could be glad, if it bent over me where it is a little bluer; like the " skyish top of blue Olympus ", which, by the way, looked very white when I last saw it.

Ever, etc.

SIR,[1] I have received your letter.   To the vague and general charge contained in it I must naturally be at a loss how to answer it—I shall therefore confine myself to the tangible fact which you are pleased to alledge as one of the motives for your present proposition.   Lady Byron received no dismissal from my house in the sense you have attached to the word.   She left London by medical advice.   She parted from me in apparent and, on my part, real harmony, though at that particular time, rather against my inclination, for I begged her to remain with the intention of myself accompanying her : when some business necessary to be arranged prevented my departure.

It is true that previous to this period I had suggested to her the expediency of a temporary residence with her parents.   My reason for this was very simple and shortly stated, viz. the embarrassment of my circumstances, and my inability to maintain our present establishment.   The truth of what is thus stated may be easily ascertained by reference to Lady B.—who is truth itself.   If she denies it, I abide by that denial.

My intention of going abroad originated in the same painful motive and was postponed from a regard to her supposed feelings on that subject.   During the last year I have had to contend with distress without and disease within.   Upon the former I have little to say—except that I have endeavoured to remove it by every sacrifice in my power ; and the latter I should not mention if I had not professional authority for saying that the disorder that I have to combat, without much impairing my apparent health, is such as to induce a morbid irritability of temper, which without recurring to external causes may have rendered me little less disagreeable to others than I am to myself.   I am, however, ignorant of any particular ill-treatment which your daughter has encountered. She may have seen me gloomy, and at times violent ; but she knows the causes too well to attribute such inequalities of disposition to herself, or even to me, if all things be fairly considered.   And now, Sir, not for your satisfaction—for I owe you none—but for my own, and in justice to Lady Byron, it is

----

[1] Byron's reply to Sir Ralph Noel's letter of the same date, announcing that Lady Byron and her parents wished for a separation.

my duty to say that there is no part of her conduct, character, temper, talents, or disposition, which could in my opinion have been changed for the better. Neither in word or deed, nor (as far as thought can be dived into) thought, can I bring to my recollection a fault on her part, or hardly even a failing. She has ever appeared to me as one of the most amiable of human beings, and nearer to perfection than I had conceived could belong to humanity in its present state of existence. Having said thus much, though more in words, less in substance, than I wished to express, I come to the point—on which subject I must for a few days decline giving a decisive answer. I will not, however, detain you longer than I can help, and as it is of some importance to your family as well as to mine, and a step which cannot be recalled when taken, you will not attribute my pause to any wish to inflict farther pain on you or yours— although there are parts of your letter which, I must be permitted to say, arrogate a right which you do not now possess ; for the present at least, your daughter is my wife ; she is the mother of my child ; and till I have her express sanction of your proceedings, I shall take leave to doubt the propriety of your interference. This will be soon ascertained, and when it is, I will submit to you my determination, which will depend very materially on hers.

I have the honour to be,

Your most obed. and very humble servt., BYRON.

TO LADY BYRON *February 5, 1816*

DEAREST BELL, No answer from you yet ; but perhaps it is as well ; only do recollect that all is at stake, the present, the future, and even the colouring of the past. My errors, or by whatever harsher name you choose to call them, you know ; but I loved you, and will not part from you without your express and expressed refusal to return to, or receive me. Only say the word that you are still mine in your heart, and

" Kate, I will buckler thee against a million."

Ever, dearest, yours most, etc., B.

TO SIR RALPH NOEL   *February 7, 1816*

Sir, I have read Lady Byron's letter, inclosed by you to Mrs. Leigh, with much surprise and more sorrow. Lady B. left London without a single hint of such feelings or intentions— neither did they transpire in her letters on the road, nor subsequent to her arrival at Kirkby. In these letters Lady Byron expresses herself to me with that playful confidence and affectionate liveliness which is perhaps a greater proof of attachment than more serious professions; she speaks to her husband of his child, like a wife and a mother. I am therefore reduced to the melancholy alternative of either believing her capable of a duplicity very foreign to my opinion of her character, or that she has lately sunk under influence, the admission of which, however respected and respectable heretofore, is not recognised in her vows at the altar.

My house, while I have one, is open to her, and my heart always—even though I should have no other shelter to offer her. I cannot suspect Lady Byron of making the grounds stated the pretext for dissolving our connection with a view to escape from my scattered fortunes; although the time chosen for this proposition, and the manner in which it was made—without inquiry, without appeal, without even a doubt, or an attempt at reconciliation—might almost excuse such a supposition. If I address you in strong language, Sir, I still wish to temper it with that respect which is required by the very duties you would persuade me to abandon, and request your candid interpretation of such expressions as circumstances have compelled me to use. I may not debase myself to implore as a suppliant the restoration of a reluctant wife, but I will not compromise my rights as a husband and as a father; I invite Lady Byron's return—I am ready to go to her should she desire or require it—and I deprecate all attempts which have been made or may be made to part us.

I have the honour to be, Sir, with great respect,
Your most obed. and very humble servant, Byron.

TO LADY BYRON   *February 8, 1816*

All I can say seems useless—and all I could say might be no less unavailing—yet I still cling to the wreck of my hopes, before they sink for ever. Were you, then, *never* happy with me? Did you never at any time or times express yourself so? Have no marks of affection of the warmest and most reciprocal attachment passed between us? or did in fact hardly a day go down without some such on one side, and generally on both? Do not mistake me : I have not denied my state of mind—but you know its causes—and were those deviations from calmness never followed by acknowledgments and repentance? Was not the last that recurred more particularly so? and had I not—had we not the days before and on the day we parted—every reason to believe that we loved each other? that we were to meet again? Were not your letters kind? Had I not acknowledged to you all my faults and follies—and assured you that some had not and could not be repeated? I do not require these questions to be answered to me, but to your own heart. The day before I received your father's letter I had fixed a day for rejoining you. If I did not write lately, Augusta did ; and as you had been my proxy in correspondence with her, so did I imagine she might be the same from me to you.

Upon your letter to me this day I surely may remark that its expressions imply a treatment which I am incapable of inflicting, and you of imputing to me, if aware of their latitude, and the extent of the inference to be drawn from them. This is not just, but I have no reproaches nor the wish to find cause for them. Will you see me?—when and where you please—in whose presence you please. The interview shall pledge you to nothing, and I will say and do nothing to agitate either. It is torture to correspond thus, and there are things to be settled and said which cannot be written.

You say it is my disposition to deem what I have worthless. Did I deem *you* so? Did I ever so express myself to you, or of you to others? You are much changed within these twenty days or you would never have thus poisoned your own better feelings and trampled on mine.

Ever your most truly and affectly.

TO LADY BYRON   *February 15, 1816*

I know not what to say, every step taken appears to bear
you farther from me, and to widen " the great gulf between
thee and me ". If it cannot be crossed I will perish in its
depth.

Two letters have been written by me to you, but I have
not sent them, and I know not well why I write this, or whether
I shall send it or no.   How far your conduct is reconcilable
to your duties and affections as a wife and a mother, must be a
question for your own reflection.   The trial has not been very
long—a year, I grant you—of distress, distemper, and misfortune ; but these fell chiefly on me, and bitter as the recollection is to me of what I have felt, it is much more so to have
made you a partner of my desolation.   On the charges to be
preferred against me I have *twice* been refused any information
by your father and his advisers.   It is now a fortnight, which
has been passed in suspense, in humiliation, in obloquy, exposed
to the most black and blighting calumnies of every kind, without even the power of contradicting conjecture and vulgar
assertion as to the accusations, because I am denied the knowledge of all, or any, particulars from the only quarter than can
afford them.   In the meantime I hope your ears are gratified
by the general rumours.

I have invited your return ; it has been refused.   I have
requested to know with what I am charged ; it is refused.   Is
this mercy or justice ?   We shall see.   And now, Bell, dearest
Bell, whatever may be the event of this calamitous difference,
whether you are returned to or torn from me, I can only say
in the truth of affliction, and without hope, motive, or end in
again saying what I have lately but vainly repeated, that I
love you, bad or good, mad or rational, miserable or content,
I love you, and shall do, to the dregs of my memory and existence.   If I can feel thus for you now under every possible
aggravation and exasperating circumstance that can corrode
the heart and inflame the brain, perhaps you may one day
know, or think at least, that I was not all you have persuaded
yourself to believe me ; but that nothing, nothing can touch
me farther.

I have hitherto avoided naming my child, but this was a

feeling you never doubted in me. I must ask of its welfare. I have heard of its beauty and playfulness, and I request, not from you, but through any other channel—Augusta, if you please— some occasional news of its wellbeing.

I am, yours, etc., B.

TO THOMAS MOORE   *February 29, 1816*

I have not answered your letter for a time; and, at present, the reply to part of it might extend to such a length, that I shall delay it till it can be made in person, and then I will shorten it as much as I can.

In the mean time, I am at war " with all the world and his wife "; or rather, " all the world and *my* wife " are at war with me, and have not yet crushed me,—whatever they *may* do. I don't know that in the course of a hair-breadth existence I was ever, at home or abroad, in a situation so completely up-rooting of present pleasure, or rational hope for the future, as this same. I say this, because I think so, and feel it. But I shall not sink under it the more for that mode of considering the question—I have made up my mind.

By the way, however, you must not believe all you hear on the subject; and don't attempt to defend me. If you succeeded in that, it would be a mortal, or an immortal, offence—who can bear refutation? I have but a very short answer for those whom it concerns; and all the activity of myself and some vigorous friends have not yet fixed on any tangible ground or personage, on which or with whom I can discuss matters, in a summary way, with a fair pretext;—though I nearly had *nailed one* yesterday, but he evaded by—what was judged by others—a satisfactory explanation. I speak of *circulators*— against whom I have no enmity, though I must act according to the common code of usage, when I hit upon those of the serious order.

Now for other matters—poesy, for instance. Leigh Hunt's poem is a devilish good one—quaint, here and there, but with the substratum of originality, and with poetry about it, that will stand the test. I do not say this because he has inscribed it to me, which I am sorry for, as I should otherwise have begged you to review it in the *Edinburgh*. It is really deserving of much praise, and a favourable critique in the *E. R.* would but do it justice, and set it up before the public eye, where it ought to be.

How are you? and where? I have not the most distant idea what I am going to do myself—or with myself—or where—or what. I had a few weeks ago, some things to say that would have made you laugh; but they tell me now that I must not laugh, and so I have been very serious—and am.

I have not been very well—with a *liver* complaint—but am much better within the last fortnight, though still under Iatrical advice. I have latterly seen a little of * *. * * I must go and dress to dine. My little girl is in the country, and, they tell me, is a very fine child, and now nearly three months old. Lady Noel (my mother-in-law, or, rather, *at* law) is at present overlooking it. Her daughter (Miss Milbanke that was) is, I believe, in London with her father. A Mrs. C.[1] (now a kind of housekeeper and spy of Lady N.'s), who, in her better days, was a washerwoman, is supposed to be—by the learned—very much the occult cause of our late domestic discrepancies.

In all this business, I am the sorriest for Sir Ralph. He and I are equally punished, though *magis pares quam similes* in our affliction. Yet it is hard for both to suffer for the fault of one, and so it is—I shall be separated from my wife; he will retain his.

Ever, etc.

TO LADY BYRON   *March 4, 1816*

I know of no offence, not merely from man to wife, nor of one human being to another, but of any being almost to God Himself, which we are not taught to believe would be expiated by the repeated atonement which I have offered even for the *unknown* faults (for to me, till stated, they are unknown to any extent which can justify such persevering rejections) I may

---

[1] " The respectable Mrs. Clermont ", Annabella Byron's former governess, her mother's companion, whom Byron suspected of having played a sinister part in his differences with his wife.

have been supposed to commit, or can have committed, against you. But since all hope is over, and instead of the duties of a wife and the mother of my child, I am to encounter accusation and implacability, I have nothing more to say, but shall act according to circumstances, though not even injury can alter the love with which (though I shall do my best to repel attack) I must ever be yours,

B.

I am told that you say *you* drew up the proposal of separation ; if so, I regret I hear it ; it appeared to me to be a kind of appeal to the supposed mercenary feelings of the person to whom it was made—" if you part with, etc., you will gain *so much now*, and so much at the death of ", etc., a matter of pounds, shillings, and pence ! No allusion to my child ; a hard, dry, attorneys' paper. Oh, Bell ! to see you thus stifling and destroying all feeling, all affections, all duties (for they are your first duties, those of a wife and a mother), is far more bitter than any possible consequences to me.

TO THOMAS MOORE   *March 8, 1816*

I rejoice in your promotion as Chairman and Charitable Steward, etc., etc. These be dignities which await only the virtuous. But then, recollect you are *six* and *thirty*, (I speak this enviously—not of your age, but the " honour—love—obedience—troops of friends ", which accompany it,) and I have eight years good to run before I arrive at such hoary perfection ; by which time,—if I *am* at all,—it will probably be in a state of grace or progressing merits.

I must set you right in one point, however. The fault was *not*—no, nor even the misfortune—in my " choice " (unless in *choosing at all*)—for I do not believe—and I must say it, in the very dregs of all this bitter business—that there ever was a better, or even a brighter, a kinder, or a more amiable and agreeable being than Lady B. I never had, nor can have, any reproach to make her, while with me. Where there is blame, it belongs to myself, and, if I cannot redeem, I must bear it.

Her nearest relatives are a * * * *—my circumstances have been and are in a state of great confusion—my health has been a good deal disordered, and my mind ill at ease for a considerable period. Such are the causes (I do not name them as excuses) which have frequently driven me into excess, and disqualified my temper for comfort. Something also may be attributed to the strange and desultory habits which, becoming my own master at an early age, and scrambling about, over and through the world, may have induced. I still, however, think that, if I had a fair chance, by being placed in even a tolerable situation, I might have gone on fairly. But that seems hopeless,—and there is nothing more to be said. At present—except my health, which is better (it is odd, but agitation or contest of any kind gives a rebound to my spirits and sets me up for the time)—I have to battle with all kinds of unpleasantnesses, including private and pecuniary difficulties, etc., etc.

I believe I may have said this before to you, but I risk repeating it. It is nothing to bear the *privations* of adversity, or, more properly, ill fortune ; but my pride recoils from its *indignities*. However, I have no quarrel with that same pride, which will, I think, buckler me through every thing. If my heart could have been broken, it would have been so years ago, and by events more afflicting than these.

I agree with you (to turn from this topic to our shop), that I have written too much. The last things were, however, published very reluctantly by me, and for reasons I will explain when we meet. I know not why I have dwelt so much on the same scenes, except that I find them fading, or *confusing* (if such a word may be) in my memory, in the midst of present turbulence and pressure, and I felt anxious to stamp before the die was worn out. I now break it. With those countries, and events connected with them, all my really poetical feelings begin and end. Were I to try, I could make nothing of any other subject, and that I have apparently exhausted. " Wo to him ", says Voltaire, " who says all he could say on any subject." There are some on which, perhaps, I could have said still more : but I leave them all, and too soon.

Do you remember the lines I sent you early last year, which you still have? I don't wish (like Mr. Fitzgerald, in the *Morning*

Post) to claim the character of " Vates " in all its translations, but were they not a little prophetic? I mean those beginning, " There's not a joy the world can ", etc., etc., on which I rather pique myself as being the truest, though the most melancholy, I ever wrote.

What a scrawl have I sent you! You say nothing of yourself, except that you are a Lancasterian churchwarden, and an encourager of mendicants. When are you out? and how is your family? My child is very well and flourishing, I hear; but I must see also. I feel no disposition to resign it to the contagion of its grandmother's society, though I am unwilling to take it from the mother. It is weaned, however, and something about it must be decided.

Ever, etc.

TO MISS MERCER ELPHINSTONE *   *April 11, 1816*

DEAR MISS MERCER,[1]—I thank you truly for yr kind acceptance of my memorial—more particularly as I felt a little apprehension that I was taking a liberty of which you might disapprove. A more useless friend you could not have, but still a very sincere and by no means a new one—altho' from circumstances you never knew (nor would it have pleased you to know) how much. These having long ceased to exist, I breathe more freely on this point, because *now* no motive can be attributed to me with regard to you of a selfish nature—at least I hope not.

I know not why I venture to talk thus, unless it be that the time is come when, whatever I may say, cannot be of importance enough to give offence; and that neither my vanity *nor my wishes* ever induced me at any time to suppose that I could by any chance have become more to you than I now am.

This may account to you for that which—however little worth accounting for—must otherwise appear inexplicable in our former acquaintance. I mean those " intermittents " at which you used to laugh, as I did too, although they caused me a serious reflection.

---

[1] At the disastrous party given by Lady Jersey after the separation, Miss Mercer Elphinstone was one of the few women who had consented to speak to Byron and his sister. Byron had expressed his gratitude by giving her a book.

But this is foolish, perhaps improper, yet it is (or rather was) the truth, and has been a silent one while it could have been supposed to proceed from hope or presumption. I am now as far removed from both by irrevocable circumstances as I always was by my own opinion and by yours, and soon shall be still further, if further be possible, by distance.

I cannot conclude without wishing you a much happier destiny not than *mine is*, for that is nothing, but than mine ever could have been, with a little common sense and prudence on my own part—no one else has been to blame. It may seem superfluous to wish *you* all this, and it would be so if our happiness always depended on ourselves; but it does not—a truth which I fear I have taught rather than learned, however unintentionally.

Ever most truly yrs, BYRON.

P.S.—This letter was intended as an answer to your note, which however required none. Will you excuse it for the sake of the paper on which it is written? It is part of the spoils of Malmaison and the Imperial bureau (as it was told me) and for this reason, you will perhaps have the kindness to accept the few sheets of it which accompany this. Their stamp is the Eagle. Adieu.

TO LADY BYRON[1]   *[April, 1816]*

More last words—not many—and such as you will attend to; answer I do not expect, nor does it import; but you will at least hear me.—I have just parted from Augusta, almost the last being whom you have left me to part with.

Wherever I may go,—and I am going far,—you and I can never meet in this world, nor in the next. Let this content or atone.—— If any accident occurs to me, be kind to Augusta; if she is then also nothing—to her children. You know that some time ago I made my will in her favour and her children, because any child of ours was provided for by other and better means. This could not be prejudice to you, for we had not

---

[1] From a copy made by Hobhouse, and endorsed by him, " Lord Byron's last letter to Lady B. on leaving England, 1816, given to Mrs. Leigh by Mr. Hobhouse ".

then differed, and even now is useless during your life by the terms of our settlements. Therefore,—be kind to her, for never has she acted or spoken towards you but as your friend. And recollect, that, though it may be an advantage to you to have lost a husband, it is sorrow to her to have the waters now, or the earth hereafter, between her and her brother. It may occur to your memory that you formerly promised me this much. I repeat it—for deep resentments have but *half* recollections. Do not deem this promise cancell'd, for it was not a vow.

I have received from Mr. Wharton a letter containing one question and two pieces of intelligence. The carriage is yours, and, as it only carried us to Halnaby, and London, and you to Kirkby, it will yet convey you many a more propitious journey.

The receipts can remain, unless you find them troublesome ; if so, let them be sent to Augusta, through whom I would also receive occasional accounts of my child. My address will be left with Mrs. Leigh ; the ring is of no lapidary value, but it contains the hair of a King and of an ancestor, and I wish it to be preserved to Miss Byron.

With regard to a subsequent letter from Mr. Wharton I have to observe that it is the " law's delay " not mine, and that, when the tenor of the bond is settled between him and Mr. H., I am ready to sign.

Yours truly, BYRON

TO THE HON. AUGUSTA LEIGH *Bruxelles,*
[Wednesday,] May 1st, 1816

MY HEART,—We are detained here for some petty carriage repairs, having come out of our way to the Rhine on purpose, after passing through Ghent, Antwerp, and Mechlin. I have written to you twice,—once from Ostend, and again from Ghent. I hope most truly that you will receive my letters, not as important in themselves, but because you wish it, and so do I. It would be difficult for me to write anything amusing ; this country has been so frequently described, and has so little for description, though a good deal for observation, that I know not what to say of it, and one don't like talking only of oneself. We saw at Antwerp the famous basons of Bonaparte for his navy, which are very superb—as all his undertakings were, and as for churches, and pictures, I have stared at them till my brains are like a guide-book :—the last (though it is heresy to say so) don't please me at all. I think Rubens a very great dauber, and prefer Vandyke a hundred times over (but then I know nothing about the matter). Rubens' women have all red gums and red shoulders—to say nothing of necks, of which they are more liberal than charming ; it may all be very fine, and I suppose it may be Art, for 'tis not Nature.

As the low Countries did not make part of my plan (except as a route), I feel a little anxious to get out of them. Level roads don't suit me, as thou knowest ; it must be up hill or down, and then I am more *au fait*. Imagine to yourself a succession of avenues with a Dutch Spire at the end of each, and you see the road ;—an accompaniment of highly cultivated farms on each side, intersected with small canals or ditches, and sprinkled with very neat and clean cottages, a village every two miles,—and you see the country ; not a rise from Ostend to Antwerp—a molehill would make the inhabitants think that the Alps had come here on a visit ; it is a perpetuity of plain and an eternity of *pavement* (on the *road*), but it is a country of great apparent comfort, and of singular though *tame* beauty, and, were it not out of my way, I should like to survey it less cursorily. The towns are wonderfully fine. The approach to Brussels is beautiful, and there is a fine palace to the right in coming.

TO JOHN CAM HOBHOUSE†   *Bruxelles, May 1st, 1816*

My dear H^E,—You will be surprised that we are not more " en avant ", and so am I, but Mr. Baxter's wheel and springs have not done their duty, for which I beg that you will abuse him like a pick-pocket (that is—*He*—the said Baxter being the *pick-pocket*) and say that I expect a deduction, having been obliged to come out of the way to this place, which was not in my route, for repairs, which however I hope to have accomplished, so as to put us in motion in a day or two.

We passed through Ghent, Antwerp, and Mechlin, and thence diverged here, having seen all the sights, pictures, docks, basins, and having climbed up steeples, etc., etc., and so forth. The first thing, after the flatness and fertility of the country, which struck me, was the beauty of the towns, Bruges first, where, you may tell Douglas Kinnaird, on entering at sunset, I overtook a crew of beggarly looking gentlemen, not unlike Oxberry, headed by a monarch with a staff, the very fac-simile, of King Clause in the said D. K.'s revived drama.

We lost our way in the dark, or rather twilight, not far from Ghent, by the stupidity of the postilion (*one* only, by the way, to four horses), which produced an alarm of intended robbery amongst the uninitiated, whom I could not convince that four or five well-armed people were not immediately to be plundered and anatomized by a single person, fortified with a horsewhip to be sure, but, nevertheless, a little encumbered with large jack boots, and a tight jacket that did not fit him. The way was found again without loss of life or limb. I thought the learned Fletcher at least would have known better after our Turkish expeditions, and defiles and banditti, and guards, etc., etc., than to have been so valorously alert, without at least a better pretext for his superfluous courage. I don't mean to say that they were frightened, but were vastly suspicious, without any cause.

At Ghent we stared at pictures; and climbed up a steeple, 450 steps in altitude, from which I had a good view and notion of these " paese bassi ".

Next day we broke down, by a damned wheel (on which Baxter should be broken) pertinaciously refusing its stipulated rotation. This becalmed us at Lo-Kristy (2 leagues from Ghent) and obliged us to return for repairs; at Lo-Kristy I came to anchor in the house of a Flemish blacksmith (who was ill of a fever for which Dr. Dori [1] physicked him—I daresay he is dead by now), and saw somewhat of Lo-Kristy; Low-country low-life, which regaled me much; besides, it being a Sunday, all the world were on their way to mass, and I had the

---

[1] Dr. John William Polidori, whom Byron took abroad with him as his personal physician.

pleasure of seeing a number of very ordinary women in extra-ordinary garments:—we found the " Contadini ", however, very good-natured and obliging, though not at all useful.

At Antwerp we pictured—churched—and steepled again, but the principal street and *bason* pleased me most—poor dear Buonaparte ! ! ! and the foundries, etc., etc. As for Rubens, I was glad to see his tomb on account of that ridiculous description (in Smollett's P. Pickle) of Pallet's absurdity at his monument—but as for his works, and his superb " tableaux ", he seems to me (who by the way know nothing of the matter) the most glaring—flaring—staring—harlotry impostor that ever passed a trick upon the senses of mankind,—it is not nature —it is not art—with the exception of some linen (which hangs over the cross in one of his pictures) which, to do it justice, looked like a very handsome table-cloth—I never saw such an assemblage of florid nightmares as his canvas contains; his portraits seem clothed in pulpit cushions.

On the way to Mechlin, a wheel, and a *spring* too gave way ; that is, the one went, and the other would not go ; so we came off here to get into dock. I hope we shall sail shortly. On to Geneva.

Will you have the goodness to get at my account with Hoares (my bankers)? I believe there must be a balance in my favour, as I did not draw a great deal previously to going : —whatever there may be, over the two thousand five hundred, they can send by you, to me in a further credit, when you come out. I wish you to enquire (for fear any tricks might be played with my drafts)—*my* banker's books, left with you, will shew you exactly what I have drawn ; and you can let them have the book, to make out the remainder of the account. All I have to urge to Hanson, or to our friend Douglas K., is to *sell* if possible.

All kind things to Scrope and the rest.

Ever yrs. most truly and obligedly, B.

P.S.—If you hear of my child let me know any good of her health and well-doing. Will you bring out a παυςανιας (Taylor's ditto) when you come. I shall bring to for you at Geneva [*sic*]. Don't forget to urge Scrope into our crew. We will buy females and found a colony—provided Scrope does

not find those ossified barriers to " the forefended place "
which cost him such a siege at Brighthelmstone.

Write at your leisure, or " ipse veni ".

TO JOHN CAM HOBHOUSE   *Evian, June 23rd, 1816*

MY DEAR H^E,—Despite of this date, address as usual to the
Genevese Poste, which awaits your answers as I await your
arrival, with that of Scrope, whose pocket appears (by your
late letter of revolutions at the Union) to have become as
" light " as his " wines ", though I suppose, on the whole, he
is still worth at least £50,000 : being what is called here a
" millionaire "—that is in francs, and such Lilliputian coinage.

I have taken a very pretty little villa in a vineyard, with the
Alps behind, and Mount Jura and the lake before—it is called
Diodati, from the name of the proprietor, who is a descendant
of the critical and illustrissimi Diodati's, and has an agreeable
house, which he lets at a reasonable rate per season or annum,
as suits the lessee. When you come out don't go to an inn, not
even to Secheron ; but come on to headquarters, where I have
rooms ready for you and Scrope, and all " appliances and
means to boot ". Bring with you also for me—some bottles of
Calcined Magnesia, a new *Sword-cane*, procured by Jackson—he
alone knows the sort (my last tumbled into this lake)—some
of Waite's *red* tooth-powder and tooth-brushes—a Taylor's
Pawrsanias—and I forget the other things.

Tell Murray I have a 3rd Canto of Childe Harold finished,
it is the longest of the three, being one hundred and eleven
stanzas. I shall send it by the first plausible conveyance.
At the present writing I am on my way on a water-tour round
the Lake Leman, and am thus far proceeded in a pretty open
boat which I bought and navigate—it is an English one, and
was brought lately from Bordeaux. I am on shore for the
night, and have just had a row with the Syndic of this town,
who wanted my passports, which I left at Diodati, not thinking
they could be wanted, except in grande route—but it seems
this is Savoy, and the dominion of his Cagliari Majesty whom
we saw at his own Opera in his own city, in 1809 ; however,
by dint of references to Geneva, and other corroborations—

together with being in a very ill-humour—truth has prevailed, wonderful to relate, and they actually take one's word for a fact, although it is credible and indubitable.

To-morrow we go to Meillerei, and Clarens, and Vevey, with Rousseau in hand, to see his scenery, according to his delineation in his Héloïse, now before me; the views have hitherto been very fine, but, I should conceive, less so than those of the remainder of the lake.

All your letters (that is *two*) have arrived—thanks, and greetings :—What—and who—and the devil is " Glenarvon "? I know nothing—nor ever heard of such a person ; and what do you mean by a brother in India ? You have none in India ; it is Scrope who has a brother in India—my remembrances to Kinnaird—and Mrs. Kinnaird—to all and everybody, and Hunt in particular, and Scrope, and Mr. Murray, and believe me

Yours ever most truly, B.

P.S.—I left the Doctor at Diodati ; he sprained his ancle.

P.S.—Will you also particularly remember to bring me a largish bottle of the strongest *Pot Ash* as before—*Mr. Le Shan* will furnish it—that child and childish Dr. Pollydolly contrived to find it broken, or to break it at Carlsruhe—so that I am in a fuss—the Genevese make it badly—it effervesces in the sulphuric acid, and it ought not—bring me some of a more quiescent character.

TO JOHN MURRAY   *Ouchy, near Lausanne, June 27, 1816*

DEAR SIR,—I am thus far (kept by stress of weather) on my way back to Diodati (near Geneva) from a voyage in my boat round the Lake ; and I enclose you a sprig of *Gibbon's Acacia* and some rose-leaves from his garden, which, with part of his house, I have just seen. You will find honorable mention, in his *Life*, made of this " Acacia ", when he walked out on the night of concluding his history. The garden and *summer-house*, where he composed, are neglected, and the last utterly decayed ; but they still show it as his " Cabinet ", and seem perfectly aware of his memory.

My route through Flanders, and by the Rhine, to Switzerland, was all I expected, and more.

I have traversed all Rousseau's ground, with the *Héloise* before me; and am struck, to a degree, with the force and accuracy of his descriptions and the beauty of their reality. Meillerie, Clarens, and Vevay, and the Château de Chillon, are places of which I shall say little, because all I could say must fall short of the impressions they stamp.

Three days ago, we were most nearly wrecked in a Squall off Meillerie, and driven to shore. I ran no risk, being so near the rocks, and a good swimmer; but our party were wet, and incommoded a good deal, the wind was strong enough to blow down some trees, as we found at landing, however, all is righted and right, and we are thus far on return.

Dr. Polidori is not here, but at Diodati, left behind in hospital with a sprained ancle, acquired in tumbling from a wall—he can't jump.

I shall be glad to hear you are well, and have received for me certain helms and swords, sent from Waterloo, which I rode over with pain and pleasure.

I have finished a third canto of *Childe Harold* (consisting of one hundred and seventeen stanzas), longer than either of the two former, and in some parts, it may be, better; but of course on that *I* cannot determine. I shall send it by the first safe-looking opportunity.

Ever very truly yours, B.

TO THE HON. DOUGLAS KINNAIRD *   *Diodati nr. Geneva,*
July 20th 1816

DEAR KINNAIRD,—I send you, not what you want, but all I can give,[1] and such as it is I give it with good will. It may be too long and if so, whatever may be cut in speaking, at least let it be published *entire*, as it is written so as not very well to endure curtailment without the sense of suffering also. Let Miss *Somerville*, (and none else) deliver it, if she has *energy*, that's the woman I want, I mean for spouting. I protest against

[1] *Monody on the Death of Sheridan*, delivered at Drury Lane Theatre.

Mrs. Davison, I protest against the *temple* or anything but an *Urn* on the scene, and above all I protest against the " Comic Muse in Mourning." If she is *Comic*, she should not be in *Mourning*, if she is in *mourning*, she ought not to be in Mourning, but should she be *comic* and in *mourning* too, the verses and Sheridan's memory (for *that* occasion at least) will go to the devil together. No, I say, an *Urn* (not a tea urn) and Miss Somerville with a little teaching. As to " Energy " I have spiced it with Cayenne all through, except a small infusion of the pathetic at starting.

I send the lines (118 in number) in a separate sheet by this post, and will send a duplicate in a day or two, for fear of you not receiving this copy in time.

Tragedy—I have none, an act, a first act of one, I had nearly finished some time before my departure from England, when events occurred which furnished me with so many real passions for time to come, that I had no attention for fictitious ones. The scenes I had scrawled are thrown with other papers and sketches into one of my trunks now in England, but into which I know not—nor care not—except that I should have been glad to have done anything you wished in my power; but I have no power nor will to recommence, and, surely, *Maturin* is your man, not I. Of what has passed in England I know but little, and have no desire to know more, except that you and my other friends are well.

I have written a third Canto of Childe Harold (of 118 Stanzas) and a (not long) poem on the Castle of Chillon, both of which I mean to send to England soon for publication, during which I could wish to ask you to *correct* the *proofs* and arrange with Murray for me. I merely wait a good opportunity to convey these to your care and if you can afford leisure and patience, perhaps G. Lamb, or some other good-natured fellow would halve it with you, though I have hardly the conscience to ask either them or you.

I have now answered you and arrived at my sheet's end— with my best remembrances to Mrs. K—— (whose silk kerchief is as precious as Othello's) believe me ever yours,

B.

TO JOHN MURRAY   *Diodati, near Geneva, July 22ᵈ, 1816*

DEAR SIR,—I wrote to you a few weeks ago, and Dr. P[olidori] received your letter; but the packet has not made its appearance, nor the epistle, of which you gave notice therein. I enclose you an advertisement, which was copied by Dr. P[olidori], and which appears to be about the most impudent imposition that ever issued from Grub Street. I need hardly say that I know nothing of all this trash, nor whence it may spring,—" Odes to St. Helena ",—" Farewells to England ", etc., etc.; and if it can be disavowed, or is worth disavowing, you have full authority to do so. I never wrote, nor conceived, a line on any thing of the kind, any more than of two other things with which I was saddled—something about " Gaul ", and another about " Mrs. La Valette "; and as to the " Lily of *France* ", I should as soon think of celebrating a turnip. On the " Morning of my Daughter's Birth ", I had other things to think of than verses; and should never have dreamed of such an invention, till Mr. Johnston and his pamphlet's advertisement broke in upon me with a new light on the Crafts and subtilties of the Demon of printing,—or rather publishing.

I did hope that some succeeding lie would have superseded the thousand and one which were accumulated during last winter. I can forgive whatever may be said *of* or against me,—but not what they make me say or sing for myself. It is enough to answer for what I have written; but it were too much for Job himself to bear what one has not. I suspect that when the Arab Patriarch wished that his " Enemy had written a book ", he did not anticipate his own name on the title-page. I feel quite as much bored with this foolery as it deserves, and more than I should be, if I had not a headache.

Of *Glenarvon*,¹ Madame de Stael told me (ten days ago, at Copet) marvellous and grievous things; but I have seen nothing of it but the Motto, which promises amiably " for us and for our tragedy ". If such be the posy, what should the ring be? " a name to all succeeding ", etc. The generous moment selected for the publication is probably its kindest accompaniment, and—truth to say—the time was well chosen.

¹ Lady Caroline Lamb's novel, which contained a romantic travesty of Byron and caricatures of Lady Holland and other Friends.

I have not even a guess at the contents, except from the very vague accounts I have heard, and I know but one thing which a woman can say to the purpose on such occasions, and that she might as well for her own sake keep to herself, which by the way they very rarely can—the old reproach against their admirers of " *Kiss* and *tell* ", bad as it is, is surely somewhat less than—and publish.

I ought to be ashamed of the Egotism of this letter. It is not my fault altogether, and I shall be but too happy to drop the subject when others will allow me. I am in tolerable plight, and in my last letter told you what I had done in the way of all rhyme. I trust that you prosper, and that your authors are in good condition. I should suppose your Stud has received some increase, by what I hear. *Bertram* must be a good horse; does he run next meeting? and does the *Quarterly* cover still at so much the mare and the groom? I hope you will beat the Row.

Yours always, very truly, B.

TO THE HON. AUGUSTA LEIGH   *Diodati, Geneva,*
                                             Septr 8th, 1816

My dearest Augusta,—By two opportunities of private conveyance, I have sent answers to your letter, delivered by Mr. H. S—— is on his return to England and may possibly arrive before this. He is charged with a few packets of seals, necklaces, balls etc. and I know not what, formed of Chrystals, Agates and other stones—*all of* and *from Mont Blanc*, bought and brought by me on and from the Spot, expressly for you to divide among yourself and the children—including also your niece Ada, for whom I selected a ball (of Granite—a *soft* substance by the way—but the only one there) wherewithal to roll and play, when she is old enough, and mischievous enough, and moreover a Chrystal necklace, and anything else you may like to add for her—the Love! The rest are for you, and the Nursery—but particularly Georgiana, who has sent me a very nice letter. I hope Scrope will carry them all safely, as he promised. There are seals and all kinds of fooleries. Pray like them, for they come from a very curious place (nothing like it hardly in all I ever saw)—to say nothing of the giver.

And so—Lady B. has been " kind to you ", you tell me— " very kind "—Umph—it is as well she should be kind to some of us—and I am glad she has the heart and the discernment to be still *your* friend—you was ever so to her. I heard the other day that she was very unwell. I was shocked enough, and sorry enough, God knows—but never mind. H. tells me, however, that she is *not* ill, that she *had* been indisposed, but is better and well to do. This is a relief. As for me, I am in good health and fair, though unequal, spirits. But, for all that, she—or rather the separation—has broken my heart : I feel as if an Elephant had trodden on it. I am convinced I shall never get over it, but I try. I had enough before I ever knew her, and more than enough. But time and agitation had done something for me. But this last wreck has affected me very differently. If it were *acutely*, it would not signify. But it is not that,—I breathe lead.

While the storm lasted and you were all piping and com- forting me with condemnation in Piccadilly, it was bad enough, and violent enough. But it's worse now; I have neither strength nor spirits, nor inclination to carry me through any- thing which will clear my brain or lighten my heart. I mean to cross the Alps at the end of this month, and go—God knows where—by Dalmatia, up to the Arnauts again, if nothing better can be done. I have still a world before me—this—or the next.

H. has told me all the strange stories in circulation of me and mine—*Not* true. I have been in some danger on the lake (near Meillerie), but nothing to speak of; and, as to all these "mistresses", Lord help me—I have had but one.[1] Now don't scold ; but what could I do?—a foolish girl, in spite of all I could say or do, would come after me, or rather went before— for I found her here—and I have had all the plague possible to persuade her to go back again ; but at last she went. Now, dearest, I do most truly tell thee, that I could not help this, that I did all I could to prevent it, and have at last put an end to it. I was not in love, nor have any love left for any ; but I could not exactly play the Stoic with a woman, who had scrambled eight hundred miles to unphilosophize me.

[1] Claire Clairmont, who had previously made his acquaintance in London.

Besides, I had been regaled of late with so many "two courses and a *desert*" (Alas!) of aversion, that I was fain to take a little love (if pressed particularly) by way of novelty. And now you know all that I know of that matter, and it's over. Pray write. I have heard nothing since your last, at least a month or five weeks ago. I go out very little, except into the *air*, and on journeys, and on the water, and to Copet, where Me de Staël has been particularly kind and friendly towards me, and (I hear) fought battles without number in my very indifferent cause. It has (they say) made quite as much noise on this as the other side of *La Manche*. Heaven knows why—but I seem destined to set people by the ears.

Don't hate me, but believe me, ever yours most affectionately,

BYRON

TO THE HON. AUGUSTA LEIGH   *Ouchy, Sep^t 17, 1816*

MY DEAREST AUGUSTA,—I am thus far on my way to the Bernese Alps and the Grindenwald, and the *Yung frau* (that is the "Wild woman" being interpreted—as it is so perverse a mountain that no other sex would suit it), which journey may occupy me about eight days or so, and then it is my intention to return to Geneva, preparatory to passing the Simplon——

Continue you to direct as usual to Geneva. I have lately written to you several letters (3 or 4 by post and two by hand) and I have received all yours very safely. I rejoice to have heard that you are well. You have been in London too lately, and H. tells me that at your levée he generally found Ld F. Bentinck—pray why is that fool so often a visitor? is he in love with you? I have recently broken through my resolution of not speaking to you of Lady B— but do not on that account name her to me. It is a relief—a partial relief to me to talk of her sometimes to you—but it would be none to hear of her. *Of* her you are to judge for yourself, but do not altogether forget that she has destroyed your brother. Whatever my faults might or may have been—*She*—was not the person marked out by providence to be their avenger. One day or another her

conduct will recoil on her own head ; *not* through *me*, for my
feelings towards her are not those of Vengeance, but—mark—
if she does not end miserably *tot ou tard*. She may think—talk
—or act as she will, and by any process of cold reasoning and
a jargon of " duty and acting for the best " etc., etc., impose
upon her own feelings and those of others for a time—but woe
unto her—the wretchedness she has brought upon the man to
whom she has been everything evil [^except in one respect (effaced)^] will flow
back into its fountain. I may thank the strength of my constitution that has enabled me to bear all this, but those who bear
the longest and the most do not suffer the least. I do not think
a human being could endure more mental torture than that
woman has directly and indirectly inflicted upon me—within
the present year.

She has (for a time at least) separated me from my child—
and from you—but I turn from the subject for the present.

To-morrow I repass Clarens and Vevey ; if in the new and
more extended tour I am making, anything that I think may
please you occurs, I will detail it.

Scrope has by this time arrived with my little presents for
you and yours and Ada. I still hope to be able to see you next
Spring, perhaps you and one or two of the children could be
spared some time next year for a little tour *here* or in France
with me of a month or two. I think I could make it pleasing
to you, and it should be no expense to L. or to yourself. Pray
think of this hint. You have no idea how very beautiful great
part of this country is—and *women* and *children* traverse it with
ease and expedition. I would return from any distance at any
time to see you, and come to England for you ; and when
you consider the chances against our—but I won't relapse into
the dismals and anticipate long absences——

The great obstacle would be that you are so admirably
yoked—and necessary as a housekeeper—and a letter writer—
and a place-hunter to that very helpless gentleman your
Cousin, that I suppose the usual self-love of an elderly person
would interfere between you and any scheme of recreation or
relaxation, for however short a period.

What a fool was I to marry—and *you* not very wise—my
dear—we might have lived so single and so happy—as old
maids and bachelors ; I shall never find any one like you—

nor you (vain as it may seem) like me. We are just formed to pass our lives together, and therefore—we—at least—I—am by a crowd of circumstances removed from the only being who could ever have loved me, or whom I can unmixedly feel attached to.

Had you been a Nun—and I a Monk—that we might have talked through a grate instead of across the sea—no matter— my voice and my heart are

ever thine—B.

A JOURNAL

Clarens, Septr 18th 1816

Yesterday September 17th 1816—I set out (with H[obhouse]) on an excursion of some days to the Mountains. I shall keep a short journal of each day's progress for my Sister Augusta.

Septr 17th

Rose at five ; left Diodati about seven, in one of the country carriages (a Charaban), our servants on horseback : weather very fine ; the Lake calm and clear ; Mont Blanc and the Aiguille of Argentières both very distinct ; the borders of the Lake beautiful. Reached Lausanne before Sunset ; stopped and slept at Ouchy.

H. went to dine with a Mr. Okeden. I remained at our Caravansera (though invited to the house of H.'s friend—too lazy or tired, or something else, to go), and wrote a letter to Augusta. Went to bed at nine—sheets damp : swore and stripped them off and flung them—Heaven knows where : wrapt myself up in the blankets, and slept like a child of a month's existence till 5 o'Clock of

Septr 18th

Called by Berger (my Courier who acts as Valet for a day or two, the learned Fletcher being left in charge of Chattels at Diodati) : got up. H. walked on before. A mile from Lausanne the road overflowed by the lake ; got on horseback and rode till within a mile of Vevay. The Colt young, but went very well : overtook H., and resumed the carriage, which is an open one. Stopped at Vevay two hours (the *second* time

I had visited it); walked to the church; view from the Churchyard superb; within it General Ludlow's (the Regicide's) monument—black marble—long inscription—Latin, but simple, particularly the latter part, in which his wife (Margaret de Thomas) records her long, her tried, and unshaken affection; he was an Exile *two and thirty years*—one of King's (Charles's) Judges—a fine fellow. I remember reading his memoirs in January 1815 (at Halnaby)—the first part of them very amusing, the latter less so: I little thought, at the time of their perusal by me, of seeing his tomb. Near him Broughton (who read King Charles's sentence to Charles Stuart) is buried, with a queer and rather canting, but still a Republican, epitaph. Ludlow's house shown; it retains still his inscription—*Omne Solum forti patria*. Walked down to the Lake side; servants, Carriage, saddle horses—all set off and left us *plantés là*, by some mistake; and we walked on after them towards Clarens: H. ran on before, and overtook them at last. Arrived the second time (1ˢᵗ time was by water) at Clarens, beautiful Clarens! Went to Chillon through Scenery worthy of I know not whom; went over the Castle of Chillon again. On our return met an English party in a carriage; a lady in it fast asleep!—fast asleep in the most anti-narcotic spot in the world—excellent! I remember, at Chamouni, in the very eyes of Mont Blanc, hearing another woman, English also, exclaim to her party " did you ever see any thing more *rural*? "—as if it was Highgate, or Hampstead, or Brompton, or Hayes,—" *Rural!* " quotha!—Rocks, pines, torrents, Glaciers, Clouds, and Summits of eternal snow far above them —and " *Rural!* " I did not know the thus exclaiming fair one, but she was a very good kind of a woman.

After a slight and short dinner, we visited the Chateau de Clarens; an English woman has rented it recently (it was not let when I saw it first): the roses are gone with their Summer; the family out, but the servants desired us to walk over the interior of the mansion. Saw on the table of the saloon Blair's sermons and somebody else's (I forget who's) sermons, and a set of noisy children. Saw all worth seeing, and then descended to the " Bosquet de Julie ", etc., etc.; our Guide full of *Rousseau*, whom he is eternally confounding with *St. Preux*, and mixing the man and the book. On the steps of a cottage in the village, I saw a young paysan*ne*, beautiful as Julie herself. Went again as far as Chillon to revisit the little torrent from the hill behind it. Sunset reflected in the lake. Have to get up at 5 tomorrow to cross the mountains on horseback—carriage to be sent round; lodged at my old Cottage—hospitable and comfortable; tired with a longish ride on the Colt, and the subsequent jolting of the Charaban, and my scramble in the hot sun. Shall go to bed, thinking of you, dearest Augusta.

Mem. The Corporal who showed the wonders of Chillon was as drunk as Blucher, and (to my mind) as great a man. He was *deaf* also, and thinking every one else so, roared out the legends of the Castle so fearfully that H. got out of humour. However, we saw all things from the Gallows to the Dungeons (the *Potence* and the *Cachots*), and returned to Clarens with more freedom than belonged to the 15th Century.

At Clarens—the only book (except the Bible), a translation of " *Cecilia* " (Miss Burney's *Cecilia*) ; and the owner of the Cottage had also called her dog (a fat Pug ten years old, and hideous as *Tip*) after Cecilia's (or rather Delville's) dog, Fidde.

Septr 19th

Rose at five: order the carriage round. Crossed the mountains to Montbovon on horseback, and on Mules, and, by dint of scrambling, on foot also ; the whole route beautiful as a Dream, and now to me almost as indistinct. I am so tired ; for though healthy, I have not the strength I possessed but a few years ago. At Mont Davant we breakfasted; afterwards, on a steep ascent dismounted, tumbled down, and cut a finger open; the baggage also got loose and fell down a ravine, till stopped by a large tree: swore; recovered baggage: horse tired and dropping; mounted Mule. At the approach of the summit of Dent Jamant dismounted again with H. and all the party. Arrived at a lake in the very nipple of the bosom of the Mountain; left our quadrupeds with a Shepherd, and ascended further; came to some snow in patches, upon which my forehead's perspiration fell like rain, making the same dints as in a sieve: the chill of the wind and the snow turned me giddy, but I scrambled on and upwards. *H.* went to the highest *pinnacle*; I did not, but paused within a few yards (at an opening of the Cliff). In coming down, the Guide tumbled

three times; I fell a laughing, and tumbled too—the descent
luckily soft, though steep and slippery: H. also fell, but
nobody hurt. The whole of the Mountain superb. A Shepherd
on a very steep and high cliff playing upon his *pipe*; very
different from *Arcadia*, (where I saw the pastors with a long
Musquet instead of a Crook, and pistols in their Girdles). Our
Swiss Shepherd's pipe was sweet, and his tune agreeable. Saw
a cow strayed; am told that they often break their necks on
and over the crags. Descended to Montbovon; pretty
scraggy village, with a wild river and a wooden bridge. H.
went to fish—caught one. Our carriage not come; our horses,
mules, etc., knocked up; ourselves fatigued; but so much the
better—I shall sleep.

The view from the highest points of to-day's journey
comprized on one side the greatest part of Lake Leman; on
the other, the valleys and mountains of the Canton of Fribourg,
and an immense plain, with the Lakes of Neuchâtel and Morat,
and all which the borders of these and of the Lake of Geneva
inherit: we had both sides of the Jura before us in one point
of view, with Alps in plenty. In passing a ravine, the Guide
recommended strenuously a quickening of pace, as the Stones
fall with great rapidity and occasional damage: the advice is
excellent, but, like most good advice, impracticable, the road
being so rough in this precise point, that neither mules, nor
mankind, nor horses, can make any violent progress. Passed
without any fractures or menace thereof.

The music of the Cows' bells (for their wealth, like the
Patriarchs', is cattle) in the pastures, (which reach to a height
far above any mountains in Britain), and the Shepherds'
shouting to us from crag to crag, and playing on their reeds
where the steeps appeared almost inaccessible, with the
surrounding scenery, realized all that I have ever heard or
imagined of a pastoral existence :—much more so than Greece
or Asia Minor, for there we are a little too much of the sabre
and musquet order; and if there is a Crook in one hand, you
are sure to see a gun in the other :—but this was pure and un-
mixed—solitary, savage, and patriarchal : the effect I cannot
describe. As we went, they played the " Ranz des Vaches "
and other airs, by way of farewell. I have lately repeopled my
mind with Nature.

Septr 20th

Up at 6. Off at 8. The whole of this day's journey at an
average of between from two thousand seven hundred to three
thousand feet above the level of the Sea. This valley, the
longest, narrowest, and considered one of the finest of the Alps,
little traversed by travellers. Saw the bridge of La Roche.
The bed of the river very low and deep, between immense rocks,
and rapid as anger;—a man and mule said to have tumbled
over without damage (the mule was lucky at any rate : unless
I knew the *man*, I should be loth to pronounce *him* fortunate).
The people looked free, and happy, and *rich* (which last im-
plies neither of the former) : the cows superb ; a Bull nearly
leapt into the Charaban—" agreeable companion in a post-
chaise " ; Goats and Sheep very thriving. A mountain with
enormous Glaciers to the right—the Kletsgerberg ; further on,
the Hockthorn—nice names—so soft !—Hockthorn, I believe,
very lofty and craggy, patched with snow only ; no Glaciers
on it, but some good epaulettes of clouds.

Passed the boundaries, out of Vaud and into Bern Canton ;
French exchanged for a bad German ; the district famous for
Cheese, liberty, property, and no taxes. H. went to fish—
caught none. Strolled to river : saw boy and kid ; kid
followed him like a dog ; kid could not get over a fence, and
bleated piteously ; tried myself to help kid, but nearly overset
both self and kid into the river. Arrived here about six in the
evening. Nine o'clock—going to bed. H. in next room
knocked his head against the door, and exclaimed of course
against doors ; not tired to-day, but hope to sleep nevertheless.
Women gabbling below : read a French translation of Schiller.
Good Night, Dearest Augusta.

Septr 21st

Off early. The valley of Simmenthal as before. Entrance
to the plain of Thoun very narrow ; high rocks, wooded to the
top ; river ; new mountains, with fine Glaciers. Lake of
Thoun ; extensive plain with a girdle of Alps. Walked down
to the Chateau de Schadau ; view along the lake : crossed the
river in a boat rowed by women : *women* went right for the
first time in my recollection. Thoun a very pretty town. The
whole day's journey Alpine and proud.

Septr 22^d

Left Thoun in a boat, which carried us the length of the lake in three hours. The lake small; but the banks fine: rocks down to the water's edge. Landed at Neuhause; passed Interlachen; entered upon a range of scenes beyond all description or previous conception. Passed a rock; inscription —2 brothers—one murdered the other; just the place for it. After a variety of windings came to an enormous rock. Girl with fruit—very pretty; blue eyes, good teeth, very fair: long but good features—reminded me rather of F^y Bought some of her pears, and patted her upon the cheek; the expression of her face very mild, but good, and not at all coquettish. Arrived at the foot of the Mountain (the Yung frau, *i.e.* the Maiden); Glaciers; torrents; one of these torrents *nine hundred feet* in height of visible descent. Lodge at the Curate's. Set out to see the Valley; heard an Avalanche fall, like thunder; saw Glacier—enormous. Storm came on, thunder, lightning, hail; all in perfection, and beautiful. I was on horseback; Guide wanted to carry my cane; I was going to give it him, when I recollected that it was a Swordstick, and I thought the lightning might be attracted towards him; kept it myself; a good deal encumbered with it, and my cloak, as it was too heavy for a whip, and the horse was stupid, and stood still with every other peal. Got in, not very wet; the Cloak being staunch. H. wet through; H. took refuge in cottage; sent man, umbrella, and cloak (from the Curate's when I arrived) after him. Swiss Curate's house very good indeed,—much better than most English Vicarages. It is immediately opposite the torrent I spoke of. The torrent is in shape curving over the rock, like the *tail* of a white horse streaming in the wind, such as it might be conceived would be that of the " *pale* horse " on which *Death* is mounted in the Apocalypse. It is neither mist nor water, but a something between both; it's immense height (nine hundred feet) gives it a wave, a curve, a spreading here, a condensation there, wonderful and indescribable. I think, upon the whole, that this day has been better than any of this present excursion.

Sept. 23^d

Before ascending the mountain, went to the torrent (7 in the morning) again; the Sun upon it forming a *rainbow* of the lower part of all colours, but principally purple and gold; the bow moving as you move; I never saw any thing like this; it is only in the Sunshine. Ascended the Wengen Mountain; at noon reached a valley on the summit; left the horses, took off my coat, and went to the summit, 7000 feet (English feet) above the level of the *sea,* and about 5000 above the valley we left in the morning. On one side, our view comprized the *Yung frau,* with all her glaciers; then the *Dent d'Argent,* shining like truth; then the *little Giant* (the Kleiner Eigher); and the great Giant (the Grosser Eigher), and last, not least, the Wetterhorn. The height of Jungfrau is 13,000 feet above the sea, 11,000 above the valley; she is the highest of this range. Heard the Avalanches falling every five minutes nearly—as if God was pelting the Devil down from Heaven with snow balls. From where we stood, on the *Wengen* Alp, we had all these in view on one side: on the other the clouds rose from the opposite valley, curling up perpendicular precipices like the foam of the Ocean of Hell, during a Springtide—it was white, and sulphury, and immeasurably deep in appearance. The side we ascended was (of course) not of so precipitous a nature; but on arriving at the summit, we looked down the other side upon a boiling sea of cloud, dashing against the crags on which we stood (these crags on one side quite perpendicular). Staid a quarter of an hour; began to descend; quite clear from cloud on that side of the mountain. In passing the masses of snow, I made a snowball and pelted H. with it.

Got down to our horses again; eat something; remounted; heard the Avalanches still; came to a morass; H. dismounted; H. got over well: I tried to pass my horse over; the horse sunk up [to] the chin, and of course he and I were in the mud together; bemired all over, but not hurt; laughed, and rode on. Arrived at the Grindenwald; dined, mounted again, and rode to the higher Glacier—twilight, but distinct—very fine Glacier, like *a frozen hurricane.* Starlight, beautiful, but a devil of a path! Never mind, got safe in; a little lightning; but the whole of the day as fine in point of weather as the day on which Paradise was made. Passed *whole woods of withered pines, all withered;* trunks stripped and barkless, branches lifeless; done by a single winter,—their appearance reminded me of me and my family.

Septr 24th.

Set out at seven; up at five. Passed the black Glacier, the Mountain Wetterhorn on the right; crossed the Scheideck mountain; came to the *Rose* Glacier, said to be the largest and finest in Switzerland. *I* think the Bossons Glacier at Chamouni as fine; H. does not. Came to the Reichenback waterfall, two hundred feet high; halted to rest the horses. Arrived in the valley of Oberhasli; rain came on; drenched a little; only 4 hours' rain, however, in 8 days. Came to Lake of Brientz, then to town of Brientz; changed. H. hurt his head against door. In the evening, four Swiss Peasant Girls of Oberhasli came and sang the airs of their country; two of the voices beautiful—the tunes also: they sing too that *Tyrolese air* and song which you love, Augusta, because I love it—and I love, because you love it; they are still singing. Dearest, you do not know how I should have liked this, were you with me. The airs are so wild and original, and at the same time of great sweetness. The singing is over: but below stairs I hear the notes of a Fiddle, which bode no good to my night's rest. The *Lard* help us—I shall go down and see the dancing.

Septr 25th

The whole town of Brientz were apparently gathered together in the rooms below; pretty music and excellent Waltzing; none but peasants; the dancing much better than in England; the English can't Waltz, never could, nor ever will. One man with his pipe in his mouth, but danced as well as the others; some other dances in pairs and in fours, and very good. I went to bed, but the revelry continued below late and early. Brientz but a village. Rose early. Embarked on the Lake of Brientz, rowed by the women in a long boat (one very young and very pretty—seated myself by her, and began to row also): presently we put to shore, and another woman jumped in. It seems it is the custom here for the boats to be *manned by women*: for of five men and three women in our bark, all the women took an oar, and but one man.

Got to Interlachen in three hours; pretty lake, not so large as that of Thoun. Dined at Interlachen. Girl gave me some flowers, and made me a speech in German, of which I know nothing : I do not know whether the speech was pretty, but as the woman was, I hope so. Saw another—very pretty too, and tall, which I prefer : I hate short women, for more reasons than one. Re-embarked on the Lake of Thoun; fell asleep part of the way : sent our horses round; found people on the shore, blowing up a rock with gunpowder : they blew it up near our boat, only telling us a minute before;—mere stupidity, but they might have broke our noddles. Got to Thoun in the Evening : the weather has been tolerable the whole day; but as the wild part of our tour is finished, it don't matter to us : in all the desirable part, we have been most lucky in warmth and clearness of Atmosphere, for which " Praise we the Lord ! ! "

Septr 26th

Being out of the mountains, my journal must be as flat as my journey. From Thoun to Bern, good road, hedges, villages, industry, property, and all sorts of tokens of insipid civilization. From Bern to Fribourg; different Canton—Catholics : passed a field of Battle; Swiss beat the French in one of the late wars against the French Republic. Bought a dog—a very ugly dog, but " *très méchant* "; this was his great recommendation in the owner's eyes and mine, for I mean him to watch the carriage. He hath no tail, and is called " *Mutz* ", which signifies " *Short-tail* " : he is apparently of the Shepherd dog genus! The greater part of this tour has been on horseback, on foot, and on mule.

The Filly (which is one of two young horses I bought of the Baron de Vincy), carried me very well : she is young and as quiet as any thing of her sex can be—very good tempered, and perpetually neighing when she wants any thing, which is every five minutes. I have called her *Biche*, because her manners are not unlike a little dog's; but she is a very tame pretty childish quadruped.

Septr 28th

Saw the tree planted in honour of the battle of Morat; 340 years old; a good deal decayed. Left Fribourg, but first saw the Cathedral; high tower. Overtook the baggage of the Nuns of La Trappe, who are removing to Normandy from their late abode in the Canton of Fribourg; afterwards a

355

coach, with a quantity of Nuns in it—Nuns old. Proceeded along the banks of the Lake of Neufchatel; very pleasing and soft, but not so mountainous—at least, the Jura, not appearing so, after the Bernese Alps. Reached Yverdun in the dusk; a long line of large trees on the border of the lake—fine and sombre: the Auberge nearly full—a German—with princess and suite; got rooms.

We hope to reach Diodati the day after tomorrow, and I wish for a letter from you, my own dearest Sis. May your sleep be soft, and your dreams of me. I am going to bed—good night.

Septr 29th

Passed through a fine and flourishing country, but not mountainous. In the evening reached Aubonne (the entrance and bridge something like that of Durham), which commands by far the fairest view of the Lake of Geneva; twilight; the Moon on the Lake; a grove on the height, and of very noble trees. Here Tavernier (the Eastern traveller) bought (or built) the Chateau, because the site resembled and equalled that of *Erivan*, (a frontier city of Persia); here he finished his voyages, and I this little excursion,—for I am within a few hours of Diodati, and have little more to see, and no more to say.

In the weather for this tour (of 13 days), I have been very fortunate—fortunate in a companion (Mr. H^e)—fortunate in our prospects, and exempt from even the little petty accidents and delays which often render journeys in a less wild country disappointing. I was disposed to be pleased. I am a lover of Nature and an admirer of Beauty. I can bear fatigue and welcome privation, and have seen some of the noblest views in the world. But in all this—the recollections of bitterness, and more especially of recent and more home desolation, which must accompany me through life, have preyed upon me here; and neither the music of the Shepherd, the crashing of the Avalanche, nor the torrent, the mountain, the Glacier, the Forest, nor the Cloud, have for one moment lightened the weight upon my heart, nor enabled me to lose my own wretched identity in the majesty, and the power, and the Glory, around, above, and beneath me.

I am past reproaches; and there is a time for all things.

I am past the wish of vengeance, and I know of none like for what I have suffered; but the hour will come, when what I feel must be felt, and the—but enough.

To you, dearest Augusta, I send, and *for* you I have kept this record of what I have seen and felt. Love me as you are beloved by me.

TO THE HON. AUGUSTA LEIGH   *Diodati, October 1ˢᵗ, 1816*

My dearest Augusta,—Two days ago I sent you in three letter-covers a journal of a mountain-excursion lately made by me and Mʳ H. in the Bernese Alps. I kept it on purpose for you thinking it might amuse you. Since my return here I have heard by an indirect Channel that Lady B. is better, or well. It is also said that she has some intention of passing the winter on the Continent. Upon this subject I want a word or two, and as you are—I understand—on terms of acquaintance with her again you will be the properest channel of communication from me to her. It regards my child. It is far from my intention now or at any future period (without misconduct on her part which I should be grieved to anticipate), to attempt to withdraw my child from its mother. I think it would be harsh; and though it is a very deep privation to me to be withdrawn from the contemplation and company of my little girl, still I would not purchase even this so very dearly; but I must strongly protest against my daughter's leaving England, to be taken over the Continent at so early a time of life and subjected to many unavoidable risks of health and comfort; more especially in so unsettled a state as we know the greater part of Europe to be in at this moment. I do not choose that my girl should be educated like Lord Yarmouth's son (or run the chance of it which a war would produce), and I make it my personal and particular request to Lady Byron that—in the event of her quitting England—the child should be left in the care of proper persons. I have no objection to its remaining with Lady Noel and Sir Ralph, (who would naturally be fond of it), but my distress of mind would be very much augmented if my daughter quitted England without my consent

357

or approbation. I beg that you will lose no time in making this known to Lady B. and I hope you will say something to enforce my request, I have no wish to trouble her more than can be helped. My whole hope—and prospect of a quiet evening (if I reach it), are wrapt up in that little creature— Ada—and you must forgive my anxiety in all which regards her even to minuteness. My journal will have told you all my recent wanderings. I am very well though I had a little accident yesterday. Being in my boat in the evening the pole of the mainsail slipped in veering round, and struck me on a nerve of one of my legs so violently as to make me faint away. M^r H^e and cold water brought me to myself, but there was no damage done—no bone hurt—and I have now no pain whatever. Some nerve or tendon was jarred—for a moment and that was all. To-day I dine at Coppet; the Jerseys are I believe to be there. Believe me ever and truly my own dearest Sis. most affectionately and entirely yours

B.

END OF VOL. I